John Henry Newman

Historical Sketches

John Henry Newman

Historical Sketches

ISBN/EAN: 9783337012199

Printed in Europe, USA, Canada, Australia, Japan

Cover: Foto ©ninafisch / pixelio.de

More available books at **www.hansebooks.com**

HISTORICAL SKETCHES

VOL. I.

THE TURKS IN THEIR RELATION TO EUROPE
MARCUS TULLIUS CICERO
APOLLONIUS OF TYANA
PRIMITIVE CHRISTIANITY

BY
JOHN HENRY NEWMAN
OF THE ORATORY
SOMETIME FELLOW OF ORIEL COLLEGE

LONDON
BASIL MONTAGU PICKERING
196 PICCADILLY
1876

TO THE

RIGHT REVEREND DAVID MORIARTY, D.D.,

BISHOP OF KERRY.

My dear Lord.

If I have not asked your Lordship for your formal leave to dedicate this Volume to you, this has been because one part of it, written by me as an Anglican controversialist, could not be consistently offered for the direct sanction of a Catholic bishop. If, in spite of this, I presume to inscribe your name in its first page, I do so because I have a freedom in this matter which you have not, because I covet much to be associated publicly with you, and because I trust to gain your forgiveness for a somewhat violent proceeding, on the plea that I may perhaps thereby be availing myself of the only opportunity given to me, if not the most suitable occasion, of securing what I so earnestly desire.

I desire it, because I desire to acknowledge the debt I owe you for kindnesses and services rendered to me through a course of years. All along, from the time that the Oratory first came to this place, you have taken a warm interest in me and in my doings. You found me out twenty-four years ago on our first start in the narrow streets of Birmingham, before we could well be said to have a home or a church. And you have never been wanting to me since, or spared time or trouble, when I had occasion in any difficulty to seek your guidance or encouragement.

Especially have I cause to remember the help you gave me, by your prudent counsels and your anxious sympathy, when I was called over to Ireland to initiate a great Catholic institution. From others also, ecclesiastics and laymen, I received a hearty welcome and a large assistance, which I ever bear in mind; but you, when I would fill the Professors' chairs, were in a position to direct me to the men whose genius, learning, and zeal became so great a part of the life and strength of the University; and, even as regards those whose high endowments I otherwise learned, or already knew myself, you had your part in my appointments, for I ever tried to guide myself by what I had gained from the conversations and correspondence which you had from time to time allowed me. To you, then, my dear Lord, more than to any other, I owe my introduction to a large circle of friends, who faithfully worked with me in the course of my seven years of connexion with the University, and who now, for twice seven years since, have generously kept me in mind, though I have been out of their sight.

There is no one, then, whom I more intimately associate with my life in Dublin than your Lordship; and thus, when I revive the recollections of what my friends there did for me, my mind naturally reverts to you; and again in making my acknowledgments to you, I am virtually thanking them.

That you may live for many years, in health, strength, and usefulness, the centre of many minds, a blessing to the Irish people, and a light in the Universal Church, is,

MY DEAR LORD,

The fervent prayer of

Your affectionate friend and servant,

JOHN HENRY NEWMAN.

BIRMINGHAM,
October 23, 1872.

I.
LECTURES ON THE HISTORY OF THE TURKS,
IN THEIR RELATION TO EUROPE.

PREFATORY NOTICE.

THE following sketch of Turkish history was the substance of Lectures delivered in the Catholic Institute of Liverpool during October, 1853. It may be necessary for its author to state at once, in order to prevent disappointment, that he only professes in the course of it to have brought together in one materials which are to be found in any ordinarily furnished library. Not intending it in the first instance for publication, but to answer a temporary purpose, he has, in drawing it up, sometimes borrowed words and phrases, to save himself trouble, from the authorities whom he has consulted; and this must be taken as his excuse, if any want of keeping is discernible in the composition. He has attempted nothing more than to group old facts in his own way; and he trusts that his defective acquaintance with historical works and travels, and the unreality of book-knowledge altogether in questions of fact, have not exposed him to superficial generalizations.

One other remark may be necessary. Such a work at the present moment, when we are on the point of undertaking a great war in behalf of the Turks, may seem without meaning, unless it conducts the reader to some definite conclusions, as to what is to be wished, what to be done, in the present state of the East; but a minister of religion may fairly protest against being made a politician. Political questions are mainly decided by political expediency, and only indirectly and under circumstances fall into the province of theology. Much less can such a question be asked of the priests of that Church, whose voice in this matter has been for five centuries unheeded by the Powers of Europe. As they have sown, so must they reap: had the advice of the Holy See been followed, there would have been no Turks in Europe for the Russians to turn out of it. All that need be said here in behalf of the Sultan is, that the Christian Powers are bound to keep such lawful promises as they have made to him. All that need be said in favour of the Czar is, that he is attacking an infamous Power, the enemy of God and man. And all that need be said by way of warning to the Catholic is, that he should beware of strengthening the Czar's cause by denying or ignoring its strong point. It is difficult to understand how a reader of history can side with the Spanish people in past centuries in their struggle with the Moors, without wishing Godspeed, in mere consistency, to any Christian Power, which aims at delivering the East of Europe from the Turkish yoke.

THE TURKS.

I. THE MOTHER COUNTRY OF THE TURKS.

LECT.	PAGE
1. The Tribes of the North	1
2. The Tartars	19

II. THE DESCENT OF THE TURKS.

3. The Tartar and the Turk	48
4. The Turk and the Saracen	74

III. THE CONQUESTS OF THE TURKS.

5. The Turk and the Christian	104
6. The Pope and the Turk	131

IV. THE PROSPECTS OF THE TURKS.

7. Barbarism and Civilization	159
8. The Past and Present of the Ottomans	183
9. The Future of the Ottomans	207
Note	230
Chronological Tables	235

I.

THE MOTHER COUNTRY OF THE TURKS.

LECTURE I.

The Tribes of the North.

I.

THE collision between Russia and Turkey, which at present engages public attention, is only one scene in that persevering conflict, which is carried on, from age to age, between the North and the South,—the North aggressive, the South on the defensive. In the earliest histories this conflict finds a place; and hence, when the inspired Prophets[1] denounce defeat and captivity upon the chosen people or other transgressing nations, who were inhabitants of the South, the North is pointed out as the quarter from which the judgment is to descend.

Nor is this conflict, nor is its perpetuity, difficult of explanation. The South ever has gifts of nature to tempt the invader, and the North ever has multitudes to be tempted by them. The North has been fitly called the storehouse of nations. Along the breadth of Asia, and thence to Europe, from the Chinese Sea on the East, to the Euxine on the West, nay to the Rhine, nay even to

---

[1] Isai. xli. 25; Jer. i. 14; vi. 1, 22; Joel ii. 20; etc., etc.

the Bay of Biscay, running between and beyond the 40th and 50th degrees of latitude, and above the fruitful South, stretches a vast plain, which has been from time immemorial what may be called the wild common and place of encampment, or again the highway, or the broad horse-path, of restless populations seeking a home. The European portion of this tract has in Christian times been reclaimed from its state of desolation, and is at present occupied by civilized communities; but even now the East remains for the most part in its primitive neglect, and is in possession of roving barbarians.

It is the Eastern portion of this vast territory which I have pointed out, that I have now, Gentlemen, principally to keep before your view. It goes by the general name of Tartary: in width from north to south it is said to vary from 400 to 1,100 miles, while in length from east to west it is not far short of 5,000. It is of very different elevations in different parts, and it is divided longitudinally by as many as three or four mountain-chains of great height. The valleys which lie between them necessarily confine the wandering savage to an eastward or westward course, and the slope of the land westward invites him to that direction rather than to the east. Then, at a certain point in these westward passages, as he approaches the meridian of the Sea of Aral, he finds the mountain-ranges cease, and open upon him the opportunity, as well as the temptation, to roam to the North or to the South also. Up in the East, from whence he came, in the most northerly of the lofty ranges which I have spoken of, is a great mountain, which some geographers have identified with the classical Imaus; it is called by the Saracens Caf, by the Turks Altai. Sometimes too it has the name of the Girdle of the Earth, from the huge appearance of the chain to which it belongs, sometimes of the Golden Mountain, from the gold, as well as other metals, with which its sides abound. It is said to be at an equal distance of 2,000 miles from the Caspian, the Frozen Sea, the North Pacific Ocean, and the Bay of Bengal: and, being in situation the furthest withdrawn from West and South, it is in fact the high capital or metropolis of the vast Tartar country, which it overlooks, and has sent forth, in the course of ages, innumerable populations into the illimitable and mysterious regions around it, regions protected by their inland character both from the observation and the civilizing influence of foreign nations.

2.

To eat bread in the sweat of his brow is the original punishment of mankind; the indolence of the savage shrinks from the obligation, and looks out for methods of escaping it. Corn, wine, and oil have no charms for him at such a price; he turns to the brute animals which are his aboriginal companions, the horse, the cow, and the sheep; he chooses to be a grazier rather than to till the ground. He feeds his horses, flocks, and herds on its spontaneous vegetation, and then in turn he feeds himself on their flesh. He remains on one spot while the natural crop yields them sustenance; when it is exhausted, he migrates to another. He adopts, what is called, the life of a *nomad*. In maritime countries indeed he must have recourse to other expedients; he fishes in the stream, or among the rocks of the beach. In the woods he betakes himself to roots and wild honey; or he has a resource in the chase, an occupation, ever ready at hand, exciting, and demanding no perseverance. But when the savage finds himself inclosed in

[1] Gibbon.

the continent and the wilderness, he draws the domestic animals about him, and constitutes himself the head of a sort of brute polity. He becomes a king and father of the beasts, and by the economical arrangements which this pretension involves, advances a first step, though a low one, in civilization, which the hunter or the fisher does not attain.

And here, beyond other animals, the horse is the instrument of that civilization. It enables him to govern and to guide his sheep and cattle; it carries him to the chase, when he is tempted to it; it transports him and his from place to place; while his very locomotion and shifting location and independence of the soil define the idea, and secure the existence, both of a household and of personal property. Nor is this all which the horse does for him; it is food both in its life and in its death; —when dead, it nourishes him with its flesh, and, while alive, it supplies its milk for an intoxicating liquor which, under the name of *koumiss*, has from time immemorial served the Tartar instead of wine or spirits. The horse then is his friend under all circumstances, and inseparable from him; he may be even said to live on horseback, he eats and sleeps without dismounting, till the fable has been current that he has a centaur's nature, half man and half beast. Hence it was that the ancient Saxons had a horse for their ensign in war; thus it is that the Ottoman ordinances are, I believe, to this day dated from "the imperial stirrup," and the display of horsetails at the gate of the palace is the Ottoman signal of war. Thus too, as the Catholic ritual measures intervals by "a Miserere," and St. Ignatius in his Exercises by "a Pater Noster," so the Turcomans and the Usbeks speak familiarly of the time of a gallop. But as to houses, on the other hand, the Tartars contemptuously called them the sepulchres of the living, and, when abroad, could hardly be persuaded to cross a threshold. Their women, indeed, and children could not live on horseback; them some kind of locomotive dwelling must receive, and a less noble animal must draw. The old historians and poets of Greece and Rome describe it, and the travellers of the middle ages repeat and enlarge the classical description of it. The strangers from Europe gazed with astonishment on huge wattled houses set on wheels, and drawn by no less than twenty-two oxen.

3.

From the age of Job, the horse has been the emblem of battle; a mounted shepherd is but one remove from a knight-errant, except in the object of his excursions; and the discipline of a pastoral station from the nature of the case is not very different from that of a camp. There can be no community without order, and a community in motion demands a special kind of organization. Provision must be made for the separation, the protection, and the sustenance of men, women, and children, horses, flocks, and cattle. To march without straggling, to halt without confusion, to make good their ground, to reconnoitre neighbourhoods, to ascertain the character and capabilities of places in the distance, and to determine their future route, is to be versed in some of the most important duties of the military art. Such pastoral tribes are already an army in the field, if not as yet against any human foe, at least against the elements. They have to subdue, or to check, or to circumvent, or to endure the opposition of earth, water, and wind, in their pursuits of the mere necessaries of life. The war with wild beasts naturally follows, and then the war on their own kind. Thus when they are at length provoked or allured to direct their fury against the inhabitants of other regions, they are ready-made soldiers. They have a soldier's qualifications in their independence of soil, freedom from local ties, and practice in discipline; nay, in one respect they are superior to any troops which civilized countries can produce. One of the problems of warfare is how to feed the vast masses which its operations require; and hence it is commonly said, that a well-managed commissariat is a chief condition of victory. Few people can fight without eating;—Englishmen as little as any. I have heard of a work of a foreign officer, who took a survey of the European armies previously to the revolutionary war; in which he praised our troops highly, but said they would not be effective till they were supported by a better commissariat. Moreover, one commonly hears, that the supply of this deficiency is one of the very merits of the great Duke of Wellington. So it is with civilized races; but the Tartars, as is evident from what I have already observed, have in their wars no need of any commissariat at all; and that, not merely from the unscrupulousness of their foraging, but because they find in the instruments of their conquests the staple of their food. "Corn is a bulky and perishable commodity," says an historian;[1] "and the large magazines, which are indispensably necessary for the subsistence of civilized troops, are difficult and slow of transport." But, not to say that even their flocks and herds were fitted for rapid movement, like the nimble sheep of Wales and the wild cattle of North Britain, the Tartars could even dispense with these altogether. If straitened for provisions, they ate the chargers which carried them to battle; indeed they seemed to account their flesh a delicacy, above the

[1] Gibbon.

reach of the poor, and in consequence were enjoying a banquet in circumstances when civilized troops would be staving off starvation. And with a view to such accidents, they have been accustomed to carry with them in their expeditions a number of supernumerary horses, which they might either ride or eat, according to the occasion. It was an additional advantage to them in their warlike movements, that they were little particular whether their food had been killed for the purpose, or had died of disease. Nor is this all: their horses' hides were made into tents and clothing, perhaps into bottles and coracles; and their intestines into bowstrings.[1]

Trained then as they are, to habits which in themselves invite to war, the inclemency of their native climate has been a constant motive for them to seek out settlements and places of sojournment elsewhere. The spacious plains, over which they roam, are either monotonous grazing lands, or inhospitable deserts, relieved with green valleys or recesses. The cold is intense in a degree of which we have no experience in England, though we lie to the north of them.[2] This arises in a measure from their distance from the sea, and again from their elevation of level, and further from the saltpetre with which their soil or their atmosphere is impregnated. The sole influence then of their fatherland, if I may apply to it such a term, is to drive its inhabitants from it to the West or to the South.

4

I have said that the geographical features of their country carry them forward in those two directions, the South and the West; not to say that the ocean forbids them going eastward, and the North does but hold out

[1] Caldecott's Baber. [2] Vid. Mitford's Greece, vol. viii. p. 86.

to them a climate more inclement than their own. Leaving the district of Mongolia in the furthermost East, high above the north of China, and passing through the long and broad valleys which I spoke of just now, the emigrants at length would arrive at the edge of that elevated plateau, which constitutes Tartary proper. They would pass over the high region of Pamer, where are the sources of the Oxus, they would descend the terrace of the Bolor, and the steeps of Badakshan, and gradually reach a vast region, flat on the whole as the expanse they had left, but as strangely depressed below the level of the sea, as Tartary is lifted above it.[1] This is the country, forming the two basins of the Aral and the Caspian, which terminates the immense Asiatic plain, and may be vaguely designated by the name of Turkistan. Hitherto the necessity of their route would force them on, in one multitudinous emigration, but now they may diverge, and have diverged. If they were to cross the Jaxartes and the Oxus, and then to proceed southward, they would come to Khorasan, the ancient Bactriana, and so to Affghanistan and to Hindostan on the east, or to Persia on the west. But if, instead, they continued their westward course, then they would skirt the north coast of the Aral and the Caspian, cross the Volga, and there would have a second opportunity, if they chose to avail themselves of it, of descending southwards, by Georgia and Armenia, either to Syria or to Asia Minor. Refusing this diversion, and persevering onwards to the west, at length they would pass the Don, and descend upon Europe across the Ukraine, Bessarabia, and the Danube.

Such are the three routes,—across the Oxus, across the Caucasus, and across the Danube,—which the pas-

[1] Pritchard's Researches.

toral nations have variously pursued at various times, when their roving habits, their warlike propensities, and their discomforts at home, have combined to precipitate them on the industry, the civilization, and the luxury of the West and of the South. And at such times, as might be inferred from what has been already said, their invasions have been rather irruptions, inroads, or, what are called, raids, than a proper conquest and occupation of the countries which have been their victims. They would go forward, 200,000 of them at once, at the rate of 100 miles a day, swimming the rivers, galloping over the plains, intoxicated with the excitement of air and speed, as if it were a fox-chase, or full of pride and fury at the reverses which set them in motion; seeking indeed their fortunes, but seeking them on no plan; like a flight of locusts, or a swarm of angry wasps smoked out of their nest. They would seek for immediate gratification, and let the future take its course. They would be bloodthirsty and rapacious, and would inflict ruin and misery to any extent; and they would do tenfold more harm to the invaded, than benefit to themselves. They would be powerful to break down; helpless to build up. They would in a day undo the labour and skill, the prosperity of years; but they would not know how to construct a polity, how to conduct a government, how to organize a system of slavery, or to digest a code of laws. Rather they would despise the sciences of politics, law, and finance; and, if they honoured any profession or vocation, it would be such as bore immediately and personally on themselves. Thus we find them treating the priest and the physician with respect, when they found such among their captives; but they could not endure the presence of a lawyer. How could it be otherwise with those who may be called the outlaws of the human race? They did but justify the seeming paradox of the traveller's exclamation, who, when at length, after a dreary passage through the wilderness, he came in sight of a gibbet, returned thanks that he had now arrived at a civilized country. "The pastoral tribes," says the writer I have already quoted, "who were ignorant of the distinction of landed property, must have disregarded the use, as well as the abuse, of civil jurisprudence; and the skill of an eloquent laywer would excite only their contempt or their abhorrence." And he refers to an outrage on the part of a barbarian of the North, who, not satisfied with cutting out a lawyer's tongue, sewed up his mouth, in order, as he said, that the viper might no longer hiss. The well-known story of the Czar Peter, himself a Tartar, is here in point. When told there were some thousands of lawyers at Westminster, he is said to have observed that there had been only two in his own dominions, and he had hung one of them.

5.

Now I have thrown the various inhabitants of the Asiatic plain together, under one description, not as if I overlooked, or undervalued, the distinction of races, but because I have no intention of committing myself to any statements on so intricate and interminable a subject as ethnology. In spite of the controversy about skulls, and skins, and languages, by means of which man is to be traced up to his primitive condition, I consider place and climate to be a sufficiently real aspect under which he may be regarded, and with this I shall content myself. I am speaking of the inhabitants of those extended plains, whether Scythians, Massagetæ, Sarmatians, Huns, Moguls, Tartars, Turks, or anything else; and whether or no any of them or all of them are identical with each other in their pedigree and antiquities. Position and climate create habits; and, since the country is called Tartary, I shall call them Tartar habits, and the populations which have inhabited it and exhibited them, Tartars, for convenience-sake, whatever be their family descent. From the circumstances of their situation, these populations have in all ages been shepherds, mounted on horseback, roaming through trackless spaces, easily incited to war, easily formed into masses, easily dissolved again into their component parts, suddenly sweeping across continents, suddenly descending on the south or west, suddenly extinguishing the civilization of ages, suddenly forming empires, suddenly vanishing, no one knows how, into their native north.

Such is the fearful provision for havoc and devastation, when the Divine Word goes forth for judgment upon the civilized world, which the North has ever had in store; and the regions on which it has principally expended its fury, are those, whose fatal beauty, or richness of soil, or perfection of cultivation, or exquisiteness of produce, or amenity of climate, makes them objects of desire to the barbarian. Such are China, Hindostan, Persia, Syria, and Anatolia or the Levant, in Asia; Greece, Italy, Sicily, and Spain, in Europe; and the northern coast of Africa.

These regions, on the contrary, have neither the inducement nor the means to retaliate upon their ferocious invaders. The relative position of the combatants must always be the same, while the combat lasts. The South has nothing to win, the North nothing to lose; the North nothing to offer, the South nothing to covet. Nor is this all: the North, as in an impregnable fortress, defies the attack of the South. Immense trackless solitudes;

no cities, no tillage, no roads ; deserts, forests, marshes; bleak table-lands, snowy mountains ; unlocated, flitting, receding populations ; no capitals, or marts, or strong places, or fruitful vales, to hold as hostages for submission ; fearful winters and many months of them ;—nature herself fights and conquers for the barbarian. What madness shall tempt the South to undergo extreme risks without the prospect or chance of a return ? True it is, ambition, whose very life is a fever, has now and then ventured on the reckless expedition ; but from the first page of history to the last, from Cyrus to Napoleon, what has the Northern war done for the greatest warriors but destroy the flower of their armies and the *prestige* of their name ? Our maps, in placing the North at the top, and the South at the bottom of the sheet, impress us, by what may seem a sophistical analogy, with the imagination that Huns or Moguls, Kalmucks or Cossacks, have been a superincumbent mass, descending by a sort of gravitation upon the fair territories which lie below them. Yet this is substantially true ;—though the attraction towards the South is of a moral, not of a physical nature, yet an attraction there is, and a huge conglomeration of destructive elements hangs over us, and from time to time rushes down with an awful irresistible momentum. Barbarism is ever impending over the civilized world. Never, since history began, has there been so long a cessation of this law of human society, as in the period in which we live. The descent of the Turks on Europe was the last instance of it, and that was completed four hundred years ago. They are now themselves in the position of those races, whom they themselves formerly came down upon.

6.

As to the instances of this conflict between North and South in the times before the Christian era, we know more of them from antiquarian research than from history. The principal of those which ancient writers have recorded are contained in the history of the Persian Empire. The wandering Tartar tribes went at that time by the name of Scythians, and had possession of the plains of Europe as well as of Asia. Central Europe was not at that time the seat of civilized nations; but from the Chinese Sea even to the Rhine or Bay of Biscay, a course of many thousand miles, the barbarian emigrant might wander on, as necessity or caprice impelled him. Darius assailed the Scythians of Europe; Cyrus, his predecessor, the Scythians of Asia.

As to Cyrus, writers are not concordant on the subject; but the celebrated Greek historian, Herodotus, whose accuracy of research is generally confessed, makes the great desert, which had already been fatal, according to some accounts, to the Assyrian Semiramis, the ruin also of the founder of the Persian Empire. He tells us that Cyrus led an army against the Scythian tribes (Massagetæ, as they were called), who were stationed to the east of the Caspian; and that they, on finding him prepared to cross the river which bounded their country to the South, sent him a message which well illustrates the hopelessness of going to war with them. They are said to have given him his choice of fighting them either three days' march within their own territory, or three days' march within his; it being the same to them whether he made himself a grave in their inhospitable deserts, or they a home in his flourishing provinces. He had with him in his army a celebrated captive, the Lydian

King Crœsus, who had once been head of a wealthy empire, till he had succumbed to the fortunes of a more illustrious conqueror; and on this occasion he availed himself of his advice. Crœsus cautioned him against admitting the barbarians within the Persian border, and counselled him to accept their permission of his advancing into their territory, and then to have recourse to stratagem. "As I hear," he says in the simple style of the historian, which will not bear translation, "the Massagetæ have no experience of the good things of life. Spare not then to serve up many sheep, and add thereunto stoups of neat wine, and all sorts of viands. Set out this banquet for them in our camp, leave the refuse of the army there, and retreat with the body of your troops upon the river. If I am not mistaken, the Scythians will address themselves to all this good cheer, as soon as they fall in with it, and then we shall have the opportunity of a brilliant exploit." I need not pursue the history further than to state the issue. In spite of the immediate success of his *ruse de guerre*, Cyrus was eventually defeated, and lost both his army and his life. The Scythian Queen Tomyris, in revenge for the lives which he had sacrificed to his ambition, is related to have cut off his head and plunged it into a vessel filled with blood, saying, "Cyrus, drink your fill." Such is the account given us by Herodòtus; and, even if it is to be rejected, it serves to illustrate the difficulties of an invasion of Scythia; for legends must be framed according to the circumstances of the case, and grow out of probabilities, if they are to gain credit, and if they have actually succeeded in gaining it.

7.

Our knowledge of the expedition of Darius in the

next generation, is more certain. This fortunate monarch, after many successes, even on the European side of the Bosphorus, impelled by that ambition, which holy Daniel had already seen in prophecy to threaten West and North as well as South, towards the end of his life directed his arms against the Scythians who inhabited the country now called the Ukraine. His pretext for this expedition was an incursion which the same barbarians had made into Asia, shortly before the time of Cyrus. They had crossed the Don, just above the sea of Azoff, had entered the country now called Circassia, had threaded the defiles of the Caucasus, and had defeated the Median King Cyaxares, the grandfather of Cyrus. Then they overran Armenia, Cappadocia, Pontus, and part of Lydia, that is, a great portion of Anatolia or Asia Minor; and managed to establish themselves in the country for twenty-eight years, living by plunder and exaction. In the course of this period, they descended into Syria, as far as to the very borders of Egypt. The Egyptians bought them off, and they turned back; however, they possessed themselves of a portion of Palestine, and gave their name to one town, Scythopolis, in the territory of Manasses. This was in the last days of the Jewish monarchy, shortly before the captivity. At length Cyaxares got rid of them by treachery; he invited the greater number of them to a banquet, intoxicated, and massacred them. Nor was this the termination of the troubles, of which they were the authors; and I mention the sequel, because both the office which they undertook and their manner of discharging it, their insubordination and their cruelty, are an anticipation of some passages in the early history of the Turks. The Median King had taken some of them into his pay, made them his huntsmen, and submitted certain noble youths to their training. Justly or unjustly they happened one day to be punished for leaving the royal table without its due supply of game: without more ado, the savages in revenge murdered and served up one of these youths instead of the venison which had been expected of them, and made forthwith for the neighbouring kingdom of Lydia. A war between the two states was the consequence.

But to return to Darius:—it is said to have been in retaliation for these excesses that he resolved on his expedition against the Scythians, who, as I have mentioned, were in occupation of the district between the Danube and the Don. For this purpose he advanced from Susa in the neighbourhood of the Persian Gulf, through Assyria and Asia Minor to the Bosphorus, just opposite to the present site of Constantinople, where he crossed over into Europe. Thence he made his way, with the incredible number of 700,000 men, horse and foot, to the Danube, reducing Thrace, the present Roumelia, in his way. When he had crossed that stream, he was at once in Scythia; but the Scythians had adopted the same sort of strategy, which in the beginning of this century was practised by their successors against Napoleon. They cut and carried off the green crops, stopped up their wells or spoilt their water, and sent off their families and flocks to places of safety. Then they stationed their outposts just a day's journey before the enemy, to entice him on. He pursued them, they retreated; and at length he found himself on the Don, the further boundary of the Scythian territory. They crossed the Don, and he crossed it too, into desolate and unknown wilds; then, eluding him altogether, from their own knowledge of the country, they made a circuit, and got back into their own land again.

Darius found himself outwitted, and came to a halt; how he had victualled his army, whatever deduction we make for its numbers, does not appear; but it is plain that the time must come, when he could not proceed. He gave the order for retreat. Meanwhile, he found an opportunity of sending a message to the Scythian chief, and it was to this effect:—" Perverse man, take your choice; fight me or yield." The Scythians intended to do neither, but contrived, as before, to harass the Persian retreat. At length an answer came; not a message, but an ominous gift; they sent Darius a bird, a mouse, a frog, and five arrows; without a word of explanation. Darius himself at first hailed it as an intimation of submission; in Greece to offer earth and water was the sign of capitulation, as, in a sale of land in our own country, a clod from the soil still passes, or passed lately, from seller to purchaser, as a symbol of the transfer of possession. The Persian king, then, discerned in these singular presents a similar surrender of territorial jurisdiction. But another version, less favourable to his vanity and his hopes, was suggested by one of his courtiers, and it ran thus: " Unless you can fly like a bird, or burrow like a mouse, or swim the marshes like a frog, you cannot escape our arrows." Whichever interpretation was the true one, it needed no message from the enemy to inflict upon Darius the presence of the dilemma suggested in this unpleasant interpretation. He yielded to imperative necessity, and hastened his escape from the formidable situation in which he had placed himself, and through great good fortune succeeded in effecting it. He crossed the sea just in time; for the Scythians came down in pursuit, as far as the coast, and returned home laden with booty.

This is pretty much all that is definitely recorded in history of the ancient Tartars. Alexander, in a later age, came into conflict with them in the region called Sogdiana which lies at the foot of that high plateau of central and eastern Asia, which I have designated as their proper home. But he was too prudent to be entangled in extended expeditions against them, and having made trial of their formidable strength, and made some demonstrations of the superiority of his own, he left them in possession of their wildernesses.

LECTURE II.

The Tartars.

I.

IF anything needs be added to the foregoing account, in illustration of the natural advantages of the Scythian or Tartar position, it is the circumstance that the shepherds of the Ukraine were divided in their counsels when Darius made war against them, and that only a portion of their tribes coalesced to repel his invasion. Indeed, this internal discord, which is the ordinary characteristic of races so barbarous, and the frequent motive of their migrations, is the cause why in ancient times they were so little formidable to their southern neighbours; and it suggests a remark to the philosophical historian, Thucydides, which, viewed in the light of subsequent history, is almost prophetic. "As to the Scythians," he says, "not only no European nation, but not even any Asiatic, would be able to measure itself with them, nation with nation, were they but of one mind." Such was the safeguard of civilization in ancient times; in modern unhappily it has disappeared. Not unfrequently, since the Christian era, the powers of the North have been under one sovereign, sometimes even for a series of years; and have in consequence been brought into combined action against the South; nay, as time has gone on, they have been thrown into more and more formidable combinations, with more and more disastrous consequences to its prosperity. Of these northern coalitions or Empires, there have been three, nay five, which demand our especial attention both from their size and their historical importance.

The first of these is the Empire of the Huns, under the sovereignty of Attila, at the termination of the Roman Empire; and it began and ended in himself. The second is in the time of the Crusades, when the Moguls spread themselves over Europe and Asia under Zingis Khan, whose power continued to the third generation, nay, for two centuries, in the northern parts of Europe. The third outbreak was under Timour or Tamerlane, a century and more before the rise of Protestantism, when the Mahometan Tartars, starting from the basin of the Aral and the fertile region of the present Bukharia, swept over nearly the whole of Asia round about, and at length seated themselves in Delhi in Hindostan, where they remained in imperial power till they succumbed to the English in the last century. Then come the Turks, a multiform and reproductive race, varied in its fortunes, complicated in its history, falling to rise again, receding here to expand there, and harassing and oppressing the world for at least a long 800 years. And lastly comes the Russian Empire, in which the Tartar element is prominent, whether in its pure blood or in the Slavonian approximation, and which comprises a population of many millions, gradually moulded into one in the course of centuries, ever growing, never wavering, looking eagerly to the South and to an unfulfilled destiny, and possessing both the energy of barbarism in its subjects and the subtlety of civilization in its rulers. The two former of these five empires were Pagan, the two next Mahometan, the last Christian, but schismatic; all have been persecutors of the Church, or, at least, instruments of evil against her children. The Russians I shall dismiss; the Turks, who form my proper subject, I shall postpone. First of all, I will take a brief survey of the three empires of the Tartars proper; of Attila and his Huns; of Zingis and his Moguls; and of Timour and his Mahometan Tartars.

I have already waived the intricate question of race, as regards the various tribes who have roamed from time immemorial, or used to roam, in the Asiatic and European wilderness, because it was not necessary to the discussion in which I am engaged. Their geographical position assimilated them to each other in their wildness, their love of wandering, their pastoral occupations, their predatory habits, their security from attack, and the suddenness and the transitoriness of their conquests, even though they descend from our first parent by different lines. However, there is no need of any reserve or hesitation in speaking of the three first empires into which the shepherds of the North developed, the Huns, the Moguls, and the Mahometan Tartars: they were the creation of Tribes, whose identity of race is as certain as their community of country.

2.

Of these the first in order is the Hunnish Empire of Attila, and if I speak of it and of him with more of historical consecutiveness than of Zingis or of Timour, it is because I think in him we see the pure undiluted Tartar, better than in the other two, and in his empire the best specimen of a Tartar rule. Nothing brings before us more vividly the terrible character of Attila than this, that he terrified the Goths themselves. These celebrated barbarians at the time of Attila inhabited the countries to the north of the Black Sea, between the Danube and the Don, the very district in which Darius so many centuries before found the Scythians. They were impending over the Roman Empire, and threatening it with destruction; their king was the great Hermanric, who, after many victories, was closing his days in the fulness of power and renown. That they themselves, the formidable Goths, should have to fear and flee, seemed the most improbable of prospects; yet it was their lot. Suddenly they heard, or rather they felt before they heard,—so rapid is the torrent of Scythian warfare,—they felt upon them and among them the resistless, crushing force of a remorseless foe. They beheld their fields and villages in flames about them, and their hearthstones deluged in the blood of their dearest and their bravest. Shocked and stunned by so unexpected a calamity, they could think of nothing better than turning their backs on the enemy, crowding to the Danube, and imploring the Romans to let them cross over, and to lodge themselves and their families in safety from the calamity which menaced them.

Indeed, the very appearance of the enemy scared them; and they shrank from him, as children before some monstrous object. It is observed of the Scythians, their ancestors, who, as I have mentioned, came down upon Asia in the Median times, that they were a frightful set of men. "The persons of the Scythians," says a living historian,[1] "naturally unsightly, were rendered hideous by indolent habits, only occasionally interrupted by violent exertions; and the same cause subjected them to disgusting diseases, in which they themselves revered the finger of Heaven." Some of these ancient tribes are said to have been cannibals, and their horrible outrage in serving up to Cyaxares human flesh for game, may be taken to confirm the account. Their sensuality was

[1] Thirlwall: Greece, vol. ii. p. 196.

unbridled, so much so that even polygamy was a licence too limited for their depravity. The Huns were worthy sons of such fathers. The Goths, the bravest and noblest of barbarians, recoiled in horror from their physical and mental deformity. Their voices were shrill, their gestures uncouth, and their shapes scarcely human. They are said by a Gothic historian to have resembled brutes set up awkwardly on their hind legs, or to the misshapen figures (something like, I suppose, the grotesque forms of medieval sculpture), which were placed upon the bridges of antiquity. Their shoulders were broad, their noses flat, and their eyes black, small, and deeply buried in their head. They had little hair on their skulls, and no beard. The report was spread and believed by the Goths, that they were not mere men, but the detestable progeny of evil spirits and witches in the wilds of the East.

As the Huns were but reproductions of the ancient Scythians, so are they reproduced themselves in various Tartar races of modern times. Tavernier, the French traveller, in the seventeenth century, gives us a similar description of the Kalmuks, some of whom at present are included in the Russian Empire. "They are robust men," he says,[1] "but the most ugly and deformed under heaven; a face so flat and broad, that from one eye to the other is a space of five or six fingers. Their eyes are very small, the nose so flat that two small nostrils is the whole of it; their knees turned out, and their feet turned in."

Attila himself did not degenerate in aspect from this unlovely race; for an historian tells us, whom I have already made use of, that "his features bore the stamp of his national origin; and the portrait of Attila exhibits

[1] Voyages, t. i. p. 456.

the genuine deformity of a modern Calmuck; a large head, a swarthy complexion, small deep-seated eyes, a flat nose, a few hairs in the place of a beard, broad shoulders, and a short square body, of nervous strength, though of a disproportioned form." I should add that the Tartar eyes are not only far apart, but slant inwards, as do the eyebrows, and are partly covered by the eyelid. Now Attila, this writer continues, "had a custom of rolling his eyes, as if he wished to enjoy the terror which he had inspired;" yet, strange to say, all this was so far from being thought a deformity by his people, that it even went for something supernatural, for we presently read, "the barbarian princes confessed, that they could not presume to gaze, with a steady eye, on the divine majesty of the King of the Huns."

I consider Attila to have been a pure Hun; I do not suppose the later hordes under Zingis and Timour to have been so hideous, as being the descendants of mixed marriages. Both Zingis himself and Timour had foreign mothers; as to the Turks, from even an earlier date than those conquerors, they had taken foreign captives to be mothers of their families, and had lived among foreign people. Borrowing the blood of a hundred tribes as they went on, they slowly made their way, in the course of six or seven centuries, from Turkistan to Constantinople. Then as to the Russians again, only a portion of the empire is strictly Tartar or Scythian; the greater portion is but Scythian in its first origin, many ages ago, and has long surrendered its wandering or nomad habits, its indolence, and its brutality.

3.

To return to Attila:—this extraordinary man is the only conqueror of ancient and modern times who has united in one empire the two mighty kingdoms of Eastern Scythia and Western Germany, that is, of that immense expanse of plain, which stretches across Europe and Asia. If we divide the inhabited portions of the globe into two parts, the land of civilization and the land of barbarism, we may call him the supreme and sole king of the latter, of all those populations who did not live in cities, who did not till the soil, who were hunters and shepherds, dwelling in tents, in waggons, and on horseback.[1] Imagination can hardly take in the extent of his empire. In the West he interfered with the Franks, and chastised the Burgundians, on the Rhine. On the East he even sent ambassadors to negotiate an equal alliance with the Chinese Empire. The north of Asia was the home of his race, and on the north of Europe he ascended as high as Denmark and Sweden. It is said he could bring into the field an army of 500,000 or 700,000 men.

You will ask perhaps how he gained this immense power; did he inherit it? the Russian Empire is the slow growth of centuries; had Attila a long line of royal ancestors, and was his empire, like that of Haroun, or Soliman, or Aurunzebe, the maturity and consummation of an eventful history? Nothing of the kind; it began, as it ended, with himself. The history of the Huns during the centuries immediately before him, will show us how he came by it. It seems that, till shortly before the Christian era, the Huns had a vast empire, from a date unknown, in the portion of Tartary to the east of Mount Altai. It was against these formidable invaders that the Chinese built their famous wall, 1,500 miles in length, which still exists as one of the wonders of the world. In spite of its protection, however, they were obliged to pay tribute to their fierce neighbours, until

[1] Gibbon.

one of their emperors undertook a task which at first sight seems an exception to what I have already laid down as if a universal law in the history of northern warfare. This Chinese monarch accomplished the bold design of advancing an army as much as 700 miles into the depths of the Tartar wilderness, and thereby at length succeeded in breaking the power of the Huns. He succeeded;—but at the price of 110,000 men. He entered Tartary with an army 140,000 strong; he returned with 30,000.

The Huns, however, though broken, had no intention at all of being reduced. The wild warriors turned their faces westward, and not knowing whither they were going, set out for Europe. This was at the end of the first century after Christ; in the course of the following centuries they pursued the track which I have already marked out for the emigrating companies. They passed the lofty Altai; they gradually travelled along the foot of the mountain-chain in which it is seated; they arrived at the edge of the high table-land which bounds Tartary on the west; then turning southward down the slopes which led to the low level of Turkistan, they found themselves close to a fertile region between the Jaxartes and the Oxus, the present Bukharia, then called Sogdiana by the Greeks, afterwards the native land of Timour. Here was the first of the three thoroughfares for a descent southwards, which I have pointed out as open to the choice of adventurers. A portion of these Huns, attracted by the rich pasture-land and general beauty of Sogdiana, took up their abode there; the main body wandered on. Persevering in their original course, they skirted Siberia and the north of the Caspian, crossed the Volga, then the Don, and thus in the fifth century of the Christian era, as I just now mentioned, came upon the Goths, who were in undisturbed possession of the country. Now it would appear that, in this long march from the wall of China to the Danube, lasting as it did through some centuries, they lost hold of no part of the tracts which they traversed. They remained on each successive encampment long enough (if I may so express myself) to sow themselves there. They left behind them at least a remnant of their own population while they went forward, like a rocket thrown up in the sky, which, while it shoots forward, keeps possession of its track by its train of fire. And hence it was that Attila, when he found himself at length in Hungary, and elevated to the headship of his people, became at once the acknowledged king of the vast territories and the untold populations which that people had been leaving behind them in its advance during the foregoing 350 years.

Such a power indeed had none of the elements of permanence in it, but it was appalling at the moment, whenever there was a vigorous and unscrupulous hand to put it into motion. Such was Attila; it was his boast, that, where his horse once trod, there grass never grew again. As he fulfilled his terrible destiny, religious men looked on with awe, and called him the "Scourge of God." He burst as a thunder-cloud upon the whole extent of country, now called Turkey in Europe, along a line of more than five hundred miles from the Black Sea to the Gulf of Venice. He defeated the Roman armies in three pitched battles, and then set about destroying the cities of the Empire. Three of the greatest, Constantinople, Adrianople, and another, escaped: but as for the rest, the barbarian fury fell on as many as seventy; they were sacked, levelled to the ground, and their inhabitants carried off to captivity. Next he turned round to the West, and rode off with his savage horsemen to the Rhine. He entered France, and stormed and sacked the greater part of its cities. At Metz he involved in one promiscuous massacre priests and children; he burned the city, so that a solitary chapel of St. Stephen was its sole remains. At length he was signally defeated by the Romans and Goths united at Chalons on the Marne, in a tremendous battle, which ended in 252,000, or, as one account says, 300,000 men being left dead on the field.

Irritated rather than humbled, as some beast of prey, by this mishap, he turned to Italy. Crossing the Alps, he laid siege to Aquileia, at that time one of the richest, most populous, and strongest of the cities on the Hadriatic coast. He took it, sacked it, and so utterly destroyed it, that the succeeding generation could scarcely trace its ruins. It is, we know, no slight work, in toil and expense, even with all the appliances of modern science, to raze a single fortress; yet the energy of these wild warriors made sport of walled cities. He turned back, and passed along through Lombardy; and, as he moved, he set fire to Padua and other cities; he plundered Vincenza, Verona, and Bergamo; and sold to the citizens of Milan and Pavia their lives and buildings at the price of the surrender of their property. There were a number of minute islands in the shallows of the extremity of the Hadriatic; and thither the trembling inhabitants of the coast fled for refuge. Fish was for a time their sole food, and salt, extracted from the sea, their sole possession. Such was the origin of the city and the republic of Venice.

4

It does not enter into my subject to tell you how this ferocious conqueror was stayed in the course of blood and fire which was carrying him towards Rome, by the great St. Leo, the Pope of the day, who undertook an embassy to his camp. It was not the first embassy which the Romans had sent to him, and their former negotiations had been associated with circumstances which could not favourably dispose the Hun to new overtures. It is melancholy to be obliged to confess that, on that occasion, the contrast between barbarism and civilization had been to the advantage of the former. The Romans, who came to Attila to treat upon the terms of an accommodation, after various difficulties and some insults, had found themselves at length in the Hunnish capital, in Hungary, the sole city of an empire which extended for some thousand miles. In the number of these ambassadors were some who were conducting an intrigue with Attila's own people for his assassination, and who actually had with them the imperial gold which was to be the price of the crime. Attila was aware of the conspiracy, and showed his knowledge of it; but, from respect for the law of nations and of hospitality, he spared the guilty instruments or authors. Sad as it is to have to record such practices of an Imperial Court professedly Christian, still, it is not unwelcome, for the honour of human nature, to discover in consequence of them those vestiges of moral rectitude which the degradation of ages had not obliterated from the Tartar character. It is well known that when Homer, 1,500 years before, speaks of these barbarians, he calls them, on the one hand, "drinkers of mare's milk;" on the other, "the most just of men." Truth, honesty, justice, hospitality, according to their view of things, are the historical characteristics, it must be granted, of Scythians, Tartars, and Turks, down to this day; and Homer, perhaps, as other authors after him, was the more struck with such virtues in these wild shepherds, in contrast with the subtlety and perfidy, which, then as since, were the qualities of his own intellectually gifted countrymen.

Attila, though aware of the treachery and of the traitor, had received the Roman ambassadors, as a barbarian indeed, but as a king; and with that strange mixture of rudeness and magnificence of which I shall have, as I proceed, to give more detailed specimens. As he entered the royal village or capital with his guests, a numerous troop of women came out to meet him, and marched in long files before him, chanting hymns in his honour. As he passed the door of one of his favourite soldiers, the wife of the latter presented wine and meat for his refreshment. He did not dismount, but a silver table was raised for his accommodation by his domestics, and then he continued his march. His palace, which was all of wood, was surrounded by a wooden wall, and contained separate houses for each of his numerous wives. The Romans were taken round to all of them to pay their respects; and they admired the singular quality and workmanship of the wooden columns, which they found in the apartments of his queen or state wife. She received them reclining on a soft couch, with her ladies round her working at embroidery. Afterwards they had an opportunity of seeing his council; the supreme tribunal was held in the gate of the palace according to Oriental custom, perpetuated even to this day in the title of the " Ottoman Porte." They were invited to two solemn banquets, in which Attila feasted with the princes and nobles of Scythia. The royal couch and table were covered with carpets and fine linen. The swords, and even the shoes of the nobles, were studded with gold and precious stones; the tables were profusely spread with gold and silver plates, goblets, and vases. Two bards stood before the King's couch, and sung of his victories. Wine was drunk in great excess; and buffoons, Scythian and Moorish, exhibited their unseemly dances before the revellers. When the Romans were to depart, Attila discovered to them his knowledge of the treachery which had been carried on against him.

Such were some of the untoward circumstances under which the great Pontiff I have mentioned undertook a new embassy to the King of the Huns. He was not, we may well conceive, to be a spectator of their barbaric festivities, or to be a listener to their licentious interludes; he was rather an object to be gazed upon, than to gaze; and in truth there was that about him, in the noble aspect and the spare youthful form, which portraits give to Pope Leo, which was adapted to arrest and subdue even Attila. Attila had seen many great men in his day; he had seen the majesty of the Cæsars, and the eagles of their legions; he had never seen before a Vicar of Christ. The place of their interview has been ascertained by antiquarians;[1] it is near the great Austrian fortress of Peschiera, where the Mincio enters the Lago di Garda, close to the farm of Virgil. It is said he saw behind the Pontiff the two Apostles St. Peter and St. Paul, as they are represented in the picture of Raffaelle; he was subdued by the influence of religion, and agreed to evacuate Italy.

A few words will bring us to the end of his career. Evil has its limit; the Scourge of God had accomplished His mission. Hardly had St. Leo retired, when the barbarian king availed himself of the brief interval in his work of blood, to celebrate a new marriage. In the deep corruption of the Tartar race, polygamy is compa-

[1] Maffei Verona, part ii. p. 6.

ratively a point of virtue: Attila's wives were beyond computation. Zingis, after him, had as many as five hundred; another of the Tartar leaders, whose name I forget, had three hundred. Attila, on the evening of his new nuptials, drank to excess, and was carried to his room. There he was found in the morning, bathed and suffocated in his blood. An artery had suddenly burst; and, as he lay on his back, the blood had flowed back upon his throat and lungs, and so he had gone to his place.

5.

And now for Zingis and Timour:—like the Huns, they and their tribes came down from the North of Asia, swept over the face of the South, obliterated the civilization of centuries, inflicted unspeakable misery on whole nations, and then were spent, extinguished, and only survived to posterity in the desolation they caused. As Attila ruled from China to the Rhine, and wasted Europe from the Black Sea to the Loire, so Zingis and his sons and grandsons occupied a still larger portion of the world's surface, and exercised a still more pitiless sway. Besides the immense range of territory, from Germany to the North Pacific Ocean, throughout which their power was felt, even if it was not acknowledged, they overran China, Siberia, Russia, Poland, Hungary, Anatolia, Syria, and Persia. During the sixty-five years of their dominion, they subdued almost all Asia and a large portion of Europe. The conquests of Timour were as sudden and as complete, if not as vast, as those of Zingis; and, if he did not penetrate into Europe, he accomplished instead the subjugation of Hindostan.

The exploits of those warriors have the air of Eastern romance; 700,000 men marched under the standard of Zingis; and in one of his battles he left 160,000 of his enemies upon the field. Before Timour died, he had had twenty-seven crowns upon his head. When he invaded Turkistan, his army stretched along a line of thirteen miles. We may conceive his energy and determination, when we are told that, for five months, he marched through wildernesses, subsisting his immense army on the fortunes of the chase. In his invasion of Hindostan he had to pass over a high chain of mountains, and, in one stage of the passage, had to be lowered by ropes on a scaffold, down a precipice of 150 cubits in depth. He attempted the operation five times before he got safely to the bottom.

These two extraordinary men rivalled or exceeded Attila in their wholesale barbarities. Attila vaunted that the grass never grew again after his horse's hoof; so it was the boast of Zingis, that when he destroyed a city, he did it so completely, that his horse could gallop across its site without stumbling. He depopulated the whole country from the Danube to the Baltic in a season; and the ruins of cities and churches were strewed with the bones of the inhabitants. He allured the fugitives from the woods, where they lay hid, under a promise of pardon and peace; he made them gather in the harvest and the vintage, and then he put them to death. At Gran, in Hungary, he had 300 noble ladies slaughtered in his presence. But these were slight excesses compared with other of his acts. When he had subdued the northern part of China, he proposed, not in the heat of victory, but deliberately in council, to exterminate all its inhabitants, and to turn it into a cattle-walk; from this project indeed he was diverted, but a similar process was his rule with the cities he conquered. Let it be understood, he came down upon cities living in peace and prosperity, as the cities of

England now, which had done him no harm, which had not resisted him, which submitted to him at discretion on his summons. What was his treatment of such? He ordered out the whole population on some adjacent plain; then he proceeded to sack their city. Next he divided them into three parts: first, the soldiers and others capable of bearing arms; these he either enlisted into his armies, or slaughtered on the spot. The second class consisted of the rich, the women, and the artizans ;—these he divided amongst his followers. The remainder, the old, infirm, and poor, he suffered to return to their rifled city. Such was his ordinary course; but when anything occurred to provoke him, the most savage excesses followed. The slightest offence, or appearance of offence, on the part of an individual, sufficed for the massacre of whole populations. The three great capitals of Khorasan were destroyed by his orders, and a reckoning made of the slain; at Maru were killed 1,300,000; at Herat, 1,600,000; and at Neisabour, 1,747,000; making a total of 4,647,000 deaths. Say these numbers are exaggerated four-fold or ten-fold; even on the last supposition you will have a massacre of towards half a million of helpless beings. After recounting such preternatural crimes, it is little to add, that his devastation of the fine countries between the Caspian and the Indus, a tract of many hundred miles, was so complete, that six centuries have been unable to repair the ravages of four years.

Timour equalled Zingis, if he could not surpass him, in barbarity. At Delhi, the capital of his future dynasty, he massacred 100,000 prisoners, because some of them were seen to smile when the army of their countrymen came in sight. He laid a tax of the following sort on the people of Ispahan, viz. to find him 70,000 human skulls, to build his towers with; and, after Bagdad had revolted, he exacted of the inhabitants as many as 90,000. He burned, or sacked, or razed to the ground, the cities of Astrachan, Carisme, Delhi, Ispahan, Bagdad, Aleppo, Damascus, Broussa, Smyrna, and a thousand others. We seem to be reading of some antediluvian giant, rather than of a medieval conqueror.

6.

The terrible races which I have been describing, like those giants of old, have ever been enemies of God and persecutors of His Church. Celts, Goths, Lombards, Franks, have been converted, and their descendants to this day are Christian; but, whether we consider Huns, Moguls, or Turks, up to this time they are in the outer darkness. And accordingly, to the innumerable Tartar tribes, and to none other, have been applied by commentators the solemn passages about Gog and Magog, who are to fight the battles of Antichrist against the faithful. "Satan shall go forth and seduce the nations which are at the four corners of the earth, Gog and Magog, and shall collect them to battle, whose number is as the sea sand." From time to time the Holy See has fulfilled its apostolic mission of sending preachers to them, but without success. The only missionaries who have had any influence upon them have been those of the Nestorian heresy, who have in certain districts made the same sort of impression on them which the Greek schism has made upon the Russians. St. Louis too sent a friar to them on an embassy, when he wished to persuade them to turn their strength upon the Turks, with whom he was at war; other European monarchs afterwards followed his pattern; and sometimes European merchants visited them for the purposes of trade.

However little influence as these various visitants, in the course of several centuries, had upon their minds, they have at least done us the service of giving us information concerning their habits and manners; and this so fully corroborates the historical account of them which I have been giving, that it will be worth while laying before you some specimens of it here.

I have said that some of these travellers were laymen travelling for gain or in secular splendour, and others were humble servants of religion. The contrast of their respective adventures is striking. The celebrated Marco Polo, who was one of a company of enterprising Venetian merchants, lived many years in Tartary in honour, and returned laden with riches; the poor friars met with hardships in plenty, and nothing besides. Not that the Poli were not good Catholics, not that they went out without a blessing from the Pope, or without friars of the order of St. Dominic of his selection; but so it was, that the Tartars understood the merchant well enough, but could not comprehend, could not set a value on the friar.

When the Pope's missionaries came in sight of the Tartar encampment on the northern frontier of Persia, they at once announced their mission and its object. It was from the Vicar of Christ upon earth, and the spiritual head of Christendom; and it was a simple exhortation addressed to the fierce conquerors before whom they stood, to repent and believe. The answer of the Tartars was equally prompt and equally intelligible. When they had fully mastered the business of their visitors, they sentenced them to immediate execution; and did but hesitate about the mode. They were to be flayed alive, their skins filled with hay, and so sent back to the Pope; or they were to be put in the first rank in the next battle with the Franks, and to die by the weapons of their own countrymen. Eventually one of the Khan's wives begged them off. They were kept in a sort of captivity for three years, and at length thought themselves happy to be sent away with their lives. So much for the friars; how different was the lot of the merchants may be understood by the scene which took place on their return to Venice. It is said that, on their arrival at their own city, after the absence of a quarter of a century, their change of appearance and poorness of apparel were such that even their nearest friends did not know them. Having with difficulty effected an entrance into their own house, they set about giving a splendid entertainment to the principal persons of the city. The banquet over, following the Oriental custom, they successively put on and then put off again, and distributed to their attendants, a series of magnificent dresses; and at length they entered the room in the same weather-stained and shabby dresses, in which, as travellers, they had made their first appearance at Venice. The assembled company eyed them with wonder; which you may be sure was not diminished, when they began to unrip the linings and the patches of those old clothes, and as the seams were opened, poured out before them a prodigious quantity of jewels. This had been their expedient for conveying their gains to Europe, and the effect of the discovery upon the world may be anticipated. Persons of all ranks and ages crowded to them, as the report spread, and they were the wonder of their day.[1]

7.

Savage cruelty, brutal gluttony, and barbarous

[1] Murray's Asia.

magnificence, are the three principal ethical characteristics of a Tartar prince, as we may gather from what has come down to us in history, whether concerning the Scythians or the Huns. The first of these three qualities has also been illustrated, from the references which I have been making to the history of Zingis and Timour, so that I think we have heard enough of it, without further instances from the report of these travellers, whether ecclesiastical or lay. I will but mention one corroboration of a barbarity, which at first hearing it is difficult to credit. When the Spanish ambassador, then, was on his way to Timour, and had got as far as the north of Persia, he there actually saw a specimen of that sort of poll-tax, which I just now mentioned. It was a structure consisting of four towers, composed of human skulls, a layer of mud and of skulls being placed alternately; and he tells us that upwards of 60,000 men were massacred to afford materials for this building. Indeed it seems a demonstration of revenge familiar to the Tartar race. Selim, the Ottoman Sultan, reared a similar pyramid on the banks of the Nile.[1]

To return to our Spanish traveller. He proceeded to his destination, which was Samarcand, the royal city of Timour, in Sogdiana, the present Bukharia, and was presented to the great conqueror. He describes the gate of the palace as lofty, and richly ornamented with gold and azure; in the inner court were six elephants, with wooden castles on their backs, and streamers, which performed gambols for the amusement of the courtiers. He was led into a spacious room, where were some boys, Timour's grandsons, and these carried the King of Spain's letters to the Khan. He then was ushered

---

[1] Thornton's Turkey. Vid. also Jenkinson's Voyage across the Caspian in 1562.

into Timour's presence, who was seated, like Attila's queen, on a sort of cushioned sofa, with a fountain playing before him. He was at that time an old man, and his eyesight was impaired.

At the entertainment which followed, the meat was introduced in leathern bags, so large as to be dragged along with difficulty. When opened, pieces were cut out and placed on dishes of gold, silver, or porcelain. One of the most esteemed, says the ambassador, was the hind quarter of a horse; I must add what I find related, in spite of its offending our ears:—our informant tells us that horse-tripe also was one of the delicacies at table. No dish was removed, but the servants of the guests were expected to carry off the remains, so that our ambassador doubtless had his larder provided with the sort of viands I have mentioned for some time to come. The drink was the famous Tartar beverage which we hear of so often, mares' milk, sweetened with sugar, or perhaps rather the *koumiss* or spirit which is distilled from it. It was handed round in gold and silver cups.

Nothing is more strange about the Tartars than the attachment they have shown to such coarse fare, from the earliest times till now. Timour, at whose royal table this most odious banquet was served, was lord of all Asia, and had the command of every refinement not only of luxury, but of gluttony. Yet he is faithful to the food which regaled the old Scythians in the heroic age of Greece, and which is prized by the Usbek of the present day. As Homer, in the beginning of the historic era, calls the Scythians "mares'-milk drinkers," so geographers of the present day describe their mode of distilling it in Russia. Tavernier speaks of it two centuries ago; the European visitors partook of it in the middle ages; and the Roman ambassadors, in the later times of the Empire. These tribes have had the command of the vine, yet they seem to have scorned or even abhorred its use; and we have a curious account in Herodotus, of a Scythian king who lost his life for presuming to take part secretly in the orgies of Bacchus. Yet it was not that they did not intoxicate themselves freely with the distillation which they had chosen; and even when they tolerated wine, they still adhered to their *koumiss*. That beverage is described by the Franciscan, who was sent by St. Louis, as what he calls biting, and leaving a taste like almond milk on the palate; though Elphinstone, on the contrary writing in this century, says "it is of a whitish colour and a sourish taste." And so of horseflesh; I believe it is still put out for sale in the Chinese markets; Lieutenant Wood, in his journey to the source of the Oxus, speaks of it among the Usbeks as an expensive food. So does Elphinstone, adding that in consequence the Usbeks are "obliged to be content with beef." Pinkerton tells us that it is made into dried hams; but this seems to be a refinement, for we hear a great deal from various authors of its being eaten more than half raw. After all, horseflesh was the most delicate of the Tartar viands in the times we are now considering. We are told that, in spite of their gold and silver, and jewels, they were content to eat dogs, foxes, and wolves; and, as I have observed before, the flesh of animals which had died of disease.

But again we have lost sight of the ambassador of Spain. After this banquet, he was taken about by Timour to other palaces, each more magnificent than the one preceding it. He speaks of the magnificent halls, painted with various colours, of the hangings of silk, of gold and silver embroidery, of tables of solid gold, and of the rubies and other precious stones. The most magnificent of these entertainments was on a plain; 20,000 pavilions being pitched around Timour's, which displayed the most gorgeous variety of colours. Two entertainments were given by the ladies of the court, in which the state queens of Timour, nine in number, sat in a row, and here pages handed round wine, not *koumiss*, in golden cups, which they were not slow in emptying.

The good friar, who went from St. Louis to the princes of the house of Zingis, several centuries earlier, gives us a similar account. When he was presented to the Khan, he went with a Bible and a Psalter in his hand; on entering the royal apartment, he found a curtain of felt spread across the room; it was lifted up, and discovered the great man at table with his wives about him, and prepared for drinking *koumiss*. The court knew something of Christianity from the Nestorians, who were about it, and the friar was asked to say a blessing on the meal; so he entered singing the Salve Regina. On another occasion he was present at the baptism of a wife of the Khan by a Nestorian priest. After the ceremony, she called for a cup of liquor, desired a blessing from the officiating minister, and drank it off. Then she drank off another, and then another; and continued this process till she could drink no more, and was put into her carriage, and taken home. At another entertainment the friar had to make a speech, in the name of the holy king he represented, to pray for health and long life to the Khan. When he looked round for his interpreter, he found him in a state of intoxication, and in no condition to be of service; then he directed his gaze upon the Khan himself, and found him intoxicated also.

I have made much mention of the wealth of the Tartars, from Attila to Timour; their foreign conquests would yield to them of course whatever of costly material their pride might require; but their native territory itself was rich in minerals. Altai in the north yielded the precious metals; the range of mountains which branches westward from the Himalaya on the south yielded them rubies and lapis lazuli. We are informed by the travellers whom I have been citing that they dressed in winter in costly furs; in summer in silk, and even in cloth of gold.[1] One of the Franciscans speaks of the gifts received by the Khan from foreign powers. They were more than could be numbered;—satin cloths, robes of purple, silk girdles wrought with gold, costly skins. We are told of an umbrella enriched with precious stones; of a train of camels covered with cloth of Bagdad; of a tent of glowing purple; of five hundred waggons full of silver, gold, and silk stuffs.

8.

It is remarkable that the three great conquerors, who have been our subject, all died in the fulness of glory. From the beginning of history to our own times, the insecurity of great prosperity has been the theme of poets and philosophers. Scripture points out to our warning in opposite ways the fortunes of Sennacherib, Nabuchodonosor, and Antiochus. Profane history tells us of Solon, the Athenian sage, coming to the court of Crœsus, the prosperous King of Lydia, whom in his fallen state I have already had occasion to mention; and, when he had seen his treasures and was asked by the exulting monarch who was the happiest of men, making answer that no one could be called happy before his death.

[1] Vid. also Jenkinson, *supr.*

And we may call to mind in confirmation the history of Cyrus, of Hannibal, of Mithridates, of Belisarius, of Bajazet, of Napoleon. But these Tartars finished a prosperous course without reverse; they died indeed and went to judgment, but, as far as the visible scene of their glory is concerned, they underwent no change. Attila was summoned suddenly, but the summons found him a triumphant king; and the case is the same with Zingis and Timour. These latter conquerors had glories besides of a different kind which increased the lustre of their rule. They were both lawgivers; it is the boast of Zingis that he laid down the principle of religious toleration with a clearness which modern philsophers have considered to rival the theory of Locke; and Timour, also established an efficient police in his dominions, and was a patron of literature. Their sun went down full and cloudless, with the merit of having shed some rays of blessing upon the earth, scorching and withering as had been its day. It is remarkable also that all three had something of a misgiving, or softening of mind, miserably unsatisfactory as it was, shortly before their deaths. Attila's quailing before the eye of the Vicar of Christ, and turning away from Italy, I have already spoken of, As to Zingis, as, laden at once with years and with the spoils of Asia, he reluctantly measured his way home at the impatient bidding of his veterans, who were tired of war, he seemed visited by a sense of the vanity of all things and a terror for the evil he had done. He showed some sort of pity for the vanquished, and declared his intention of rebuilding the cities he had destroyed. Alas! it is ever easier to pull down than to build up. His wars continued; he was successful by his lieutenants when he could not go to battle himself; he left his power to his children and grandchildren, and he died.

9.

Such was the end of Zingis, a pagan, who had some notion of Christianity in a corrupted form, and who once almost gave hopes of becoming a Christian, but who really had adopted a sort of indifference towards religious creeds altogether. Timour was a zealous Mahometan, and had been instructed in more definite notions of moral duty. He too felt some misgivings about his past course towards the end of his life; and the groans and shrieks of the dying and the captured in the sack of Aleppo awoke for a while the stern monitor within him. He protested to the cadhi his innocence of the blood which he had shed. "You see me here," he said, "a poor, lame, decrepit mortal; yet by my arm it has pleased the Almighty to subdue the kingdoms of Iran, Touran, and Hindostan. I am not a man of blood; I call God to witness, that never, in all my wars, have I been the aggressor, but that my enemies have ever been the authors of the calamities which have come upon them."[1]

This was the feeling of a mind sated with conquest, sated with glory, aware at length that he must go further and look deeper, if he was to find that on which the soul could really feed and live, and startled to find the entrance to that abode of true greatness and of glory sternly shut against him. He looked towards the home of his youth, and the seat of his long prosperity, across the Oxus, to Sogdiana, to Samarcand, its splendid capital, with its rich groves and smiling pastures, and there the old man went to die. Not that he directly thought of death; for still he yearned after military success: and he went thither for but a short repose,

[1] Gibbon.

between his stupendous victories in Asia Minor and a projected campaign in China. But Samarcand was a fitting halt in that long march; and there for the last time he displayed the glory of his kingdom, receiving the petitions or appeals of his subjects, ostentatiously judging between the deserving and the guilty, inspecting plans for the erection of palaces and temples, and giving audience to ambassadors from Russia, Spain, Egypt, and Hindostan. An English historian, whom I have already used, has enlarged upon this closing scene, and I here abridge his account of it. "The marriage of six of the Emperor's grandsons," he says, "was esteemed an act of religion as well as of paternal tenderness; and the pomp of the ancient caliphs was revived in their nuptials. They were celebrated in the garden of Canighul, where innumerable tents and pavilions displayed the luxury of a great city and the spoils of a victorious camp. Whole forests were cut down to supply fuel for the kitchens; the plain was spread with pyramids of meat and vases of every liquor, to which thousands of guests were courteously invited. The orders of the state and the nations of the earth were marshalled at the royal banquet. The public joy was testified by illuminations and masquerades; the trades of Samarcand passed in review; and every trade was emulous to execute some quaint device, some marvellous pageant, with the materials of their peculiar art. After the marriage contracts had been ratified by the cadhies, nine times, according to the Asiatic fashion, were the bridegrooms and their brides dressed and undressed; and at each change of apparel, pearls and rubies were showered on their heads, and contemptuously abandoned to their attendants."

. You may recollect the passage in Milton's Paradise

Lost, which has a reference to the Oriental ceremony here described. It is in his account of Satan's throne in Pandemonium. "High on a throne," the poet says,

> "High on a throne of royal state, which far
> Outshone the wealth of Ormus or of Ind,
> Or where the gorgeous East, with richest hand,
> Showers on her kings barbaric pearl and gold,
> Satan exulting sat, by merit raised
> To that bad eminence."

So it is; the greatest magnificence of this world is but a poor imitation of the flaming throne of the author of evil. But let us return to the history:—"A general indulgence was proclaimed, and every law was relaxed, every pleasure was allowed; the people were free, the sovereign was idle; and the historian of Timour may remark, that after devoting fifty years to the attainment of empire, the only happy period of his life was the two months in which he ceased to exercise his power. But he was soon awakened to the cares of government and war. The standard was unfurled for the invasion of China; the emirs made the report of 200,000, the select and veteran soldiers of Iran and Touran; the baggage and provisions were transported by 500 great waggons, and an immense train of horses and camels; and the troops might prepare for a long absence, since more than six months were employed in the tranquil journey of a caravan from Samarcand to Pekin. Neither age, nor the severity of winter, could retard the impatience of Timour; he mounted on horseback, passed the Sihun" (or Jaxartes) "on the ice, marched 300 miles from his capital, and pitched his last camp at Otrar, where he was expected by the angel of death. Fatigue and the indiscreet use of iced water accelerated the progress of his fever; and the conqueror of Asia expired in the seventieth year of his age; his designs were lost; his armies were disbanded; China was saved."

But the wonderful course of human affairs rolled on. Timour's death was followed at no long interval by the rise of John Basilowich in Russia, who succeeded in throwing off the Mogul yoke, and laid the foundation of the present mighty empire. The Tartar sovereignty passed from Samarcand to Moscow.

II.

THE DESCENT OF THE TURKS.

LECTURE III.

The Tartar and the Turk.

YOU may think, Gentlemen, I have been very long in coming to the Turks, and indeed I have been longer than I could have wished; but I have thought it necessary, in order to your taking a just view of them, that you should survey them first of all in their original condition. When they first appear in history they are Huns or Tartars, and nothing else; they are indeed in no unimportant respects Tartars even now; but, had they never been made something more than Tartars, they never would have had much to do with the history of the world. In that case, they would have had only the fortunes of Attila and Zingis; they might have swept over the face of the earth, and scourged the human race, powerful to destroy, helpless to construct, and in consequence ephemeral; but this would have been all. But this has not been all, as regards the Turks; for, in spite of their intimate resemblance or relationship to the Tartar tribes, in spite of their essential barbarism to this day, still they, or at least great portions of the race, have been put under education; they have been submitted to a slow course of change, with a long history and a profitable discipline and fortunes of a peculiar kind; and thus they have gained those qualities of mind, which alone enable a nation to wield and to consolidate imperial power.

I.

I have said that, when first they distinctly appear on the scene of history, they are indistinguishable from Tartars. Mount Altai, the high metropolis of Tartary, is surrounded by a hilly district, rich not only in the useful, but in the precious metals. Gold is said to abound there; but it is still more fertile in veins of iron, which indeed is said to be the most plentiful in the world. There have been iron works there from time immemorial, and at the time that the Huns descended on the Roman Empire (in the fifth century of the Christian era), we find the Turks nothing more than a family of slaves, employed as workers of the ore and as blacksmiths by the dominant tribe. Suddenly in the course of fifty years, soon after the fall of the Hunnish power in Europe, with the sudden development peculiar to Tartars, we find these Turks spread from East to West, and lords of a territory so extensive, that they were connected, by relations of peace or war, at once with the Chinese, the Persians, and the Romans. They had reached Kamtchatka on the North, the Caspian on the West, and perhaps even the mouth of the Indus on the South. Here then we have an intermediate empire of Tartars, placed between the eras of Attila and Zingis; but in this sketch it has no place, except as belonging to Turkish history, because it was contained within the limits of Asia, and, though it lasted for 200 years, it only faintly affected the political transactions of Europe. However, it was not without some sort of influence on Christendom, for the Romans interchanged embassies with its sovereign in the reign of the then Greek Emperor Justin the younger (A.D. 570), with the view of engaging him in a warlike alliance against Persia. The account of one of these embassies remains, and the picture it presents of the Turks is important, because it seems clearly to identify them with the Tartar race.

For instance, in the mission to the Tartars from the Pope, which I have already spoken of, the friars were led between two fires, when they approached the Khan, and they at first refused to follow, thinking they might be countenancing some magical rite. Now we find it recorded of this Roman embassy, that, on its arrival, it was purified by the Turks with fire and incense. As to incense, which seems out of place among such barbarians, it is remarkable that it is used in the ceremonial of the Turkish court to this day. At least Sir Charles Fellows, in his work on the Antiquities of Asia Minor, in 1838, speaks of the Sultan as going to the festival of Bairam with incense-bearers before him. Again, when the Romans were presented to the great Khan, they found him in his tent, seated on a throne, to which wheels were attached and horses attachable, in other words, a Tartar waggon. Moreover, they were entertained at a banquet which lasted the greater part of the day; and an intoxicating liquor, not wine, which was sweet and pleasant, was freely presented to them; evidently the Tartar *koumiss*.[1] The next day they had a second entertainment in a still more splendid tent; the hangings were of embroidered silk, and the throne, the cups, and the vases were of gold. On the third day, the pavilion, in which they were received, was supported on gilt columns; a couch of massive gold was raised on four gold peacocks; and before the entrance to the tent was what

[1] Univ. Hist. Modern, vol. iii. p. 346.

might be called a sideboard, only that it was a sort of barricade of waggons, laden with dishes, basins, and statues of solid silver. All these points in the description,—the silk hangings, the gold vessels, the successively increasing splendour of the entertainments,—remind us of the courts of Zingis and Timour, 700 and 900 years afterwards.

This empire, then, of the Turks was of a Tartar character; yet it was the first step of their passing from barbarism to that degree of civilization which is their historical badge. And it was their first step in civilization, not so much by what it did in its day, as (unless it be a paradox to say so), by its coming to an end. Indeed it so happens, that those Turkish tribes which have changed their original character and have a place in the history of the world, have obtained their *status* and their qualifications for it, by a process very different from that which took place in the nations most familiar to us. What this process has been I will say presently; first, however, let us observe that, fortunately for our purpose, we have still specimens existing of those other Turkish tribes, which were never submitted to this process of education and change, and, in looking at them as they now exist, we see at this very day the Turkish nationality in something very like its original form, and are able to decide for ourselves on its close approximation to the Tartar. You may recollect I pointed out to you, Gentlemen, in the opening of these lectures, the course which the pastoral tribes, or nomads as they are often called, must necessarily take in their emigrations. They were forced along in one direction till they emerged from their mountain valleys, and descended their high plateau at the end of Tartary, and then they had the opportunity of turning south. If they did not avail themselves of this opening, but went on still westward, their next southern pass would be the defiles of the Caucasus and Circassia, to the west of the Caspian. If they did not use this, they would skirt the top of the Black Sea, and so reach Europe. Thus in the emigration of the Huns from China, you may recollect a tribe of them turned to the South as soon as they could, and settled themselves between the high Tartar land and the sea of Aral, while the main body went on to the furthest West by the north of the Black Sea. Now with this last passage into Europe we are not here concerned, for the Turks have never introduced themselves to Europe by means of it;[1] but with those two southward passages which are Asiatic, viz., that to the east of the Aral, and that to the west of the Caspian. The Turkish tribes have all descended upon the civilized world by one or other of these two roads; and I observe, that those which have descended along the east of the Aral have changed their social habits and gained political power, while those which descended to the west of the Caspian remain pretty much what they ever were. The former of these go among us by the general name of Turks; the latter are the Turcomans or Turkmans.

2.

Now, first, I shall briefly mention the Turcomans, and dismiss them, because, when they have once illustrated the original state of their race, they have no place in this sketch. I have said, then, that the ancient Turco-Tartar empire, to which the Romans sent their embassy in the sixth century, extended to the Caspian and towards the Indus. It was in the beginning of the

---

[1] I am here assuming that the Magyars are not of the Turkish stock; vid. Gibbon and Pritchard.

next century that the Romans, that is, the Greco-Romans of Constantinople, found them in the former of these neighbourhoods; and they made the same use of them in the defence of their territory, to which they had put the Goths before the overthrow of the Western Empire. It was a most eventful era at which they addressed themselves to these Turks of the Caspian. It was almost the very year of the Hegira, which marks the rise of the Mahometan imposture and rule. As yet, however, the Persians were in power, and formidable enemies to the Romans, and at this very time in possession of the Holy Cross, which Chosroes, their powerful king, had carried away from Jerusalem twelve years before. But the successful Emperor Heraclius was already in the full tide of those brilliant victories, which in the course of a few years recovered it; and, to recall him from their own soil, the Persians had allied themselves with the barbarous tribes of Europe, (the Russians, Sclavonians, Bulgarians, and others,) which, then as now, were pressing down close upon Constantinople from the north. This alliance suggested to Heraclius the counterstroke of allying himself with the Turkish freebooters, who in like manner, as stationed above the Caspian, were impending over Persia. Accordingly the horde of Chozars, as this Turkish tribe was called, at the Emperor's invitation, transported their tents from the plains of the Volga through the defiles of the Caucasus into Georgia. Heraclius showed them extraordinary attention; he put his own diadem on the head of the barbarian prince, and distributed gold, jewels, and silk to his officers; and, on the other hand, he obtained from them an immediate succour of 40,000 horse, and the promise of an irruption of their brethren into Persia from the far East, from the quarter of the

Sea of Aral, which I have pointed out as the first of the passages by which the shepherds of Tartary came down upon the South. Such were the allies, with which Heraclius succeeded in utterly overthrowing and breaking up the Persian power; and thus, strange to say, the greatest of all the enemies of the Church among the nations of the earth, the Turk, began his career in Christian history by coöperating with a Christian Emperor in the recovery of the Holy Cross, of which a pagan, the ally of Russia, had got possession. The religious aspect, however, of this first era of their history, seems to have passed away without improvement; what they gained was a temporal advantage, a settlement in Georgia and its neighbourhood, which they have held from that day to this.

This horde of Turks, the Chozars, was nomad and pagan; it consisted of mounted shepherds, surrounded with their flocks, living in tents and waggons. In the course of the following centuries, under the shadow of their more civilized brethren, other similar hordes were introduced, nomad and pagan still; they might indeed happen sometimes to pass down from the east of the Caspian as well as from the west, hastening to the south straight from Turkistan along the coast of the Aral; —either road would lead them down to the position which the Chozars were the first to occupy in Georgia and Armenia,—but still there would be but one step in their journey between their old native sheep-walk and horse-path and the fair region into which they came. It was a sudden Tartar descent, accompanied with no national change of habits, and promising no permanent stability. Nor would they have remained there, I suppose, as they did remain, were it not that they have been protected, as they were originally introduced, by neighbouring states which have made use of them. There, however, in matter of fact, they remain to this day, the successors of the Chozars, in Armenia, in Syria, in Asia Minor, even as far west as the coast of the Archipelago and its maritime cities and ports, being pretty much what they were a thousand years ago, except that they have taken up the loose profession of Mahometanism, and have given up some of the extreme peculiarities of their Tartar state, such as their attachment to horse-flesh and mares' milk. These are the Turcomans.

3.

The writer in the Universal History divides them into eastern and western. Of the Eastern, with which we are not concerned, he tells us that [1] "they are tall and robust, with square flat faces, as well as the western; only they are more swarthy, and have a greater resemblance to the Tartars. Some of them have betaken themselves to husbandry. They are all Mohammedans; they are very turbulent, very brave, and good horsemen." And of the Western, that they once had two dynasties in the neighbourhood of Armenia, and were for a time very powerful, but that they are now subjects of the Turks, who never have been able to subdue their roving habits; that they dwell in tents of thick felt, without fixed habitation; that they profess Mahomedanism, but perform its duties no better than their brethren in the East; that they are governed by their own chiefs according to their own laws; that they pay tribute to the Ottoman Porte, and are bound to furnish it with horsemen; that they are great robbers, and are in perpetual warfare with their neighbours the Kurds; that they

[1] Vol. v. p. 248.

march sometimes two or three hundred families together, and with their droves cover sometimes a space of two leagues, and that they prefer the use of the bow to that of fire-arms.

This account is drawn up from writers of the sixteenth and seventeenth centuries. Precisely the same report of their habits is made by Dr. Chandler in his travels in Asia Minor in the middle of the last century; he fell in with them in his journey between Smyrna and Ephesus. "We were told here," he says, "that the road farther on was beset with Turcomans, a people supposed to be descended from the Nomades Scythæ or Shepherd Scythians; busied, as of old, in breeding and nurturing cattle, and leading, as then, an unsettled life; not forming villages and towns with stable habitations, but flitting from place to place, as the season and their convenience directs; choosing their stations, and overspreading without control the vast neglected pastures of this desert empire. . . We set out, and . . . soon after came to a wild country covered with thickets, and with the black booths of the Turcomans, spreading on every side, innumerable, with flocks and herds and horses and poultry feeding round them."[1]

I may seem to be making unnecessary extracts, but I have two reasons for multiplying them; in order, first, to show the identity in character of the various tribes of the Tartar and the Turkish stock, and next, in order to impress upon your imagination what that character is; for it is not easy to admit into the mind the very idea of a people of this kind, dwelling too, and that for ages, in some of the most celebrated and beautiful regions of the world, such as Syria and Asia Minor. With this view I will read what Volney says of them, as he found

[1] P. 127, ed. 1817.

them in Syria towards the close of the last century. "The Turkmans," he says,[1] "are of the number of those Tartar hordes, who, in the great revolutions of the Empire of the Caliphs, emigrated from the eastward of the Caspian Sea, and spread themselves over the vast plains of Armenia and Asia Minor. Their language is the same as that of the Turks, and their mode of life nearly resembles that of the Bedouin Arabs. Like them, they are shepherds, and consequently obliged to travel over immense tracts of land to procure subsistence for their numerous herds. . . . Their whole occupation consists in smoking and looking after their flocks. Perpetually on horseback, with their lances on their shoulders, their crooked sabres by their sides, and their pistols in their belts, they are expert horsemen and indefatigable soldiers . . . A great number of these tribes pass in the summer into Armenia and Caramania, where they find grass in great abundance, and return to their former quarters in the winter. The Turkmans are reputed to be Moslem . . . but they trouble themselves little about religion."

While I was collecting these passages, a notice of these tribes appeared in the columns of the *Times* newspaper, sent home by its Constantinople correspondent, apropos of the present concentration of troops in that capital in expectation of a Russian war. His statement enables us to carry down our specimens of the Tartar type of the Turkish race to the present day. "From the coast of the Black Sea," he writes home, "to the Taurus chain of mountains, a great part of the population is nomad, and besides the Turks or Osmanlis," that is, the Ottoman or Imperial Turks, "consists of two distinct races;—the Turcomans, who possessed them-

[1] Travels in Syria, vol. i. p. 369, ed. 1787.

selves of the land before the advent of the Osmanlis, and who wander with their black tents up to the shores of the Bosphorus; and the Curds." With the Curds we are not here concerned. He proceeds: "The Turcomans, who are spread over the whole of Asia Minor, are a most warlike people. Clans, numbering many thousand, acknowledge the Sultan as the representative of the Caliphs and the Sovereign Lord of Islam, from whom all the Frank kings receive their crowns; but they are practically independent of him, and pay no taxes but to their own chiefs. In the neighbourhood of Cæsarea, Kusan Oghlou, a Turcoman chief, numbers 20,000 armed horsemen, rules despotically over a large district, and has often successfully resisted the Sultan's arms. These people lead a nomad life, are always engaged in petty warfare, are well mounted, and armed with pistol, scimitar, spear, or gun, and would always be useful as irregular troops."

4

And now I have said enough, and more than enough, of the original state of the Turkish race, as exhibited in the Chozars and Turcomans:—it is time to pursue the history of that more important portion of it with which we are properly engaged, which received some sort of education, and has proved itself capable of social and political union. I observed just now, that that education was very different in its mode and circumstances from that which has been the lot of the nations with which we are best acquainted. Other nations have been civilized in their own homes, and, by their social progress, have immortalized a country as well as a race. They have been educated by their conquests, or by subjugation, or by the intercourse with foreigners which commerce or colonization has opened; but in every case they have been true to their father-land, and are children of the soil. The Greeks sent out their colonies to Asia Minor and Italy, and those colonies reacted upon the mother country. Magna Græcia and Ionia showed their mother country the way to her intellectual supremacy. The Romans spread gradually from one central city, and when their conquests reached as far as Greece, "the captive," in the poet's words, " captivated her wild conqueror, and introduced arts into unmannered Latium."[1] England was converted by the Roman See and conquered by the Normans, and was gradually civilized by the joint influences of religion and of chivalry. Religion indeed, though a depraved religion, has had something to do, as we shall see, with the civilization of the Turks; but. the circumstances have been altogether different from those which we trace in the history of England, Rome, or Greece. The Turks present the spectacle of a race poured out, as it were, upon a foreign material, interpenetrating all its parts, yet preserving its individuality, and at length making its way through it, and reappearing, in substance the same as before, but charged with the qualities of the material through which it has been passed, and modified by them. They have been invaded by no conqueror, they have brought no captive arts or literature home, they have undergone no conversion in mass, they have been taught by no commerce, by no international relationship; but they have in the course of centuries slowly soaked or trickled, if I may use the words, through the Saracenic populations with which they came in contact, and after being nationally lost to the world, as far as history goes, for long periods and through different countries, eventually they have come

[1] Hor. Epist. ii. 1, 155.

to the face of day with that degree of civilization which they at present possess, and at length have usurped a place within the limits of the great European family. And this is why the path southwards to the east of the Aral was, in matter of fact, the path of civilization, and that by the Caucasus the path of barbarism; this is why the Turks who took the former course could found an empire, and those who took the latter have remained Tartars or Turcomans, as they were originally; because the way of the Caucasus was a sheer descent from Turkistan into the country which they occupy, but the way of the Aral was a circuitous course, leading them through many countries—through Sogdiana, Khorasan, Zabulistan, and Persia,—with many fortunes, under many masters, for many hundred years, before they came round to the region to which their Turcoman brethren attained so easily, but with so little eventual advantage. My meaning will be clearer, as I proceed.

5.

1. First of all, we may say that the very region into which they came, tended to their civilization. Of course the peculiarities of soil, climate, and country are not by themselves sufficient for a social change, else the Turcomans would have the best right to civilization; yet, when other influences are present too, climate and country are far from being unimportant. You may recollect that I have spoken more than once of the separation of a portion of the Huns from the main body, when they were emigrating from Tartary into Europe, in the time of the Goths.[1] These turned off sharp to the South immediately on descending the high table-land; and, crossing the Jaxartes, found themselves in a fertile

---
[1] *Supr.* p. 26.

and attractive country, between the Aral and their old country, where they settled. It is a peculiarity of Asia that its regions are either very hot or very cold. It has the highest mountains in the world, bleak table-lands, vast spaces of burning desert, tracts stretched out beneath the tropical sun. Siberia goes for a proverb for cold: India is a proverb for heat. It is not adequately supplied with rivers, and it has little of inland sea. In these respects it stands in singular contrast with Europe. If then the tribes which inhabit a cold country have, generally speaking, more energy than those which are relaxed by the heat, it follows that you will have in Asia two descriptions of people brought together in extreme, sometimes in sudden, contrariety with each other, the strong and the weak. Here then, as some philosophers have argued,[1] you have the secret of the despotisms and the vast empires of which Asia has been the seat; for it always possesses those who are naturally fitted to be tyrants, and those also whose nature it is to tremble and obey. But we may take another, perhaps a broader, view of the phenomenon. The sacred writer says: "Give me neither riches nor beggary:" and, as the extremes of abundance and of want are prejudicial to our moral well-being, so they seem to be prejudicial to our intellectual nature also. Mental cultivation is best carried on in temperate regions. In the north men are commonly too cold, in the south too hot, to think, read, write, and act. Science, literature, and art refuse to germinate in the frost, and are burnt up by the sun.

Now it so happened that the region in which this party of Huns settled themselves was one of the fairest and most fruitful in Asia. It is bounded by deserts, it

[1] Montesquieu.

is in parts encroached on by deserts; but viewed in its length and breadth, in its produce and its position, it seems a country equal, or superior, to any which that vast continent, as at present known, can show. Its lower portion is the extensive territory of Khorasan, the ancient Bactriana; going northwards across the Oxus, we come into a spacious tract, stretching to the Aral and to the Jaxartes, and measuring a square of 600 miles. It was called in ancient times Sogdiana; in the history of the middle ages Transoxiana, or "beyond the Oxus;" by the Eastern writers Maver-ul-nere, or Mawer-al-nahar, which is said to have the same meaning; and it is now known by the name Bukharia. To these may be added a third province, at the bottom of the Aral, between the mouth of the Oxus and the Caspian, called Kharasm. These, then, were the regions in which the Huns in question took up their abode.

The two large countries I first mentioned are celebrated in all ages for those characteristics which render a spot desirable for human habitation. As to Sogdiana, or Maver-ul-nere, the region with which we are specially concerned, the Orientals, especially the Persians, of the medieval period do not know how to express in fit terms their admiration of its climate and soil. They do not scruple to call it the Paradise of Asia. "It may be considered," says a modern writer,[1] "as almost the only example of the finest temperate climate occurring in that continent, which presents generally an abrupt transition from burning tropical heat to the extreme cold of the north." According to an Arabian author, there are just three spots in the globe which surpass all the rest in beauty and fertility; one of them is near Damascus, another seems to be the valley of a river on the Persian

[1] Murray.

Gulf, and the third is the plain of Sogdiana. Another writer says: "I have cast my eyes around Bokhara, and never have I seen a verdure more fresh or of wider extent. The green carpet mingles in the horizon with the azure of the sky."[1] Abulfeda in like manner calls it "the most delightful of all places God has created." Some recent writer, I think, speaks in disparagement of it.[2] And I can quite understand, that the deserts which must be passed to reach it from the south or the north may betray the weary traveller into an exaggerated praise, which is the expression both of his recruited spirits and of his gratitude. But all things are good only by comparison; and I do not see why an Asiatic, having experience of the sands which elsewhere overspread the face of his continent, should for that reason be ill qualified to pronounce that Sogdiana affords a contrast to them. Moreover, we have the experience of other lands, as Asia Minor, which have presented a very different aspect in different ages. A river overflows and turns a fruitful plain into a marsh; or it fails, and turns it into a sandy desert. Sogdiana is watered by a number of great rivers, which make their way across it from the high land on its east to the Aral or Caspian. Now we read in history of several instances of changes, accidental or artificial, in the direction or the supply of these great water-courses. I think I have read somewhere, but cannot recover my authority, of some emigration of the inhabitants of those countries, caused by a failure of the stream on which they depended. And we know for certain that the Oxus has been changed in its course, accidentally or artificially, more than once. Disputes have arisen before now between the Russian Government and the Tartars, on the subject of one of these diversions of the bed of

[1] Caldecott's Baber.   [2] Vid. Quarterly Review, vol. lii. p. 396-7.

a river.[1] One province of Khorasan, which once was very fertile, is in consequence now a desert. It may be questioned, too, whether the sands of the adjacent deserts, which are subject to violent agitation from the action of the wind, may not have encroached upon Sogdiana. Nor should it be overlooked that this rich country has been subjected to the same calamities which have been the desolation of Asia Minor; for, as the Turcomans have devastated the latter, so, as I have already had occasion to mention, Zingis swept round the sea of Aral, and destroyed the fruits of a long civilization.

Even after the ravages of that conqueror, however, Timour and the Emperor Baber, who had a right to judge of the comparative excellence of the countries of the East, bear witness to the beauty of Sogdiana. Timour, who had fixed his imperial seat in Samarcand, boasted he had a garden 120 miles in extent. Baber expatiates on the grain and fruit and game of its northern parts; of the tulips, violets, and roses of another portion of it; of the streams and gardens of another. Its plains are said by travellers to abound in wood, its rivers in fish, its valleys in fruit-trees, in wheat and barley, and in cotton.[2] The quince, pomegranate, fig, apricot, and almond all flourish in it. Its melons are the finest in the world. Mulberries abound, and provide for a considerable manufacture of silk. No wine, says Baber, is equal to the wine of Bokhara. Its atmosphere is so clear and serene, that the stars are visible even to the verge of the horizon. A recent Russian traveller says he came to a country so smiling, well cultivated, and thickly peopled, with fields, canals, avenues of trees, villages, and gardens, that he thought

[1] Univ. Hist. mod. vol. v. p. 262, etc.
[2] Ibid. vol. iv. p. 353.

himself in an enchanted country. He speaks in raptures of its melons, pomegranates, and grapes.[1] Its breed of horses is celebrated; so much so that a late British traveller[2] visited the country with the special object of substituting it for the Arab in our Indian armies. Its mountains abound in useful and precious produce. Coal is found there; gold is collected from its rivers; silver and iron are yielded by its hills; we hear too of its mines of turquoise, and of its cliffs of lapis lazuli,[3] and its mines of rubies, which to this day are the object of the traveller's curiosity.[4] I might extend my remarks to the country south of the Oxus and of its mountain range, the modern Affghanistan. Though Cabul is 6,000 feet above the level of the sea, it abounds in pomegranates, mulberries, apples, and fruit of every kind. Grapes are so plentiful, that for three months of the year they are given to the cattle.

6.

This region, favoured in soil and climate, is favoured also in position. Lying at the mouth of the two great roads of emigration from the far East, the valleys of the Jaxartes and the Oxus, it is the natural mart between High Asia and Europe, receiving the merchandize of East and North, and transporting it by its rivers, by the Caspian, the Kur, and the Phasis, to the Black Sea. Thus it received in former days the silk of China, the musk of Thibet, and the furs of Siberia, and shipped them for the cities of the Roman Empire. To Samarcand, its metropolis, we owe the art of transforming linen into paper, which the Sogdian merchants are said to have gained from China, and thence diffused by means of their own manufacturers over the western

---

[1] Meyendorff. [2] Moorcroft. [3] Vid. Elphinstone. [4] Wood's Oxus.

world. A people so circumstanced could not be without civilization; but that civilization was of a much earlier date. It must not be forgotten that the celebrated sage, Zoroaster, before the times of history, was a native, and, as some say, king of Bactriana. Cyrus had established a city in the same region, which he called after his name. Alexander conquered both Bactriana and Sogdiana, and planted Grecian cities there. There is a long line of Greco-Bactrian kings; and their coins and pateræ have been brought to light within the last few years. Alexander's name is still famous in the country; not only does Marco Polo in the middle ages speak of his descendants as still found there, but even within the last fifteen years Sir Alexander Burns found a man professing that descent in the valley of the Oxus, and Lieutenant Wood another in the same neighbourhood.

Nor was Greek occupation the only source of the civilization of Sogdiana. Centuries rolled on, and at length the Saracens renewed, on their own peculiar basis, the mental cultivation which Sogdiana had received from Alexander. The cities of Bokhara and Samarcand have been famous for science and literature. Bokhara was long celebrated as the most eminent seat of Mahometan learning in central Asia; its colleges were, and are, numerous, accommodating from 60 to 600 students each. One of them gained the notice and the pecuniary aid of the Russian Empress Catharine.[1] Samarcand rivals Bokhara in fame; its university even in the last century was frequented by Mahometan youth from foreign countries. There were more than 300 colleges for students, and there was an observatory, celebrated in the middle ages, the ruins of which remain. Here lies the body of Timour,

[1] Elphinstone's Cabul.

under a lofty dome, the sides of which are enriched with agate. "Since the time of the Holy Prophet," that is, Mahomet, says the Emperor Baber, "no country has produced so many Imaums and eminent divines as Mawar-al-nahar," that is, Sogdiana. It was celebrated for its populousness. At one time it boasted of being able to send out 300,000 foot, and as many horse, without missing them. Bridges and caravansaries abounded; the latter, in the single province attached to its capital, amounted to 2,000. In Bactriana, the very ruins of Balkh extend for a circuit of 20 miles, and Sir A. Burns wound through three miles of them continuously.

Such is the country, seated at present between the British and the Russian Empires, and such as regards its previous and later state, which the savage Huns, in their emigration from Tartary, had necessarily encountered; and it cannot surprise us that one of their many tribes had been persuaded to settle there, instead of seeking their fortunes farther west. The effect upon these settlers in course of time was marvellous. Though it was not of course the mere climate of Sogdiana that changed them, still we cannot undervalue the influence which is necessarily exerted on the mind by the idea of property, when once recognised and accepted, by the desire of possession and by the love of home, and by the sentiment of patriotism which arises in the mind, especially with the occupation of a rich and beautiful country. Moreover, they became the guests or masters of a people, who, however rude, at least had far higher claims to be called civilized than they themselves, and possessed among them the remains of a more civilized era. They found a race, too, not Tartar, more capable of civilization, more gifted with intellect, and more comely in person. Settling down among the inhabitants, and intermarrying with them, in the course of generations their Tartar characteristics were sensibly softened. For a thousand years this restless people remained there, as if chained to the soil. They still had the staple of barbarism in them, but so polished were they for children of a Tartar stock, that they are called in history the White Huns of Sogdiana. They took to commerce, they took to literature; and when, at the end of a few centuries, the Turks, as I have already described, spread abroad from the iron works and forges of Mount Altai to Kamtchatka, the Volga, and the Indus, and overran these White Huns in the course of their victories, they could find no parties more fitted than them to act as their diplomatists and correspondents in their negotiations with the Romans.

Such was the influence of Sogdiana on the Huns; is it wonderful that it exerted some influence on the Turks, when they in turn got possession of it? History justifies the anticipation; as the Huns of the second or third centuries settled around the Aral, so the Turks in the course of the sixth or seventh centuries overran them, and descended down to the modern Affghanistan and the Indus; and as the fair region and its inhabitants, which they crossed and occupied, had begun at the former era the civilization of the first race of Tartars, so did it at the latter era begin the education of the second.

7.

2. But a more direct and effective instrument of social education was accorded to the Turks on their occupation of Sogdiana. You may recollect I spoke of their first empire as lasting for only 200 years,[1] about 90 of which measures the period of that occupation. Their

---

[1] *Supr.* p. 59.

power then came to an end; what was the consequence of their fall? were they driven out of Sogdiana again? were they massacred? did they take refuge in the mountains or deserts? were they reduced to slavery? Thus we are introduced to a famous passage of history: the case was as follows:—At the very date at which Heraclius called the Turcomans into Georgia, at the very date when their Eastern brethren crossed the northern border of Sogdiana, an event of most momentous import had occurred in the South. A new religion had arisen in Arabia. The impostor Mahomet, announcing himself the Prophet of God, was writing the pages of that book, and moulding the faith of that people, which was to subdue half the known world. The Turks passed the Jaxartes southward in A.D. 626; just four years before Mahomet had assumed the royal dignity, and just six years after, on his death, his followers began the conquest of the Persian Empire. In the course of 20 years they effected it; Sogdiana was at its very extremity, or its borderland; there the last king of Persia took refuge from the south, while the Turks were pouring into it from the north. There was little to choose for the unfortunate prince between the Turk and the Saracen; the Turks were his hereditary foe; they had been the giants and monsters of the popular poetry; but he threw himself into their arms. They engaged in his service, betrayed him, murdered him, and measured themselves with the Saracens in his stead. Thus the military strength of the north and south of Asia, the Saracenic and the Turkish, came into memorable conflict in the regions of which I have said so much. The struggle was a fierce one, and lasted many years; the Turks striving to force their way down to the ocean, the Saracens to drive them back into their Scythian deserts. They first fought this issue in Bactriana or Khorasan; the Turks got the worst of the fight, and then it was thrown back upon Sogdiana itself, and there it ended again in favour of the Saracens. At the end of 90 years from the time of the first Turkish descent on this fair region, they relinquished it to their Mahometan opponents. The conquerors found it rich, populous, and powerful; its cities, Carisme, Bokhara, and Samarcand, were surrounded beyond their fortifications by a suburb of fields and gardens, which was in turn protected by exterior works; its plains were well cultivated, and its commerce extended from China to Europe. Its riches were proportionally great; the Saracens were able to extort a tribute of two million gold pieces from the inhabitants; we read, moreover, of the crown jewels of one of the Turkish princesses; and of the buskin of another, which she dropt in her flight from Bokhara, as being worth two thousand pieces of gold.[1] Such had been the prosperity of the barbarian invaders, such was its end; but not *their* end, for adversity did them service, as well as prosperity, as we shall see.

It is usual for historians to say, that the triumph of the South threw the Turks back again upon their northern solitudes; and this might easily be the case with some of the many hordes, which were ever passing the boundary and flocking down; but it is no just account of the historical fact, viewed as a whole. Not often indeed do the Oriental nations present us with an example of versatility of character; the Turks, for instance, of this day are substantially what they were four centuries ago. We cannot conceive, were Turkey overrun by the Russians at the present moment, that the fanatical tribes, which are pouring into Constantinople from Asia Minor, would submit to the foreign yoke,

[1] Gibbon.

take service under their conquerors, become soldiers, custom-officers, police, men of business, attachés, statesmen, working their way up from the ranks and from the masses into influence and power; but, whether from skill in the Saracens, or from far-reaching sagacity in the Turks (and it is difficult to assign it to either cause), so it was, that a process of this nature followed close upon the Mahometan conquest of Sogdiana. It is to be traced in detail to a variety of accidents. Many of the Turks probably were made slaves, and the service to which they were subjected was no matter of choice. Numbers had got attached to the soil; and inheriting the blood of Persians, White Huns, or aboriginal inhabitants for three generations, had simply unlearned the wildness of the Tartar shepherd. Others fell victims to the religion of their conquerors, which ultimately, as we know, exercised a most remarkable influence upon them. Not all at once, but as tribe descended after tribe, and generation followed generation, they succumbed to the creed of Mahomet; and they embraced it with the ardour and enthusiasm which Franks and Saxons so gloriously and meritoriously manifested in their conversion to Christianity.

8.

3. Here again was a very powerful instrument in modification of their national character. Let me illustrate it in one particular. If there is one peculiarity above another, proper to the savage and to the Tartar, it is that of excitability and impetuosity on ordinary occasions; the Turks, on the other hand, are nationally remarkable for gravity and almost apathy of demeanour. Now there are evidently elements in the Mahometan creed, which would tend to change them from the one

temperament to the other. Its sternness, its coldness, its doctrine of fatalism; even the truths which it borrowed from Revelation, when separated from the truths it rejected, its monotheism untempered by mediation, its severe view of the divine attributes, of the law, and of a sure retribution to come, wrought both a gloom and also an improvement in the barbarian, not very unlike the effect which some forms of Protestantism produce among ourselves. But whatever was the mode of operation, certainly it is to their religion that this peculiarity of the Turks is ascribed by competent judges. Lieutenant Wood in his journal gives us a lively account of a peculiarity of theirs, which he unhesitatingly attributes to Islamism. "Nowhere," he says, "is the difference between European and Mahomedan society more strongly marked than in the lower walks of life. . . . A Kasid, or messenger, for example, will come into a public department, deliver his letters in full durbar, and demean himself throughout the interview with so much composure and self-possession, that an European can hardly believe that his grade in society is so low. After he has delivered his letters, he takes his seat among the crowd, and answers, calmly and without hesitation, all the questions which may be addressed to him, or communicates the verbal instructions with which he has been entrusted by his employer, and which are often of more importance than the letters themselves. Indeed, all the inferior classes possess an innate self-respect, and a natural gravity of deportment, which differs as far from the suppleness of a Hindustani as from the awkward rusticity of an English clown." . . . "Even children," he continues, "in Mahomedan countries have an unusual degree of gravity in their deportment. The boy, who can but lisp his 'Peace be with you,' has imbibed this portion of the national character. In passing through a village, these little men will place their hands upon their breasts, and give the usual greeting. Frequently have I seen the children of chiefs approach their father's durbar, and stopping short at the threshold of the door, utter the shout of 'Salam Ali-Kum,' so as to draw all eyes upon them; but nothing daunted, they marched boldly into the room, and sliding down upon their knees, folded their arms and took their seat upon the musnad with all the gravity of grown-up persons."

As Islamism has changed the demeanour of the Turks, so doubtless it has in other ways materially innovated on their Tartar nature. It has given an aim to their military efforts, a political principle, and a social bond. It has laid them under a sense of responsibility, has moulded them into consistency, and taught them a course of policy and perseverance in it. But to treat this part of the subject adequately to its importance would require, Gentlemen, a research and a fulness of discussion unsuitable to the historical sketch which I have undertaken. I have said enough for my purpose upon this topic; and indeed on the general question of the modification of national character to which the Turks were at this period subjected.

LECTURE IV.

The Turk and the Saracen.

I.

MERE occupation of a rich country is not enough for civilization, as I have granted already. The Turks came into the pleasant plains and valleys of Sogdiana; the Turcomans into the well-wooded mountains and sunny slopes of Asia Minor. The Turcomans were brought out of their dreary deserts, yet they retained their old habits, and they remain barbarians to this day. But why? it must be borne in mind, they neither subjugated the inhabitants of their new country on the one hand, nor were subjugated by them on the other. They never had direct or intimate relations with it; they were brought into it by the Roman Government at Constantinople as its auxiliaries, but they never naturalized themselves there. They were like gipseys in England, except that they were mounted freebooters instead of pilferers and fortune-tellers. It was far otherwise with their brethren in Sogdiana; they were there first as conquerors, then as conquered. First they held it in possession as their prize for 90 or 100 years; they came into the usufruct and enjoyment of it. Next, their political ascendancy over it involved, as in the case of the White Huns, some sort of moral surrender of themselves to it. What was the first consequence of this? that, like the White Huns, they intermarried with the races they found there. We know the custom of the Tartars and Turks; under such circumstances they would avail themselves of their national practice of polygamy to its full extent of licence. In the course of twenty years a new generation would arise of a mixed race; and these in turn would marry into the native population, and at the end of ninety or a hundred years we should find the great-grandsons or the great-great-grandsons of the wild marauders who first crossed the Jaxartes, so different from their ancestors in features both of mind and body, that they hardly would be recognized as deserving the Tartar name. At the end of that period their power came to an end, the Saracens became masters of them and of their country, but the process of emigration southward from the Scythian desert, which had never intermitted during the years of their domination, continued still, though that domination was no more.

Here it is necessary to have a clear idea of the nature of that association of the Turkish tribes from the Volga to the Eastern Sea, to which I have given the name of Empire:—it was not so much of a political as of a national character; it was the power, not of a system, but of a race. They were not one well-organized state, but a number of independent tribes, acting generally together, acknowledging one leader or not, according to circumstances, combining and coöperating from the identity of object which acted on them, and often jealous of each other and quarrelling with each other on account of that very identity. Each tribe made its way down to the south as it could; one blocked up the way of the other for a time; there were stoppages and collisions, but there was a continual movement and progress. Down they came one after another, like wolves after their prey; and as the tribes which came first became partially civilized, and as a mixed generation arose, these would naturally be desirous of keeping back their less polished uncles or cousins, if they could; and would do so successfully for awhile: but cupidity is stronger than conservatism; and so, in spite of delay and difficulty, down they would keep coming, and down they did come, even after and in spite of the overthrow of their Empire; crowding down as to a new world, to get what they could, as adventurers, ready to turn to the right or the left, prepared to struggle on anyhow, willing to be forced forward into countries farther still, careless what might turn up, so that they did but get down. And this was the process which went on (whatever were their fortunes when they actually got down, prosperous or adverse) for 400, nay, I will say for 700 years. The storehouse of the north was never exhausted; it sustained the never-ending run upon its resources.

2.

I was just now referring to a change in the Turks, which I have mentioned before, and which had as important a bearing as any other of their changes upon their subsequent fortunes. It was a change in their physiognomy and shape, so striking as to recommend them to their masters for the purposes of war or of display. Instead of bearing any longer the hideous exterior which in the Huns frightened the Romans and Goths, they were remarkable, even as early as the ninth century, when they had been among the natives of Sogdiana only two hundred years, for the beauty of their persons. An important political event was the result: hence the introduction of the Turks into the heart of the Saracenic empire. By this time the Caliphs had removed from Damascus to Bagdad; Persia was the imperial province, and into Persia they were introduced for the reason I have mentioned, sometimes as slaves, sometimes as captives taken in war, sometimes as mercenaries for the Saracenic armies: at length they were enrolled as guards to the Caliph, and even appointed to offices in the palace, to the command of the forces, and to governorships in the provinces. The son of the celebrated Harun al Raschid had as many as 50,000 of these troops in Bagdad itself. And thus slowly and silently they made their way to the south, not with the pomp and pretence of conquest, but by means of that ordinary intercommunion which connected one portion of the empire of the Caliphs with another. In this manner they were introduced even into Egypt.

This was their history for a hundred and fifty years, and what do we suppose would be the result of this importation of barbarians into the heart of a flourishing empire? Would they be absorbed as slaves or settlers in the mass of the population, or would they, like mercenaries elsewhere, be fatal to the power that introduced them? The answer is not difficult, considering that their very introduction argued a want of energy and resource in the rulers whom they served. To employ them was a confession of weakness; the Saracenic power indeed was not very aged, but the Turkish was much younger, and more vigorous;—then too must be considered the difference of national character between the Turks and the Saracens. A writer of the beginning of the present century,[1] compares the Turks to the Romans; such parallels are generally fanciful and fallacious; but, if we must accept it in the present instance, we may complete the picture by likening the Saracens and Persians to the Greeks, and we know what was the result of the collision between Greece and Rome. The

[1] Thornton.

Persians were poets, the Saracens were philosophers. The mathematics, astronomy, and botany were especial subjects of the studies of the latter. Their observatories were celebrated, and they may be considered to have originated the science of chemistry. The Turks, on the other hand, though they are said to have a literature, and though certain of their princes have been patrons of letters, have never distinguished themselves in exercises of pure intellect; but they have had an energy of character, a pertinacity, a perseverance, and a political talent, in a word, they then had the qualities of mind necessary for ruling, in far greater measure, than the people they were serving. The Saracens, like the Greeks, carried their arms over the surface of the earth with an unrivalled brilliancy and an unchequered success; but their dominion, like that of Greece, did not last for more than 200 or 300 years. Rome grew slowly through many centuries, and its influence lasts to this day; the Turkish race battled with difficulties and reverses, and made its way on amid tumult and complication, for a good 1,000 years from first to last, till at length it found itself in possession of Constantinople, and a terror to the whole of Europe. It has ended its career upon the throne of Constantine; it began it as the slave and hireling of the rulers of a great empire, of Persia and Sogdiana.

3.

As to Sogdiana, we have already reviewed one season of power and then in turn of reverse which there befell the Turks; and next a more remarkable outbreak and its reaction mark their presence in Persia. I have spoken of the formidable force, consisting of Turks, which formed the guard of the Caliphs immediately after the time of

Harun al Raschid:—suddenly they rebelled against their master, burst into his apartment at the hour of supper, murdered him, and cut his body into seven pieces. They got possession of the symbols of imperial power, the garment and the staff of Mahomet, and proceeded to make and unmake Caliphs at their pleasure. In the course of four years they had elevated, deposed, and murdered as many as three. At their wanton caprice, they made these successors of the false prophet the sport of their insults and their blows. They dragged them by the feet, stripped them, and exposed them to the burning sun, beat them with iron clubs, and left them for days without food. At length, however, the people of Bagdad were roused in defence of the Caliphate, and the Turks for a time were brought under; but they remained in the country, or rather, by the short-sighted policy of the moment, were dispersed throughout it, and thus became in the sequel ready-made elements of revolution for the purposes of other traitors of their own race, who, at a later period, as we shall presently see, descended on Persia from Turkistan.

Indeed, events were opening the way slowly, but surely, to their ascendancy. Throughout the whole of the tenth century, which followed, they seem to disappear from history; but a silent revolution was all along in progress, leading them forward to their great destiny. The empire of the Caliphate was already dying in its extremities, and Sogdiana was one of the first countries to be detached from his power. The Turks were still there, and, as in Persia, filled the ranks of the army and the offices of the government; but the political changes which took place were not at first to their visible advantage. What first occurred was the revolt of the Caliph's viceroy, who made himself a great kingdom or empire out of the provinces around, extending it from the Jaxartes, which was the northern boundary of Sogdiana, almost to the Indian ocean, and from the confines of Georgia to the mountains of Affghanistan. The dynasty thus established lasted for four generations and for the space of ninety years. Then the successor happened to be a boy; and one of his servants, the governor of Khorasan, an able and experienced man, was forced by circumstances to rebellion against him. He was successful, and the whole power of this great kingdom fell into his hands; now he was a Tartar or Turk; and thus at length the Turks suddenly appear in history, the acknowledged masters of a southern dominion.

4.

This is the origin of the celebrated Turkish dynasty of the Gaznevides, so called after Gazneh, or Ghizni, or Ghuznee, the principal city, and it lasted for two hundred years. We are not particularly concerned in it, because it has no direct relations with Europe; but it falls into our subject, as having been instrumental to the advance of the Turks towards the West. Its most distinguished monarch was Mahmood, and he conquered Hindostan, which became eventually the seat of the empire. In Mahmood the Gaznevide we have a prince of true Oriental splendour. For him the title of Sultan or Soldan was invented, which henceforth became the special badge of the Turkish monarchs; as Khan is the title of the sovereign of the Tartars, and Caliph of the sovereign of the Saracens. I have already described generally the extent of his dominions: he inherited Sogdiana, Carisme, Khorasan, and Cabul; but, being a zealous Mussulman, he obtained the title of Gazi, or champion, by his reduction of Hindostan, and his destruction of its idol temples.

There was no need, however, of religious enthusiasm to stimulate him to the war: the riches, which he amassed in the course of it, were a recompense amply sufficient. His Indian expeditions in all amounted to twelve, and they abound in battles and sieges of a truly Oriental cast. "Never," says a celebrated historian,[1] "was the Mussulman hero dismayed by the inclemency of the seasons, the height of the mountains, the breadth of the rivers, the barrenness of the desert, the multitudes of the enemy," or their elephants of war. One of the sovereigns of the country brought against him as many as 2,500 elephants; the borderers on the Indus resisted him with 4,000 war-boats. He was successful in every direction; he levelled to the ground many hundreds of pagodas, and carried off their treasures. In one of his campaigns[2] he took prisoner the prince of Lahore, round whose neck alone were sixteen strings of jewels, valued at £320,000 of our money. At Mutra he found five great idols of pure gold, with eyes of rubies; and a hundred idols of silver, which, when melted down, loaded a hundred camels with bullion.

These stories, which sound like the fables in the Arabian Nights, are but a specimen of the wonderful fruits of the victories of this Mahmood. His richest prize was the great temple of Sunnat, or Somnaut, on the promontory of Guzerat, between the Indus and Bombay It was a place as diabolically wicked as it was wealthy, and we may safely regard Mahmood as the instrument of divine vengeance upon it. But here I am only concerned with its wealth, for which grave writers are the vouchers. When this temple was taken, Mahmood entered a great square hall, having its lofty roof supported with 56 pillars, curiously turned and set with

[1] Gibbon.   Vid. Dow's Hindostan.

precious stones. In the centre stood the idol, made of stone, and five feet high. The conqueror began to demolish it. He raised his mace, and struck off the idol's nose. The Brahmins interposed, and are said to have offered the fabulous sum, as Mill considers it, of ten millions sterling for its ransom. His officers urged him to accept it, and the Sultan himself was moved; but recovering himself, he observed that it was somewhat more honourable to destroy idols than to traffic in them, and proceeded to repeat his blows at the trunk of the figure. He broke it open; it was found to be hollow, and at once explained the prodigality of the offer of the Brahmins. Inside was found an incalculable treasure of diamonds, rubies, and pearls. Mahmood took away the lofty doors of sandal-wood, which belonged to this temple, as a trophy for posterity. Till a few years ago, they were the decoration of his tomb near Gazneh, which is built of white marble with a cupola, and where Moollas' are still maintained to read prayers over his grave.[1] There too once hung the ponderous mace, which few but himself could wield; but the mace has disappeared, and the sandal gates, if genuine, were carried off about twelve years since by the British Governor-General of India, and restored to their old place, as an acceptable present to the impure idolaters of Guzerat.[2]

It is not wonderful that this great conqueror should have been overcome by the special infirmity, to which such immense plunder would dispose him; he has left

---

[1] Caldecott's Baber. Vid. also Elphinstone, vol. ii. p. 366.

[2] "Our victorious army bears the gates of the temple of Somnauth in triumph from Affghanistan, and the despoiled tomb of Sultan Mahmood looks upon the ruins of Ghuznee. The insult of 800 years is at last avenged," etc., etc.—*Proclamation of the Governor-General to all the princes, chiefs, and people of India.*

behind him a reputation for avarice. He desired to be a patron of literature, and on one occasion he promised a court poet a golden coin for every verse of an heroic poem he was writing. Stimulated by the promise, "the divine poet," to use the words of the Persian historian, "wrote the unparalleled poem called the Shah Namna, consisting of 60,000 couplets." This was more than had been bargained for by the Sultan, who, repenting of his engagement, wished to compromise the matter for 60,000 rupees, about a sixteenth part of the sum he had promised. The indignant author would accept no remuneration at all, but wrote a satire upon Mahmood instead; but he was merciful in his revenge, for he reached no more than the seven-thousandth couplet.

There is a melancholy grandeur about the last days of this victorious Sultan, which seems to show that even then the character of his race was changed from the fierce impatience of Hun and Tartar to the grave, pensive, and majestic demeanour of the Turk. Tartar he was in his countenance, as he was painfully conscious, but his mind had a refinement, to which the Tartar was a stranger. Broken down by an agonizing complaint, he perceived his life was failing, and his glory coming to an end. Two days before his death, he commanded all the untold riches of his treasury, his sacks of gold and silver, his caskets of precious stones, to be brought out and placed before him. Having feasted his eyes upon them, he burst into tears; he knew they would not long be his, but he had not the heart to give any part of them away. The next day he caused to be drawn up before his travelling throne, for he observed still the Tartar custom, his army of 100,000 foot and 55,000 horse, his chariots, his camels, and his 1,300 elephants of war; and again he wept, and, overcome with grief, retired to his palace. Next day he died, after a prosperous reign of more than thirty years.

But, to return to the general history. It will be recollected that Mahmood's dominions stretched very far to the west, as some say, even round the Caspian to Georgia; and it is not wonderful that, while he was adding India to them, he found a difficulty in defending his frontier towards Persia. Meantime, as before, his own countrymen kept streaming down upon him without intermission from the north, and he thought he could not do better than employ these dangerous visitors in garrison duty against his western enemies. They took service under him, but did not fulfil his expectations. Indeed, what followed may be anticipated from the history which I have been giving of the Caliphs: it was an instance of workmen emancipating themselves from their employer. The fierce barbarians who were defending the province of Khorasan so well for another, naturally felt that they could take as good care of it for themselves; and when Mahmood was approaching the end of his life, he became sensible of the error he had committed in introducing them. He asked one of their chiefs what force he could lend him: "If you sent one of the arrows into our camp," was the answer, "50,000 of us will mount to do thy bidding." "But what if I want more?" inquired Mahmood; "send this arrow into the camp of Balik, and you will have another 50,000." The Sultan asked again: "But what if I require your whole forces?" "Send round my bow," answered the Turk, "and the summons will be obeyed by 200,000 horse."[1] The foreboding, which disclosures such as this inspired, was fulfilled the year before his death. The Turks came into collision with his lieutenants, and defeated one of them

[1] Gibbon. Universal Hist.

in a bloody action; and though he took full reprisals, and for a while cleared the country of them, yet in the reign of his son they succeeded in wresting from his dynasty one-half of his empire, and Hindostan, the acquisition of Mahmood, became henceforth its principal possession.

5.

We have now arrived at what may literally be called the turning-point of Turkish history. We have seen them gradually descend from the north, and in a certain degree become acclimated in the countries where they settled. They first appear across the Jaxartes in the beginning of the seventh century; they have now come to the beginning of the eleventh. Four centuries or thereabout have they been out of their deserts, gaining experience and educating themselves in such measure as was necessary for playing their part in the civilized world. First they came down into Sogdiana and Khorasan, and the country below it, as conquerors; they continued in it as subjects and slaves. They offered their services to the race which had subdued them; they made their way by means of their new masters down to the west and the south; they laid the foundations for their future supremacy in Persia, and gradually rose upwards through the social fabric to which they had been admitted, till they found themselves at length at the head of it. The sovereign power which they had acquired in the line of the Gaznevides, drifted off to Hindostan; but still fresh tribes of their race poured down from the north, and filled up the gap; and while one dynasty of Turks was established in the peninsula, a second dynasty arose in the former seat of their power.

Now I call the era at which I have arrived the

turning-point of their fortunes, because, when they had descended down to Khorasan and the countries below it, they might have turned to the East or to the West, as they chose. They were at liberty to turn their forces eastward against their kindred in Hindostan, whom they had driven out of Ghizni and Affghanistan, or to face towards the west, and make their way thither through the Saracens of Persia and its neighbouring countries. It was an era which determined the history of the world. I recollect once hearing a celebrated professor of geology attempt to draw out the consequences which would have occurred, had there not been an outlet for the Thames, which exists in fact, at a certain point of its course. He said that, had the range of hills been unbroken, it would have streamed off to the north-east, and have run into the sea at the Wash in Lincolnshire. An utter change in the political events which came after, another history of England, and nothing short of it, would have been the result. An illustration such as this will at least serve to express what I would say of the point at which we now stand in the history of the Turks. Mahmood turned to the east; and had the barbarian tribes which successively descended done the same, they might have conquered the Gaznevide dynasty, they might have settled themselves, like Timour, at Delhi, and their descendants might have been found there by the British in their conquests during the last century; but they would have been unknown to Europe, they would have been strange to Constantinople, they would have had little interest for the Church. They had rebelled against Mahmood, they had driven his family to the East; but they did not pursue him thither; he had strength enough to keep them off the rich territory he had appropriated; he was the obstacle which turned the stream westward; in consequence, they looked towards Persia, where their brethren had been so long settled, and they directed their course for good and all towards Europe.

But this era was a turning-point in their history in another and more serious respect. In Sogdiana and Khorasan, they had become converts to the Mahometan faith. You will not suppose I am going to praise a religious imposture, but no Catholic need deny that it is, considered in itself, a great improvement upon Paganism. Paganism has no rule of right and wrong, no supreme and immutable judge, no intelligible revelation, no fixed dogma whatever; on the other hand, the being of one God, the fact of His revelation, His faithfulness to His promises, the eternity of the moral law, the certainty of future retribution, were borrowed by Mahomet from the Church, and are steadfastly held by his followers. The false prophet taught much which is materially true and objectively important, whatever be its subjective and formal value and influence in the individuals who profess it. He stands in his creed between the religion of God and the religion of devils, between Christianity and idolatry, between the West and the extreme East. And so stood the Turks, on adopting his faith, at the date I am speaking of; they stood between Christ in the West, and Satan in the East, and they had to make their choice; and, alas! they were led by the circumstances of the time to oppose themselves, not to Paganism, but to Christianity. A happier lot indeed had befallen poor Sultan Mahmood than befell his kindred who followed in his wake. Mahmood, a Mahomedan, went eastward and found a superstition worse than his own, and fought against it, and smote it; and the sandal doors which he tore away from the idol temple and hung up at his tomb at Gazneh, almost seemed to plead for him through centuries as the soldier and the instrument of Heaven. The tribes which followed him, Moslem also, faced westward, and found, not error but truth, and fought against it as zealously, and in doing so, were simply tools of the Evil One, and preachers of a lie, and enemies, not witnesses of God. The one destroyed idol temples, the other Christian shrines. The one has been saved the woe of persecuting the Bride of the Lamb; the other is of all races the veriest brood of the serpent which the Church has encountered since she was set up. For 800 years did the sandal gates remain at Mahmood's tomb, as a trophy over idolatry; and for 800 years have Seljuk and Othman been our foe, singled out as such, and denounced by successive Vicars of Christ.

6.

The year 1048 of our era is fixed by chronologists as the date of the rise of the Turkish power, as far as Christendom is interested in its history.[1] Sixty-three years before this date, a Turk of high rank, of the name of Seljuk, had quarrelled with his native prince in Turkistan, crossed the Jaxartes with his followers, and planted himself in the territory of Sogdiana. His father had been a chief officer in the prince's court, and was the first of his family to embrace Islamism; but Seljuk, in spite of his creed, did not obtain permission to advance into Sogdiana from the Saracenic government, which at that time was in possession of the country. After several successful encounters, however, he gained admission into the city of Bokhara, and there he settled. As time went on, he fully recompensed the tardy hos-

[1] Baronius, Pagi.

pitality which the Saracens had shown him ; for his feud with his own countrymen, whom he had left, took the shape of a religious enmity, and he fought against them as pagans and infidels, with a zeal, which was both an earnest of the devotion of his people to the faith of Mahomet, and a training for the exercise of it. He died, it is said, in battle against the pagans, and at the wonderful age of 107. Of his five sons, whom he left behind him, one, Michael, was cut off prematurely in battle against the infidels also, and has obtained the name of Shadid or the Martyr; for in a religion where the soldier is the missionary, the soldier is the martyr also. The other sons became rich and powerful; they had numerous flocks and fertile pastures in Sogdiana, till at length they attracted the notice of the Sultan Mahmood, who, having dispossessed the Saracens of the country where Seljuk had placed himself, looked about for mercenary troops to keep his possession of it. It was one of Seljuk's family, who at a later date alarmed Mahmood by telling him he could bring 200,000 horsemen from the Scythian wilderness, if he sent round his bow to summon them ; it was Seljuk's horde and retainers that ultimately forced back Mahmood's son into the south and the east, and got possession of Sogdiana and Khorasan. Having secured this acquisition, they next advanced into Persia, and this was the event, which is considered to fix the date of their entrance into ecclesiastical history. It was the date of their first steadily looking westward ; it determined their destiny ; they began to be enemies of the Cross in the year 1048, under the leading of Michael the Martyr's son, Togrul Beg.

It is the inconvenience of any mere sketch of historical transactions, that a multiplicity of objects successively passes over the field of view, not less independent in themselves, though not less connected in the succession of events, than the pictures of a magic lantern. I am aware of the weariness and the perplexity which are in consequence inflicted on the attention and the memory of the hearer; but what can I do but ask your indulgence, Gentlemen, for a circumstance which is inherent in any undertaking like the present? I have in the course of an hour to deal with a series of exploits and fortunes, which begin in the wilds of Turkistan, and conclude upon the Bosphorus; in which, as I may say, time is no measure of events, one while from the obscurity in which they lie, at another from their multitude and consequent confusion. For four centuries the Turks are little or hardly heard of; then suddenly in the course of as many tens of years, and under three Sultans, they make the whole world resound with their deeds; and, while they have pushed to the East through Hindostan, in the West they have hurried down to the coasts of the Mediterranean and the Archipelago, have taken Jerusalem, and threatened Constantinople. In their long period of silence they had been sowing the seeds of future conquests; in their short period of action they were gathering the fruit of past labours and sufferings. The Saracenic empire stood apparently as before; but, as soon as a Turk showed himself at the head of a military force within its territory, he found himself surrounded by the armies of his kindred which had been so long in its pay; he was joined by the tribes of Turcomans, to whom the Romans in a former age had shown the passes of the Caucasus; and he could rely on the reserve of innumerable swarms, ever issuing out of his native desert, and following in his track. Such was the state of Western Asia in the middle of the eleventh century.

7.

I have said there were three great Sultans of the race of Seljuk, by whom the conquest of the West of Asia was begun and completed; their names are Togrul Beg, Alp Arslan, and Malek Shah. I have not to write their histories, but I may say a few words of their characters and their actions.

1. The first, Togrul, was the son and grandson of Mahometan Martyrs, and he inherited that fanaticism, which made the old Seljuk and the young Michael surrender their lives in their missionary warfare against the enemies of their faith. Each day he repeated the five prayers prescribed for the disciples of Islam; each week he gave two days to fasting; in every city which he made his own, he built a mosque before he built his palace. He introduced vast numbers of his wild countrymen into his provinces, and suffered their nomadic habits, on the condition of their becoming proselytes to his creed. He was the man suited to his time; mere material power was not adequate to the overthrow of the Saracenic sovereignty: rebellion after rebellion had been successful against the Caliph; and at the very time I speak of he was in subjection to a family of the old Persian race. But then he was spiritual head of the Empire as well as temporal; and, though he lay in his palace wallowing in brutal sensuality, he was still a sort of mock-Pope, even after his armies and his territories had been wrested from his hands; but it was the reward of Togrul's zeal to gain from him this spiritual prerogative, retaining which the Caliph could never have fallen altogether. He gave to Togrul the title of Rocnoddîn, or "the firm pillar of religion;" and, what was more to the purpose, he made him his vicegerent over the whole

Moslem world. Armed with this religious authority, which was temporal in its operation, he went to war against the various insurgents who troubled the Caliph's repose, and substituted himself for them, a more powerful and insidious enemy than any or all. But even Mahomet, the Caliph's predecessor, would not have denied that Togrul was worthy of his hire; he turned towards Armenia and Asia Minor, and began that terrible war against the Cross, which was to last 500 years. The prodigious number of 130,000 Christians, in battle or otherwise, is said to be the sacrifice he offered up to the false prophet. On his victorious return, he was again recognized by his grateful master as his representative. He made his public entry into the imperial city on horseback. At the palace gate he showed the outward deference to the Caliph's authority which was his policy. He dismounted, his nobles laid aside their arms, and thus they walked respectfully into the recesses of the palace. According to the Saracenic ceremonial, the Caliph received them behind his black veil, the black garment of his family was cast over his shoulders, and the staff of Mahomet was in his hand. Togrul kissed the ground, and waited modestly, till he was led to the throne, and was there allowed to seat himself, and to hear the commission publicly declaring him invested with the authority of the Vicar of the Arch-deceiver. He was then successively clothed in seven robes of honour, and presented with seven slaves, the natives of the seven climates of the Saracenic Empire. His veil was perfumed with musk; two crowns were set upon his head; two scimitars were girded on his side, in token of his double reign over East and West. He twice kissed the Caliph's hand; and his titles were proclaimed by the voice of heralds and the applause of the Moslem.

Such was Togrul Beg, and such was his reward. After these exploits, he marched against his brother (for these Turkish tribes were always quarrelling over their prey), deposed him, strangled him and put to death a number of his adherents, married the Caliph's daughter, and then died without children. His power passed to his nephew Alp Arslan.

2. Alp Arslan, the second Sultan of the line of Seljuk, is said to signify in Turkish "the courageous lion:" and the Caliph gave its possessor the Arabic appellation of Azzaddin, or "Protector of Religion." It was the distinctive work of his short reign to pass from humbling the Caliph to attacking the Greek Emperor. Togrul had already invaded the Greek provinces of Asia Minor, from Cilicia to Armenia, along a line of 600 miles, and here it was that he had achieved his tremendous massacres of Christians. Alp Arslan renewed the war; he penetrated to Cæsarea in Cappadocia, attracted by the gold and pearls which encrusted the shrine of the great St. Basil. He then turned his arms against Armenia and Georgia, and conquered the hardy mountaineers of the Caucasus, who at present give such trouble to the Russians. After this he encountered, defeated, and captured the Greek Emperor. He began the battle with all the solemnity and pageantry of a hero of romance. Casting away his bow and arrows, he called for an iron mace and scimitar; he perfumed his body with musk, as if for his burial, and dressed himself in white, that he might be slain in his winding-sheet. After his victory, the captive Emperor of New Rome was brought before him in a peasant's dress; he made him kiss the ground beneath his feet, and put his foot upon his neck. Then, raising him up, he struck or patted him three times with his hand, and gave him his life and, on a large ransom, his liberty.

At this time the Sultan was only forty-four years of age, and seemed to have a career of glory still before him. Twelve hundred nobles stood before his throne; two hundred thousand soldiers marched under his banner. As if dissatisfied with the South, he turned his arms against his own paternal wildernesses, with which his family, as I have related, had a feud. New tribes of Turks seem to have poured down, and were wresting Sogdiana from the race of Seljuk, as the Seljukians had wrested it from the Gaznevides. Alp had not advanced far into the country, when he met his death from the hand of a captive. A Carismian chief had withstood his progress, and, being taken, was condemned to a lingering execution. On hearing the sentence, he rushed forward upon Alp Arslan; and the Sultan, disdaining to let his generals interfere, bent his bow, but, missing his aim, received the dagger of his prisoner in his breast. His death, which followed, brings before us that grave dignity of the Turkish character, of which we have already had an example in Mahmood. Finding his end approaching, he has left on record a sort of dying confession:—" In my youth," he said, "I was advised by a sage to humble myself before God, to distrust my own strength, and never to despise the most contemptible foe. I have neglected these lessons, and my neglect has been deservedly punished. Yesterday, as from an eminence, I beheld the numbers, the discipline, and the spirit of my armies; the earth seemed to tremble under my feet, and I said in my heart, Surely thou art the king of the world, the greatest and most invincible of warriors. These armies are no longer mine; and, in the confidence of my personal strength, I now fall by the hand of an assassin." On his tomb was engraven an inscription, conceived in a similar spirit. " O ye, who have seen the glory of Alp Arslan exalted to the heavens, repair to Maru, and you will behold it buried in the dust."[1] Alp Arslan was adorned with great natural qualities both of intellect and of soul. He was brave and liberal: just, patient, and sincere: constant in his prayers, diligent in his alms, and, it is added, witty in his conversation ;— but his gifts availed him not.

3. It often happens in the history of states and races, in which there is found first a rise and then a decline, that the greatest glories take place just then when the reverse is beginning or begun. Thus, for instance, in the history of the Ottoman Turks, to which I have not yet come, Soliman the Magnificent is at once the last and greatest of a series of great Sultans. So was it as regards this house of Seljuk. Malek Shah, the son of Alp Arslan, the third sovereign, in whom its glories ended, is represented to us in history in colours so bright and perfect, that it is difficult to believe we are not reading the account of some mythical personage. He came to the throne at the early age of seventeen; he was well-shaped, handsome, polished both in manners and in mind; wise and courageous, pious and sincere. He engaged himself even more in the consolidation of his empire than in its extension. He reformed abuses; he reduced the taxes; he repaired the high roads, bridges, and canals; he built an imperial mosque at Bagdad; he founded and nobly endowed a college. He patronised learning and poetry, and he reformed the calendar. He provided marts for commerce; he upheld the pure administration of justice, and protected the helpless and the innocent. He established wells and cisterns in great numbers along the road of pilgrimage to Mecca; he fed the pilgrims, and distributed immense sums among the poor.

[1] Gibbon.

He was in every respect a great prince; he extended his conquests across Sogdiana to the very borders of China. He subdued by his lieutenants Syria and the Holy Land, and took Jerusalem. He is said to have travelled round his vast dominions twelve times. So potent was he, that he actually gave away kingdoms, and had for feudatories great princes. He gave to his cousin his territories in Asia Minor, and planted him over against Constantinople, as an earnest of future conquests; and he may be said to have finally allotted to the Turcomans the fair regions of Western Asia, over which they roam to this day.

All human greatness has its term; the more brilliant was this great Sultan's rise, the more sudden was his extinction; and the earlier he came to his power, the earlier did he lose it. He had reigned twenty years, and was but thirty-seven years old, when he was lifted up with pride and came to his end. He disgraced and abandoned to an assassin his faithful vizir, at the age of ninety-three, who for thirty years had been the servant and benefactor of the house of Seljuk. After obtaining from the Caliph the peculiar and almost incommunicable title of "the commander of the faithful," unsatisfied still, he wished to fix his own throne in Bagdad, and to deprive his impotent superior of his few remaining honours. He demanded the hand of the daughter of the Greek Emperor, a Christian, in marriage. A few days, and he was no more; he had gone out hunting, and returned indisposed; a vein was opened, and the blood would not flow. A burning fever took him off, only eighteen days after the murder of his vizir, and less than ten before the day when the Caliph was to have been removed from Bagdad.

8.

Such is human greatness at the best, even were it ever so innocent; but as to this poor Sultan, there is another aspect even of his glorious deeds. If I have seemed here or elsewhere in these Lectures to speak of him or his with interest or admiration, only take me, Gentlemen, as giving the external view of the Turkish history, and that as introductory to the determination of its true significance. Historians and poets may celebrate the exploits of Malek; but what were they in the sight of Him who has said that whoso shall strike against His corner-stone shall be broken; but on whomsoever it shall fall, shall be ground to powder? Looking at this Sultan's deeds as mere exhibitions of human power, they were brilliant and marvellous; but there was another judgment of them formed in the West, and other feelings than admiration roused by them in the faith and the chivalry of Christendom. Especially was there one, the divinely appointed shepherd of the poor of Christ, the anxious steward of His Church, who from his high and ancient watch tower, in the fulness of apostolic charity, surveyed narrowly what was going on at thousands of miles from him, and with prophetic eye looked into the future age; and scarcely had that enemy, who was in the event so heavily to smite the Christian world, shown himself, when he gave warning of the danger, and prepared himself with measures for averting it. Scarcely had the Turk touched the shores of the Mediterranean and the Archipelago, when the Pope detected and denounced him before all Europe. The heroic Pontiff, St. Gregory the Seventh, was then upon the throne of the Apostle; and though he was engaged in one of the severest conflicts which Pope has ever sustained, not only against the secular power, but against bad bishops and priests, yet at a time when his very life was not his own, and present responsibilities so urged him, that one would fancy he had time for no other thought, Gregory was able to turn his mind to the consideration of a contingent danger in the almost fabulous East. In a letter written during the reign of Malek Shah, he suggested the idea of a crusade against the misbeliever, which later popes, carried out. He assures the Emperor of Germany, whom he was addressing, that he had 50,000 troops ready for the holy war, whom he would fain have led in person. This was in the year 1074.

In truth, the most melancholy accounts were brought to Europe of the state of things in the Holy Land. A rude Turcoman ruled in Jerusalem; his people insulted there the clergy of every profession; they dragged the patriarch by the hair along the pavement, and cast him into a dungeon, in hopes of a ransom; and disturbed from time to time the Latin Mass and office in the Church of the Resurrection. As to the pilgrims, Asia Minor, the country through which they had to travel in an age when the sea was not yet safe to the voyager, was a scene of foreign incursion and internal distraction. They arrived at Jerusalem exhausted by their sufferings, and sometimes terminated them by death, before they were permitted to kiss the Holy Sepulchre.

9.

Outrages such as these were of frequent occurrence, and one was very like another. In concluding, however, this Lecture, I think it worth while to set before you, Gentlemen, the circumstances of one of them in detail, that you may be able to form some ideas of the state both of Asia Minor and of a Christian pilgrimage, under the dominion of the Turks. You may recollect, then, that Alp Arslan, the second Seljukian Sultan, invaded Asia Minor, and made prisoner the Greek Emperor. This Sultan came to the throne in 1062, and appears to have begun his warlike operations immediately. The next year, or the next but one, a body of pilgrims, to the number of 7,000, were pursuing their peaceful way to Jerusalem, by a route which at that time lay entirely through countries professing Christianity.[1] The pious company was headed by the Archbishop of Mentz, the Bishops of Utrecht, Bamberg, and Ratisbon, and, among others, by a party of Norman soldiers and clerks, belonging to the household of William Duke of Normandy, who made himself, very soon afterwards, our William the Conqueror. Among these clerks was the celebrated Benedictine Monk Ingulphus, William's secretary, afterwards Abbot of Croyland in Lincolnshire, being at that time a little more than thirty years of age. They passed through Germany and Hungary to Constantinople, and thence by the southern coast of Asia Minor or Anatolia, to Syria and Palestine. When they got on the confines of Asia Minor towards Cilicia, they fell in with the savage Turcomans, who were attracted by the treasure, which these noble persons and wealthy churchmen had brought with them for pious purposes and imprudently displayed. Ingulphus's words are few, but so graphic that I require an apology for using them. He says then, they were "exenterated" or "cleaned out of the immense sums of money they carried with them, together with the loss of many lives."

A contemporary historian gives us fuller particulars of the adventure, and he too appears to have been a party to the expedition.[2] It seems the prelates celebrated the

---
[1] Baronius, Gibbon.   [2] Vid. Cave's Hist. Litterar. in nom. *Lambertus*.

rites of the Church with great magnificence, as they went along, and travelled with a pomp which became great dignitaries. The Turcomans in consequence set on them, overwhelmed them, stripped them to the skin, and left the Bishop of Utrecht disabled and half dead upon the field. The poor sufferers effected their retreat to a village, where they fortified an enclosure and took possession of a building which stood within it. Here they defended themselves courageously for as many as three days, though they are said to have had nothing to eat. At the end of that time they expressed a wish to surrender themselves to the enemy, and admitted eighteen of the barbarian leaders into their place of strength, with a view of negotiating the terms. The Bishop of Bamberg, who is said to have had a striking presence, acted for the Christians, and bargained for nothing more than their lives. The savage Turcoman, who was the speaker on the other side, attracted by his appearance, unrolled his turban, and threw it round the Bishop's neck, crying out: "You and all of you are mine." The Bishop made answer by an interpreter: "What will you do to me?" The savage shrieked out some unintelligible words, which, being explained to the Bishop, ran thus: "I will suck that blood which is so ruddy in your throat, and then I will hang you up like a dog at your gate." "Upon which," says the historian, "the Bishop, who had the modesty of a gentleman, and was of a grave disposition, not bearing the insult, dashed his fist into the Turcoman's face with such vigour as to fell him to the ground, crying out that the profane wretch should rather be the sufferer, for laying his unclean hands upon a priest."

This was the signal for an exploit so bold, that it seemed, if I may so express myself, like a particular

inspiration. The Christians, unarmed as they were,
started up, and though, as I have observed, they may be
said to have scarcely tasted food for three days, rushed
upon the eighteen Turcomans, bound their arms behind
their backs, and showing them in this condition to their
own troops who surrounded the house, protested that
they would instantly put them all to death, unless they
themselves were let go. It is difficult to see how this
complication would have ended, in which neither side
were in a condition either to recede or to advance, had
not a third party interfered with a considerable force in
the person of the military governor, himself a Pagan,[1]
of a neighbouring city; and though, as our historian
says, the Christians found it difficult to understand how
Satan could cast out Satan, so it was, that they found
themselves at liberty and their enemies marched off to
punishment, on the payment of a sum of money to their
deliverers. I need not pursue the history of these
pilgrims further than to say, that, of 7,000 who set out,
only 2,000 returned to Europe.

Much less am I led to enter into the history of the
Crusades which followed. How the Holy See, twenty
years after St. Gregory, effected that which St. Gregory
attempted without result; how, along the very way
which the pilgrims I have described journeyed, 100,000
men at length appeared cased in complete armour and
on horseback; how they drove the Turk from Nicæa
over against Constantinople, where he had fixed his
imperial city, to the farther borders of Asia Minor; how,

[1] Gibbon makes this the Fatimite governor of some town in Galilee,
laying the scene in Palestine. The name Capernaum is doubtfully
mentioned in the history, but the occurrence is said to have taken place on
the borders of Lycia. Anyhow, there were Turcomans in Palestine. Part
of the account in the text is taken from Marianus Scotus.

after defeating him in a pitched battle at Dorylæum, they went on and took Antioch, and then at length, after a long pilgrimage of three years, made conquest of Jerusalem itself, I need not here relate. To one point only is it to our present purpose to direct attention. It is commonly said that the Crusades failed in their object; that they were nothing else but a lavish expenditure of men and treasure ; and that the possession of the Holy Places by the Turks to this day is a proof of it. Now I will not enter here into a very intricate controversy; this only will I say, that, if the tribes of the desert, under the leadership of the house of Seljuk, turned their faces to the West in the middle of the eleventh century; if in forty years they had advanced from Khorasan to Jerusalem and the neighbourhood of Constantinople; and if in consequence they were threatening Europe and Christianity ; and if, for that reason, it was a great object to drive them back or break them to pieces ; if it were a worthy object of the Crusades to rescue Europe from this peril and to reassure the anxious minds of Christian multitudes;—then were the Crusades no failure in their issue, for this object was fully accomplished. The Seljukian Turks were hurled back upon the East, and then broken up, by the hosts of the Crusaders.[1] The lieutenant of Malek Shah, who had been established as Sultan of Roum (as Asia Minor was called by the Turks), was driven to an obscure town, where his dynasty lasted, indeed, but gradually dwindled away. A similar fate attended the house of Seljuk in other parts of the Empire, and internal quarrels increased and perpetuated its weakness. Sudden as was its rise, as sudden was its fall ; till the terrible Zingis, descending

---

[1] I should observe that the Turks were driven out of Jerusalem by the Fatimites of Egypt, two years before the Crusaders appeared.

on the Turkish dynasties, like an avalanche, coöperated effectually with the Crusaders and finished their work; and if Jerusalem was not protected from other enemies, at least Constantinople was saved, and Europe was placed in security, for three hundred years.[1]

[1] I am pleased to see that Mr. Sharon Turner takes the same view strongly.—*England in Middle Ages*, i. 9. Also Mr. Francis Newman; "The See of Rome," he says, "had not forgotten, if Europe had, how deadly and dangerous a war Charles Martel and the Franks had had to wage against the Moors from Spain. A new and redoubtable nation, the Seljuk Turks, had now appeared on the confines of Europe, as a fresh champion of the Mohammedan Creed; and it is not attributing too much foresight or too sagacious policy to the Court of Rome, to believe, that they wished to stop and put down the Turkish power before it should come too near. Be this as it may, such was the result. The might of the Seljukians was crippled on the plains of Palestine, and did not ultimately reach Europe. . . . A large portion of Christendom, which disowned the religious pretensions of Rome, was afterwards subdued by another Turkish tribe, the Ottomans or Osmanlis; but Romish Christendom remained untouched : Poland, Germany, and Hungary, saved her from the later Turks, even during the schism of the Reformation, as the Franks had saved her from the Moors. On the whole, it would seem that to the Romish Church we have been largely indebted for that union between European nations, without which Mohammedanism might perhaps not have been repelled. I state this as probable, not at all as certain."—*Lectures at Manchester*, 1846.

III.

THE CONQUESTS OF THE TURKS.

LECTURE V.

The Turk and the Christian.

I SAID in my last Lecture, that we are bound to judge of persons and events in history, not by their outward appearance, but by their inward significancy. In speaking of the Turks, we may for a moment yield to the romance which attends on their name and their actions, as we may admire the beauty of some beast of prey; but, as it would be idle and puerile to praise its shape or skin, and form no further judgment upon it, so in like manner it is unreal and unphilosophical to interest ourselves in the mere adventures and successes of the Turks, without going on to view them in their moral aspect also. No race casts so broad and dark a shadow on the page of ecclesiastical history, and leaves so painful an impression on the minds of the reader, as the Turkish. The fierce Goths and Vandals, and then again the Lombards, were converted to Catholicism. The Franks yielded to the voice of St. Remigius, and Clovis, their leader, became the eldest son of the Church. The Anglo-Saxons gave up their idols at the preaching of St. Augustine and his companions. The German tribes acknowledged Christ amid their forests, though they martyred St. Boniface and other English and Irish missionaries who came to them. The Magyars in Hungary were led to faith through loyalty to their temporal monarch, their royal missioner St. Stephen. The heathen Danes reappear as the chivalrous Normans, the haughty but true sons and vassals of St. Peter. The Saracens even, who gave birth to an imposture, withered away at the end of 300 or 400 years, and had not the power, though they had the will, to persevere in their enmity to the Cross. The Tartars had both the will and the power, but they were far off from Christendom, or they came down in ephemeral outbreaks, which were rather those of freebooters than of persecutors, or they directed their fury as often against the enemies of the Church as against her children. But the unhappy race, of whom I am speaking, from the first moment they appear in the history of Christendom, are its unmitigated, its obstinate, its consistent foes. They are inexhaustible in numbers, pouring down upon the South and West, and taking one and the same terrible mould of misbelief, as they successively descend. They have the populousness of the North, with the fire of the South; the resources of Tartars, with the fanaticism of Saracens. And when their strength declines, and age steals upon them, there is no softening, no misgiving; they die and make no sign. In the words of the Wise Man, "Being born, they forthwith ceased to be; and have been able to show no mark of virtue, but are consumed in wickedness." God's judgments, God's mercies, are inscrutable; one nation is taken, another is left. It is a mystery; but the fact stands; since the year 1048 the Turks have been the great Antichrist among the races of men.

I say since this date, because then it was that Togrul Beg finally opened the gates of the North to those descents, which had taken place indeed at intervals before, but then became the habit of centuries. In vain was the power of his dynasty overthrown by the Crusaders; in vain do the Seljukians disappear from the annals of the world; in vain is Constantinople respited; in vain is Europe saved. Christendom in arms had not yet finished, it had but begun the work, in which it needed the grace to persevere. Down came the savage hordes, as at first, upon Sogdiana and Khorasan, so then upon Syria and its neighbouring countries. Sometimes they remain wild Turcomans, sometimes they fall into the civilization of the South; but there they are, in Egypt, in the Holy Land, in Armenia, in Anatolia, forming political bodies of long or short duration, breaking up here to form again there, in all cases trampling on Christianity, and beating out its sacred impression from the breasts of tens of thousands. Nor is this all; scarcely is the race of Seljuk quite extinct, or rather when it is on its very death-bed, after it had languished and shrunk and dwindled and flickered and kept on dying through a tedious two hundred years, when its sole remaining heir was just in one obscure court, from that very court we discern the birth of another empire, as dazzling in its rise, as energetic and impetuous in its deeds as that of Togrul, Alp, and Malek, and far more wide-spreading, far more powerful, far more lasting than the Seljukian. This is the empire of the great (if I must measure it by a human standard) and glorious race of Othman; this is the dynasty of the Ottomans or Osmanlis; once the admiration, the terror of nations, now, even in its downfall, an object of curiosity, interest, anxiety, and even respect; but, whether high or low, in all cases to the Christian the inveterate and hateful enemy of the Cross.

I.

There is a certain remarkable parallel and contrast between the fortunes of these two races, the Seljukian and the Ottoman. In the beginning of the twelfth century, the race of Seljuk all but took Constantinople, and overran the West, and did not; in the beginning of the fifteenth, the Ottoman Turks were all but taking the same city, and then were withheld from taking it, and at length did take it, and have it still. In each case a foe came upon them from the north, still more fierce and vigorous than they, and humbled them to the dust.

These two foes, which came upon the Seljukian Turks and the Ottoman Turks respectively, are names by this time familiar to us; they are Zingis and Timour. Zingis came down upon the Seljukians, and Timour came down upon the Ottomans. Timour pressed the Ottomans even more severely than Zingis pressed the Seljukians; yet the Seljukians did not recover the blow of Zingis; but the Ottomans survived the blow of Timour, and rose more formidable after it, and have long outlived the power which inflicted it.

Zingis and Timour were but the blind instruments of divine vengeance. They knew not what they did. The inward impulse of gigantic energy and brutal cupidity urged them forward; ambition, love of destruction, sensual appetite, frenzied them, and made them both more and less than men. They pushed eastward, westward, southward; they confronted promptly and joyfully every peril, every obstacle which lay in their course. They smote down all rival pride and greatness of man; and therefore, by the law (as I may call it) of their nature and destiny, not on politic reason or far-reaching plan, but because they came across him, they smote the Turk.

These then were one class of his opponents; but there was another adversary, stationed against him, of a different order, one whose power was not material, but mental and spiritual; one whose enmity was not random, or casual, or temporary, but went on steadily from age to age, and lasts down to this day, except so far as the Turk's decrepitude has at length disarmed anxiety and opposition. I have spoken of him already; of course I mean the Vicar of Christ. I mean the zealous, the religious enmity to every anti-Christian power, of him who has outlasted Zingis and Timour, who has outlasted Seljuk, who is now outlasting Othman. He incited Christendom against the Seljukians, and the Seljukians, assailed also by Zingis, sunk beneath the double blow. He tried to rouse Christendom against the Ottomans also, but in vain; and therefore in vain did Timour discharge his overwhelming, crushing force against them. Overwhelmed and crushed they were, but they revived. The Seljukians fell, in consequence of the united zeal of the great Christian commonwealth moving in panoply against them; the Ottomans succeeded by reason of its deplorable divisions, and its decay of faith and heroism.

2.

Whether indeed in the long run, and after all his disappointments and reverses, the Pope was altogether unsuccessful in his warfare against the Ottomans, we shall see by-and-by; but certainly, if perseverance merited a favourable issue, at least he has had a right to expect it. War with the Turks was his uninterrupted cry for seven or eight centuries, from the eleventh to the eighteenth; it is a solitary and singular event in the history of the Church. Sylvester the Second was the originator of the scheme of a union of Christian nations against them. St. Gregory the Seventh collected 50,000 men to repel them. Urban the Second actually set in motion the long crusade. Honorius the Second instituted the order of Knight Templars to protect the pilgrims from their assaults. Eugenius the Third sent St. Bernard to preach the Holy War. Innocent the Third advocated it in the august Council of the Lateran. Nicholas the Fourth negotiated an alliance with the Tartars for its prosecution. Gregory the Tenth was in the Holy Land in the midst of it, with our Edward the First, when he was elected Pope. Urban the Fifth received and reconciled the Greek Emperor with a view to its renewal. Innocent the Sixth sent the Blessed Peter Thomas the Carmelite to preach in its behalf. Boniface the Ninth raised the magnificent army of French, Germans, and Hungarians, who fought the great battle of Nicopolis. Eugenius the Fourth formed the confederation of Hungarians and Poles who fought the battle of Varna. Nicholas the Fifth sent round St. John Capistran to urge the princes of Christendom against the enemy. Callixtus the Third sent the celebrated Hunniades to fight with them. Pius the Second addressed to their Sultan an apostolic letter of warning and denunciation. Sixtus the Fourth fitted out a fleet against them. Innocent the Eighth made them his mark from the beginning of his Pontificate to the end. St. Pius the Fifth added the "Auxilium Christianorum" to our Lady's Litany in thankfulness for his victory over them. Gregory the Thirteenth with the same purpose appointed the Festival of the Rosary. Clement the Ninth died of grief on account of their successes. The venerable Innocent the Eleventh appointed the Festival of the Holy Name of Mary, for their rout before Vienna. Clement the Eleventh extended the Feast of the Rosary to the whole Church for the great victory over them near Belgrade. These are but some of the many instances which might be given; but they are enough for the purpose of showing the perseverance of the Popes.

Nor was their sagacity in this matter less remarkable than their pertinacity. The Holy See has the reputation, even with men of the world, of seeing instinctively what is favourable, what is unfavourable, to the interests of religion and of the Catholic Faith. Its undying opposition to the Turks is not the least striking instance of this divinely imparted gift. From the very first it pointed at them as an object of alarm for all Christendom, in a way in which it had marked out neither Tartars nor Saracens. It exposed them to the reprobation of Europe, as a people, with whom, if charity differ from merciless ferocity, tenderness from hardness of heart, depravity of appetite from virtue, and pride from meekness and humility, the faithful never could have sympathy, never alliance. It denounced, not merely an odious outlying deformity, painful simply to the moral sight and scent, but an energetic evil, an aggressive, ambitious, ravenous foe, in whom foulness of life and cruelty of policy were methodized by system, consecrated by religion, propagated by the sword. I am not insensible, I wish to do justice, to the high qualities of the Turkish race. I do not altogether deny to its national character the grandeur, the force and originality, the valour, the truthfulness and sense of justice, the sobriety and gentleness, which historians and travellers speak of; but, in spite of all that has been done for them by nature and by the European world, Tartar still is the staple of their composition, and their gifts and attainments, whatever they may be, do but make them the more efficient foes of faith and civilization.

3.

It was said by a Prophet of old, in the prospect of a fierce invader, "a day of clouds and whirlwinds, a numerous and strong people, as the morning spread upon the mountains. The like to it hath not been from the beginning, nor shall be after it, even to the years of generation and generation. Before the face thereof a devouring fire, and behind it a burning flame. The land is like a garden of pleasure before it, and behind it a desolate wilderness; neither is there any one can escape it." Now I might, in illustration of the character which the Turks bear in history, suitably accommodate these words to the moral, or the social, or the political, or the religious calamities, of which they were the authors to the Christian countries they overran; and so I might bring home to you the meaning and drift of that opposition with which the Holy See has met them in every age. I might allude (if I dare, but I dare not, nor does any one dare),—else, allusion might be made to those unutterable deeds which brand the people which allows them, even in the natural judgment of men, as the most flagitious, the most detestable of nations. I might enlarge on the reckless and remorseless cruelty which, had they succeeded in Europe, as they succeeded in Asia, would have decimated or exterminated her children; I might have reminded you, for instance, how it has been almost a canon of their imperial policy for centuries, that their Sultan, on mounting the throne, should destroy his nearest of kin, father, brother, or cousin, who might rival him in his sovereignty; how he is surrounded, and his subjects according to their wealth, with slaves carried off from their homes, men and boys, living monuments of his barbarity towards the work of God's hands; how he has at his remorseless will and in the sudden breath of his mouth the life or death of all his subjects; how he multiplies his despotism by giving to his lieutenants in every province, a like prerogative; how little scruple those governors have ever felt in exercising this prerogative to the full, in executions on a large scale, and sudden overwhelming massacres, shedding blood like water, and playing with the life of man as though it were the life of a mere beast or reptile. I might call your attention to particular instances of such atrocities, such as that outrage perpetrated in the memory of many of us,—how, on the insurrection of the Greeks at Scio, their barbarian masters carried fire and sword throughout the flourishing island till it was left a desert, hurrying away women and boys to an infamous captivity, and murdering youths and grown men, till out of 120,000 souls, in the spring time, not 900 were left there when the crops were ripe for the sickle. If I do not go into scenes such as these in detail, it is because I have wearied and troubled you more than enough already, in my account of the savage perpetrations of Zingis and Timour.

Or I might, in like manner, still more obviously insist on their system of compulsory conversion, which, from the time of the Seljukian Sultans to the present day, have raised the indignation and the compassion of the Christian world; how, when the lieutenants of Malek Shah got possession of Asia Minor, they profaned the churches, subjected Bishops and Clergy to the most revolting outrages, circumcised the youth, and led off their sisters to their profligate households;—how, when the Ottomans conquered in turn, and added an infantry,

I mean the Janizaries, to their Tartar horse, they formed that body of troops, from first to last, for near five hundred years, of boys, all born Christian, a body of at first 12,000, at last 40,000 strong, torn away year by year from their parents, circumcised, trained to the faith and morals of their masters, and becoming in their turn the instruments of the terrible policy of which they had themselves been victims; and how, when at length lately they abolished this work of their hands, they ended it by the slaughter of 20,000 of the poor renegades whom they had seduced from their God. I might remind you how within the last few years a Protestant traveller tells us that he found the Nestorian Christians, who had survived the massacres of their race, living in holes and pits, their pastures and tillage land forfeited, their sheep and cattle driven away, their villages burned, and their ministers and people tortured; and how a Catholic missionary has found in the neighbourhood of Broussa the remnant of some twenty Catholic families, who, in consequence of repudiating the Turkish faith, had been carried all the way from Servia and Albania across the sea to Asia Minor; the men killed, the women disgraced, the boys sold, till out of a hundred and eighty persons but eighty-seven were left, and they sick, and famished, and dying among their unburied dead. I could of course continue this topic also to any extent, and draw it out as an illustration of the words of the Prophet which I have quoted. But I prefer to take those words literally, as expressive of the desolation spread by an infidel foe over the face of a flourishing country; and then I shall be viewing the Turkish rule under an aspect addressed to the senses, not admitting of a question, calculated to rouse the sensibilities of Christians of whatever caste of opinion, and explanatory by itself of the determined front which the Holy See has ever made against it.

4

The Catholic Church was in the first instance a wanderer on the earth, and had nothing to attach her to its soil; but no sooner did persecution cease, and territory was allowed to her, than she began to exert a beneficent influence upon the face of the land, and on its cultivators. She shed her consolations, and extended her protection, over the serf and the slave; and, while she gradually relaxed his fetters, she sent her own dearest children to bear his burden with him, and to aid him in the cultivation of the soil. Under the loving assiduity of the Benedictine Monk, the ravages of war were repaired, the plantation throve, the river diffused itself in rills and channels, and hill and dale and plain rejoiced in corn land and pasture. And when in a later time a world was to be created, not restored, when the deep forests of the North were to be cleared, and the unwholesome marsh to be drained, who but the missionaries from the same great Order were to be the ministers of temporal, as well as spiritual, benefits to the rude tribes they were converting? And then again, when history moved on into the era of the first Turkish outbreak, who but St. Bernard, the very preacher of the Crusade, who but he led on his peaceful Cistercians, after the pattern of his master, St. Stephen, to that laborious but cheerful husbandry, which they continue in the wild places of the earth even to this day? Never has Holy Church forgotten,—abhorrent, as she is, from the Pantheistic tendencies which in all ages have surrounded her,—never has she forgotten the interests of that mighty mother on whose bosom we feed in life, into whose arms we drop in death; never has she forgotten that that mother is the special creature of God, and to be honoured, in leaf and flower, in lofty tree and pleasant stream, for His sake, as well as for our own; that while it is our primeval penalty to till the earth, she lovingly repays us for our toil; that Adam was a gardener even in Paradise, and that Noe inaugurated his new world by "beginning to be a husbandman, and by planting a vineyard."

Such is the genius of the true faith; and it might have been thought, that, though not Christians, even of very gratitude, the barbarous race, which owed a part of whatever improvement of mind or manners they had received to the fair plains of Sogdiana, would, on seizing on their rich and beautiful lands on the north, east, and south of the Mediterranean, have felt some sort of reverence for their captive, and, while enjoying her gifts, would have been merciful to the giver. But the same selfish sensuality, with which they regard the rational creation of God, possesses them in their conduct towards physical nature. They have made the earth their paramour, and are heartless towards her dishonour and her misery. We have lately been reminded in this place of the Doge of Venice[1] making the Adriatic his bride, and claiming her by a ring of espousal; but the Turk does not deign to legitimatize his possession of the soil he has violently seized, or to gain a title to it by any sacred tie; caring for no better right to it than the pirate has to the jurisdiction of the high seas. Let the Turcoman ride up and down Asia Minor or Syria for a thousand years, how is the trampling of his horse-hoofs a possession of those countries, more than a

[1] Vid. a beautiful passage in Cardinal Wiseman's late lecture at Liverpool.

Scythian raid or a Tartar gallop across it? The imperial Osmanli sits and smokes long days in his pavilion, without any thought at all of his broad domain except to despise and to plunder and impoverish its cultivators; and is his title made better thereby than the Turcoman's, to be the heir of Alexander and Seleucus, of the Ptolemies and Massinissa, of Constantine and Justinian? What claim does it give him upon Europe, Asia, and Africa, upon Greece, Palestine, and Egypt, that he has frustrated the munificence of nature and demolished the works of man?

5.

Asia Minor especially, the peninsula which lies between the Black Sea, the Archipelago, and the Mediterranean, was by nature one of the most beautiful, and had been made by art one of the most fertile of countries. It had for generations contained flourishing marts of commerce, and it had been studded with magnificent cities, the ruins of which now stand as a sepulchre of the past. No country perhaps has seen such a succession of prosperous states, and had such a host of historical reminiscences, under such distinct eras and such various distributions of territory. It is memorable in the beginning of history for its barbarian kings and nobles, whose names stand as commonplaces and proverbs of wealth and luxury. The magnificence of Pelops imparts lustre even to the brilliant dreams of the mythologist. The name of Crœsus, King of Lydia, whom I have already had occasion to mention, goes as a proverb for his enormous riches. Midas, King of Phrygia, had such abundance of the precious metals, that he was said by the poets to have the power of turning whatever he touched into gold. The tomb of

Mausolus, King of Caria, was one of the seven wonders of the ancient world. It was the same with the Greek colonies which were scattered along its coasts; they are renowned for opulence, for philosophy, and for the liberal and the fine arts. Homer among the poets, Thales among philosophers, Herodotus, the father of history, Hippocrates, the oracle of physicians, Apelles, the prince of painters, were among their citizens; and Pythius, who presented one of the Persian Kings with a plane-tree and a vine of massive gold, was in his day, after those kings, the richest man in the known world.

Then come the many splendid cities founded by the successors of Alexander, through its extent; and the powerful and opulent kingdoms, Greek or Barbarian, of Pontus, and Bithynia, and Pergamus—Pergamus, with its library of 200,000 choice volumes. Later still, the resources of the country were so well recognised, that it was the favourite prey of the Roman statesmen, who, after involving themselves in enormous debts in the career of ambition, needed by extortion and rapine to set themselves right with their creditors. Next it became one of the first seats of Christianity; St. Luke in the Acts of the Apostles relates to us the apostolic labours of St. Paul there in town and country; St. John wrote the Apocalypse to the Churches of seven of its principal cities; and St. Peter, his first Epistle to Christians scattered through its provinces. It was the home of some of the greatest Saints, Martyrs, and Doctors of the early ages: there first, in Bithynia, the power of Christianity manifested itself over a heathen population; there St. Polycarp was martyred, there St. Gregory Thamaturgus converted the inhabitants of Pontus; there St. Gregory Nazianzen, St. Gregory Nyssen, St.

Basil, and St. Amphilochius preached and wrote. There were held three of the first four Councils of the Church, at Chalcedon, at Ephesus, and at Nicæa, the very city afterwards profaned by the palace of the Sultan. It abounded in the gifts of nature, for food, utility, or ornament; its rivers ran with gold, its mountains yielded the most costly marbles; it had mines of copper, and especially of iron; its plains were fruitful in all kinds of grain, in broad pastures and luxuriant woods, while its hills were favourable to the olive and the vine.

Such was that region, once celebrated for its natural advantages, for its arts, its splendour, as well as for its gifts of grace; and the misery and degradation which are at present imprinted on the very face of the soil are the emblems of that worse ruin which has overtaken the souls of its children. I have already referred to the journal of Dr. Chandler, who saw it, even in its western coast, overrun by the hideous tents of the Turcomans. Another traveller of late years[1] tells us of that ancient Bithynia, which runs along the Black Sea, a beautiful and romantic country, intersected with lofty mountains and fertile valleys, and abounding in rivers and forests. The luxuriance of the pastures, he says, and the richness of the woods, often reminded him of an English gentleman's park. Such is it as nature has furnished it for the benefit of man; but he found its forests covered with straggling Turcomans and numerous flocks of goats. As he was passing through Phrygia, the inhabitants smiled, when he asked for ruins, assuring him that the whole country was overspread with them. There too again he found a great part of its face covered with the roving Turcomans, "a boisterous and ignorant race,

[1] Vid. Murray's Asia.

though much more honourable and hospitable," he adds, "than the inhabitants of the towns." Mr. Alison tells us that when the English fleet, in 1801, was stationed on the southern coast, some sailors accidentally set fire to a thick wood, and the space thus left bare was studded all along with the ruins of temples and palaces.

A still more recent traveller[1] corroborates this testimony. Striking inland from Smyrna, he found "the scenery extremely beautiful, and the land," he continues, "which is always rich, would be valuable, if sufficiently cultivated, but it is much neglected." In another part of the country, he "rode for at least three miles through a ruined city, which was one pile of temples, theatres, and buildings, vying with each other in splendour." Now here, you will observe, I am not finding fault with the mere circumstance that the scenes of ancient grandeur should abound in ruins. Buildings will decay; old buildings will not answer new uses; there are ruins enough in Europe; but the force of the argument lies in this, that in these countries there are ruins and nothing else; that the old is gone, and has not been replaced by the new. So was it about Smyrna; and so too about Sardis: "Its situation," he says, "is very beautiful, but the country over which it looks is now almost deserted, and the valley is become a swamp. Its little rivers of clear water, after turning a mill or two, serve only to flood, instead of draining and beautifying the country." His descriptions of the splendour of the scenery, yet of the desolation of the land, are so frequent that I should not be able to confine my extracts within bounds, did I attempt to give them all. He speaks of his route as lying through "a rich wilderness" of ruins. Sometimes the landscape "so far exceeded the beauty of nature, as to

[1] Sir Charles Fellows.

seem the work of magic." Again, "the splendid view passed like a dream; for the continual turns in the road, and the increasing richness of the woods and vegetation, soon limited my view to a mere foreground. Nor was this without interest; on each projecting rock stood an ancient sarcophagus; and the trees half concealed the lids and broken sculpture of innumerable tombs."

The gifts of nature remain; he was especially struck with the trees. "We traversed the coast," he says, "through woods of the richest trees, the planes being the handsomest to be found in this or perhaps any other part of the world. I have never seen such stupendous arms to any trees." Everything was running wild; "the underwood was of myrtle, growing sometimes twenty feet high, the beautiful daphne laurel, and the arbutus; and they seemed contending for preëminence with the vine, clematis, and woodbine, which climbed to the very tops, and in many instances bore them down into a thicket of vegetation, impervious except to the squirrels and birds, which, sensible of their security in these retreats, stand boldly to survey the traveller." Elsewhere he found the ground carpeted with the most beautiful flowers. A Protestant Missionary,[1] in like manner, travelling in a different part of the country, speaks of the hedges of wild roses, the luxuriant gardens and fruit-trees, principally the cherry, the rich soil, the growth of beech, oak, and maple, the level meadows and swelling hills covered with the richest sward, and the rivulets of the purest water. No wonder that, as he tells us, "sitting down under a spreading walnut-tree, by the side of a murmuring mill stream, he was led by the charming woodland scenery around to reflect upon that mysterious Providence, by which so beautiful a country

[1] Vid. Smith and Dwight's Travels.

has been placed under such a blighting government, in the hands of so ignorant and barbarous a people."

The state of the population is in keeping with the neglected condition of the country. It is, down to the present time, wasting away; and that there are inhabitants at all seems in the main referable to merely accidental causes. On the road from Angora to Constantinople there were old people, twenty years since, who remembered as many as forty or fifty villages, where now there are none; and in the middle of the last century two hundred places had become forsaken in the tract lying between those two cities and Smyrna.[1]

This desolation is no accident of a declining empire; it dates from the very time that a Turk first came into the country, from the era of the Seljukian Sultans, eight hundred years ago. We have indirect but clear proof of it in the course of history following their expulsion from the country by the Crusaders. For a while the Greeks recovered their dominion in its western portion, and fixed their imperial residence at Nicæa, which had been the capital of the Seljukians. A vigorous prince mounted the throne, and the main object of his exertions and the special work of his reign was the recovery of the soil. We are told by an English historian,[2] that he found the most fertile lands without either cultivation or inhabitants, and he took them into his own management. It followed that, in the course of some years, the imperial domain became the granary and garden of Asia; and the sovereign made money without impoverishing his people. According to the nature of the soil, he sowed it with corn, or planted it with vines, or laid it down in grass: his pastures abounded with herds and flocks, horses and swine; and his speculation, as it may

[1] Eclectic Review, Dec., 1839.   [2] Gibbon.

be called, in poultry was so happy, that he was able to present his empress with a crown of pearls and diamonds out of his gains. His example encouraged his nobles to imitation; and they learned to depend for their incomes on the honourable proceeds of their estates, instead of oppressing their people, and seeking favours from the court. Such was the immediate consequence when man coöperated with the bountifulness of nature in this fruitful region; and it brings out prominently by its contrast the wretchedness of the Turkish domination.

6.

That wretchedness is found, not in Asia Minor only, but wherever Turks are to be found in power. Throughout the whole extent of their territory, if you believe the report of travellers, the peasantry are indigent, oppressed, and wretched.[1] The great island of Crete or Candia would maintain four times its present population; once it had a hundred cities; many of its towns, which were densely populous, are now obscure villages. Under the Venetians it used to export corn largely; now it imports it. As to Cyprus, from holding a million of inhabitants, it now has only 30,000. Its climate was that of a perpetual spring; now it is unwholesome and unpleasant; its cities and towns nearly touched one another, now they are simply ruins. Corn, wine, oil, sugar, and the metals are among its productions; the soil is still exceedingly rich; but now, according to Dr. Clarke, in that "paradise of the Levant, agriculture is neglected, inhabitants are oppressed, population is destroyed." Cross over to the continent, and survey Syria and its neighbouring cities; at this day the Turks themselves are dying out; Diarbekr, which numbered 400,000 souls

[1] Alison on Population, vol. i. p. 309, etc.

in the middle of last century, forty years afterwards had dwindled to 50,000. Mosul had lost half its inhabitants; Bagdad had fallen from 130,000 to 20,000; and Bassora from 100,000 to 8,000.

If we pass on to Egypt, the tale is still the same. "In the fifteenth century," says Mr. Alison, "Egypt, after all the revolutions which it had undergone, was comparatively rich and populous; but since the fatal era of Turkish conquest, the tyranny of the Pashas has expelled industry, riches, and the arts." Stretch across the width of Africa to Barbary, wherever there is a Turk, there is desolation. What indeed have the shepherds of the desert, in the most ambitious effort of their civilization, to do with the cultivation of the soil? "That fertile territory," says Robertson, "which sustained the Roman Empire, still lies in a great measure uncultivated; and that province, which Victor called *Speciositas totius terrœ florentis*, is now the retreat of pirates and banditti."

End your survey at length with Europe, and you find the same account is to be given of its Turkish provinces. In the Morea, Chateaubriand, wherever he went, beheld villages destroyed by fire and sword, whole suburbs deserted, often fifteen leagues without a single habitation. "I have travelled," says Mr. Thornton, "through several provinces of European Turkey, and cannot convey an idea of the state of desolation in which that beautiful country is left. For the space of seventy miles, between Kirk Kilise and Carnabat, there is not an inhabitant, though the country is an earthly paradise. The extensive and pleasant village of Faki, with its houses deserted, its gardens overrun with weeds and grass, its lands waste and uncultivated, and now the resort of robbers, affects the traveller with the most painful sensations."[1] Even in Wallachia and Moldavia the population has been gradually decreasing, while of that rich country not more than a fortieth part is under tillage. In a word, the average population in the whole Empire is not a fifth of what it was in ancient times.

7.

Here I am tempted to exclaim (though the very juxtaposition of two countries so different from each other in their condition needs an apology), I cannot help exclaiming, how different is the condition of that other peninsula in the centre of which is placed the See of Peter! I am ashamed of comparing, or even contrasting, Italy with Asia Minor—the seat of Christian governments with the seat of a barbarian rule—except that, since I have been speaking of the tenderness which the Popes have shown, according to their means, for the earth and its cultivators, there is a sort of fitness in pointing out that the result is in their case conformable to our just anticipation. Besides, so much is uttered among us in disparagement of the governments of that beautiful country, that there is a reason for pressing the contrast on the attention of those, who in their hearts acknowledge little difference between the rulers of Italy and of Turkey. I think it will be instructive, then, to dwell upon the account given us of Italy by an intelligent and popular writer of this day; nor need we, in doing so, concern ourselves with questions which he elsewhere discusses, such as whether Italy has received the last improvements in agriculture, or in civil economy, or in finance, or in politics, or in mechanical contrivances; in short, whether the art of life is carried there to its perfection. Systems and codes are to be tested by their

[1] Vol. i., p. 66, note.

results; let us put aside theories and disputable points; let us survey a broad, undeniable, important fact; let us look simply at the state both of the land and of the population in Italy; let us take it as our gauge and estimate of political institutions; let us, by way of contrast, put it side by side of the state of land and population, as reported to us by travellers in Turkey.

Mr. Alison, then, in his most diligent and interesting history of Europe,[1] divides the extent of Italy into three great districts, of mountain, plain, and marsh. The region of marsh lies between the Apennines and the Mediterranean; and here, I confess, he finds fault with the degree of diligence in reclaiming it exerted by its present possessors. He notices with dissatisfaction that the marshes of Volterra are still as pestilential as in the days of Hannibal; moreover, that the Campagna of Rome, once inhabited by numerous tribes, is now an almost uninhabited desert, and that the Pontine Marshes, formerly the abode of thirty nations, are now a pestilential swamp. I will not stop to remind you that the irruptions of barbarians like the Turks, have been the causes of this desolation, that the existing governments had nothing to do with it, and that, on the contrary, they have made various efforts to overcome the evil. For argument's sake, I will allow them to be a reproach to the government, for they will be found to be only exceptions to the general state of the country. Even as regards this low tract, he speaks of one portion of it, the plain of the Clitumnus, as being rich, as in ancient days, in herds and flocks; and he enlarges upon the Campagna of Naples as "still the scene of industry, elegance, and agricultural riches. There," he says, "still, as in ancient times, an admirable cultivation brings to perfection the

[1] Alison, ch. xx., § 28.

choicest gifts of nature. Magnificent crops of wheat and maize cover the rich and level expanse; rows of elms or willows shelter their harvests from the too scorching rays of the sun; and luxuriant vines, clustering to the very tops of the trees, are trained in festoons from one summit to the other. On its hills the orange, the vine, and the fig-tree flourish in luxuriant beauty; the air is rendered fragrant by their ceaseless perfume; and the prodigy is here exhibited of the fruit and the flower appearing at the same time on the same stem."

So much for that portion of Italy which owes least to the labours of the husbandman: the second portion is the plain of Lombardy, which stretches three hundred miles in length by one hundred and twenty in breadth, and which, he says, "beyond question is the richest and the most fertile in Europe." This great plain is so level, that you may travel two hundred miles in a straight line, without coming to a natural eminence ten feet high; and it is watered by numerous rivers, the Ticino, the Adda, the Adige, and others, which fall into the great stream of the Po, the "king of rivers," as Virgil calls it, which flows majestically through its length from west to east till it finds its mouth in the Adriatic. It is obvious, from the testimony of the various travellers in the East, whom I have cited, what would be the fate of this noble plain under a Turkish government; it would become nothing more or less than one great and deadly swamp. But Mr. Alison observes: "It is hard to say, whether the cultivation of the soil, the riches of nature, or the structures of human industry in this beautiful region, are most to be admired. An unrivalled system of agriculture, from which every nation in Europe might take a lesson, has long been established over its whole surface, and two, and sometimes three successive crops annually reward the labours of the husbandman. Indian corn is produced in abundance, and by its return, quadruple that of wheat, affords subsistence for a numerous and dense population. Rice arrives at maturity to a great extent in the marshy districts; and an incomparable system of irrigation, diffused over the whole, conveys the waters of the Alps to every field, and in some places to every ridge, in the grass lands. It is in these rich meadows, stretching round Lodi, and from thence to Verona, that the celebrated Parmesan cheese, known over all Europe for the richness of its flavour, is made. The vine and the olive thrive in the sunny slopes which ascend from the plain to the ridges of the Alps; and a woody zone of never-failing beauty lies between the desolation of the mountain and the fertility of the plain."

8.

Such is his language concerning the cultivation at present bestowed upon the great plain of Italy; but after all it is for the third or mountainous region of the country, where art has to supply the deficiencies of nature, that he reserves his enthusiastic praises. After speaking of what nature really does for it in the way of vegetation and fruits, he continues: "An admirable terrace-cultivation, where art and industry have combined to overcome the obstacles of nature, has everywhere converted the slopes, naturally sterile and arid, into a succession of gardens, loaded with the choicest vegetable productions. A delicious climate there brings the finest fruits to maturity; the grapes hang in festoons from tree to tree; the song of the nightingale is heard in every grove; all nature seems to rejoice in the paradise which the industry of man has created. To this incomparable system of horticulture, which appears to have been unknown to the ancient Romans, and to have been introduced into Europe by the warriors who returned from the Crusades, the riches and smiling aspect of Tuscany and the mountain-region of Italy are chiefly to be ascribed; for nothing can be more desolate by nature than the waterless declivities, in general almost destitute of soil, on which it has been formed. The earth required to be brought in from a distance, retaining walls erected, the steep slopes converted into a series of gentle inclinations, the mountain-torrent diverted or restrained, and the means of artificial irrigation, to sustain nature during the long droughts of summer, obtained. By the incessant labour of centuries this prodigy has been completed, and the very stony sterility of nature converted into the means of heightening, by artificial means, the heat of summer. . . . No room is lost in these little but precious freeholds; the vine extends its tendrils along the terrace walls . . . in the corners formed by their meeting, a little sheltered nook is found, where fig-trees are planted, which ripen delicious fruit under their protection. The owner takes advantage of every vacant space to raise melons and vegetables. Olives shelter it from the rains; so that, within the compass of a very small garden, he obtains olives, figs, grapes, pomegranates, and melons. Such is the return which nature yields under this admirable system of management, that half the crop of seven acres is sufficient in general for the maintenance of a family of five persons, and the whole produce supports them all in rustic affluence. Italy, in this delightful region, still realizes the glowing description of her classic historian three hundred years ago."

The author I have quoted goes on next to observe that this diligent cultivation of the rock accounts for what at first sight is inexplicable, viz., the vast population, which is found, not merely in the valleys, but over the greater part of the ridges of the Apennines, and the endless succession of villages and hamlets which are perched on the edge or summit of rocks, often, to appearance, scarcely accessible to human approach. He adds that the labour never ends, for, if a place goes out of repair, the violence of the rain will soon destroy it. "Stones and torrents wash down the soil; the terraces are broken through; the heavy rains bring down a shapeless mass of ruins; everything returns rapidly to its former state." Thus it is that parts of Palestine at present exhibit such desolate features to the traveller, who wonders how it ever could have been the rich land described in Scripture; till he finds that it was this sort of cultivation which made it what it was, that this it was the Crusaders probably saw and imported into Europe, and this that the ruthless Turks in great measure laid waste.

Lastly, he speaks of the population of Italy; as to the towns, it has declined on account of the new channels of commerce which nautical discovery has opened, to the prejudice of the marts and ports of the middle ages. In spite of this, however, he says, "that the provinces have increased both in riches and inhabitants, and the population of Italy was never, either in the days of the Emperors, or of the modern Republics, so considerable as it is at the present moment. In the days of Napoleon, it gave 1,237 to the square marine league, a density greater than that of either France or England at that period. This populousness of Italy," he adds, "is to be explained by the direction of its capital to agricultural investment, and the increasing industry with which, during a long course of centuries, its inhabitants have overcome the sterility of nature."

Such is the contrast between Italy under its present governments and Asia Minor under the Turks; and can we doubt at all, that, if the Turks had conquered Italy, they would have caused the labours of the agriculturist and the farmer to cease, and have reduced it to the level of their present dominions?

LECTURE VI.

The Pope and the Turk.

I.

AND now, having dwelt upon the broad contrast which exists between Christendom and Turkey, I proceed to give you some general idea of the Ottoman Turks, who are at present in power, as I have already sketched the history of the Seljukian. We left off with the Crusaders victorious in the Holy Land, and the Seljukian Sultan, the cousin of Malek Shah, driven back from his capital over against Constantinople, to an obscure town on the Cilician border of Asia Minor. This is that Sultan Soliman, who plays so conspicuous a part in Tasso's celebrated Poem of "Jerusalem Delivered,"—

> That Solyman, than whom there was not any
>   Of all God's foes more rebel an offender;
> Nay, nor a giant such, among the many
>   Whom earth once bore, and might again engender;
> The Turkish Prince, who first the Greeks expelling,
> Fixed at Nicæa his imperial dwelling.
>
> And then he made his infidel advances
>   From Phrygian Sangar to Meander's river;
> Lydia and Mysia, humbled in war's chances,
>   Bithynia, Pontus, hymned the Arch-deceiver;
> But when to Asia passed the Christian lances,
>   To battle with the Turk and misbeliever,
> He, in two fields, encountered two disasters,
> And so he fled, and the vexed land changed masters.

Two centuries of military effort followed, and then

the contest seemed over; the barbarians of the North destroyed, and Europe free. It seemed as though the Turks had come to their end and were dying out, as the Saracens had died out before them, when suddenly, when the breath of the last Seljukian Sultan was flitting at Iconium, and the Crusaders had broken their last lance for the Holy Sepulchre, on the 27th of July, 1301, the rule and dynasty of the Ottomans rose up from his death-bed.

2.

Othman, the founder of the line and people, who take from him the name of Ottoman or Osmanli, was the grandson of a nomad Turk, or Turcoman, who, descending from the North by Sogdiana and the Oxus, took the prescriptive course (as I may call it) towards social and political improvement. His son, Othman's father, came into the service of the last Sultan of the Seljukian line, and governed for fifty-two years a horde of 400 families. That line of sovereigns had been for a time in alliance with the Greek Emperors; but Othman inherited the fanaticism of the desert, and, when he succeeded to his father's power, he proclaimed a gazi, or holy war, against the professors of Christianity. Suddenly, like some beast of prey, he managed to leap the mountain heights which separated the Greek Province from the Mahomedan conquests, and he pitched himself in Broussa, in Bithynia, which remained from that time the Turkish capital, till it was exchanged for Adrianople and Constantinople. This was the beginning of a long series of conquests lasting about 270 years, till the Ottomans became one of the first, if not the first power, not only of Asia, but of the world.

These conquests were achieved during the reigns of ten great Sultans, the average length of whose reigns is as much as twenty-six years, an unusual period for military sovereigns, and both an evidence of the stability, and a means of the extension, of their power. Then came the period of their decline, and we are led on through the space of another 270 years, up to our own day, when they seem on the verge of some great reverse or overthrow. In this second period they have had as many as twenty-one Sultans, whose average reigns are only half the length of those who preceded them, and afford as cogent an argument of their national disorder and demoralization. Of these twenty-one, five have been strangled, three have been deposed, and three have died of excess; of the remaining ten, four only have attained the age of man, and these come together in the course of the last century; two others have died about the age of thirty, and three about the age of fifty. The last, the thirty-first from Othman, is the present Sultan, who came to the throne as a boy, and is described at that time by an English traveller, as one of the most "sickly, pale, inanimate, and unmanly youths he ever saw,"[1] and who has this very year just reached the average length of the reign of his twenty predecessors.

The names of the Ottoman Sultans are more familiar to us and more easy to recollect than other Oriental sovereigns, partly from their greater euphony as Europeans read them, partly from their recurrence again and again in the catalogue. There are four Mahomets, four Mustaphas, four Amuraths or Murads, three Selims, three Achmets, three Othmans, two Mahmoods, two Solimans, and two Bajazets.[2]

I have already described Othman, the founder of the

[1] Formby's Visit to the East.
[2] The three remaining of the thirty are Orchan, Ibrahim, and Abdoul Achmet.

line, as a soldier of fortune in the Seljukian service; and, in spite of the civilizing influences of the country, the people, and the religion, to which he had attached himself, he had not as yet laid aside the habits of his ancestors, but was half shepherd, half freebooter. Nor is it likely that any of his countrymen would be anything else, as long as they were still in war and in subordinate posts. Peace must precede the enjoyment, and power the arts of government; and the very readiness with which his followers left their nomad life, as soon as they had the opportunity, shows that the means of civilization which they had enjoyed, had not been thrown away on them. The soldiers of Zingis, when laden with booty, and not till then, cried out to be led back, and would fight no more; Tamerlane, at the end of fifty years, began to be a magnificent king. In like manner, Othman observed the life of a Turcoman, till he became a conqueror; but, as soon as he had crossed Mount Olympus, and found himself in the Greek territory as a master, he was both willing and able to accommodate himself to a pomp and luxury to which a mere Turcoman was unequal. He bade adieu to his fastnesses in the heights, and he began to fortify the towns and castles which he had heretofore pillaged. Conquest and civilization went hand in hand; his successor, Orchan, selected a capital, which he ornamented with a mosque, a hospital, a mint, and a college; he introduced professors of the sciences, and, what was as great a departure from Tartar habits, he raised a force of infantry, among his captives (in anticipation of the Janizaries, formed soon after), and he furnished himself with a train of battering engines. More strange still, he gained the Greek Emperor's daughter in marriage, a Christian princess; and lastly, he crossed over into Europe under cover of friendship to the court of Constantinople, and possessed himself of Gallipoli, the key of the Hellespont. His successors gained first Roumelia, that is, the country round Constantinople, as far as the Balkan, with Adrianople for a capital; then they successively swept over Moldavia, Servia, Bulgaria, Greece, and the Morea. Then they gained a portion of Hungary; then they took Constantinople, just 400 years ago this very year. Meanwhile they had extended their empire into Syria, Egypt, and along the coast of Africa. And thus at length they more than half encompassed the Mediterranean, from the straits of Gibraltar to the Gulf of Venice, and reigned in three quarters of the world.

3.

Now you may ask me, what were Christians doing in Europe all this while? What was the Holy Father about at Rome, if he did not turn his eyes, as heretofore, on the suffering state of his Asiatic provinces, and oppose some rampart to the advance of the enemy upon Constantinople? and how has he been the enduring enemy of the Turk, if he acquiesced in the Turk's long course of victories? Alas! he often looked towards the East, and often raised the alarm, and often, as I have said, attempted by means of the powers of Christendom, what his mission did not give him arms to do himself. But he was impeded and embarrassed by so many and such various difficulties, that, if I proposed to go through them, I should find myself engaged in a history of Europe during those centuries. I will suggest some of them, though I can do no more.

1. First of all, then, I observe generally, that the Pope, in attempting to save Constantinople and its Empire, was attempting to save a fanatical people, who

had for ages set themselves against the Holy See and the Latin world, and who had for centuries been under a sentence of excommunication. They hated and feared the Catholics, as much as they hated and feared the Turks, and they contemned them too, for their comparative rudeness and ignorance of literature; and this hatred and fear and contempt were grafted on a cowardly, crafty, insincere, and fickle character of mind, for which they had been notorious from time immemorial. It was impossible to save them without their own cordial coöperation; it was impossible to save them in spite of themselves.

These odious traits and dispositions had, in the course of the two hundred years during which the Crusades lasted, borne abundant fruits and exhibited themselves in results intolerable to the warlike multitudes who had come to their assistance. For two hundred years "each spring and summer had produced a new emigration of pilgrim warriors for the defence of the Holy Land;"[1] and what had been the effect upon the Greeks of such prodigality of succour? what satisfaction, what gratitude had they shown for an undertaking on the part of the West, which ought properly to have been their own, and which the West commenced, because the East asked it? When the celebrated Peter the Hermit was in Constantinople, he would have addressed himself first of all to its imperial master; and not till the Patriarch of the day showed the hopelessness of seeking help from a vicious and imbecile court, did he cry out: "I will rouse the nations of Europe in your cause." The Emperors sought help themselves instead of lending it. Again and again, in the course of the Holy Wars, did they selfishly betake themselves to the European capitals; and they made

[1] Gibbon.

their gain of the successes of the Crusaders, as far as they had opportunity, as the jackal follows the lion; but from the very first, their pride was wounded, and their cowardice alarmed, at the sight of their protectors in their city and provinces, and they took every means to weaken and annoy the very men whom they had invited. In the great council of Placentia, summoned by Urban the Second, before the Crusades were yet begun, in the presence of 200 Latin Bishops, 4,000 inferior clergy, and 30,000 laity, the ambassadors of the Greek Emperor had been introduced, and they pleaded the distress of their sovereign and the danger of their city, which the misbelievers already were threatening.[1] They insisted on its being the policy of the Latin princes to repel the barbarian in Asia rather than when he was in the heart of Europe, and drew such a picture of their own miseries, that the vast assembly burst into tears, and dismissed them with the assurance of their most zealous coöperation.

Yet what, I say, was the reception which the cowardly suppliants had given to their avengers and protectors? From the very first, they threw difficulties in the way of their undertaking. When the heroic Godfrey and his companions in arms arrived in the neighbourhood of Constantinople, they found themselves all but betrayed into a dangerous position, where they might either have been starved, or been easily attacked. When at length they had crossed over into Asia, the Crusaders found themselves without the means of sustenance. They had bargained for a fair market in the Greek territories; but the Imperial Court allowed the cities which they passed by to close their gates upon them, to let down to them from the wall an insufficient supply of food, to mix

[1] Gibbon.

poisonous ingredients in their bread, to give them base coin, to break down the bridges before them, and to fortify the passes, and to mislead them by their guides, to give information of their movements to the Turk, to pillage and murder the stragglers, and to hang up their dead bodies on gibbets along the highway. The Greek clergy preached against them as heretics and schismatics and dogs; the Patriarch and the Bishops spoke of their extermination as a merit, and their priests washed and purified the altars where the Latin priests had said mass. Nay, the Emperors formed a secret alliance with Turks and Saracens against them, and the price at which they obtained it, was the permission of erecting a mosque in Constantinople.

As time went on, they did not stop even here. A number of Latin merchants had settled at Constantinople, as our own merchants now are planted all over the cities of the Continent. The Greek populace rose against them ; and the Emperor did not scruple to send his own troops to aid the rioters. The Latins were slaughtered in their own homes and in the streets; their clergy were burned in the churches, their sick in the hospitals, and their whole quarter reduced to ashes ; nay, 4,000 of the survivors were sold into perpetual slavery to the Turks. They cut off the head of the Cardinal Legate, and tied it to the tail of a dog, and then chanted a *Te Deum*. What could be said to such a people ? What could be made of them ? The Turks might be a more powerful and energetic, but could not be a more virulent, a more unscrupulous foe. It did not seem to matter much to the Latin whether Turk or Greek was lord of Constantinople ; and the Greek justified the indifference of the Latin by declaring that he would rather have the Turban in Constantinople than the Tiara.

2. It is the nature of crime to perpetuate itself, and the atrocities of the Greeks brought about a retaliation from the Latins. Twenty years after the events I have been relating, the Crusading hosts turned their arms against the Greeks, and besieged and gained possession of Constantinople; and, though their excesses seem to have been inferior to those which provoked them, it is not to be supposed that a city could be taken by a rude and angry multitude, without the occurrence of innumerable outrages. It was pillaged and disfigured; and the Pope had to publish an indignant protest against the work of his own adherents and followers. He might well be alarmed and distressed, not only for the crime itself, but for its bearing on the general course of the Crusades; for, if it was difficult under any circumstances to keep the Greeks in a right course, it was doubly difficult, when they had been injured, even though they were the original offenders.

4.

3. But there were other causes, still less satisfactory than those I have mentioned, tending to nullify all the Pope's efforts to make head against the barbarian power. I have said that the period of the Ottoman growth was about 270 years; and this period, viz., the fourteenth and fifteenth and first half of the sixteenth centuries, was the most disastrous and melancholy in the internal history of the Church of any that can be named. It was that miserable period, which directly prepared the way for Protestantism. The resistance to the Pope's authority, on the part of the states of Europe generally, is pretty nearly coincident with the rise of the Ottomans. Heresy followed; in the middle of the fourteenth century, the teaching of Wickliffe gained ground in England;

Huss and others followed on the Continent; and they were succeeded by Luther. That energy of Popes, those intercessions of holy men, which hitherto had found matter in the affairs of the East, now found a more urgent incentive in the troubles which were taking place at home.

4. The increase of national prosperity and strength, to which the alienation of kings and states from the Holy See must be ascribed, in various ways indisposed them to the continuance of the war against the misbelievers. Rulers and people, who were increasing in wealth, did not like to spend their substance on objects both distant and spiritual. Wealth is a present good, and has a tendency to fix the mind on the visible and tangible, to the prejudice of both faith and secular policy. The rich and happy will not go to war, if they can help it; and trade, of course, does not care for the religious tenets of those who offer to enter into relations with it, whether of interchange or of purchase. Nor was this all; when nations began to know their own strength, they had a tendency to be jealous of each other, as well as to be indifferent to the interests of religion; and the two most valiant nations of Europe, France and England, gave up the Holy Wars, only to go to war one with another. As in the twelfth century, we read of Cœur de Lion in Palestine, and in the thirteenth, of St. Louis in Egypt, so in the fourteenth do we read the sad tale of Poitiers and Cressy, and in the fifteenth of Agincourt. People are apt to ask what good came of the prowess shown at Ascalon or Damietta; forgetting that they should rather ask themselves what good came of the conquests of our Edwards and Henries, of which they are so proud. If Richard's prowess ended in his imprisonment in Germany, and St. Louis died in Africa, yet there is another history which

ends as ingloriously in the Maid of Orleans, and the expulsion of tyrants from a soil they had usurped. In vain did the Popes attempt to turn the restless destructiveness of the European commonwealth into a safer channel. In vain did the Legates of the Holy See interpose between Edward of England and the French king; in their very presence was a French town delivered over by the English conqueror to a three days' pillage.[1] In vain did one Pope take a vow of never-dying hostility to the Turks; in vain did another, close upon his end, repair to the fleet, that "he might, like Moses, raise his hands to God during the battle;"[2] Christian was to war with Christian, not with infidel.

The suppliant Greek Emperor in one of his begging missions, as they may be called, came to England: it was in the reign of Henry the Fourth, but Henry could do nothing for him. He had usurped the English Crown, and could not afford to rescue the Holy Sepulchre, with so precarious a position at home. However, he was under some kind of promise to take the Cross, which is signified in the popular story, that he had expected to die at Jerusalem, whereas he died in his palace at Westminster instead, in the Jerusalem chamber. It is said, too, that he was actually meditating a Crusade, and had ordered galleys to be prepared, when he came to his end.[3] His son, Henry the Fifth, crossed the Channel to conquer France, just at the very, the only time, when the Ottoman reverses gave a fair hope of the success of Christendom. When premature death overtook him, and he had but two hours to live,[4] he ordered his confessor to recite the Seven Penitential Psalms; and, when the verse was read about building the walls of Jerusalem, the word caught his ear; he stopped the reader, and

[1] Hume's History. [2] Ranke, vol. i. [3] Turner's History. [4] Ibid.

observed that he had proposed to conquer Jerusalem, and to have rebuilt it, had God granted him life. Indeed, he had already sent a knight to take a survey of the towns and country of Syria, which is still extant. Alas, that good intentions should only become strong in moments of sickness or of death!

A like necessary or unnecessary attention, as the case might be, to national concerns and private interests, prevailed all over Europe. In the same century[1] Charles the Seventh of France forbade the preaching of a Crusade in his dominions, lest it should lay him open to the attacks of the English. Alfonso of Portugal promised to join in a Holy War, and retracted. Alfonso of Arragon and Sicily took the Cross, and used the men and money raised for its objects in a war against the Genoese. The Bohemians would not fight, unless they were paid; and the Germans affected or felt a fear that the Pope would apply the sums they contributed for some other purpose.

5. Alas! more must be said; it seldom happens that the people go wrong, without the rulers being somewhere in fault, nor is the portion of history to which I am referring an exception. It must be confessed that, at the very time the Turks were making progress, the Christian world was in a more melancholy state than it had ever been either before or since. The sins of nations were accumulating that heavy judgment which fell upon them in the Ottoman conquests and the Reformation. There were great scandals among Bishops and Priests, as well as heresy and insubordination. As to the Pontiffs who filled the Holy See during that period, I will say no more than this, that it did not please the good Providence of God to raise up for His Church such

[1] Gieseler's Text Book.

heroic men as St. Leo, of the fifth, and St. Gregory, of the eleventh century. For a time the Popes removed from Italy to France; then, when they returned to Rome, there was a schism in the Papacy for nearly forty years, during which time the populations of Europe were perplexed to find the real successor of St. Peter, or even took the pretended Pope for the true one.

5.

Such was the condition of Christendom, thus destitute of resources, thus weakened by internal quarrels, thus bribed and retained (so to speak) by the temptations of the world, at the very time when the Ottomans were pressing on its outposts. One moment occurred, and just one, in their history, when they might have been resisted with success. You will recollect that the Seljukians were broken, not simply by the Crusaders, but also, though not so early, by the terrible Zingis. What Zingis was to the Seljukians, such, and more than such, was Timour to the Ottomans. It was in their full career of victory, and when everything seemed in their power, when they had gained the whole province of Roumelia, which is round about Constantinople, that a terrible reverse befell them. The Sultan then on the throne was Bajazet, surnamed Ilderim, or the Lightning, from the rapidity of his movements. He had extended his empire, or his sensible influence, from the Carpathians to the Euphrates; he had destroyed the remains of rival dynasties in Asia Minor, had carried his arms down to the Morea, and utterly routed an allied Christian army in Hungary. Elated with these successes, he put no bounds to his pride and ambition. He vaunted that he would subdue, not Hungary only, but Germany and Italy besides; and that he would feed his horse with a bushel of oats on the altar of St. Peter's, at Rome. The Apostle heard the blasphemy; and this mighty conqueror was not suffered to leave this world for his eternal habitation without Divine infliction in evidence that He who made him, could unmake him at His will. The Disposer of all things sent against him the fierce Timour, of whom I have already said so much. One would have thought the two conquerors could not possibly have come into collision—Timour, the Lord of Persia, Khorasan, Sogdiana, and Hindostan, and Bajazet, the Sultan of Syria, Asia Minor, and Greece. They were both Mahomedans; they might have turned their backs on each other, if they were jealous of each other, and might have divided the world between them. Bajazet might have gone forward towards Germany and Italy, and Timour might have stretched his conquests into China.

But ambition is a spirit of envy as well as of covetousness; neither of them could brook a rival greatness. Timour was on the Ganges, and Bajazet was besieging Constantinople, when they interchanged the words of hatred and defiance. Timour called Bajazet a pismire, whom he would crush with his elephants; and Bajazet retaliated with a worse insult on Timour, by promising that he would capture his retinue of wives. The foes met at Angora in Asia Minor; Bajazet was defeated and captured in the battle, and Timour secured him in an iron-barred apartment or cage, which, according to Tartar custom, was on wheels, and he carried him about, as some wild beast, on his march through Asia. Can imagination invent a more intolerable punishment upon pride? is it not wonderful that the victim of it was able to live as many as nine months under such a visitation?

This was at the beginning of the fifteenth century, shortly before young Harry of Monmouth, the idol of

English poetry and loyalty, crossed the sea to kill the French at Agincourt; and an opportunity was offered to Christendom to destroy an enemy, who never before or since has been in such extremity of peril. For fourteen years a state of interregnum, or civil war, lasted in the Ottoman empire; and the capture of Constantinople, which was imminent at the time of Bajazet's downfall, was anyhow delayed for full fifty years. Had a crusade been attempted with the matured experience and subdued enthusiasm, which the trials of three hundred years had given to the European nations, the Ottomans, according to all human probability, would have perished, as the Seljukians before them. But, in the inscrutable decree of Heaven, no such attempt was made; one attempt indeed was made too soon, and a second attempt was made too late, but none at the time.

1. The first of these two was set on foot when Bajazet was in the full tide of his victories; and he was able, not only to defeat it, but, by defeating, to damp the hopes, and by anticipation, to stifle the efforts, which might have been used against him with better effect in the day of his reverses. In the year 1394, eight years before Bajazet's misfortunes, Pope Boniface the Ninth proclaimed a Crusade, with ample indulgences for those who engaged in it, to the countries which were especially open to the Ottoman attack. In his Bull, he bewails the sins of Christendom, which had brought upon them that scourge which was the occasion of his invitation. He speaks of the massacres, the tortures, and slavery which had been inflicted on multitudes of the faithful. "The mind is horrified," he says, "at the very mention of these miseries; but it crowns our anguish to reflect, that the whole of Christendom, which, if in concord, might put an end to these and even greater evils, is either in

open war, country with country, or, if in apparent peace, is secretly wasted by mutual jealousies and animosities."[1]

The Pontiff's voice, aided by the imminent peril of Hungary and its neighbouring kingdoms, was successful. Not only from Germany, but even from France, the bravest knights, each a fortress in himself, or a man-of-war on land (as he may be called), came forward in answer to his call, and boasted that, even were the sky to fall, they would uphold its canopy upon the points of their lances. They formed the flower of the army of 100,000 men, who rallied round the King of Hungary in the great battle of Nicopolis. The Turk was victorious; the greater part of the Christian army were slain or driven into the Danube; and a part of the French chivalry of the highest rank were made prisoners. Among these were the son of the Duke of Burgundy; the Sire de Coucy, who had great possessions in France and England; the Marshal of France (Boucicault), who afterwards fell on the field of Agincourt; and four French princes of the blood. Bajazet spared twenty-five of his noblest prisoners, whom their wealth and station made it politic to except; then, summoning the rest before his throne, he offered them the famous choice of the Koran or the sword. As they came up one by one, they one by one professed their faith in Christ, and were beheaded in the Sultan's presence. His royal and noble captives he carried about with him in his march through Europe and Asia, as he himself was soon to grace the retinue of Timour. Two of the most illustrious of them died in prison in Asia. As to the rest, he exacted a heavy ransom from them; but, before he sent them away, he gave them a grand entertainment, which displayed both the barbarism and the magnificence of the Asiatic. He

[1] Baronius.

exhibited before them his hunting and hawking equipage, amounting to seven thousand huntsmen and as many falconers; and, when one of his chamberlains was accused before him of drinking a poor woman's goat's milk, he literally fulfilled the "castigat auditque" of the poet, by having the unhappy man ripped open, in order to find in his inside the evidence of the charge.

Such was the disastrous issue of the battle of Nicopolis; nor is it wonderful that it should damp the zeal of the Christians and weaken the influence of the Pope, for a long time to come; anyhow, it had this effect till the critical moment of the Turkish misfortunes was over, and the race of Othman was recovering itself after the captivity and death of its Sultan. "Whereas the Turks might have been expelled from Greece on the loss of their Sultan," says Rainaldus, "Christians, torn to pieces by their quarrels and by schism, lost a fit and sufficient opportunity. Whence it followed, that the wound inflicted upon the beast was not unto death, but he revived more ferocious for the devouring of the faithful."

2. However, Christendom made a second attempt still, but when it was too late. The grandson of Bajazet was then on the throne, one of the ablest of the Sultans; and, though the allied Christian army had considerable success against him at first, in vain was the bravery of Hunniades, and the preaching of St. John Capistran: the Turk managed to negotiate with its leaders, to put them in the wrong, to charge them with perjury, and then to beat them in the fatal battle of Varna, in which the King of Hungary and Poland and the Pope's Legate were killed, with 10,000 men. In vain after this was any attempt to make head against the enemy; in vain did Pope after Pope raise his warning voice and point to the judgment which hung over Christendom; Constantinople fell.

6.

Thus things did but go on worse and worse for the interest of Christendom. Even the taking of Constantinople was not the limit of the Ottoman successes. Mahomet the Conqueror, as he is called, was but the seventh of the great Sultans, who carried on the fortunes of the barbarian empire. An eighth, a ninth followed. The ninth, Selim, returned from his Eastern conquests with the last of the Caliphs in his company, and made him resign to himself the prerogatives of Pontiff and Lawgiver, which the Caliph inherited from Mahomet. Then came a tenth, the greatest perhaps of all, Soliman the Magnificent, the contemporary of the Emperor Charles, Francis the First of France, and Henry the Eighth of England. And an eleventh might have been expected, and a twelfth, and the power of the enemy would have become greater and greater, and would have afflicted the Church more and more heavily; and what was to be the end of these things? What was to be the end? why, not a Christian only, but any philosopher of this world would have known what was to be the end, in spite of existing appearances. All earthly power has an end; it rises to fall, it grows to die; and the depth of its humiliation issues out of the pride of its lifting up. This is what even a philosopher would say; he would not know whether Soliman, the tenth conqueror, was also to be the last; but if not the tenth, he would be bold to say it would be the twelfth, who would close their victories, or the fifteenth, or the twentieth. But what a philosopher could not say, what a Christian knows and enjoys, is this, that one earthly power there is which is something more than earthly, and which, while it dies in the individual, for he is human, is immortal in its succession, for it is divine.

It was a remarkable question addressed by the savage Tartars of Zingis to the missionaries whom the Pope sent them in the thirteenth century: "Who was the Pope?" they asked; "was he not an old man, five hundred years of age?"[1] It was their one instinctive notion of the religion of the West; and the Turks in their own history have often had cause to lament over its truth. Togrul Beg first looked towards the West, in the year 1048; twenty years later, between the years 1068 and 1074,[2] his successor, Malek Shah, attracted the attention of the great St. Gregory the Seventh. Time went on; they were thrown back by the impetuosity of the Crusaders; they returned to the attack. Fresh and fresh multitudes poured down from Turkistan; the furious deluge of the Tartars under Zingis spread itself and disappeared; the Turks sunk in it, but emerged; the race seemed indestructible; then Othman began a new career of victory, as if there had never been an old one, and founded an empire, more stable, more coherent than any Turkish rule before it. Then followed Sultan after Sultan, each greater than his predecessor, while the line of Popes had indeed many bright names to show, Pontiffs of learning, and of piety, and of genius, and of zeal and energy; but still where was the destined champion of Christendom, the holy, the inflexible, the lion-hearted, the successor of St. Gregory, who in a luxurious and a self-willed age, among his other high duties and achievements, had the mission, by his prayers and by his efforts, of stopping the enemy in his full career, and of rescuing Catholicism from the pollution of the blasphemer? The five hundred years were not yet completed.

But the five hundred years at length were run out; the long-expected champion was at hand. He appeared

[1] Bergeron. [2] Gibbon says twenty years; Sharon Turner gives 1074.

at the very time when the Ottoman crescent had passed its zenith and was beginning to descend the sky. The Turkish successes began in the middle of the eleventh century; they ended in the middle of the sixteenth; in the middle of the sixteenth century, just five hundred years after St Gregory and Malek Shah, Selim the Sot came to the throne of Othman, and St. Pius the Fifth to the throne of the Apostle; Pius became Pope in 1566, and Selim became Sultan in that very same year.

O what a strange contrast, Gentlemen, did Rome and Constantinople present at that era! Neither was what it had been, but they had changed in opposite directions. Both had been the seat of Imperial Power; Rome, where heresy never throve, had exchanged its Emperors for the succession of St. Peter and St. Paul; Constantinople had passed from secular supremacy into schism, and thence into a blasphemous apostasy. The unhappy city, which with its subject provinces had been successively the seat of Arianism, of Nestorianism, of Photianism, now had become the metropolis of the false Prophet; and, while in the West the great edifice of the Vatican Basilica was rising anew in its wonderful proportions and its costly materials, the Temple of St. Sophia in the East was degraded into a Mosque! O the strange contrast in the state of the inhabitants of each place! Here in the city of Constantine a God-denying misbelief was accompanied by an impure, man-degrading rule of life, by the slavery of woman, and the corruption of youth. But there, in the city which Apostles had consecrated with their blood, the great and true reformation of the age was in full progress. There the determinations in doctrine and discipline of the great Council of Trent had lately been promulgated. There for twenty years past had laboured our own dear saint, St. Philip, till he earned the title of Apostle of Rome, and yet had still nearly thirty years of life and work in him. There, too, the romantic royal-minded saint, Ignatius Loyola, had but lately died. And there, when the Holy See fell vacant, and a Pope had to be appointed in the great need of the Church, a saint was present in the conclave to find in it a brother saint, and to recommend him for the Chair of St. Peter, to the suffrages of the Fathers and Princes of the Church.

7.

St. Carlo Borromeo,[1] the Cardinal Archbishop of Milan, was the nephew of the Pope who was just dead, and though he was only twenty-five years of age at the time, nevertheless, by the various influences arising out of the position which he held, and from the weight attached to his personal character, he might be considered to sway the votes of the College of Cardinals, and to determine the election of a new Pontiff. It is remarkable that Cardinal Alessandrino, as St. Pius was then called, (from Alexandria, in North Italy, near which he was born,) was not the first object of his choice. His eyes were first turned on Cardinal Morone, who was in many respects the most illustrious of the Sacred College, and had served the Church on various occasions with great devotion, and with distinguished success. From his youth he had been reared up in public affairs, he had held many public offices, he had great influence with the German Emperor, he had been Apostolical Legate at the Council of Trent. He had great virtue, judgment, experience, and sagacity. Such, then, was the choice of St. Carlo, and the votes were taken; but it seemed otherwise to the Holy Ghost. He wanted four to make

[1] Bollandist. Mai. 5.

up the sufficient number of votes. St. Carlo had to begin again; and again, strange to say, the Cardinal Alessandrino still was not his choice. He chose Cardinal Sirleto, a man most opposite in character and history to Morone. He was not nobly born, he was no man of the world, he had ever been urgent with the late Pope not to make him Cardinal. He was a first-rate scholar in Hebrew, Greek, and Latin; versed in the Scriptures, ready as a theologian. Moreover, he was of a character most unblemished, of most innocent life, and of manners most popular and winning. St. Pius as well as St. Carlo advocated the cause of Cardinal Sirleto, and the votes were given a second time; a second time they came short. It was like holy Samuel choosing Eliab instead of David. Then matters were in confusion; one name and another were mentioned, and no progress was made.

At length and at last, and not till all others were thought of who could enter into the minds of the electors, the Cardinal Alessandrino himself began to attract attention. He seems not to have been known to the Fathers of the conclave in general; a Dominican Friar, of humble rank, ever taken up in the duties of his rule and his special employments, living in his cell, knowing little or nothing of mankind—such a one St. Carlo, the son of a prince and the nephew of a Pope, had no means of knowing; and the intimacy, consequent on their coöperation in behalf of Cardinal Sirleto, was the first real introduction which the one Saint had to the other. It was just at this moment that our own St. Philip was in his small room at St. Girolamo, with Marcello Ferro, one of his spiritual children, when, lifting up his eyes to heaven, and going almost into an ecstasy, he said: "The Pope will be elected on Monday." On one of the following days, as they were walking together, Marcello asked him who was to be Pope. Philip answered, "Come, I will tell you; the Pope will be one whom you have never thought of, and whom no one has spoken of as likely; and that is Cardinal Alessandrino; and he will be elected on Monday evening without fail." The event accomplished the prediction; the statesman and the man of the world, the accomplished and exemplary and amiable scholar, were put aside to make way for the Saint. He took the name of Pius.

I am far from denying that St. Pius was stern and severe, as far as a heart burning within and melting with the fulness of divine love could be so; and this was the reason that the conclave was so slow in electing him. Yet such energy and vigour as his was necessary for his times. He was emphatically a soldier of Christ in a time of insurrection and rebellion, when, in a spiritual sense, martial law was proclaimed. St. Philip, a private priest, might follow his bent, in casting his net for souls, as he expressed himself, and enticing them to the truth; but the Vicar of Christ had to right and to steer the vessel, when it was in rough waters, and among breakers. A Protestant historian on this point does justice to him. "When Pope," he says, "he lived in all the austerity of his monastic life, fasted with the utmost rigour and punctuality, would wear no finer garments than before ... arose at an extremely early hour in the morning, and took no *siesta*. If we doubted the depth of his religious earnestness, we may find a proof of it in his declaration, that the Papacy was unfavourable to his advance in piety; that it did not contribute to his salvation and to his attainment of Paradise; and that, but for prayer, the burden had been too heavy for him. The happiness of a fervent devotion, which often moved him to tears, was granted him to the end of his life. The people were excited to enthusiasm, when they saw him walking in procession, barefooted and bareheaded, with the expression of unaffected piety in his countenance, and with his long snow-white beard falling on his breast. They thought there had never been so pious a Pope; they told each other how his very look had converted heretics. Pius was kind, too, and affable; his intercourse with his old servants was of the most confidential kind. At a former period, before he was Pope, the Count della Trinità had threatened to have him thrown into a well, and he had replied, that it must be as God pleased. How beautiful was his greeting to this same Count, who was now sent as ambassador to his court! 'See,' said he, when he recognized him, 'how God preserves the innocent.' This was the only way in which he made him feel that he recollected his enmity. He had ever been most charitable and bounteous; he kept a list of the poor of Rome, whom he regularly assisted according to their station and their wants." The writer, after proceeding to condemn what he considers his severity, ends thus: "It is certain that his deportment and mode of thinking exercised an incalculable influence on his contemporaries, and on the general development of the Church of which he was the head. After so many circumstances had concurred to excite and foster a religious spirit, after so many resolutions and measures had been taken to exalt it to universal dominion, a Pope like this was needed, not only to proclaim it to the world, but also to reduce it to practice; his zeal and his example combined produced the most powerful effect."[1]

8.

It is not to be supposed that a Saint on whom lay the

[1] Ranke's Hist. of the Popes.

"solicitude of all the churches," should neglect the tradition, which his predecessors of so many centuries had bequeathed to him, of zeal and hostility against the Turkish power. He was only six years on the Pontifical throne; and the achievement of which I am going to speak was among his last; he died the following year. At this time the Ottoman armies were continuing their course of victory; they had just taken Cyprus, with the active coöperation of the Greek population of the island, and were massacring the Latin nobility and clergy, and mutilating and flaying alive the Venetian governor. Yet the Saint found it impossible to move Christendom to its own defence. How, indeed, was that to be done, when half Christendom had become Protestant, and secretly perhaps felt as the Greeks felt, that the Turk was its friend and ally? In such a quarrel England, France, and Germany were out of the question. At length, however, with great effort, he succeeded in forming a holy league between himself, King Philip of Spain, and the Venetians. Don John, of Austria, King Philip's half brother, was appointed commander-in-chief of the forces, and Colonna admiral. The treaty was signed on the 24th of May; but such was the cowardice and jealousy of the parties concerned, that the autumn had arrived, and nothing of importance was accomplished. With difficulty were the armies united; with difficulty were the dissensions of the commanders brought to a settlement. Meanwhile, the Ottomans were scouring the Gulf of Venice, blockading the ports, and terrifying the city itself.

But the holy Pope was securing the success of his cause by arms of his own, which the Turks understood not. He had been appointing a Triduo of supplication at Rome, and had taken part in the procession himself.

He had proclaimed a jubilee to the whole Christian world, for the happy issue of the war. He had been interesting the Holy Virgin in his cause. He presented to his admiral, after High Mass in his chapel, a standard of red damask, embroidered with a crucifix, and with the figures of St. Peter and St. Paul, and the legend, "*In hoc signo vinces.*" Next, sending to Messina, where the allied fleet lay, he assured the general-in-chief and the armament, that "if, relying on divine, rather than on human help, they attacked the enemy, God would not be wanting to His own cause. He augured a prosperous and happy issue; not on any light or random hope, but on a divine guidance, and by the anticipations of many holy men." Moreover, he enjoined the officers to look to the good conduct of their troops; to repress swearing, gaming, riot, and plunder, and thereby to render them more deserving of victory. Accordingly, a fast of three days was proclaimed for the fleet, beginning with the Nativity of our Lady; all the men went to confession and communion, and appropriated to themselves the plentiful indulgences which the Pope attached to the expedition. Then they moved across the foot of Italy to Corfu, with the intention of presenting themselves at once to the enemy; being disappointed in their expectations, they turned back to the Gulf of Corinth; and there at length, on the 7th of October, they found the Turkish fleet, half way between Lepanto and the Echinades on the North, and Patras, in the Morea, on the South; and, though it was towards evening, strong in faith and zeal, they at once commenced the engagement.

 The night before the battle, and the day itself, aged as he was, and broken with a cruel malady, the Saint had passed in the Vatican in fasting and prayer. All through the Holy City the monasteries and the colleges were in prayer too. As the evening advanced, the Pontifical treasurer asked an audience of the Sovereign Pontiff on an important matter. Pius was in his bedroom, and began to converse with him; when suddenly he stopped the conversation, left him, threw open the window, and gazed up into heaven. Then closing it again, he looked gravely at his official, and said, "This is no time for business; go, return thanks to the Lord God. In this very hour our fleet has engaged the Turkish, and is victorious." As the treasurer went out, he saw him fall on his knees before the altar in thankfulness and joy.

And a most memorable victory it was: upwards of 30,000 Turks are said to have lost their lives in the engagement, and 3,500 were made prisoners. Almost their whole fleet was taken. I quote from Protestant authorities when I say that the Sultan, on the news of the calamity, neither ate, nor drank, nor showed himself, nor saw any one for three days; that it was the greatest blow which the Ottomans had had since Timour's victory over Bajazet, a century and a half before; nay, that it was the turning-point in the Turkish history;[1] and that, though the Sultans have had isolated successes since, yet from that day they undeniably and constantly declined, that they have lost their *prestige* and their self-

[1] "The battle of Lepanto arrested for ever the danger of Mahometan invasion in the south of Europe."—Alison's Europe, vol. ix. p. 95. "The powers of the Turks and of their European neighbours were now nearly balanced; in the reign of Amurath the Third, who succeeded Selim, the advantages became more evidently in favour of the Christians; and since that time, though the Turks have sometimes enjoyed a transitory success, the real stability of their affairs has constantly declined."—Bell's Geography, vol. ii., part 2. Vid. also Ranke, vol. i., pp. 381-2. It is remarkable that it should be passed over by Professor Creasy in his "Fifteen Decisive Battles.

confidence, and that the victories gained over them since are but the complements and the reverberations of the overthrow at Lepanto.

Such was the catastrophe of this long and anxious drama; the hosts of Turkistan and Tartary had poured down from their wildernesses through ages, to be withstood, and foiled, and reversed by an old man. It was a repetition, though under different circumstances, of the history of Leo and the Hun. In the contrast between the combatants we see the contrast of the histories of good and evil. The Enemy, as the Turks in this battle, rushing forward with the terrible fury of wild beasts; and the Church, ever combating with the energetic perseverance and the heroic obstinacy of St. Pius.

IV.

THE PROSPECTS OF THE TURKS.

LECTURE VII.

Barbarism and Civilization.

1.

MY object in the sketch which I have been attempting, of the history of the Turks, has been to show the relation of this celebrated race to Europe and to Christendom. I have not been led to speak of them by any especial interest in them for their own sake, but by the circumstances of the present moment, which bring them often before us, oblige us to speak of them, and involve the necessity of entertaining some definite sentiments about them. With this view I have been considering their antecedents; whence they came, how they came, where they are, and what title they have to be there at all. When I now say, that I am proceeding to contemplate their future, do not suppose me to be so rash as to be hazarding any political prophecy; I do but mean to set down some characteristics in their existing state (if I have any right to fancy, that in any true measure we at the distance of some thousand miles know it), which naturally suggest to us to pursue their prospective history in one direction, not in another.

Now it seems safe to say, in the first place, that some time or other the Ottomans will come to an end. All human power has its termination sooner or later; states rise to fall; and, secure as they may be now, so one day they will be in peril and in course of overthrow. Nineveh, Tyre, Babylon, Persia, Egypt, and Greece each has had its day; and this was so clear to mankind 2,000 years ago, that the conqueror of Carthage wept, as he gazed upon its flames, for he saw in them the conflagration of her rival, his own Rome. "*Fuit Ilium.*" The Saracens, the Moguls, have had their day; those European states, so great three centuries ago, Spain and Poland, Venice and Genoa, are now either extinct or in decrepitude. What is the lot of all states, is still more strikingly fulfilled in the case of empires; kingdoms indeed are of slow growth, but empires commonly are but sudden manifestations of power, which are as short-lived as they are sudden. Even the Roman empire, which is an exception, did not last beyond five hundred years; the Saracenic three hundred; the Spanish three hundred; the Russian has lasted about a hundred and fifty, that is, since the Czar Peter; the British not a hundred; the Ottoman has reached four or five. If there be an empire which does not at all feel the pressure of this natural law, but lasts continuously, repairs its losses, renews its vigour, and with every successive age emulates its antecedent fame, such a power must be more than human, and has no place in our present inquiry. We are concerned, not with any supernatural power, to which is promised perpetuity, but with the Ottoman empire, famous in history, vigorous in constitution, but, after all, human, and nothing more. There is, then, neither risk nor merit in prophesying the eventual fall of the Osmanlis, as of the Seljukians, as of the Gaznevides before them; the only wonder is that they actually have lasted as much as four hundred years.

Such will be the issue and the sum of their whole history; but, certain as this is, and confidently as it may be pronounced, nothing else can be prudently asserted about their future. Times and moments are in the decrees of the All-wise, and known to Him alone; and so are the occurrences to which they give birth. The only further point open to conjecture, as being not quite destitute of data for speculating upon it, is the particular course of events and quality of circumstances, which will precede the downfall of the Turkish power; for, granting that that downfall is to come, it is reasonable to think it will take place in that particular way, for which in their present state we see an existing preparation, if such can be discerned, or in a way which at least is not inconsistent with the peculiarities of that present state.

2.

Hence, in speculating on this question, I shall take this as a reasonable assumption first of all, that the catastrophe of a state is according to its antecedents, and its destiny according to its nature; and therefore, that we cannot venture on any anticipation of the instruments or the conditions of its death, until we know something about the principle and the character of its life. Next I lay down, that, whereas a state is in its very idea a society, and a society is a collection of many individuals made one by their participation in some common possession, and to the extent of that common possession, the presence of that possession held in common constitutes the life, and the loss of it constitutes the dissolution, of a state. In like manner, whatever avails or tends to withdraw that common possession, is either fatal or prejudicial to the social union. As regards the Ottoman power, then, we have to inquire what its life consists in, and what are the dangers to which that life, from the nature of its constitution, is exposed.

Now, states may be broadly divided into *barbarous* and *civilized;* their common possession, or life, is some object either of *sense* or of *imagination;* and their bane and destruction is either *external* or *internal*. And, to speak in general terms, without allowing for exceptions or limitations (for I am treating the subject scientifically only so far as is requisite for my particular inquiry), we may pronounce that *barbarous* states live in a common *imagination*, and are destroyed *from without;* whereas *civilized* states live in some common object of *sense*, and are destroyed from *within*.

By *external* enemies I mean foreign wars, foreign influence, insurrection of slaves or of subject races, famine, accidental enormities of individuals in power, and other instruments analogous to what, in the case of an individual, is called a violent death; by *internal* I mean civil contention, excessive changes, revolution, decay of public spirit, which may be considered analogous to natural death.

Again, by objects of *imagination*, I mean such as religion, true or false (for there are not only false imaginations but true), divine mission of a sovereign or of a dynasty, and historical fame; and by objects of *sense*, such as secular interests, country, home, protection of person and property.

I do not allude to the conservative power of habit when I speak of the social bond, because habit is rather the necessary result of possessing a common object, and protects all states equally, barbarous and civilized. Nor do I include moral degeneracy among the instruments of their destruction, because this too attaches to all states, civilized and barbarous, and is rather a disposition exposing them to the influence of what is their bane, than a direct cause of their ruin in itself.

3.

But what is meant by the words *barbarous* and *civilized*, as applied to political bodies? this is a question which it will take more time to answer, even if I succeed in satisfying it at all. By "barbarism," then, I suppose, in itself is meant a state of nature; and by "civilization," a state of mental cultivation and discipline. In a state of nature man has reason, conscience, affections, and passions, and he uses these severally, or rather is influenced by them, according to circumstances; and whereas they do not one and all necessarily move in the same direction, he takes no great pains to make them agree together, but lets them severally take their course, and, if I may so speak, jostle into a sort of union, and get on together, as best they can. He does not improve his talents; he does not simplify and fix his motives; he does not put his impulses under the control of principle, or form his mind upon a rule. He grows up pretty much what he was when a child; capricious, wayward, unstable, idle, irritable, excitable; with not much more of habituation than that which experience of living unconsciously forces even on the brutes. Brutes act upon instinct, not on reason; they are ferocious when they are hungry; they fiercely indulge their appetite; they gorge themselves; they fall into torpor and inactivity. In a like, but a more human way, the savage is drawn by the object held up to him, as if he could not help following it; an excitement rushes on him, and he yields to it without a struggle;

he acts according to the moment, without regard to consequences; he is energetic or slothful, tempestuous or calm, as the winds blow or the sun shines. He is one being to-day, another to-morrow, as if he were simply the sport of influences or circumstances. If he is raised somewhat above this extreme state of barbarism, just one idea or feeling occupies the narrow range of his thoughts, to the exclusion of others.

Moreover, brutes differ from men in this; that they cannot invent, cannot progress. They remain in the use of those faculties and methods, which nature gave them at their birth. They are endowed by the law of their being with certain weapons of defence, and they do not improve on them. They have food, raiment, and dwelling, ready at their command. They need no arrow or noose to catch their prey, nor kitchen to dress it; no garment to wrap round them, nor roof to shelter them. Their claws, their teeth, their viscera, are their butcher and their cook; and their fur is their wardrobe. The cave or the jungle is their home; or if it is their nature to exercise some architectural craft, they have not to learn it. But man comes into the world with the capabilities, rather than the means and appliances, of life. He begins with a small capital, but one which admits of indefinite improvement. He is, in his very idea, a creature of progress. He starts, the inferior of the brute animals, but he surpasses them in the long run; he subjects them to himself, and he goes forward on a career, which at least hitherto has not found its limit.

Even the savage of course in some measure exemplifies this law of human nature, and is lord of the brutes; and what he is and man is generally, compared with the inferior animals, such is man civilized compared with the barbarian. <u>Civilization</u> is that state to which man's nature points and tends; it is the systematic use, improvement, and combination of those faculties which are his characteristic; and, viewed in its idea, it is the perfection, the happiness of our mortal state. It is the development of art out of nature, and of self-government out of passion, and of certainty out of opinion, and of faith out of reason. It is the due disposition of the various powers of the soul, each in its place, the subordination or subjection of the inferior, and the union of all into one whole. Aims, rules, views, habits, projects; prudence, foresight, observation, inquiry, invention, resource, resolution, perseverance, are its characteristics. Justice, benevolence, expedience, propriety, religion, are its recognized, its motive principles. Supernatural truth is its sovereign law. Such is it in its true idea, synonymous with Christianity; and, not only in idea, but in matter of fact also, is Christianity ever civilization, as far as its influence prevails; but, unhappily, in matter of fact, civilization is not necessarily Christianity. If we would view things as they really are, we must bear in mind that, true as it is, that only a supernatural grace can raise man towards the perfection of his nature, yet it is possible,—without the cultivation of its spiritual part, which contemplates objects subtle, distant, delicate of apprehension, and slow of operation, nay, even with an actual contempt of faith and devotion, in comparison of objects tangible and present,—possible it is, I say, to combine in some sort the other faculties of man into one, and to progress forward, with the substitution of natural religion for faith, and a refined expediency or propriety for true morality, just as with practice a man might manage to run without an arm or without sight, and as the defect of one organ is sometimes supplied to a certain extent by the preternatural action of another.

And this is, in fact, what is commonly understood by civilization, and it is the sense in which the word must be used here; not that perfection which nature aims at, and requires, and cannot of itself reach; but a second-rate perfection of nature, being what it is, and remaining what it is, without any supernatural principle, only with its powers of ratiocination, judgment, sagacity, and imagination fully exercised, and the affections and passions under sufficient control. Such was it, in its higher excellences, in heathen Greece and Rome, where the perception of moral principles, possessed by the cultivated and accomplished intellect, by the mind of Plato or Isocrates, of Cleanthes, Seneca, Epictetus, or Antoninus, rivalled in outward pretensions the inspired teaching of the Apostle of the Gentiles. Such is it at the present day, not only in its reception of the elements of religion and morals (when Christianity is in the midst of it as an inexhaustible storehouse for natural reason to borrow from), but especially in a province peculiar to these times, viz., in science and art, in physics, in politics, in economics, and mechanics. And great as are its attainments at present, still, as I have said, we are far from being able to discern, even in the distance, the limit of its advancement and of its perfectibility.

4.

It is evident from what has been said, that barbarism is a principle, not of society, but of isolation; he who will not submit even to himself, is not likely to volunteer a subjection to others; and this is more or less the price which, from the nature of the case, the members of society pay individually for the security of that which they hold in common. It follows, that no polity can be simply barbarous; barbarians may indeed combine in small bodies, as they have done in Gaul, Scythia, and America, from the gregariousness of our nature, from fellowship of blood, from accidental neighbourhood, or for self-preservation; but such societies are not bodies or polities; they are but the chance result of an occasion, and are destitute of a common life. Barbarism has no individuality, it has no history; quarrels between neighbouring tribes, grudges, blood-shedding, exhaustion, raids, success, defeat, the same thing over and over again, this is not the action of society, nor the subject-matter of narrative; it neither interests the curiosity, nor leaves any impression on the memory. "*Labitur et labetur;*" it forms and breaks again, like the billows of the sea, and is but a mockery of unity. When I speak of barbarian states, I mean such as consist of members not simply barbarous, but just so far removed from the extreme of savageness that they admit of having certain principles in common, and are able to submit themselves individually to the system which rises out of those principles; that they do recognize the ideas of government, property, and law, however imperfectly; though they still differ from civilized polities in those main points, which I have set down as analogous to the difference between brutes and the human species.

As instinct is perfect after its kind at first, and never advances, whereas the range of the intellect is ever growing, so barbarous states are pretty much the same from first to last, and this is their characteristic; and civilized states, on the other hand, though they have had a barbarian era, are ever advancing further and further from it, and thus their distinguishing badge is progress. So far my line of thought leads me to concur in the elaborate remarks on the subject put forth by the celebrated M. Guizot, in his "Lectures on European Civilization."

Civilized states are ever developing into a more perfect organization, and a more exact and more various operation; they are ever increasing their stock of thoughts and of knowledge: ever creating, comparing, disposing, and improving. Hence, while bodily strength is the token of barbarian power, mental ability is the honourable badge of civilized states. The one is like Ajax, the other like Ulysses; civilized nations are constructive, barbarous are destructive. Civilization spreads by the ways of peace, by moral suasion, by means of literature, the arts, commerce, diplomacy, institutions; and, though material power never can be superseded, it is subordinate to the influence of mind. Barbarians can provide themselves with swift and hardy horses, can sweep over a country, rush on with a shout, use the steel and firebrand, and frighten and overwhelm the weak or cowardly; but in the wars of civilized countries, even the implements of carnage are scientifically constructed, and are calculated to lessen or supersede it; and a campaign becomes co-ordinately a tour of *savants*, or a colonizing expedition, or a political demonstration. When Sesostris marched through Asia to the Euxine, he left upon his road monuments of himself, which have not utterly disappeared even at this day; and the memorials of the rule of the Pharaohs are still engraved on the rocks of Libya and Arabia. Alexander, again, in a later age, crossed from Macedonia to Asia with the disciples of Aristotle in his train. His march was the diffusion of the arts and commerce, and the acquisition of scientific knowledge; the countries he passed through were accurately described, as he proceeded, and the intervals between halt and halt regularly measured.[1] His naval armaments explored nearly the whole distance from

[1] Murray's Asia.

Attock on the Upper Indus to the Isthmus of Suez : his philosophers noted down the various productions and beasts of the unknown East; and his courtiers were the first to report to the western world the singular institutions of Hindostan.

Again, while Attila boasted that his horse's hoof withered the grass it trod on, and Zingis could gallop over the site of the cities he had destroyed, Seleucus, or Ptolemy, or Trajan, covered the range of his conquests vith broad capitals, marts of commerce, noble roads, and spacious harbours. Lucullus collected a magnificent library in the East, and Cæsar converted his northern expeditions into an antiquarian and historical research.

Nor is this an accident in Roman annals. She was a power pre-eminently military; yet what is her history but the most remarkable instance of a political development and progress? More than any power, she was able to accommodate and expand her institutions according to the circumstances of successive ages, extending her municipal privileges to the conquered cities, yielding herself to the literature of Greece, and admitting into her bosom the rites of Egypt and Phrygia. At length, by an effort of versatility unrivalled in history, she was able to reverse one main article of her policy, and,.as she had already acknowledged the intellectual supremacy of Greece, so did she humble herself in a still more striking manner before a religion which she had persecuted.

5.

If these remarks upon the difference between barbarism and civilization be in the main correct, they have prepared the way for answering the question which I have raised concerning the principle of life and the mode of dissolution proper or natural to barbarous and civilized powers respectively. Ratiocination and its kindred processes, which are the necessary instruments of political progress, are, taking things as we find them, hostile to imagination and auxiliary to sense. It is true that a St. Thomas can draw out a whole system of theology from principles impalpable and invisible, and fix upon the mind by pure reason a vast multitude of facts and truths which have no pretence to a bodily form. But, taking man as he is, we shall commonly find him dissatisfied with a demonstrative process from an undemonstrated premiss, and, when he has once begun to reason, he will seek to prove the point from which his reasoning starts, as well as that at which it arrives. Thus he will be forced back from immediate first principles to others more remote, nor will he be satisfied till he ultimately reaches those which are as much within his own handling and mastery as the reasoning apparatus itself. Hence it is that civilized states ever tend to substitute objects of sense for objects of imagination, as the basis of their existence. The Pope's political power was greater when Europe was semi-barbarous; and the divine right of the successors of the English St. Edward received a death-blow in the philosophy of Bacon and Locke. At present, I suppose, our own political life, as a nation, lies in the supremacy of the law; and that again is resolvable into the internal peace, and protection of life and property, and freedom of the individual, which are its result; and these I call objects of sense.

For the very same reason, objects of this nature will not constitute the life of a barbarian community; prudence, foresight, calculation of consequences do not enter into its range of mental operations; it has no talent for analysis; it cannot understand expediency; it is impressed and affected by what is direct and absolute.

Religion, superstition, belief in persons and families, objects, not proveable, but vivid and imposing, will be the bond which keeps its members together. I have already alluded to the divinity which in the imagination of the Huns encircled the hideous form of Attila. Zingis claimed for himself or his ancestry a miraculous conception, and received from a prophet, who ascended to heaven, the dominion of the earth. He called himself the son of God; and when the missionary friars came to his immediate successor from the Pope, that successor made answer to them, that it was the Pope's duty to do him homage, as being earthly lord of all by divine right. It was a similar pretension, I need hardly say, which was the life of the Mahometan conquests, when the wild Saracen first issued from the Arabian desert. So, too, in the other hemisphere, the Caziques of aboriginal America were considered to be brothers of the Sun, and received religious homage as his representatives. They spoke as the oracles of the divinity, and claimed the power of regulating the seasons and the weather at their will. This was especially the case in Peru; "the whole system of policy," says Robertson, "was founded on religion. The Incas appeared, not only as a legislator, but as the messenger of heaven."[1] Elsewhere, the divine virtue has been considered to rest, not on the monarch, but on the code of laws, which accordingly is the social principle of the nation. The Celts ascribed their legislation to Mercury;[2] as Lycurgus and Numa in Sparta and Rome appealed to a divine sanction in behalf of their respective institutions.

This being the case, imperfect as is the condition of barbarous states, still what is there to overthrow them? They have a principle of union congenial to the state of

[1] Robertson's America, books vi. and vii. [2] Univ. Hist. Anc., vol. xvi.

their intellect, and they have not the ratiocinative habit to scrutinize and invalidate it. Since they admit of no mental progress, what serves as a bond to-day will be equally serviceable to-morrow; so that apparently their dissolution cannot come from themselves. It is true, a barbarous people, possessed of a beautiful country, may be relaxed in luxury and effeminacy; but such degeneracy has no obvious tendency to weaken their faith in the objects in which their political unity consists, though it may render them defenceless against external attacks. And here indeed lies their real peril at all times; they are ever vulnerable from without. Thus Sparta, formed deliberately on a barbarian pattern, remained faithful to it, without change, without decay, while its intellectual rival was the victim of successive revolutions. At length its power was broken externally by the Theban Epaminondas; and by the restoration of Messenia, the insurrection of the Laconians, and the emancipation of the Helots. Agesilaus, at the time of its fall, was as good a Spartan as any of his predecessors. Again, the ancient Empire of the Huns in Asia is said to have lasted 1,500 years; at length its wanton tyranny was put an end to by the Chinese King plunging into the Tartar desert, and thus breaking their power. Thrace, again, a barba rous country, lasted many centuries, with kings of great vigour, with much external prosperity, and then succumbed, not to internal revolution, but to the permanent ascendancy of Rome. Similar too is the instance of Pontus, and again of Numidia and Mauritania; they may have had great or accomplished sovereigns, but they have no history, except in the wars of their conquerors. Great leaders are necessary for the prosperity, as great enemies for the destruction, of barbarians; they thrive, as they come to nought, by means of agents external to themselves. So again Malek Shah died, and his empire fell to pieces. Hence, too, the unexpected and utter catastrophes which befall barbarous people, analogous to a violent death, which I have alluded to in speaking of the sudden rise and fall of Tartar dynasties; for no one can anticipate results, which, instead of being the slow evolution of political principles, proceed from the accident of external quarrels and of the relative condition of rival powers.

6.

Far otherwise is the history of those states, in which the intellect, not prescription, is recognized as the ultimate authority, and where the course of time is necessarily accompanied by a corresponding course of change. Such polities are ever in progress; at first from worse to better, and then from better to worse. In all human things there is a *maximum* of advance, and that *maximum* is not an established state of things, but a point in a career. The cultivation of reason and the spread of knowledge for a time develop and at length dissipate the elements of political greatness; acting first as the invaluable ally of public spirit, and then as its insidious enemy. Barbarian minds remain in the circle of ideas which sufficed their forefathers; the opinions, principles, and habits which they inherited, they transmit. They have the *prestige* of antiquity and the strength of conservatism; but where thought is encouraged, too many will think, and will think too much. The sentiment of sacredness in institutions fades away, and the measure of truth or expediency is the private judgment of the individual. An endless variety of opinion is the certain though slow result; no overpowering majority of judgments is found to decide what is good and what is bad;

political measures become acts of compromise; and at length the common bond of unity in the state consists in nothing really common, but simply in the unanimous wish of each member of it to secure his own interests. Thus the veterans of Sylla, comfortably settled in their farms, refused to rally round Pompey in his war with Cæsar.[1] Thus the municipal cities in the provinces refused to unite together in a later age for the defence of the Empire, then evidently on the way to dissolution.[2] Selfishness takes the place of loyalty, patriotism, and faith; parties grow and strengthen themselves; classes and ranks withdraw from each other more and more; the national energy becomes but a self-consuming fever, and but enables the constituent parts to be their own mutual destruction; and at length such union as is necessary for political life is found to be impossible. Meanwhile corruption of morals, which is common to all prosperous countries, completes the internal ruin, and, whether an external enemy appears or not, the nation can hardly be considered any more a state. It is but like some old arch, which, when its supports are crumbled away, stands by the force of cohesion, no one knows how. It dies a natural death, even though some Alaric or Genseric happens to be at hand to take possession of the corpse. And centuries before the end comes, patriots may see it coming, though they cannot tell its hour; and that hour creates surprise, not because it at length is come, but because it has been so long delayed.

I have been referring to the decline, as I before spoke of the progress, of the Romans: the career of that people through twelve centuries is a drama of sustained interest and equable and majestic evolution; it has

[1] Merivale's Rome, vol. ii.   [2] Guizot's European Civilization.

given scope for the most ingenious researches into its internal history. There one age is the parent of another; the elements and principles of its political system are brought out into a variety of powers with mutual relations; external events act and react with domestic affairs; manners and views change; excess of prosperity becomes the omen of misfortune to come; till in the words of the poet, "*Suis et ipsa Roma viribus ruit.*" For how many philosophical histories has Greece afforded opportunity! while the constitutional history of England, as far as it has hitherto gone, is a recognized subject-matter of scientific and professional teaching. The case is the same with the history of the medieval Italian cities, of the medieval Church, and of the Saracenic empire. As regards the last of these instances, I am not alluding merely to the civil contentions and wars which took place in it, for such may equally happen to a barbarian state. Cupidity and ambition are inherent in the nature of man; the Gauls and British, the tribes of Scythia, the Seljukian Turks, consisted each of a number of mutually hostile communities or kingdoms. What is relevant to my purpose in the history of the Saracens is, that their quarrels often had an intellectual basis, and arose out of their religion. The white, the green, and the black factions, who severally reigned at Cordova, Cairo, and Bagdad, excommunicated each other, and claimed severally to be the successors of Mahomet. Then came the fanatical innovation of the Carmathians, who pretended to a divine mission to complete the religion of Mahomet, as Mahomet had completed Christianity.[1] They relaxed the duties of ablution, fasting, and pilgrimage; admitted the use of wine, and protested against the worldly pomp

[1] Gibbon, vol. x.

of the Caliphs. They spread their tents along the coast of the Persian Gulf, and in no long time were able to bring an army of 100,000 men into the field. Ultimately they took up their residence on the borders of Assyria, Syria, and Egypt. As time went on, and the power of the Caliphs was still further reduced, religious contention broke out in Bagdad itself, between the rigid and the lax parties, and the followers of the Abbassides and of Ali.

If we consult ancient history, the case is the same; the Jews, a people of progress, were ruined, as appears on the face of Scripture, by internal causes; they split into sects, Pharisees, Sadducees, Herodians, Essenes, as soon as the Divine Hand retired from the direct government of their polity; and they were fighting together in Jerusalem when the Romans were beleaguering its walls. Nay, even the disunion, which was a special and divine punishment for their sins, was fulfilled according to this natural law which I am illustrating; it was the splendid reign of Solomon, the era of literature, commerce, opulence, and general prosperity, which was the antecedent of fatal revolutions. If we turn to civilized nations of an even earlier date, the case is the same; we are accustomed indeed to associate Chinese and Egyptians with ideas of perpetual untroubled stability; but a philosophical historian, whom I shall presently cite, speaks far otherwise of those times when the intellect was prominently active. China was for many centuries the seat of a number of petty principalities, which were limited, not despotic; about 200 years before our era it became one absolute monarchy. Till then idolatry was unknown, and the doctrines of Confucius were in honour: the first Emperor ordered a general burning of books, burning at the same time between 400 and 500 of the followers of Confucius, and persecuting the men of letters. A rationalist philosophy succeeded, and this again gave way to the introduction of the religion of Buddha or Fo, just about the time of our Lord's Crucifixion. At later periods, in the fifth and in the thirteenth centuries, the country was divided into two distinct kingdoms, north and south; and such was its state when Marco Polo visited it. It has been several times conquered by the Tartars, and it is a remarkable proof of its civilization, that it has ever obliged them to adopt its manners, laws, and even language. China, then, has a distinct and peculiar internal history, and has paid to the full the penalty which, in the course of centuries, goes along with the blessings of civilization. "The whole history of China, from beginning to end," says Frederic Schlegel, "displays one continued series of seditions, usurpations, anarchy, changes of dynasty, and other violent revolutions and catastrophes."[1]

The history of Egypt tells the same tale; "Civil discord," he says, "existed there under various forms. The country itself was often divided into several kingdoms; and, even when united, we observe a great conflict of interests between the agricultural province of Upper Egypt, and the commercial and manufacturing province of the Lower: as, indeed, a similar clashing of interests is often to be noticed in modern states. In the period immediately preceding the Persian conquest, the caste of warriors, or the whole class of nobility, were decidedly opposed to the monarchs, because they imagined them to promote too much the power of the priesthood;"—in other words, their national downfall was not owing directly to an external cause, but to an internal collision of parties and interests;—" in the same way," continues

[1] Philosophy of History; Robertson's translation.

the author I am quoting, "as the history of India presents a similar rivalry or political hostility between the Brahmins and the caste of the Cshatriyas. In the reign of Psammatichus, the disaffection of the native nobility obliged this prince to take Greek soldiers into his pay; and thus at length was the defence of Egypt entrusted to an army of foreign mercenaries." He adds, which is apposite to my purpose, for I suppose he is speaking of civilized nations, "In general, states and kingdoms, before they succumb to a foreign conqueror, are, if not outwardly and visibly, yet secretly and internally, undermined."

So much on the connexion between the civilization of a state and its overthrow from internal causes, or, what may be called, its succumbing to a natural death. I will only add, that I am but attempting to set down general rules, to which there may be exceptions, explicable or not. For instance, Venice is one of the most civilized states of the middle age; but, by a system of jealous and odious tyranny, it continued to maintain its ground without revolution, when revolutions were frequent in the other Italian cities; yet the very necessity of so severe a despotism shows us what would have happened there, if natural causes had been left to work unimpeded.

7.

I feel I owe you, Gentlemen, an apology for the time I have consumed in an abstract discussion; it is drawing to an end, but it still requires the notice of two questions, on which, however, I have not much to say, even if I would. First, can a civilized state become barbarian in course of years? and secondly, can a barbarian state ever become civilized?

As to the former of these questions, considering the

human race did start with society, and did not start with barbarism, and barbarism exists, we might be inclined at first sight to answer it in the affirmative; again, since Christianity implies civilization, and is the recovery of the whole race of Adam, we might answer the second in the affirmative also; but such resolutions of the inquiry are scarcely to the point. Doubtless the human race may degenerate, doubtless it may make progress; doubtless men, viewed as individuals or as members of races or tribes, or as inhabitants of certain countries, may change their state from better to worse, or from worse to better: this, however, is not the question; but whether a given state, which has a certain political unity, can change the principle of that unity, and, without breaking up into its component parts, become barbarian instead of civilized, and civilized instead of barbarian.

(1.) Now as to the latter of these questions, it still must be answered in the affirmative under circumstances: that is, all civilized states have started with barbarism, and have gradually in the course of ages developed into civilization, unless there be any political community in the world, as China has by some been considered, representative of Noe; and unless we consider the case of colonies, as Constantinople or Venice, fairly to form an exception. But the question is very much altered, when we contemplate a change in one or two generations from barbarism to civilization. The substitution of one form of political life for another, when it occurs, is the sort of process by which fossils take the place of animal substances, or strata are formed, or carbon is crystallized, or boys grow into men. Christianity itself has never, I think, suddenly civilized a race; national habits and opinions cannot be cast off at will without miracle.

Hence the extreme jealousy and irritation of the members of a state with innovators, who would tamper with what the Greeks called νόμιμα, or constitutional and vital usages. Hence the fury of Pentheus against the Mænades, and of the Scythians against their King Scylas, and the agitation created at Athens by the destruction of the Mercuries. Hence the obstinacy of the Roman statesmen of old, and of the British constituency now, against the Catholic Church; and the feeling is so far justified, that projected innovations often turn out, if not simply nugatory, nothing short of destructive; and though there is a great notion just now that the British Constitution admits of being fitted upon every people under heaven, from the Blacks to the Italians, I do not know what has occurred to give plausibility to the anticipation. England herself once attempted the costume of republicanism, but she found that monarchy was part of her political essence.

(2.) Still less can the possibility be admitted of a civilized polity really relapsing into barbarism; though a state of things may be superinduced, which in many of its features may be thought to resemble it. In truth, I have not yet traced out the ultimate result of those internal revolutions which I have assigned as the incidental but certain evils, in the long run, attendant on civilization. That result is various: sometimes the over-civilized and degenerate people is swept from the face of the earth, as the Roman populations in Africa by the Vandals; sometimes it is reduced to servitude, as the Egyptians by the Ptolemies, or the Greeks by the Turks; sometimes it is absorbed or included in new political combinations, as the northern Italians by the Lombards and Franks; sometimes it remains unmolested on its own territory, and lives by the momentum, or the repute, or the habit, or the tradition of its former civilization. This last of course is the only case which bears upon the question I am considering; and I grant that a state of things does then ensue, which in some of its phenomena is like barbarism; China is an example in point. No one can deny its civilization; its diligent care of the soil, its cultivation of silk and of the tea-tree, its populousness, its canals, its literature, its court ceremonial, its refinement of manners, its power of persevering so loyally in its old institutions through so many ages, abundantly vindicate it from the reproach of barbarism. But at the same time there are tokens of degeneracy, which are all the stronger for being also tokens, still more striking than those I have hitherto mentioned, of its high civilization in times past. It has had for ages the knowledge of the more recent discoveries and institutions of the West, which have done so much for Europe, yet it has been unable to use them, the magnetic needle, gunpowder, and printing. The littleness of the national character, its self-conceit, and its formality, are further instances of an effete civilization. They remind the observer vividly of the picture which history presents to us of the Byzantine Court before the taking of Constantinople; or, again, of that *material* retention of Christian doctrine (to use the theological word), of which Protestantism in its more orthodox exhibitions, and still more, of which the Greek schism affords the specimen. Either a state of deadness and mechanical action, or a restless ebb and flow of opinion and sentiment, is the symptom of that intellectual exhaustion and decrepitude, whether in politics or religion, which, if old age be a second childhood, may in some sense be called barbarism, and of which, at present, we are respectively reminded in China on the one hand, and in some southern states of Europe on the other.

These are the principles, whatever modifications they may require, which, however rudely adumbrated, I trust will suffice to enable me to contemplate the future of the Ottoman Empire.

LECTURE VIII.

The Past and Present of the Ottomans.

WHATEVER objections in detail may stand against the account I have been giving of barbarism and civilization—and I trust there are none which do not admit of removal—so far, I think, is clear, that, if my account be only in the main correct, the Turkish power certainly is not a civilized, and is a barbarous power. The barbarian lives without principle and without aim; he does but reflect the successive outward circumstances in which he finds himself, and he varies with them. He changes suddenly, when their change is sudden, and is as unlike what he was just before, as one fortune or external condition is unlike another. He moves when he is urged by appetite; else, he remains in sloth and inactivity. He lives, and he dies, and he has done nothing, but leaves the world as he found it. And what the individual is, such is his whole generation; and as that generation, such is the generation before and after. No generation can say what it has been doing; it has not made the state of things better or worse; for retrogression there is hardly room; for progress, no sort of material. Now I shall show that these characteristics of the barbarian are rudimental points, as I may call them, in the picture of the Turks, as drawn by those who have studied them. I shall principally avail myself of the information supplied by Mr. Thornton and M. Volney, men of name and ability, and for various reasons preferable as authorities to writers of the present day.

I.

"The Turks," says Mr. Thornton, who, though not blind to their shortcomings, is certainly favourable to them, "the Turks are of a grave and saturnine cast ... patient of hunger and privations, capable of enduring the hardships of war, but not much inclined to habits of industry.... They prefer apathy and indolence to active enjoyments; but when moved by a powerful stimulus they sometimes indulge in pleasures in excess." "The Turk," he says elsewhere, "stretched at his ease on the banks of the Bosphorus, glides down the stream of existence without reflection on the past, and without anxiety for the future. His life is one continued and unvaried reverie. To his imagination the whole universe appears occupied in procuring him pleasures.... Every custom invites to repose, and every object inspires an indolent voluptuousness. Their delight is to recline on soft verdure under the shade of trees, and to muse without fixing the attention, lulled by the trickling of a fountain or the murmuring of a rivulet, and inhaling through their pipe a gently inebriating vapour. Such pleasures, the highest which the rich can enjoy, are equally within the reach of the artizan or the peasant."

M. Volney corroborates this account of them:— "Their behaviour," he says, "is serious, austere, and melancholy; they rarely laugh, and the gaiety of the French appears to them a fit of delirium. When they speak, it is with deliberation, without gestures and without passion; they listen without interrupting you; they are silent for whole days together, and they by no means pique themselves on supporting conversation. If they walk, it is always leisurely, and on business. They have no idea of our troublesome activity, and our walks backwards and forwards for amusement. Continually seated, they pass whole days smoking, with their legs crossed, their pipes in their mouths, and almost without changing their attitude." Englishmen present as great a contrast to the Ottoman as the French; as a late English traveller brings before us, apropos of seeing some Turks in quarantine: "Certainly," he says, "Englishmen are the least able to wait, and the Turks the most so, of any people I have ever seen. To impede an Englishman's locomotion on a journey, is equivalent to stopping the circulation of his blood; to disturb the repose of a Turk on his, is to re-awaken him to a painful sense of the miseries of life. The one nation at rest is as much tormented as Prometheus, chained to his rock, with the vulture feeding on him; the other in motion is as uncomfortable as Ixion tied to his ever-moving wheel."[1]

2.

However, the barbarian, when roused to action, is a very different being from the barbarian at rest. "The Turk," says Mr. Thornton, "is usually placid, hypochondriac, and unimpassioned; but, when the customary sedateness of his temper is ruffled, his passions . . . . are furious and uncontrollable. The individual seems possessed with all the ungovernable fury of a multitude; and all ties, all attachments, all natural and moral obligations, are forgotten or despised, till his rage subsides." A similar remark is made by a writer of the day: "The Turk on horseback has no resemblance to the Turk reclining on his carpet. He there assumes a vigour,

[1] Formby's Visit, p. 70.

and displays a dexterity, which few Europeans would be capable of emulating; no horsemen surpass the Turks; and, with all the indolence of which they are accused, no people are more fond of the violent exercise of riding."[1]

So was it with their ancestors, the Tartars; now dosing on their horses or their waggons, now galloping over the plains from morning to night. However, these successive phases of Turkish character, as reported by travellers, have seemed to readers as inconsistencies in their reports; Thornton accepts the inconsistency. "The national character of the Turks," he says, "is a composition of contradictory qualities. We find them brave and pusillanimous; gentle and ferocious; resolute and inconstant; active and indolent; fastidiously abstemious, and indiscriminately indulgent. The great are alternately haughty and humble, arrogant and cringing, liberal and sordid." What is this but to say in one word that we find them barbarians?

According to these distinct moods or phases of character, they will leave very various impressions of themselves on the minds of successive beholders. A traveller finds them in their ordinary state in repose and serenity; he is surprised and startled to find them so different from what he imagined; he admires and extols them, and inveighs against the prejudice which has slandered them to the European world. He finds them mild and patient, tender to the brute creation, as becomes the children of a Tartar shepherd, kind and hospitable, self-possessed and dignified, the lowest classes sociable with each other, and the children gamesome. It is true; they are as noble as the lion of the desert, and as gentle and as playful as the fireside cat. Our traveller observes all

[1] Bell's Geography.

this ;[1] and seems to forget that from the humblest to the highest of the feline tribe, from the cat to the lion, the most wanton and tyrannical cruelty alternates with qualities more engaging or more elevated. Other barbarous tribes also have their innocent aspects — from the Scythians in the classical poets and historians down to the Lewchoo islanders in the pages of Basil Hall.

3.

2. But whatever be the natural excellences of the Turks, progressive they are not. This Sir Charles Fellows seems to allow: "My intimacy with the character of the Turks," he says, "which has led me to think so highly of their moral excellence, has not given me the same favourable impression of the development of their mental powers. Their refinement is of manners and affections; there is little cultivation or activity of mind among them." This admission implies a great deal, and brings us to a fresh consideration. Observe, they were in the eighth century of their political existence when Thornton and Volney lived among them, and these authors report of them as follows:—"Their buildings," says Thornton, "are heavy in their proportions, bad in detail, both in taste and execution, fantastic in decoration, and destitute of genius. Their cities are not decorated with public monuments, whose object is to enliven or to embellish." Their religion forbids them every sort of painting, sculpture, or engraving; thus the fine arts cannot exist among them. They have no music but vocal; and know of no accompaniment except a bass of one note like that of the bagpipe. Their singing is in a great measure recitative, with little variation of note. They have scarcely any notion of medicine

[1] Vid. Sir Charles Fellows' Asia Minor.

or surgery; and they do not allow of anatomy. As to science, the telescope, the microscope, the electric battery, are unknown, except as playthings. The compass is not universally employed in their navy, nor are its common purposes thoroughly understood. Navigation, astronomy, geography, chemistry, are either not known, or practised only on antiquated and exploded principles. As to their civil and criminal codes of law, these are unalterably fixed in the Koran. Their habits require very little furniture; "the whole inventory of a wealthy family," says Volney, "consists in a carpet, mats, cushions, mattresses, some small cotton clothes, copper and wooden platters for the table, a mortar, a portable mill, a little porcelain, and some plates of copper tinned. All our apparatus of tapestry, wooden bedsteads, chairs, stools, glasses, desks, bureaus, closets, buffets with their plate and table services, all our cabinet and upholstery-work are unknown." They have no clocks, though they have watches. In short, they are hardly more than dismounted Tartars still; and, if pressed by the Powers of Christendom, would be able, at very short warning, to pack up and turn their faces northward to their paternal deserts. You find in their cities barbers and mercers; saddlers and gunsmiths; bakers and confectioners; sometimes butchers; whitesmiths and ironmongers; these are pretty nearly all their trades. Their inheritance is their all; their own acquisition is nought. Their stuffs are from the classical Greeks; their dyes are the old Tyrian; their cement is of the age of the Romans; and their locks may be traced back to Solomon. They do not commonly engage either in agriculture or in commerce; of the cultivators of the soil I have said quite enough in a foregoing Lecture, and their commerce seems to be generally in the hands of Franks,

Greeks, or Armenians, as formerly in the hands of the Jews.[1]

The White Huns took to commerce and diplomacy in the course of a century or two; the Saracens in a shorter time unlearned their barbarism, and became philosophers and experimentalists; what have the Turks to show to the human race for their long spell of prosperity and power?

As to their warfare, their impracticable and unprogressive temperament showed itself even in the era of their military and political ascendancy, and had much to do, as far as human causes are concerned, with their defeat at Lepanto. "The signal for engaging was no sooner given," says the writer in the "Universal History," "than the Turks with a hideous cry fell on six galeasses, which lay at anchor near a mile ahead of the confederate fleet." "With a hideous cry,"—this was the true barbarian onset; we find it in the Red Indians and the New Zealanders; and it is noticed of the Seljukians, the predecessors of the Ottomans, in their celebrated engagement with the Crusaders at Dorylæum. "With horrible howlings," says Mr. Turner, "and loud clangour of drums and trumpets, the Turks rushed on;" and you may recollect, the savage who would have murdered the Bishop of Bamberg, began with a shriek. However, as you will see directly, such an onset was as ignorant as it was savage, for it was made with a haughty and wilful blindness to the importance of firearms under their circumstances. The Turks, in the hey-day of their victories and under their most sagacious leaders,

---

[1] The correspondent of the *Times* in February, 1854, speaking of the great arsenal of Rustchuk, observes: "All the heavy smith work was done by Bulgarians, the light iron work by gipsies, the carpenters were all Turks, the sawyers Bulgarians, the tinmen all Jews."

had scorned and ignored the use of the then newly invented instruments of war. In truth, they had shared the prejudice against firearms which had been in the first instance felt by the semi-barbarous chivalry of Europe. The knight-errant, as Ariosto draws and reflects him, disdained so dishonourable a means of beating a foe. He looked upon the use of gunpowder, as Mr. Thornton reminds us, as "cruel, cowardly, and murderous;" because it gave an unfair and disgraceful advantage to the feeble or the unwarlike. Such was the sentiment of the Ottomans even in the reign of their great Soliman. Shortly before the battle of Lepanto, a Dalmatian horseman rode express to Constantinople, and reported to the Divan, that 2,500 Turks had been surprised and routed by 500 musqueteers. Great was the indignation of the assembly against the unfortunate troops, of whom the messenger was one. But he was successful in his defence of himself and his companions. "Do you not hear," he said, "that we were overcome by guns? We were routed by fire, not by the enemy. It would have been otherwise, had it been a contest of courage. They took fire to their aid; fire is one of the elements; what is man that he should resist their shock?" They did not dream of the apophthegm that knowledge is power; and that we become strong by subduing nature to our will.

Accordingly, their tactics by sea was a sort of land engagement on deck, as it was with our ancestors, and with the ancients. First, they charged the adverse vessel, with a view of taking it; if that would not do, they boarded it. They fought hand to hand, and each captain might pretty much exercise his own judgment which ship to attack, as Homer's heroes chose their combatants on the field of Troy. However, the Christian galeasses at Lepanto,—for to these we must at length return,—were vessels of larger dimensions than the Ottomans had ever built; they were fortified, like castles, with heavy ordnance, and were so disposed as to cover the line of their own galleys. The consequence was, that as the Turks advanced in order of battle, these galeasses kept up a heavy and destructive fire upon them, and their barbarian energy availed them as little as their howlings. It was the triumph of civilization over brute force, as well as of faith over misbelief. "While discipline and attention to the military exercises could insure success in war, the Turks," says Thornton, "were the first of military nations. When the whole art of war was changed, and victory or defeat became matter of calculation, the rude and illiterate Turkish warriors experienced the fatal consequences of ignorance without suspecting the cause; accustomed to employ no other means than force, they sunk into despondency, when force could no longer avail."

Another half century has passed since this was written, and the Turkish power has now completed its eighth century since Togrul Beg, the first Seljukian Sultan; and what has been the fruit of so long a duration? Just about the time of Togrul Beg, flourished William, Duke of Normandy; he passed over to take possession of England; compare the England of the Conquest with the England of this day. Again, compare the Rome of Junius Brutus to the Rome of Constantine, 800 years afterwards. In each of these polities there was a continuous progression, and the end was unlike the beginning; but the Turks, except that they have gained the faculty of political union, are pretty much what they were when they crossed the Jaxartes and Oxus. Again, at the time of Togrul Beg, the Greek schism also took place; now from Michael Cerularius, in 1054, to Anthimus, in 1853, Patriarchs of Constantinople, eight centuries have passed of religious deadness and insensibility: a longer time has passed in China of a similar political inertness: yet China has preserved at least the civilization, and Greece the ecclesiastical science, with which they respectively passed into their long sleep; but the Turks of this day are still in the less than infancy of art; literature, philosophy, and general knowledge; and we may fairly conclude that, if they have not learned the very alphabet of science in eight hundred years, they are not likely to set to work on it in the nine hundredth.

Moreover, it is remarkable that with them, as with the ancient Medes and Persians, change of law and government is distinctly prohibited. The greatest of their Sultans, and the last of the great ten, Soliman, known in European history as the Magnificent, is called by his compatriots the Regulator, on account of the irreversible sanction which he gave to the existing administration of affairs. "The magnitude and the splendour of the military achievements of Soliman," says Mr. Thornton, "are surpassed in the judgment of his people by the wisdom of his legislation. He has acquired the name of Canuni, or institutor of rules . . . on account of the order and police which he established in his Empire. He caused a compilation to be made of all the maxims and regulations of his predecessors on subjects of political and military economy. He strictly defined the duties, the powers, and the privileges of all governors, commanders, and public functionaries. He regulated the levies, the services, the equipments, and the pay of the military and maritime force of the Empire. He prescribed the mode of collecting, and of applying, the public revenue. He assigned to every officer his rank at court, in the city, and in the army; and the observance of his regulations was enforced on his successors by the sanction of his authority. The work, which his ancestors had begun, and which his care had completed, seemed to himself and his contemporaries the compendium of human wisdom. Soliman contemplated it with the fondness of a parent; and, conceiving it not to be susceptible of further improvement, he endeavoured to secure its perpetual duration." The author, after pointing out that this was done at the very time when a new hemisphere was in course of exploration, when the telescope was mapping for mankind the heavens, when the Baconian philosophy was about to convert discovery and experiment into instruments of science, printing was carrying knowledge and literature into the heart of society, and the fine arts were receiving one of their most remarkable developments, proceeds: " The institutions of Soliman placed a barrier between his subjects and future improvement. He beheld with complacency and exultation the eternal fabric which his hands had reared; and the curse denounced against pride has reduced the nation, which participated in his sentiments, to a state of inferiority to the present level of civilized men." The result is the same, though we say that Soliman only recognized and affirmed that barbarism was the law of the Ottoman power.

4

3. It is true that in the last quarter of a century efforts have been made by the government of Constantinople to innovate on the existing condition of its people; and it has addressed itself in the first instance to certain details of daily Turkish life. We must take it for granted that it began with such changes as were easiest;

if so, its failure in these small matters suggests how little ground there is for hope of success in other advances more important and difficult. Every one knows that in the details of dress, carriage, and general manners, the Turks are very different from Europeans: so different, and so consistently different, that the contrariety would seem to arise from some difference of essential principle. "This dissimilitude," says Mr. Thornton, "which pervades the whole of their habits, is so general, even in things of apparent insignificance, as almost to indicate design rather than accident. The whole exterior of the Oriental is different from ours." And then he goes on to mention some specimens, to which we are able to add others from Volney and Bell. For instance:—The European stands firm and erect; his head drawn back, his chest advanced, his toes turned out, his knees straight. The attitude of the Turk, in each of these particulars, is different, and, to express myself by an antithesis, is more conformable to nature, and less to reason. The European wears short and close garments, the Turk long and ample. The one uncovers the head, when he would show reverence; with the other, a bared head is a sign of folly. The one salutes by an inclination, the other by raising himself. The one passes his life upright, the other sitting. The one sits on raised seats, the other on the ground. In inviting a person to approach, the one draws his hand to him, the other thrusts it from him. The host in Europe helps himself last; in Turkey, first. The one drinks to his company, or at least to some toast; the other drinks silently, and his guests congratulate him. The European has a night dress, the Turk lies down in his clothes. The Turkish barber pushes the razor from him; the Turkish carpenter draws the saw to him; the Turkish mason sits as he builds;

and he begins a house at the top, and finishes at the bottom, so that the upper rooms are inhabited, when the bottom is a framework.

Now it would seem as if this multitude of little usages hung together, and were as difficult to break through as the meshes of some complicated web. However, the Sultan found it the most favourable subject-matter of his incipient reformation; and his consequent attempt and the omens of its ultimate issue are interestingly recounted in the pages of Sir Charles Fellows, the panegyrist both of Mahmood and his people. "The Turk," he says, "proud of his beard, comes up from the province a candidate for, or to receive, the office of governor. The Sultan gives him an audience, passes his hand over his own short-trimmed beard; the candidate takes the hint, and appears the next day shorn of his honoured locks. The Sultan, who is always attired in a plain blue frock coat, asks of the aspirant for office if he admires it; he, of course, praises the costume worn by his patron; whereupon the Sultan suggests that he would look well in it, as also in the red unturbaned fez. The following day the officer again attends to receive or lose his appointment; and, to promote the progress of his suit, throws off his costly and beautiful costume, and appears like the Sultan in the dull unsightly frock."

Such is the triumph of loyalty and self-interest, and such is its limit. "A regimental cloak," continues our author, "may sometimes be seen covering a fat body inclosed in all the robes of the Turkish costume; the whole bundle, including the fur-lined gown, being strapped together round the waist. Some of the figures are literally as broad as long, and have a laughable effect on horseback. The saddles for the upper classes are now generally made of the European form; but the people, who cannot give up their accustomed love of finery for plain leather, have them mostly of purple or crimson velvet, embroidered with silver or gold, the holsters ornamented with beautiful patterns." After a while, he continues: "One very unpopular reform which the Sultan tried to effect in the formation of his troops was that of their wearing braces, a necessary accompaniment to the trousers; and why? because these form a cross, the badge of the infidel, upon the back. Many, indeed, will submit to severe punishment, and even death, for disobedience to military orders, rather than bear upon their persons this sign hostile to their religion."

In another place he continues this subject with an amusing accuracy of analysis:—"The mere substitution of trousers for their loose dress interferes seriously with their old habits; they all turn in their toes, in consequence of the Turkish manner of sitting, and they walk wide, and with a swing, from being habituated to the full drapery: this gait has become natural to them, and in their European trousers they walk in the same manner. They wear wide-topped loose boots, which push up their trousers. Wellington boots would be still more inconvenient, as they must slip them off six times a day for prayers. In this new dress they cannot with comfort sit or kneel on the ground, as is their custom; and they will thus be led to use chairs; and with chairs they will want tables. But, were these to be introduced, their houses would be too low, for their heads would almost touch the ceiling. Thus by a little innovation might their whole usages be unhinged."

5.

4. In these failures, however, should they turn out to be such, the *vis inertiæ* of habit is not the whole account of

the matter ; an antagonistic principle is at work, characteristic of the barbarian, and intimately present to the mind of a Turk—national pride. All nations, indeed, are proud of themselves; but, as being the first and the best, not as being the solitary existing perfection, among the inhabitants of the earth. Civilized nations allow that foreigners have their specific excellences, and such excellences as are a lesson to themselves. They may think too well of their own proficiency, and may lose by such blindness ; but they admit enough about others to allow of their own emulation and advance ; whereas the barbarian, in his own estimate, is perfect already ; and what is perfect cannot be improved. Hence he cherishes in his heart a self-esteem of a very peculiar kind, and a special contempt of others. He views foreigners, either as simply unworthy of his attention, or as objects of his legitimate dominion. Thus, too, he justifies his sloth, and places his ignorance of all things human and divine on a sort of intellectual basis.

Robertson, in his history of America, enlarges on this peculiarity of the savage. "The Tartar," he says, "accustomed to roam over extensive plains, and to subsist on the produce of his herds, imprecates upon his enemy, as the greatest of all curses, that he may be condemned to reside in one place, and to be nourished with the top of a weed. The rude Americans . . . far from complaining of their own situation, or viewing that of men in a more improved state with admiration or envy, regard themselves as the standard of excellence, as beings the best entitled, as well as the most perfectly qualified, to enjoy real happiness. . . . Void of foresight, as well as free from care themselves, and delighted with that state of indolent security, they wonder at the anxious precautions, the unceasing industry, and complicated arrangements of Europeans, in guarding against distant evils, or providing for future wants; and they often exclaim against their preposterous folly, in thus multiplying the troubles, and increasing the labour of life. . . . The appellation which the Iroquois give to themselves is, 'The chief of men.' Caraibe, the original name of the fierce inhabitants of the Windward Islands, signifies 'The warlike people.' The Cherokees, from an idea of their own superiority, call the Europeans 'Nothings,' or 'The accursed race,' and assume to themselves the name of 'The beloved people.' . . . They called them the froth of the sea, men without father or mother. They suppose that either they have no country of their own, and, therefore, invaded that which belonged to others; or that, being destitute of the necessaries of life at home, they were obliged to roam over the ocean, in order to rob such as were more amply provided."[1]

It is easy to see that an intense self-adoration, such as is here suggested, is, in the case of a martial people, to a certain point a principle of strength; it gives a sort of intellectual force to the impetuosity and obstinacy of their attacks; while, on the other hand, it is in the long run a principle of debility, as blinding them to the most evident and imminent dangers, and, after defeat, burdening and precipitating their despair.

Now, is it possible to trace this attribute of barbarism among the Turks? If so, what does it do for them, and whence is it supplied? You will recollect, I have not been unwilling in a former Lecture to acknowledge what is salutary in Mahometanism; certainly it embodies in it some ancient and momentous truths, and is undeniably beneficial so far as their proper influence extends. But, after all, looked at as a religion, it is as debasing to

[1] Lib. iv. fin.

the populations which receive it as it is false; and, as it arose among barbarians, it is not wonderful that it subserves the reign of barbarism. This it certainly does in the case of the Turks; already three great departments of intellectual activity in civilized countries have incidentally come before us, which are forbidden ground to its professors. The first is legislation; for the criminal and civil code of the Mahometan is unalterably fixed in the Koran. The second is the modern system of money transactions and finance; for "in obedience to their religion," says an author I have been lately quoting,[1] "which, like the Jewish law, forbids taking interest for money, the Turks abstain from carrying on many lucrative trades connected with the lending of money. Hence other nations, generally the Armenians, act as their bankers." The third is the department of the Fine Arts for, it being unlawful to represent the human form, nay, any natural substance whatever, as fruit or flowers, sculpture loses its solitary object, painting is almost extinguished, while architecture has been obliged to undergo a sort of revolution in its decorative portions to accommodate it to the restriction. These, however, are matters of detail, though of very high importance; what I wish rather to point out is the general tendency of Mahometanism, as such, to foster those very faults in the barbarian which keep him from ameliorating his condition. Here something might be said on what seems to be the acknowledged effect of its doctrine of fatalism, viz., in encouraging a barbarian recklessness of mind both in special seasons of prosperity and adversity, and in the ordinary business of life; but this is a point which it is difficult to speak of without a more intimate knowledge of its circumstances than can be gained at a distance; I prefer

[1] Sir C. Fellows.

to show how the Religion is calculated to act upon that extravagant self-conceit, which Robertson tells us is so congenial to uncivilized man. While, on the one hand, it closes the possible openings and occasions of internal energy and self-education, it has no tendency to compensate for this mischief, on the other, by inculcating any docile attention to the instruction of foreigners.

6.

To learn from others, you must entertain a respect for them; no one listens to those whom he contemns. Christian nations make progress in secular matters, because they are aware they have many things to learn, and do not mind from whom they learn them, so that he be able to teach. It is true that Christianity, as well as Mahometanism, which imitated it, has its visible polity, and its universal rule, and its especial prerogatives and powers and lessons, for its disciples. But, with a divine wisdom, and contrary to its human copyist, it has carefully guarded (if I may use the expression) against extending its revelations to any point which would blunt the keenness of human research or the activity of human toil. It has taken those matters for its field in which the human mind, left to itself, could not profitably exercise itself, or progress, if it would; it has confined its revelations to the province of theology, only indirectly touching on other departments of knowledge, so far as theological truth accidentally affects them; and it has shown an equally remarkable care in preventing the introduction of the spirit of caste or race into its constitution or administration. Pure nationalism it abhors; its authoritative documents pointedly ignore the distinction of Jew and Gentile, and warn us that the first often becomes the last; while its subsequent history has illustrated this great principle, by its awful, and absolute, and inscrutable, and irreversible passage from country to country, as its territory and its home. Such, then, it has been in the divine counsels, and such, too, as realized in fact; but man has ways of his own, and, even before its introduction into the world, the inspired announcements, which preceded it, were distorted by the people to whom they were given, to minister to views of a very different kind. The secularized Jews, relying on the supernatural favours locally and temporally bestowed on themselves, fell into the error of supposing that a conquest of the earth was reserved for some mighty warrior of their own race, and that, in compensation of the reverses which befell them, they were to become an imperial nation.

What a contrast is presented to us by these different ideas of a universal empire! The distinctions of race are indelible; a Jew cannot become a Greek, or a Greek a Jew; birth is an event of past time; according to the Judaizers, their nation, as a nation, was ever to be dominant; and all other nations, as such, were inferior and subject. What was the necessary consequence? There is nothing men more pride themselves on than birth, for this very reason, that it is irrevocable; it can neither be given to those who have it not, nor taken away from those who have. The Almighty can do anything which admits of doing; He can compensate every evil; but a Greek poet says that there is one thing impossible to Him—to undo what is done. Without throwing the thought into a shape which borders on the profane, we may see in it the reason why the idea of national power was so dear and so dangerous to the Jew. It was his consciousness of inalienable superiority that led him to regard Roman and Greek, Syrian and Egyptian, with ineffable arrogance and scorn. Christians, too, are accustomed to think of those who are not Christians as their inferiors; but the conviction which possesses them, that they have what others have not, is obviously not open to the temptation which nationalism presents. According to their own faith, there is no insuperable gulf between themselves and the rest of mankind; there is not a being in the whole world but is invited by their religion to occupy the same position as themselves, and, did he come, would stand on their very level, as if he had ever been there. Such accessions to their body they continually receive, and they are bound under obligation of duty to promote them. They never can pronounce of any one, now external to them, that he will not some day be among them; they never can pronounce of themselves that, though they are now within, they may not some day be found outside, the divine polity. Such are the sentiments inculcated by Christianity, even in the contemplation of the very superiority which it imparts; even there it is a principle, not of repulsion between man and man, but of good fellowship; but as to subjects of secular knowledge, since here it does not arrogate any superiority at all, it has in fact no tendency whatever to centre its disciple's contemplation on himself, or to alienate him from his kind. He readily acknowledges and defers to the superiority in art or science of those, if so be, who are unhappily enemies to Christianity. He admits the principle of progress on all matters of knowledge and conduct on which the Creator has not decided the truth already by revealing it; and he is at all times ready to learn, in those merely secular matters, from those who can teach him best. Thus it is that Christianity, even negatively, and without contemplating its positive influences, is the religion of civilization.

7.

But I have here been directing your attention to Christianity with no other view than to illustrate, by the contrast, the condition of the Mahometan Turks. Their religion is not far from embodying the very dream of the Judaizing zealots of the Apostolic age. On the one hand, there is in it the profession of a universal empire, and an empire by conquest; nay, military success seems to be considered the special note of its divine origin. On the other hand, I believe it is a received notion with them that their religion is not even intended for the north of the earth, for some reasons connected with its ceremonial; nor is there in it any public recognition, as in intercessory prayer, of the duty of converting infidels. Certainly, the idea of Mahometan missions and missionaries, unless an army in the field may be considered to be such, is never suggested to us by Eastern historian or traveller, as entering into their religious system. Though the Caliphate, then, may be transferred from Saracen to Turk, Mahometanism is essentially a consecration of the principle of nationalism; and thereby is as congenial to the barbarian as Christianity is congenial to man civilized. The less a man knows, the more conceited he is of his proficiency; and, the more barbarous is a nation, the more imposing and peremptory are its claims. Such was the spirit of the religion of the Tartars, whatever was the nature of its tenets in detail. It deified the Tartar race; Zingis Khan was "the son of God, mild and venerable;" and "God was great and exalted over all, and immortal, but Zingis Khan was sole lord upon the earth."[1] Such, too, is the strength of the Greek schism, which there only flourishes

[1] Bergeron, t. 1.

where it can fasten on barbarism, and extol the prerogatives of an elect nation. The Czar is the divinely-appointed source of religious power; his country is "Holy Russia;" and the high office committed to him and to it is to extend what it considers the orthodox faith. The Osmanlis are not behind Tartar or Russ in pretending to a divine mission; the Sultan, in his treaties with Christian Powers, calls himself "Refuge of Sovereigns, Distributor of Crowns to the Kings of the earth, Master of Europe, Asia, and Africa, and shadow of God upon earth."

We might smile at such titles, were they not claimed in good earnest, and professed in order to be used. It is said to be the popular belief among the Turks, that the monarchs of Europe are, as this imperial style declares, the feudatories of the Sultan. We should smile, too, at the very opposite titles which they apply to Europeans, did they not here, too, mean what they say, and strengthen and propagate their own scorn and hatred of us by using them. "The Mussulmans, courteous and humane in their intercourse with each other," says Thornton, "sternly refuse to unbelievers the salutation of peace." Not that they necessarily insult the Christian, he adds, by this refusal; nay, he even insists that polished Turks are able to practise condescension; and then, as an illustration of their courtesy, he tells us that "Mr. Eton, pleasantly and accurately enough, compared the general behaviour of a Turk to a Christian with that of a German baron to his vassal." However, he allows that at least "the common people, more bigoted to their dogmas, express more bluntly their sense of superiority over the Christians." "Their usual salutation addressed to Christians," says Volney, "is 'good morning;' but it is well if it be not accompanied with a Djaour, Kafer, or

Kelb, that is, impious, infidel, dog, expressions to which Christians are familiarized." Sir C. Fellows is an earnest witness for their amiableness; but he does not conceal that the children "hoot after a European, and call him Frank dog, and even strike him;" and on one occasion a woman caught up a child and ran off from him, crying out against the Ghiaour; which gives him an opportunity of telling us that the word "Ghiaour" means a man without a soul, without a God. A writer in a popular Review, who seems to have been in the East, tells us that "their hatred and contempt of the Ghiaour and Frangi is as burning as ever; perhaps even more so, because they are forced to implore his aid. The Eastern seeks Christian aid in the same spirit and with the same disgust as he would eat swine's flesh, were it the only means of securing him from starvation."[1] Such conduct is indeed only consistent with their faith, and the untenableness of that faith is not my present question; here I do but ask, are these barbarians likely to think themselves inferior in any respect to men without souls? are they likely to receive civilization from the nations of the West, whom, according to the well-known story, they definitively divide into the hog and the dog?

I have not time for more than an allusion to what is the complement of this arrogance, and is a most pregnant subject of thought, whenever the fortunes of the Ottomans are contemplated; I mean the despair which takes its place in their minds, consistently with the barbarian temperament, upon the occurrence of any considerable reverses. A passage from Mr. Thornton just now quoted refers to this characteristic. The overthrow at Lepanto, though they rallied from their consternation for a while, was a far more serious and permanent

[1] Edinburgh Rev. 1853.

misfortune in its moral than in its material consequences. And, on any such national calamity, the fatalism of their creed, to which I have already referred, consecrates and fortifies their despair.

I have been proving a point, which most persons would grant me, in thus insisting on the essential barbarism of the Turks; but I have thought it worth while to insist on it under the feeling, that to prove it is at the same time to describe it, and many persons will vaguely grant that they are barbarous without having any clear idea what barbarism means. With this view I draw out my formal conclusion :—If civilization be the ascendancy of mind over passion and imagination; if it manifests itself in consistency of habit and action, and is characterised by a continual progress or development of the principles on which it rests; and if, on the other hand, the Turks alternate between sloth and energy, self-confidence and despair,—if they have two contrary characters within them, and pass from one to the other rapidly, and when they are the one, are as if they could not be the other;—if they think themselves, notwithstanding, to be the first nation upon earth, while at the end of many centuries they are just what they were at the beginning;—if they are so ignorant as not to know their ignorance, and so far from making progress that they have not even started, and so far from seeking instruction that they think no one fit to teach them;—there is surely not much hazard in concluding, that, apart from the consideration of any supernatural intervention, barbarians they have lived, and barbarians they will die.

LECTURE IX.

The Future of the Ottomans.

SCIENTIFIC anticipations are commonly either truisms or failures; failures, if, as is usually the case, they are made upon insufficient data; and truisms, if they succeed, for conclusions, being always contained in their premisses, never can be discoveries. Yet, as mixed mathematics correct, without superseding, the pure science, so I do not see why I may not allowably take a sort of pure philosophical view of the Turks and their position, though it be but abstract and theoretical, and require correction when confronted by the event. There is a use in investigating what ought to be, under given suppositions and conditions, even though speculation and fact do not happen to keep pace together.

As to myself, having laid down my premisses, as drawn from historical considerations, I must needs go on, whether I will or no, to the conjectures to which they lead; and that shall be my business in this concluding discussion. My line of argument has been as follows:—First, I stated some peculiarities of civilized and of barbarian communities; I said that it is a general truth that civilized states are destroyed from within, and barbarian states from without; that the very causes, which lead to the greatness of civilized communities, at length by continuing become their ruin, whereas the causes of barbarian greatness uphold that greatness, as long as they continue, and by ceasing to act, not by continuing, lead the way to its overthrow. Thus the intellect of Athens first was its making and then its unmaking; while the warlike prowess of the Spartans maintained their pre-eminence, till it succumbed to the antagonist prowess of Thebes.

1.

I laid down this principle as a general law of human society, open to exceptions and requiring modifications in particular cases, but true on the whole. Next, I went on to show that the Ottoman power was of a barbarian character. The conclusion is obvious; viz., that it has risen, and will fall, not by anything within it, but by agents external to itself; and this conclusion, I certainly think, is actually confirmed by Turkish history, as far as it has hitherto gone. The Ottoman state seems, in matter of fact, to be most singularly constructed, so as to have nothing inside of it, and to be moved solely or mainly by influences from without. What a contrast, for instance, to the German race! In the earliest history of that people, we discern an element of civilization, a vigorous action of the intellect residing in the body, independent of individuals, and giving birth to great men, rather than created by them. Again, in the first three centuries of the Church, we find martyrs indeed in plenty, as the Turks might have soldiers; but (to view the matter humanly) perhaps there was not one great mind, after the Apostles, to teach and to mould her children. The highest intellects, Origen, Tertullian, and Eusebius, were representatives of a philosophy not hers; her greatest bishops, such as St. Gregory, St. Dionysius, and St. Cyprian, so little exercised a doctor's office, as to incur, however undeservedly, the imputation of doctrinal inaccuracy. Vigilant as was the Holy See then, as in every age, yet there is no Pope, I may say, during that period, who has impressed his character upon his generation; yet how well instructed, how precisely informed, how self-possessed an oracle of truth, nevertheless, do we find the Church to be, when the great internal troubles of the fourth century required it! how unambiguous, how bold is the Christianity of the great Pontiffs, St. Julius, St. Damasus, St. Siricius, and St. Innocent; of the great Doctors, St. Athanasius, St. Basil, St. Ambrose, and St. Augustine! By what channels, then, had the divine philosophy descended down from the Great Teacher through three centuries of persecution? First through the See and Church of Peter, into which error never intruded (though Popes might be little more than victims, to be hunted out and killed, as soon as made), and to which the faithful from all quarters of the world might have recourse when difficulties arose, or when false teachers anywhere exalted themselves. But intercommunion was difficult, and comparatively rare in days like those, and of nothing is there less pretence of proof than that the Holy See, while persecution raged, imposed a faith upon the ecumenical body. Rather, in that earliest age, it was simply the living spirit of the myriads of the faithful, none of them known to fame, who received from the disciples of our Lord, and husbanded so well, and circulated so widely, and transmitted so faithfully, generation after generation, the once delivered apostolic faith; who held it with such sharpness of outline and explicitness of detail, as enabled even the unlearned instinctively to discriminate between truth and error, spontaneously to reject the very shadow of heresy, and to be proof against the fascination of the most brilliant intellects, when they would lead them out of the narrow way. Here, then, is a luminous instance of what I mean by an energetic action from within.

Take again the history of the Saracenic schools and parties, on which I have already touched. Mr. Southgate considers the absence of religious controversy among the Turks, contrasted with its frequency of old among the Saracens, as a proof of the decay of the spirit of Islam. I should rather refer the present apathy to the national temperament of the Turks, and set it down, with other instances I shall mention presently, as a result of their barbarism. Saracenic Mahometanism, on the contrary, gives me an apposite illustration of what I mean by an "interior" people, if I may borrow a devotional word to express a philosophical idea. A barbarous nation has no "interior," but the Saracens show us what a national "interior" is. "In former ages," says the author to whom I have referred, Mr. Southgate, "the bosom of Islamism was riven with numerous feuds and schisms, some of which have originated from religious controversy, and others from political ambition. During the first centuries of its existence, and while Mussulman learning flourished under the patronage of the Caliphs, religious questions were discussed by the learned with all the proverbial virulence of theological hatred. The chief of these questions respected the origin of the Koran, the nature of God, predestination and free will, and the grounds of human salvation. The question, whether the Koran was created or eternal, rent for a time the whole body of Islamism into twain, and gave rise to the most violent persecutions. . . . Besides these religious contentions, which divided the Mussulmans into parties, but seldom gave birth to sects, there have sprung up, at different 'periods, avowed heresies, which flourished for a time, and for the most part died with their authors. Others, stimulated by ambition only, have reared the standard of revolt, and under cover of some new religious dogma, propounded only to shield a selfish end, have sought to raise themselves to power. Most of these, whether theological disputes, heresies, or civil rebellions, cloaked under the name of religion, arose previously to the sixteenth century."[1]

2.

Such is that internal peculiarity, the presence of which constitutes a civilized, the absence a barbarous people; which makes a people great, and small again; and which, just consistently with the notion of their being barbarians, I cannot discern, for strength or for weakness, in the Turks. On the contrary, almost all the elements of their success, and instruments of their downfall, are external to themselves. For instance, their religion, one of their principal bonds, owes nothing to them; it is, not only in substance, but in concrete shape, just what it was when it came to them. I cannot find that they have commented upon it; I cannot find that they are the channels of any of those famous traditions by which the Koran is interpreted, and which they themselves accept; or that they have exercised their minds upon it at all, except so far as they have been obliged, in a certain degree, to do so in the administration of the law. It is true also that they have been obliged to choose to be Sunnites and not Shiahs; but, considering the latter sect arose in Persia, since the date of the Turkish occupation of Constantinople, it was really no choice at all. They have but remained as they were. Besides, the Shiahs

[1] Tour through Armenia, etc.

maintain the hereditary transmission of the Caliphate, which would exclude the line of Othman from the succession—good reason then the Turks should be Sunnites; and the dates of the two events so nearly coincide, that one could even fancy that the Shiahs actually arose in consequence of the Sultan Selim's carrying off the last of the Abassides from Egypt, and gaining the transference of the Caliphate from his captive. Besides, if it is worth while pursuing the point, did they not remain Sunnites, they would have to abandon the traditional or oral law, and must cease to use the labours of its four great doctors, which would be to bring upon themselves an incalculable extent of intellectual toil; for without recognized comments on the Koran, neither the religion nor the civil state could be made to work.

The divine right of the line of Othman is another of their special political bonds, and this too is shown by the following extract from a well-known historian,[1] if it needs showing, to be simply external to themselves: "The origin of the Sultans," he says, "is obscure; but this sacred and indefeasible right" to the throne, "which no time can erase, and no violence can infringe, was soon and unalterably implanted in the minds of their subjects. A weak or vicious Sultan may be deposed and strangled, but his inheritance devolves to an infant or an idiot; nor has the most daring rebel presumed to ascend the throne of his lawful sovereign. While the transient dynasties of Asia have been continually subverted by a crafty visir in the palace, or a victorious general in the camp, the Ottoman succession has been confirmed by the practice of five centuries, and is now incorporated with the vital principle of the Turkish nation." Here we have on the one hand the imperial succession described as an element

[1] Gibbon.

of the political life of the Osmanlis—on the other as an appointment over which they have no power; and obviously it is from its very nature independent of them. It is a form of life external to the community it vivifies.

Probably it was the wonderful continuity of so many great Sultans in their early ages, which wrought in their minds the idea of a divine mission as the attribute of the dynasty; and its acquisition of the Caliphate would fix it indelibly within them. And here again, we have another special instrument of their imperial greatness, but still an external one. I have already had occasion to observe, that barbarians make conquests by means of great men, in whom they, as it were, live; ten successive monarchs, of extraordinary vigour and talent, carried on the Ottomans to empire. Will any one show that those monarchs can be fairly called specimens of the nation, any more than Zingis was the specimen of the Tartars? Have they not rather acted as the *Deus è machinâ*, carrying on the drama, which has languished or stopped, since the time when they ceased to animate it? Contrast the Ottoman history in this respect with the rise of the Anglo-Indian Empire, or with the military successes of Great Britain under the Regency; or again with the literary eminence of England under Charles the Second or even Anne, which owed little to those monarchs. Kings indeed at various periods have been most effective patrons of art and science; but the question is, not whether English or French literature has ever been indebted to royal encouragement, but whether the Ottomans can do anything at all, as a nation, without it.

Indeed, I should like it investigated what internal history the Ottomans have at all; what inward development of any kind they have made since they crossed Mount Olympus and planted themselves in Broussa; how they have changed shape and feature, even in lesser matters, since they were a state, or how they are a year older than when they first came into being. We see among them no representative of Confucius, Chi-hoagti, and the sect of Ta-osse; no magi; no Pisistratus and Harmodius; no Socrates and Alcibiades; no patricians and plebeians; no Cæsar; no invasion or adoption of foreign mysteries; no mythical impersonation of an Ali; no Suffeeism; no Guelphs and Gibellines; nothing really on the type of Catholic religious orders; no Luther; nothing, in short, which, for good or evil, marks the presence of a life internal to the political community itself. Some authors indeed maintain they have a literature; but I cannot ascertain what the assertion is worth. Rather the tenor of their annals runs thus :—Two Pachas make war against each other, and a kat-sherif comes from Constantinople for the head of the one or the other; or a Pacha exceeds in pillaging his province, or acts rebelliously, and is preferred to a higher government and suddenly strangled on his way to it; or he successfully maintains himself, and gains an hereditary settlement, still subject, however, to the feudal tenure, which is the principle of the political structure, continuing to send his contingent of troops, when the Sultan goes to war, and remitting the ordinary taxes through his agent at Court. Such is the staple of Turkish history, whether amid the hordes of Turkistan, or the feudatory Turcomans of Anatolia, or the imperial Osmanlis.

3.

The remark I am making applies to them, not only as a nation, but as a body politic. When they descended on horseback upon the rich territories which they occupy, they had need to become agriculturists, and miners, and civil engineers, and traders; all which they were not; yet I do not find that they have attempted any of these functions themselves. Public works, bridges, and roads, draining, levelling, building, they seem almost entirely to have neglected; where, however, to do something was imperative, instead of applying themselves to their new position, and manifesting native talent for each emergency, they usually have had recourse to foreign assistance to execute what was uncongenial or dishonourable to themselves. The Franks were their merchants, the Armenians their bankers, the subject races their field labourers, and the Greeks their sailors. "Almost the whole business of the ship," says Thornton, "is performed by the slaves, or by the Greeks who are retained upon wages."

The most remarkable instance of this reluctance to develop from within—remarkable, both for the originality, boldness, success, and permanence of the policy adopted, and for its appositeness to my purpose—is the institution of the Janizaries, detestable as it was in a moral point of view. I enlarge upon it here because it is at the same time a palmary instance of the practical ability and wisdom of their great Sultans, exerted in compensation of the resourceless impotence of the barbarians whom they governed. The Turks were by nature nothing better than horsemen; infantry they could not be; an infantry their Sultans hardly attempted to form out of them; but since infantry was indispensable in European warfare, they availed themselves of passages in their own earlier history, and provided themselves with a perpetual supply of foot soldiers from without. Of this procedure they were not, strictly speaking, the originators; they took the idea of it from the Saracens. You may recollect that, when their ancestors were defeated by the latter people in Sogdiana, instead of returning to their deserts, they suffered themselves to be diffused and widely located through the great empire of the Caliphs. Whether as slaves, or as captives, or as mercenaries, they were taken into favour by the dominant nation, and employed as soldiers or civilians. They were chosen as boys or youths for their handsome appearance, turned into Mahometans, and educated for the army or other purposes. And thus the strength of the empire which they served was always kept fresh and vigorous, by the continual infusion into it of new blood to perform its functions; a skilful policy, if the servants could be hindered from becoming masters.

Masters in time they did become, and then they adopted a similar system themselves; we find traces of it even in the history of the Gaznevide dynasty. In the reign of the son of the great Mahmood, we read of an insurrection of the slaves; who, conspiring with one of his nobles, seized his best horses, and rode off to his enemies. "By slaves," says Dow, in translating this history, "are meant the captives and young children, bought by kings, and educated for the offices of state. They were often adopted by the Emperors, and very frequently succeeded to the Empire. A whole dynasty of these possessed afterwards the throne in Hindostan."

The same system appears in Egypt, about or soon after the time of the celebrated Saladin. Zingis, in his dreadful expedition from Khorasan to Syria and Russia, had collected an innumerable multitude of youthful captives, who glutted, as we may say, the markets of Asia. This gave the conquerors of Egypt an opportunity of forming a mercenary or foreign force for their defence, on a more definite idea than seems hitherto to have been acted upon. Saladin was a Curd, and, as such, a neighbour of the Caucasus; hence the Caucasian tribes became for many centuries the store-houses of Egyptian mercenaries. A detestable slave trade has existed with this object, especially among the Circassians, since the time of the Moguls; and of these for the most part this Egyptian force, Mamlouks, as they are called, has consisted. After a time, these Mamlouks took matters into their own hands, and became a self-elective body, or sort of large corporation. They were masters of the country, and of its nominal ruler, and they recruited their ranks continually, and perpetuated their power, by means of the natives of the Caucasus, slaves like themselves, and of their own race.

"During the 500 or 600 years," says Volney, "that there have been Mamlouks in Egypt, not one of them has left subsisting issue; there does not exist one single family of them in the second generation; all their children perish in the first and second descent. The means therefore by which they are perpetuated and multiplied were of necessity the same by which they were first established." These troops have been massacred and got rid of in the memory of the last generation; towards the end of last century they formed a body of above 8,500 men. The writer I have just been quoting adds the following remarks:—"Born for the most part in the rites of the Greek Church, and circumcised the moment they are bought, they are considered by the Turks themselves as renegades, void of faith and of religion. Strangers to each other, they are not bound by those natural ties which unite the rest of mankind. Without parents, without children, the past has nothing to do for them, and they do nothing for the future. Ignorant and superstitious from education, they become ferocious from the murders they commit, and corrupted by the most horrible debauchery." On the other hand, they had every sort of incentive and teaching to prompt them to rapacity and lawlessness. "The young peasant, sold in Mingrelia or Georgia, no sooner arrives in Egypt, than his ideas undergo a total alteration. A new and extraordinary scene opens before him, where everything conduces to awaken his audacity and ambition. Though now a slave, he seems destined to become a master, and already assumes the spirit of his future condition. No sooner is a slave enfranchised, than he aspires to the principal employments; and who is to oppose his pretensions? and he will be no less able than his betters in the art of governing, which consists only in taking money, and giving blows with the sabre."

In describing the Mamlouks I have been in a great measure describing the Janizaries, and have little to add to the picture. When Amurath, one of the ten Sultans, had made himself master of the territory round Constantinople, as far as the Balkan, he passed northwards, and subdued the warlike tribes which possessed Bulgaria, Servia, Bosnia, and the neighbouring provinces. These countries had neither the precious metals in their mountains, nor marts of commerce; but their inhabitants were a brave and hardy race, who had been for ages the terror of Constantinople. It was suggested to the Sultan, that, according to the Mahometan law, he was entitled to a fifth part of the captives, and he made this privilege the commencement of a new institution. Twelve thousand of the strongest and handsomest youths were selected as his share; he formed them into a military force; he made them abjure Christianity, he consecrated them with a religious rite, and named them Janizaries. The discipline to which they were submitted was peculiar, and in some respects severe. They were in the first instance made over to the peasantry to assist them in the labours of the field, and thus were prepared by penury and hard fare for the privations of a military life. After this introduction, they were drafted into the companies of the Janizaries, but only in order to commence a second noviciate. Sometimes they were employed in the menial duties of the palace, sometimes in the public works, sometimes in the dockyards, and sometimes in the imperial gardens. Meanwhile they were taught their new religion, and were submitted to the drill. When at length they went on service, the road to promotion was opened upon them; nor were military honours the only recompense to which they might aspire. There are examples in history, of men from the ranks attaining the highest dignities in the state, and at least of one of them marrying the sister of the Sultan.

This corps has constituted the main portion of the infantry of the Ottoman armies for a period of nearly five hundred years; till, in our own day, on account of its repeated turbulence, it was annihilated, as the Mamlouks before it, by means of a barbarous massacre. Its end was as strange as its constitution; but here it comes under our notice as a singular exemplification of the unproductiveness, as I may call it, of the Turkish intellect. It was nothing else but an external institution devised to supply a need which a civilized state would have supplied from its own resources; and it fell perhaps without any essential prejudice to the integrity of the power which it had served. That power is just what it was before the Janizaries were formed. They may still fall back upon the powerful cavalry, which carried them all the way from Turkistan; or they may proceed to employ a mercenary force; anyhow their primitive social type remains inviolate.

Such is the strange phenomenon, or rather portent, presented to us by the barbarian power which has been for centuries seated in the very heart of the old world; which has in its brute clutch the most famous countries of classical and religious antiquity, and many of the most fruitful and beautiful regions of the earth; which stretches along the course of the Danube, the Euphrates, and the Nile; which embraces the Pindus, the Taurus, the Caucasus, Mount Sinai, the Libyan mountains, and the Atlas, as far as the Pillars of Hercules; and which, having no history itself, is heir to the historical names of Constantinople and Nicæa, Nicomedia and Cæsarea, Jerusalem and Damascus, Nineveh and Babylon, Mecca and Bagdad, Antioch and Alexandria, ignorantly holding in possession one-half of the history of the whole world. There it lies and will not die, and has not in itself the elements of death, for it has the life of a stone, and, unless pounded and pulverized, is indestructible. Such is it in the simplicity of its national existence, while that mode of existence remains, while it remains faithful to its religion and its imperial line. Should its fidelity to either fail, it would not merely degenerate or decay; it would simply cease to be.

4

But we have dwelt long enough on the internal peculiarities of the Ottomans; now let us shift the scene, and view them in the presence of their enemies, and in their external relations both above and below them; and then at once a very different prospect presents itself for our contemplation. However, the first remark I have to make is one which has reference still to their internal condition, but which does not properly come into consideration, till we place them in the presence of rival and hostile nations and races. Moral degeneracy is not, strictly speaking, a cause of political ruin, as I have already said; but its existence is of course a point of the gravest importance, when we would calculate the chance which a people has of standing the brunt of war and insurrection. It is a natural question to ask whether the Osmanlis, after centuries of indulgence, have the physical nerve and mental vigour which carried them forward through such a course of fortunes, till it enthroned them in three quarters of the world. Their numbers are diminished and diminishing; their great cities are half emptied; their villages have disappeared; I believe that even out of the fraction of Mahometans to be found amid their European population, but a miserable minority are Osmanlis. Too much stress, however, must not be laid on this circumstance. Though the Osmanlis are the conquering race, it requires to be shown that they have ever had much to do, as a race, with the executive of the Empire. While there are some vigorous minds at the head of affairs, while there is a constant introduction of foreigners into posts of authority and power, while Curd and Turcoman supply the cavalry, while Egypt and other Pachalics send their contingents, while the government can manage to combine, or to steer between, the fanaticism of its subjects and the claims of European diplomacy, there is a certain counterbalance in the State to the depravity and worthlessness, whatever it be, of those who have the nominal power.

A far more formidable difficulty, when we survey their external prospects, is that very peculiarity, which, internally considered, is so much in their favour—the simplicity of their internal unity, and the individuality of their political structure. The Turkish races, as being conquerors, of course are only a portion of the whole population of their empire; for four centuries they have remained distinct from Slavonians, Greeks, Copts, Armenians, Curds, Arabs, Jews, Druses, Maronites, Ansarians, Motoualis; and they never can coalesce with them. Like other Empires, they have kept their sovereign position by the insignificance, degeneracy, or mutual animosities of the several countries and religions which they rule, and by the ruthless tyranny of their government. Were they to relax that tyranny, were they to relinquish their ascendancy, were they to place their Greek subjects, for instance, on a civil equality with themselves, how in the nature of things could two incommunicable races coexist beside each other in one political community? Yet if, on the other hand, they refuse this enfranchisement of their subjects, they will have to encounter the displeasure of united Christendom.

Nor is it a mere question of political practicability or expedience: will the Koran, in its laxest interpretation, admit of that toleration, on which the Frank kingdoms insist? yet what and where are they without the Koran?

Nor do we understand the full stress of the dilemma in which they are placed, until we have considered what is meant by the demands and the displeasure of the European community. Pledged by the very principle of their existence to barbarism, the Turks have to cope with civilized governments all around them, ever advancing in the material and moral strength which civilization gives, and ever feeling more and more vividly that the Turks are simply in the way. They are in the way of the progress of the nineteenth century. They are in the way of the Russians, who wish to get into the Mediterranean; they are in the way of the English, who wish to cross to the East; they are in the way of the French, who, from the Crusades to Napoleon, have felt a romantic interest in Syria; they are in the way of the Austrians, their hereditary foes. There they lie, unable to abandon their traditionary principles, without simply ceasing to be a state; unable to retain them, and retain the sympathy of Christendom;—Mahometans, despots, slave merchants, polygamists, holding agriculture in contempt, Europe in abomination, their own wretched selves in admiration, cut off from the family of nations,[1] existing by ignorance and fanaticism, and tolerated in existence by the mutual jealousies of Christian powers as well as of their own subjects, and by the recurring excitement of military and political combinations, which cannot last for ever.

5.

And, last of all, as if it were not enough to be unable to procure the countenance of any Christian power, except on specific conditions prejudicial to their existence, still further, as the alternative of their humbling themselves before the haughty nations of the West whom they abhor, they have to encounter the direct cupidity, hatred, and overpowering pressure of the multitudinous North, with its fanaticism almost equal, and its numbers superior, to their own; a peril more awful in imagination, from the circumstance that its descent has been for so many centuries foretold and commenced, and of late years so widely acquiesced in as inevitable. Seven centuries and a half have passed, since, at the very beginning

[1] Since this was written, they have been taken into the European family by the Treaty of 1856, and the Sultan has become a Knight of the Garter. This strange phenomenon is not for certain to the advantage of their political position.

of the Crusades, a Greek writer still extant turns from the then menacing inroads of the Turks in the East, and the long centuries of their triumph which lay in prospect, to record a prophecy, old in his time, relating to the North, to the effect that in the last days the Russians should be masters of Constantinople. When it was uttered no one knows; but it was written on an equestrian statue, in his day one of the special monuments of the Imperial City, which had one time been brought thither from Antioch. That statue, whether of Christian or pagan origin is not known, has a name in history, for it was one of the works of art destroyed by the Latins in the taking of Constantinople; and the prediction engraven on it bears at least a remarkable evidence of the congruity in itself, if I may use the word, of that descent of the North upon Constantinople, which, though not as yet accomplished, generation after generation grows more probable.

It is now a thousand years since this famous prophecy has been illustrated by the actual incursions of the Russian hordes. Such was the date of their first expedition against Constantinople; their assaults continued through two centuries; and, in the course of that period, they seemed to be nearer the capture of the city than they have been at any time since. They descended the Dnieper in boats, coasted along the East of the Black Sea, and so came round by Trebizond to the Bosphorus, plundering the coast as they advanced. At one time their sovereign had got possession of Bulgaria, to the south of the Danube. Barbarians of other races flocked to his standard; he found himself surrounded by the luxuries of the East and West, and he marched down as far as Adrianople, and threatened to go further. Ultimately he was defeated; then followed the conversion of his people to Christianity, which for a period restrained their barbarous rapacity; after this, for two centuries, they were under the yoke and bondage of the Tartars; but the prophecy, or rather the omen, remains, and the whole world has learned to acquiesce in the probability of its fulfilment. The wonder rather is, that that fulfilment has been so long delayed. The Russians, whose wishes would inspire their hopes, are not solitary in their anticipations: the historian from whom I have borrowed this sketch of their past attempts,[1] writing at the end of last century, records his own expectation of the event. "Perhaps," he says, "the present generation may yet behold the accomplishment of a rare prediction, of which the style is unambiguous and the date unquestionable." The Turks themselves have long been under the shadow of its influence; even as early as the middle of the seventeenth century, when they were powerful, and Austria and Poland also, and Russia distant and comparatively feeble, a traveller tells us that, "of all the princes of Christendom, there was none whom the Turks so much feared as the Czar of Muscovy." This apprehension has ever been on the increase; in favour of Russia, they made the first formal renunciation of territory which had been consecrated to Islam by the solemnities of religion,—a circumstance which has sunk deep into their imaginations; there is an enigmatical inscription on the tomb of the Great Constantine, to the effect that "the yellow-haired race shall overthrow Ismael;" moreover, ever since their defeats by the Emperor Leopold, they have had a surmise that the true footing of their faith is in Asia; and so strong is the popular feeling on the subject, that in consequence their favourite cemetery is at Scutari on the Asiatic coast.[2]

[1] Gibbon.   [2] Thornton, ii. 89; Formby, p. 24; Eclectic Rev., Dec., 1828'.

6.

It seems likely, then, at no very remote day, to fare ill with the old enemy of the Cross. However, we must not undervalue what is still the strength of his position. First, no well-authenticated tokens come to us of the decay of the Mahometan faith. It is true that in one or two cities, in Constantinople, perhaps, or in the marts of commerce, laxity of opinion and general scepticism may to a certain extent prevail, as also in the highest class of all, and in those who have most to do with Europeans; but I confess nothing has been brought home to me to show that this superstition is not still a living, energetic principle in the Turkish population, sufficient to bind them together in one, and to lead to bold and persevering action. It must be recollected that a national and local faith, like the Mahometan, is most closely connected with the sentiments of patriotism, family honour, loyalty towards the past, and party spirit; and this the more in the case of a religion which has no articles of faith at all, except those of the Divine Unity and the mission of Mahomet. To these must be added more general considerations: that they have ever prospered under their religion, that they are habituated to it, that it suits them, that it is their badge of a standing antagonism to nations they abhor, and that it places them, in their own imagination, in a spiritual position relatively to those nations, which they would simply forfeit if they abandoned it. It would require clear proof of the fact, to credit in their instance the report of a change of mind, which antecedently is so improbable.

And next it must be borne in mind that, few as may be the Osmanlis, yet the raw material of the Turkish nation, represented principally by the Turcomans, extends over half Asia; and, if it is what it ever has been, might under circumstances be combined or concentrated into a formidable Power. It extends at this day from Asia Minor, in a continuous tract, to the Lena, towards Kamtchatka, and from Siberia down to Khorasan, the Hindu Cush, and China. The Nogays on the north-east of the Danube, the inhabitants of the Crimea, the populations on each side of the Don and Wolga, the wandering Turcomans who are found from the west of Asia, along the Euxine, Caspian, and so through Persia into Bukharia, the Kirghies on the Jaxartes, are said to speak one tongue, and to have one faith.[1] Religion is a bond of union, and language is a medium of intercourse; and, what is still more, they are all Sunnites, and recognize in the Sultan the successor of Mahomet.

Without a head, indeed, to give them a formal unity, they are only one in name. Nothing is less likely than a resuscitation of the effete family of Othman; still, supposing the Ottomans driven into Asia, and a Sultan of that race to mount the throne, such as Amurath, Mahomet, or Selim, it is not easy to set bounds to the influence the Sovereign Pontiff of Islam might exert, and to the successes he might attain, in rallying round him the scattered members of a race, warlike, fanatical, one in faith, in language, in habits, and in adversity. Nay, even supposing the Turkish Caliph, like the Saracenic of old, still to slumber in his seraglio, he might appoint a vicegerent, Emir-ul-Omra, or Mayor of the Palace, such as Togrul Beg, to conquer with his authority in his stead.

But, supposing great men to be wanting to the

[1] Pritchard.

Turkish race, and the despair, natural to barbarians, to rush upon them, and defeat, humiliation, and flight to be their lot; supposing the rivalries and dissensions of Pachas, in themselves arguing no disaffection to their Sultan and Caliph, should practically lead to the success of their too powerful foes, to the divulsion of their body politic, and the partition of their territory; should this be the distant event to which the present complications tend, then the fiercer spirits, I suppose, would of their free will return into the desert, as a portion of the Kalmucks have done within the last hundred years. Those, however, who remained, would lead the easiest life under the protection of Russia. She already is the sovereign ruler of many barbarian populations, and, among them, Turks and Mahometans; she lets them pursue their wandering habits without molestation, satisfied with such service on their part as the interests of the empire require. The Turcomans would have the same permission, and would hardly be sensible of the change of masters. It is a more perplexing question how England or France, did they on the other hand become their masters, would be able to tolerate them in their reckless desolation of a rich country. Rather, such barbarians, unless they could be placed where they would answer some political purpose, would eventually share the fate of the aboriginal inhabitants of North America; they would, in the course of years, be surrounded, pressed upon, divided, decimated, driven into the desert by the force of civilization, and would once more roam in freedom in their old home in Persia or Khorasan, in the presence of their brethren, who have long succeeded them in its possession.

Many things are possible; one thing is inconceivable,

—that the Turks should, as an existing nation, accept of modern civilization; and, in default of it, that they should be able to stand their ground amid the encroachments of Russia, the interested and contemptuous patronage of Europe, and the hatred of their subject populations.

NOTE ON PAGE 109.

CARDINAL FISHER, in his *Assert. Luther. Confut.*, fol. clxi., gives the following list of Popes who, up to his time, had called on the Princes of Christendom to direct their arms against the Turks:—Urban II., Paschal II., Gelasius II., Calistus II., Eugenius III., Lucius III., Gregory VIII., Clement III., Cœlestine III., Innocent III., Honorius III., Gregory IX., Innocent IV., Alexander IV., Gregory X., John XXII., Martin IV., Nicolas IV., Innocent VI., Urban V.

NOTE ON PAGE 124, ETC.

THE following passages, as being upon the subject of the foregoing Lectures, are extracted from the lively narrative of an Expedition to the Jordan and Dead Sea by Commander Lynch, of the United States Navy.

1. He was presented to Sultan Abdoul Medjid in February, 1848. He says: "On the left hung a gorgeous crimson velvet curtain, embroidered and fringed with gold" [the ancient Tartar one was of felt], "and towards it the secretary led the way. His countenance and his manner exhibited more awe than I had ever seen depicted in the human countenance. He seemed to hold his breath; and his step was so soft and stealthy, that once or twice I stopped, under the impression that I had left him behind, but found him ever beside me. There were three of us in close proximity, and the stairway was lined with officers and attendants; but such was the death-like stillness that I could distinctly hear my own foot-fall. If it had been a wild beast slumbering in his lair that we were about to visit, there could not have been a silence more deeply hushed."

2. "I presented him, in the name of the President of the United States, with some biographies and prints, illustrative of the character and habits of our North American Indians, the work of American artists. He looked at some of them. . . and said that he considered them as evidences of the advancement of the United States in *civilization*, and would treasure them as a

souvenir of the good feeling of its Government towards him. At the word 'civilization,' pronounced in French, I started, for it seemed singular, coming from the lips of a Turk, and applied to our country." The author accounts for it by observing that the Sultan is but a beginner in French, and probably meant by "civilization" arts and sciences.

3. He saw the old Tartar throne, which puts one in mind of Attila's queen, Zingis's lieutenant, and Timour. "The old divan, upon which the Sultans formerly reclined when they gave audience, looks like an overgrown four-poster, covered with carbuncles, turquoise, amethysts, topaz, emeralds, ruby, and diamond: the couch was covered with Damascus silk and Cashmere shawls."

4. "Anchored in the Bay of Scio. In the afternoon, the weather partially moderating, visited the shore. From the ship we had enjoyed a view of rich orchards and green fields; but on landing we found ourselves amid a scene of desolation. . . . We rode into the country. . . . What a contrast between the luxuriant vegetation, the bounty of nature, and the devastation of man! Nearly every house was unroofed and in ruins, not one in ten inhabited, although surrounded with thick groves of orange-trees loaded with the weight of their golden fruit."

"While weather-bound, we availed ourselves of the opportunity to visit the ruins [of Ephesus]. There are no trees and but very few bushes on the face of this old country, but the mountain-slopes and the valleys are enamelled with thousands of beautiful flowers. . . . Winding round the precipitous crest of a mountain, we saw the river Cayster . . . flowing through the alluvial plain to the sea, and on its banks the black tents of herdsmen, with their flocks of goats around them." As Chandler had seen them there ninety years ago.

5. "The tomb of Mahmood is a sarcophagus about eight feet high and as many long, covered with purple cloth embroidered in gold, and many votive shawls of the richest cashmere thrown over it. . . . At the head is the crimson tarbouch which the monarch wore in life, with a lofty plume, secured by a large and lustrous aigrette of diamonds. The following words are inscribed in letters of gold on the face of the tomb:— 'This is the tomb of the layer of the basis of the civilization of his empire; of the monarch of exalted place, the Sultan victorious and just, Mahmood Khan, son of the victorious Abd' al Hamid Khan. May the Almighty make his abode in the gardens of Paradise! Born,' etc."

"From the eager employment of Franks, the introduction of foreign machinery, and the adoption of improved modes of cultivating the land, the present Sultan gives the strongest assurance of his anxiety to promote the welfare of his people."

San Stefano "possesses two things in its near vicinity, of peculiar interest to an American—a model farm and an agricultural school. The farm consists of about 2,000 acres of land, especially appropriated to the culture of the cotton-plant. Both farm and school are under the superintendence of Dr. Davis of South Carolina. . . . Besides the principal culture, he is sedulously engaged in the introduction of seeds, plants, domestic animals, and agricultural instruments. The school is held in one of the kiosks of the Sultan, which overlooks the sea."

At Jaffa, Dr. Kayat, H.B.M. Consul, "has encouraged the culture of the vine; has introduced that of the mulberry and of the Irish potato; and by word and example is endeavouring to prevail on the people in the adjacent plain to cultivate the sweet potato. . . . In the court-yard we observed an English plough of improved construction."

He speaks in several places of the remains of the terrace cultivation (vid. above, p. 128) of Palestine.

6. "We visited the barracks, where a large number of Turkish soldiers, shaved and dressed like Europeans, except the moustache and the tarbouch, received us with the Asiatic salute. . . . The whole caserne was scrupulously clean, the bread dark coloured, but well baked and sweet. The colonel, who politely accompanied us, said that the bastinado had been discontinued, on account of its injuring the culprit's eyes."

. ... "Here," in the Palace, "we saw the last of the White Eunuchs; the present enlightened Sultan having pensioned off those on hand, and discontinued their attendance for ever."

"In an extensive, but nearly vacant building, was an abortive attempt at a museum."

"It is said, but untruly, that the slave market of Constantinople has been abolished. An edict, it is true, was some years since promulgated, which declared the purchase and sale of slaves to be unlawful; the prohibition, however, is only operative against the Franks, under which term the Greeks are included."

7. "Every coloured person, employed by the Government, receives monthly wages; and, if a slave, is emancipated at the expiration of seven years, when he becomes eligible to any office beneath the sovereignty. Many of the high dignitaries of the empire were originally slaves; the present Governor of the Dardanelles is a black, and was, a short time since, freed from servitude."

"The secretary had the most prepossessing countenance of any Turk I had yet seen, and in conversation evinced a spirit of inquiry and an amount of intelligence that far surpassed my expectations. . . . His history is a pleasing one. He was a poor boy, a charity scholar in one of the public schools. The late Sultan Mahmood requiring a page to fill a vacancy in his suite, directed the appointment to be given to the most intelligent pupil. The present secretary was the fortunate one; and by his abilities, his suavity and discretion, has risen to the highest office near the person of majesty."

CHRONOLOGICAL TABLES.

[The dates, as will be seen, are fixed on no scientific principle, but are taken as they severally occur in approved authors.]

OUTLINES OF TURKISH CHRONOLOGY.

		A.D.
I.	Tartar Empire of the Turks in the north and centre of Asia	500-700
II.	Their subjection, education, and silent growth, under the Saracens	700-1000
III.	Their Gaznevide Empire in Hindostan	1000-1200
IV.	Their Seljukian Empire in Persia and Asia Minor	1048-1100
V.	Decline of the Seljukians, yet continuous descent of their kindred tribes to the West	1100-1300
VI.	Their Ottoman Empire in Asia, Africa, and Europe, growing for 270 years	1300-1571
VII.	Their Ottoman Empire declining for 270 years	1571-1841

CHRONOLOGICAL EVENTS INTRODUCED INTO THE FOREGOING LECTURES.

	B.C.
Semiramis lost in the Scythian desert p. 13	—
The Scythians celebrated by Homer pp. 29, 39	900
The Scythians occupy for twenty-eight years the Median kingdom in the time of Cyaxares pp. 15, 22 (*Prideaux*)	633
Cyrus loses his life in an expedition against the Scythian Massagetæ p. 14 (*Clinton*)	529
Darius invades Scythia north of the Danube, p. 16 (*Clinton*)	508
Zoroaster p. 66 (*Prideaux*)	492
Alexander's campaign in Sogdiana p. 18 (*Clinton*)	329

	A.D.
Ancient Empire of the Huns in further Asia ends; their consequent emigration westward p. 26 (*Gibbon*)	100
The White Huns of Sogdiana pp. 26, 34, 52, 60, 67	after 100
Main body of the Huns invade the Goths on the north of the Danube p. 22 (*L'Art de vérifier les dates*)	375

Chronological Tables. 237

	A.D.
Attila and his Huns ravage the Roman Empire pp. 27, 28	441-452
Mission of St. Leo to Attila pp. 29, 31	453
Tartar Empire of the Turks pp. 49-52 (*L'Art*, etc., *Gibbon*), about	500-700
Chosroes the Second captures the Holy Cross p. 53 (*L'Art*, etc.)	614
Mahomet assumes the royal dignity. The Hegira p. 69 (*L'Art*)	622
The Turks from the Wolga settled by the Emperor Heraclius in Georgia against the Persians p. 53 (*Gibbon*)	626
The Turks invade Sogdiana p. 68 (*Gibbon*)	626
Heraclius recovers the Holy Cross p. 53 (*L'Art*, etc.)	628
Death of Mahomet p. 69 (*L'Art*)	632
Yezdegerde, last King of Persia, flying from the Saracens, is received and murdered by the Turks in Sogdiana p. 69 (*Universal History*)	654
The Saracens reduce the Turks in Sogdiana p. 70 (*L'Art*, and *Univ. Hist.*)	705-716
The Caliphate transferred from Damascus to Bagdad p. 76 (*L'Art*)	762
Harun al Raschid p. 77 (*L'Art*)	786
The Turks taken into the pay of the Caliphs p. 77 (*L'Art*)	833, etc.
The Turks tyrannize over the Caliphs p. 79 (*L'Art*)	862-870
The Caliphs lose Sogdiana p. 80 (*L'Art*)	873
The Turkish dynasty of the Gaznevides in Khorasan and Sogdiana p. 80 (*Dow*)	977
Mahmood the Gaznevide pp. 80-84 (*Dow*)	997
Seljuk the Turk pp. 84-89 (*Univ. Hist.*)	985
The Seljukian Turks wrest Sogdiana and Khorasan from the Gaznevides p. 89 (*Dow*)	1041
Togrul Beg, the Seljukian, turns to the West pp. 89, 92 (*Baronius*)	1048
Sufferings of Christians on pilgrimage to Jerusalem pp. 98-101 (*Baronius*)	1064
Alp Arslan's victory over the Emperor Diogenes p. 93 (*Baronius*)	1071
St. Gregory the Seventh's letter against the Turks p. 98 (*Sharon Turner*)	1074
Jerusalem in possession of the Turks p. 98 (*L'Art*)	1076
Soliman, the Seljukian Sultan of Roum, establishes himself at Nicæa p. 131 (*L'Art*)	1082
The Council of Placentia under Urban the Second pp. 109, 137 (*L'Art*)	1095
The first Crusade p. 109 (*L'Art*)	1097

Chronological Tables.

	A.D.
Conquests of Zingis Khan and the Moguls pp. 32-34 (*L'Art*)	1176-1259
Richard Cœur de Lion in Palestine p. 140 (*L'Art*)	1190
Institution of Mamlooks p. 217	about 1200
Constantinople taken by the Latins p. 139 (*L'Art*)	1203
Greek Empire of Nicæa p. 121 (*L'Art*)	1206
The Greek Emperor Vataces encourages agriculture in Asia Minor p. 121 (*L'Art*)	1222-1255
The Moguls subjugate Russia p. 225 (*L'Art*)	1236
Mission of St. Louis to the Moguls pp. 35-41 (*L'Art*)	1253
The Turks attack the north and west coast of Asia Minor p. 93 (*Univ. Hist.*)	1266-1296
Marco Polo p. 37	1270
End of the Seljukian kingdom of Roum p. 132 (*L'Art*)	1294
Othman p. 132	1301
The Popes retire to Avignon for seventy years p. 143 (*L'Art*)	1305
Orchan, successor to Othman, originates the institution of Janizaries p. 134 (*L'Art*)	1326-1360
Battle of Cressy p. 140	1346
Battle of Poitiers, p. 140	1356
Wicliffe, p. 139	1360
Amurath institutes the Janizaries pp. 113, 215, 218 (*Gibbon*)	1370
Conquests of Timour p. 32 (*L'Art*)	1370, etc.
Schismatical Pontiffs for thirty-eight years p. 143 (*L'Art*)	1378-1417
Battle of Nicopolis p. 146 (*L'Art*)	1393
Timour defeats and captures Bajazet p. 144 (*L'Art*)	1402
Timour at Samarcand pp. 38, 45 (*L'Art*)	1404
Timour dies on his Chinese expedition p. 46	1405
Henry the Fourth of England dies, p. 141	1413
Battle of Agincourt pp. 140, 145	1415
Huss p. 140	1415
Henry the Fifth of England dies p. 142	1422
Maid of Orleans p. 141	1428
Battle of Varna p. 147 (*L'Art*)	1442
Constantinople taken by the Ottomans p. 147	1453
John Basilowich rescues Russia from the Moguls p. 47 (*L'Art*)	about 1480
Luther p. 140	1517
Soliman the Great pp. 148, 192	1520
St. Pius the Fifth p. 153	1568
Battle of Lepanto pp. 156, 189	1571

II.
PERSONAL AND LITERARY CHARACTER OF CICERO.

(*From the* ENCYCLOPÆDIA METROPOLITANA *of* 1824.)

PREFATORY NOTICE.

IF the following sketch of Cicero's life and writings be thought unworthy of so great a subject, the Author must plead the circumstances under which it was made.

In the spring of 1824, when his hands were full of work, Dr. Whately paid him the compliment of asking him to write it for the *Encyclopædia Metropolitana*, to which he was at that time himself contributing. Dr. Whately explained to him that the Editor had suddenly been disappointed in the article on Cicero which was to have appeared in the *Encyclopædia*, and that in consequence he could not allow more than two months for the composition of the paper which was to take its place; also, that it must contain such and such subjects. The Author undertook and finished it under these conditions.

In the present Edition (1872) he has in some places availed himself of the excellent translations of its Greek and Latin passages, made by the Reverend Henry Thompson in the Edition of 1852.

MARCUS TULLIUS CICERO.

		PAGE
1.	CHIEF EVENTS IN THE LIFE OF CICERO, §§ 1-4	245
2.	HIS LITERARY POSITION, § 5	259
3.	THE NEW ACADEMY AND HIS RELATION TO IT, §§ 6-7	264
4.	HIS PHILOSOPHICAL WRITINGS, §§ 8-10	275
5.	HIS LETTERS, HIS HISTORICAL AND POETICAL COMPOSITIONS, § 10	289
6.	HIS ORATIONS, § 11	291
7.	HIS STYLE, § 12	295
8.	THE ORATORS OF ROME, § 13	297

MARCUS TULLIUS CICERO.

I.

MARCUS TULLIUS CICERO was born at Arpinum, the native place of Marius,[1] in the year of Rome 648 (A.C. 106), the same year which gave birth to the Great Pompey. His family was ancient and of Equestrian rank, but had never taken part in the public affairs of Rome,[2] though both his father and grandfather were persons of consideration in the part of Italy to which they belonged.[3] His father, being a man of cultivated mind himself, determined to give his two sons the advantage of a liberal education, and to fit them for the prospect of those public employments which a feeble constitution incapacitated himself from undertaking. Marcus, the elder of the two, soon displayed indications of a superior intellect, and we are told that his schoolfellows carried home such accounts of him, that their parents often visited the school for the sake of seeing a youth who gave such promise of future eminence.[4] One of his earliest masters was the poet Archias, whom he defended afterwards in his Consular year; under his instructions he was able to compose a poem, though yet a boy, on the fable of Glaucus, which had formed the subject of one of the tragedies of Æschylus. Soon after

[1] De Legg. i. 1, ii. 1.
[2] Contra Rull. ii. 1.
[3] De Legg. ii. 1, iii. 16; de Orat. ii. 66.
[4] Plutarch, in Vitâ.

he assumed the manly gown he was placed under the care of Scævola, the celebrated lawyer, whom he introduces so beautifully into several of his philosophical dialogues ; and in no long time he gained a thorough knowledge of the laws and political institutions of his country.[1]

This was about the time of the Social war ; and, according to the Roman custom, which made it a necessary part of education to learn the military art by personal service, Cicero took the opportunity of serving a campaign under the Consul Pompeius Strabo, father of Pompey the Great. Returning to pursuits more congenial to his natural taste, he commenced the study of Philosophy under Philo the Academic, of whom we shall speak more particularly hereafter.[2] But his chief attention was reserved for Oratory, to which he applied himself with the assistance of Molo, the first rhetorician of the day ; while Diodotus the Stoic exercised him in the argumentative subtleties for which the disciples of Zeno were so generally celebrated. At the same time he declaimed daily in Greek and Latin with some young noblemen, who were competitors with him in the same race of political honours.

Of the two professions,[3] which, from the contentiousness of human nature, are involved in the very notion of society, while that of arms, by its splendour and importance, secures the almost undivided admiration of a rising and uncivilized people, legal practice, on the other hand, becomes the path to honours in later and more civilized ages, by reason of the oratorical accomplishments to which it usually gives scope. The date of Cicero's birth fell precisely during that intermediate state of things, in which

---

[1] Middleton's Life, vol. i. p. 13. 4to ; de Clar. Orat. 89.
[2] Ibid.   [3] Pro Muræna, 11 ; de Orat. i. 9.

the glory of military exploits lost its pre-eminence by means of the very opulence and luxury which were their natural issue; and he was the first Roman who found his way to the highest dignities of the State with no other recommendation than his powers of eloquence and his merits as a civil magistrate.[1]

The first cause of importance he undertook was his defence of Sextus Roscius; in which he distinguished himself by his spirited opposition to Sylla, whose favourite Chrysogonus was prosecutor in the action. This obliging him, according to Plutarch, to leave Rome on prudential motives, he employed his time in travelling for two years under pretence of his health, which, he tells us,[2] was as yet unequal to the exertion of pleading. At Athens he met with T. Pomponius Atticus, whom he had formerly known at school, and there renewed with him a friendship which lasted through life, in spite of the change of interests and estrangements of affection so common in turbulent times.[3] Here too he attended the lectures of Antiochus, who, under the name of Academic, taught the dogmatic doctrines of Plato and the Stoics. Though Cicero felt at first considerable dislike of his philosophical views,[4] he seems afterwards to have adopted the sentiments of the Old Academy, which they much resembled; and not till late in life to have relapsed into the sceptical tenets of his former instructor Philo.[5] After visiting the principal philosophers and rhetoricians of Asia, in his thirtieth year he returned to Rome, so strengthened and improved both

[1] In Catil. iii. 6; in Pis. 3; pro Sylla, 30; pro Dom. 37; de Harusp. resp. 23; ad Fam. xv. 4.
[2] De Clar. Orat. 91.   [3] Middleton's Life, vol. i. p. 42, 4to.
[4] Plutarch, in Vitâ.
[5] Warburton, Div. Leg. lib. iii. sec. 3; and Vossius, de Nat. Logic. c. viii. sec. 22.

in bodily and mental powers, that he soon eclipsed in his oratorical efforts all his competitors for public favour. So popular a talent speedily gained him the suffrage of the Commons; and, being sent to Sicily as Quæstor, at a time when the metropolis itself was visited with a scarcity of corn, he acquitted himself in that delicate situation with such address as to supply the clamorous wants of the people without oppressing the province from which the provisions were raised.[1] Returning thence with greater honours than had ever been before decreed to a Roman Governor, he ingratiated himself still farther in the esteem of the Sicilians by undertaking his celebrated prosecution of Verres; who, though defended by the influence of the Metelli and the eloquence of Hortensius, was at length driven in despair into voluntary exile.

Five years after his Quæstorship, Cicero was elected Ædile, a post of considerable expense from the exhibition of games connected with it. In this magistracy he conducted himself with singular propriety;[2] for, it being customary to court the people by a display of splendour in these official shows, he contrived to retain his popularity without submitting to the usual alternative of plundering the provinces or sacrificing his private fortune. The latter was at this time by no means ample; but, with the good sense and taste which mark his character, he preserved in his domestic arrangements the dignity of a literary and public man, without any of the ostentation of magnificence which often distinguished the candidate for popular applause.[3]

After the customary interval of two years, he was

---

[1] Pro Planc. 26; in Ver. vi. 14.   [2] Pro Dom. 57, 58.
[3] De Offic. ii. 17; Middleton.

returned at the head of the list as Prætor;[1] and now made his first appearance in the rostrum in support of the Manilian law. About the same time he defended Cluentius. At the expiration of his Prætorship, he refused to accept a foreign province, the usual reward of that magistracy;[2] but, having the Consulate full in view, and relying on his interest with Cæsar and Pompey, he allowed nothing to divert him from that career of glory for which he now believed himself to be destined.

2.

It may be doubted, indeed, whether any individual ever rose to power by more virtuous and truly honourable conduct; the integrity of his public life was only equalled by the correctness of his private morals; and it may at first sight excite our wonder that a course so splendidly begun should afterwards so little fulfil its early promise. Yet it was a failure from the period of his Consulate to his Pro-prætorship in Cilicia, and each year is found to diminish his influence in public affairs, till it expires altogether with the death of Pompey. This surprise, however, arises in no small degree from measuring Cicero's political importance by his present reputation, and confounding the authority he deservedly possesses as an author with the opinions entertained of him by his contemporaries as a statesman. From the consequence usually attached to passing events, a politician's celebrity is often at its zenith in his own generation; while the author, who is in the highest repute with posterity, may perhaps have been little valued or courted in his own day. Virtue indeed so conspicuous as that of Cicero, studies so dignified, and oratorical powers so commanding, will

[1] In Pis. 1. [2] Pro Muræna, 20.

always invest their possessor with a large portion of reputation and authority; and this is nowhere more apparent than in the enthusiastic welcome with which he was greeted on his return from exile. But unless other qualities be added, more peculiarly necessary for a statesman, they will hardly of themselves carry that political weight which some writers have attached to Cicero's public life, and which his own self-love led him to appropriate.

The advice of the Oracle,[1] which had directed him to make his own genius, not the opinion of the people, his guide to immortality (which in fact pointed at the above-mentioned distinction between the fame of a statesman and of an author), at first made a deep impression on his mind; and at the present day he owes his reputation principally to those pursuits which, as Plutarch tells us, exposed him to the ridicule and even to the contempt of his contemporaries as a "pedant and a professor."[2] But his love of popularity overcame his philosophy, and he commenced a career which gained him one triumph and ten thousand mortifications.

It is not indeed to be doubted that in his political course he was more or less influenced by a sense of duty. To many it may even appear that a public life was best adapted for the display of his particular talents; that, at the termination of the Mithridatic war, Cicero was in fact marked out as the very man to adjust the pretensions of the rival parties in the Commonwealth, to withstand the encroachments of Pompey, and to baffle the arts of Cæsar. And if the power of swaying and controlling the popular assemblies by his eloquence; if the circumstances of his rank, Equestrian as far as family was concerned, yet almost Patrician from the splendour of his personal

---

[1] Plutarch, in Vitâ. [2] Γραικὸς καὶ σχολαστικός. Plutarch, in Vitâ.

honours; if the popularity derived from his accusation of Verres, and defence of Cornelius, and the favour of the Senate acquired by the brilliant services of his Consulate; if the general respect of all parties which his learning and virtue commanded; if these were sufficient qualifications for a mediator between contending factions, Cicero was indeed called upon by the voice of his country to that most arduous and honourable post. And in his Consulate he had seemed sensible of the call: "All through my Consulate," he declares in his speech against Piso, "I made a point of doing nothing without the advice of the Senate and the approval of the People. I ever defended the Senate in the Rostrum, in the Senate House the People, and united the populace with the leading men, the Equestrian order with the Senate."

Yet, after that eventful period, we see him resigning his high station to Cato, who, with half his abilities, little foresight, and no address,[1] possessed that first requisite for a statesman, firmness. Cicero, on the contrary, was irresolute, timid, and inconsistent.[2] He talked indeed largely of preserving a middle course,[3] but he was continually vacillating from one to the other extreme; always too confident or too dejected; incorrigibly vain of success, yet meanly panegyrizing the government of an usurper. His foresight, sagacity, practical good sense, and singular tact, were lost for want of that strength of mind which points them steadily to one object. He was never decided, never (as has sometimes been observed) took an important step without afterwards repenting of it. Nor can we account for the firmness and resolution of

---

[1] Ad Atticum, i. 18, ii. 1.
[2] See Montesquieu, Grandeur des Romains, ch. xii.
[3] Ad Atticum, i. 19.

his Consulate, unless we discriminate between the case of resisting and exposing a faction, and that of balancing contending interests. Vigour in repression differs widely from steadiness in mediation; the latter requiring a coolness of judgment, which a direct attack upon a public foe is so far from implying, that it even inspires minds naturally timid with unusual ardour.

3.

His Consulate was succeeded by the return of Pompey from the East, and the establishment of the First Triumvirate; which, disappointing his hopes of political power, induced him to resume his forensic and literary occupations. From these he was recalled, after an interval of four years, by the threatening measures of Clodius, who at length succeeded in driving him into exile. This event, which, considering the circumstances connected with it, was one of the most glorious of his life, filled him with the utmost distress and despondency. He wandered about Greece bewailing his miserable fortune, refusing the consolations which his friends attempted to administer, and shunning the public honours with which the Greek cities were eager to load him.[1] His return, which took place in the course of the following year, reinstated him in the high station he had filled at the termination of his Consulate, but the cir-

---

[1] Ad Atticum, lib. iii.; ad Fam. lib. xiv.; pro Sext. 22; pro Dom. 36; Plutarch, in Vitâ. It is curious to observe how he converts the alleviating circumstances of his case into exaggerations of his misfortune: he writes to Atticus: "As to your many fierce objurgations of me, for my weakness of mind, I ask you, what aggravation is wanting to my calamity? Who else has ever fallen from so high a position, in so good a cause, with so large an intellect, influence, popularity, with all good men so powerfully supporting him, as I?"—iii. 10. Other persons would have reckoned the justice of their cause, and the countenance of good men, alleviations of their distress; and so, when others were concerned, he himself thought. Vid. pro Sext. 12.

cumstances of the times did not allow him to retain it. We refer to Roman history for an account of his vacillations between the several members of the Triumvirate; his defence of Vatinius to please Cæsar; and of his bitter political enemy Gabinius, to ingratiate himself with Pompey. His personal history in the meanwhile furnishes little worth noticing, except his election into the college of Augurs, a dignity which had been a particular object of his ambition. His appointment to the government of Cilicia, which took place about five years after his return from exile, was in consequence of Pompey's law, which obliged those Senators of Consular or Prætorian rank, who had never held any foreign command, to divide the vacant provinces among them. This office, which we have above seen him decline, he now accepted with feelings of extreme reluctance, dreading perhaps the military occupations which the movements of the Parthians in that quarter rendered necessary. Yet if we consider the state and splendour with which the Proconsuls were surrounded, and the opportunities afforded them for almost legalized plunder and extortion, we must confess that this insensibility to the common objects of human cupidity was the token of no ordinary mind. The singular disinterestedness and integrity of his administration, as well as his success against the enemy, also belong to the history of his times. The latter he exaggerated from the desire, so often instanced in eminent men, of appearing to excel in those things for which nature has not adapted them.

His return to Italy was followed by earnest endeavours to reconcile Pompey with Cæsar, and by very spirited behaviour when Cæsar required his presence in the Senate. On this occasion he felt the glow of self-approbation with which his political conduct seldom repaid him: he writes to Atticus, "I believe I do not please Cæsar, but I am pleased with myself, which has not happened to me for a long while." However, this effort at independence was but transient. At no period of his public life did he display such miserable vacillation as at the opening of the civil war.² We find him first accepting a commission from the Republic; then courting Cæsar; next, on Pompey's sailing for Greece, resolving to follow him thither; presently determining to stand neuter; then bent on retiring to the Pompeians in Sicily; and, when after all he had joined their camp in Greece, discovering such timidity and discontent as to draw from Pompey the bitter reproof, "I wish Cicero would go over to the enemy, that he may learn to fear us."³

On his return to Italy, after the battle of Pharsalia, he had the mortification of learning that his brother and nephew were making their peace with Cæsar, by throwing on himself the blame of their opposition to the conqueror. And here we see one of those elevated points of character which redeem the weaknesses of his political conduct; for, hearing that Cæsar had retorted on Quintus Cicero the charge which the latter had brought against himself, he wrote a pressing letter in his favour, declaring his brother's safety was not less precious to him than his own, and representing him not as the leader, but as the companion of his voyage.⁴

Now too the state of his private affairs reduced him to much perplexity; a sum he had advanced to Pompey had impoverished him, and he was forced to

---

¹ Ad Atticum, ix. 18.
² Ibid. vii. 11, ix. 6, x. 8 and 9, xi, 9, etc.
³ Macrobius, Saturnalia, ii. 3.
⁴ Ad Atticum, xi. 8, 9, 10 and 12.

stand indebted to Atticus for present assistance.[1] These difficulties led him to take a step which it has been customary to regard with great severity; the divorce of his wife Terentia, though he was then in his sixty-second year, and his marriage with his rich ward Publilia, who of course was of an age disproportionate to his own.[2] Yet, in reviewing this proceeding, we must not adopt the modern standard of propriety, forgetful of a condition of society which reconciled actions even of moral turpitude with a reputation for honour and virtue. Terentia was a woman of a most imperious and violent temper, and (what is more to the purpose) had in no slight degree contributed to his present embarrassments by her extravagance in the management of his private affairs.[3] By her he had two children, a son, born a year before his Consulate, and a daughter whose loss he was now fated to deplore. To Tullia he was tenderly attached, not only from the excellence of her disposition, but from her literary tastes; and her death tore from him, as he so pathetically laments to Sulpicius, the only comfort which the course of public events had left him.[4] At first he was inconsolable; and, retiring to a little island near his estate at Antium, he buried himself in the woods, to avoid the sight of man.[5] His distress was increased by the conduct of his new wife Publilia; whom he soon divorced for testifying joy at the death of her stepdaughter. On this occasion he wrote his Treatise on Consolation, with a view to alleviate his grief; and, with the same object, he determined on dedicating a temple to his daughter, as a memorial of her virtues and his affection. His friends were assiduous in their attentions; and Cæsar, who had treated him with extreme kindness

---

[1] Ibid. xi. 13. [2] Ad Fam. iv. 14; Middleton, vol. ii. p. 149.
[3] Ibid. [4] Ad Fam. iv. 6. [5] Ad Atticum, xii. 15, etc.

on his return from Egypt, signified the respect he bore his character by sending him a letter of condolence from Spain,[1] where the remains of the Pompeian party still engaged him. Cæsar, moreover, had shortly before given a still stronger proof of his favour, by replying to a work which Cicero had drawn up in praise of Cato;[2] but no attentions, however considerate, could soften Cicero's vexation at seeing the country he had formerly saved by his exertions now subjected to the tyranny of one master. His speeches, indeed, for Marcellus and Ligarius, exhibit traces of inconsistency; but for the most part he retired from public business, and gave himself up to the composition of those works which, while they mitigated his political sorrows, have secured his literary celebrity.

4.

The murder of Cæsar, which took place in the following year, once more brought him on the stage of public affairs; but as our present paper is but supplemental to the history of the times, we leave to others to relate what more has to be told of him, his unworthy treatment of Brutus, his coalition with Octavius, his orations against Antonius, his proscription, and his violent death, at the age of sixty-four. Willingly would we pass over his public life altogether; for he was as little of a great statesman as of a great commander. His merits are of another kind and in a higher order of excellence. Antiquity may be challenged to produce a man more virtuous, more perfectly amiable than Cicero. None interest more in their life, none excite more painful emotions in their death. Others, it is true, may be found of loftier and more heroic character, who awe and subdue the mind by the grandeur of their views, or the intensity of their exertions. But

---

[1] Ad Atticum, xiii. 20.   [2] Ibid. xii. 40 and 41.

Cicero engages our affections by the integrity of his public conduct, the correctness of his private life, the generosity,[1] placability, and kindness of his heart, the playfulness of his wit, the warmth of his domestic attachments. In this respect his letters are invaluable. "Here," says Middleton, "we may see the genuine man without disguise or affectation, especially in his letters to Atticus; to whom he talked with the same frankness as to himself, opened the rise and progress of each thought; and never entered into any affair without his particular advice."[2]

It must be confessed, indeed, that this private correspondence discloses the defects of his political conduct, and shows that they were partly of a moral character. Want of firmness has been repeatedly mentioned as his principal failing; and insincerity is the natural attendant on a timid and irresolute mind. On the other hand, it must not be forgotten that openness and candour are rare qualities in a statesman at all times, and while the duplicity of weakness is despised, the insincerity of a powerful but crafty mind, though incomparably more odious, is too commonly regarded with feelings of indulgence. Cicero was deficient, not in honesty, but in moral courage; his disposition, too, was conciliatory and forgiving; and much which has been referred to inconsistency should be attributed to the generous temper which induced him to remember the services rather than the neglect of Plancius, and to relieve the exiled and indigent Verres.[3] Much too may be traced to his professional habits as a pleader; which led him to introduce

---

[1] His want of jealousy towards his rivals was remarkable; this was exemplified in his esteem for Hortensius, and still more so in his conduct towards Calvus. See Ad Fam. xv. 21.

[2] Vol. ii. p. 525, 4to. [3] Pro Planc.; Middleton, vol. i. p. 108.

the licence of the Forum into deliberative discussions, and (however inexcusably) even into his correspondence with private friends.

Some writers, as Lyttelton, have considered it an aggravation of Cicero's inconsistencies, that he was so perfectly aware, as his writings show, of what was philosophically and morally upright and honest. It might be sufficient to reply, that there is a wide difference between calmly deciding on an abstract point, and acting on that decision in the hurry of real life; that Cicero in fact was apt to fancy (as all will fancy when assailed by interest or passion) that the circumstances of his case constituted it an exception to the broad principles of duty. Besides, he considered it to be actually the duty of a statesman to accommodate theoretical principle to the exigencies of existing circumstances. "Surely," he says in his defence of Plancius, "it is no mark of inconsistency in a statesman to determine his judgment and to steer his course by the state of the political weather. This is what I have been taught, what I have experienced, what I have read; this is what is recorded in history of the wisest and most eminent men, whether at home or abroad; namely, that the same man is not bound always to maintain the same opinions, but those, whatever they may be, which the state of the commonwealth, the direction of the times, and the interests of peace may demand."[1] Moreover, he claimed for himself especially the part of mediator between political rivals; and he considered it to be a mediator's duty alternately to praise and blame both parties, even to exaggeration, if by such means it was possible either to flatter or frighten them into an adoption of temperate measures.[2] "Cicero," says

[1] C. 39. [2] Ad Fam. vi. 6, vii. 3.

Plutarch, "used to give them private advice, keeping up a correspondence with Cæsar, and urging many things upon Pompey himself, soothing and persuading each of them."[1]

5.

But such criticism on Cicero as Lyttelton's proceeds on an entire misconception of the design and purpose with which the ancients prosecuted philosophical studies. The motives and principles of morals were not so seriously acknowledged as to lead to a practical application of them to the conduct of life. Even when they proposed them in the form of precept, they still regarded the perfectly virtuous man as the creature of their imagination rather than a model for imitation—a character whom it was a mental recreation rather than a duty to contemplate; and if an individual here or there, as Scipio or Cato, attempted to conform his life to his philosophical conceptions of virtue, he was sure to be ridiculed for singularity and affectation.

Even among the Athenians, by whom philosophy was, in many cases, cultivated to the exclusion of every active profession, intellectual amusement, not the discovery of Truth, was the principal object of their discussions. That we must thus account for the ensnaring questions and sophistical reasonings of which their disputations consisted, has been noticed by writers on Logic;[2] and it was their extension of this system to the case of morals which brought upon their Sophists the irony of Socrates and the sterner rebuke of Aristotle. But if this took place in a state of society in which the love of speculation pervaded all ranks, much more was it

---

[1] Plutarch, in Vitâ Cic. See also in Vitâ Pomp.
[2] Vid. Dr. Whately in the Encyclopædia Metropolitana.

to be expected among the Romans, who, busied as they were in political enterprises, and deficient in philosophical acuteness, had neither time nor inclination for abstruse investigations; and who considered philosophy simply as one of the many fashions introduced from Greece, "a sort of table furniture," as Warburton well expresses it, a mere refinement in the arts of social enjoyment.[1] This character it bore both among friends and enemies. Hence the popularity which attended the three Athenian philosophers who had come to Rome on an embassy from their native city; and hence the inflexible determination with which Cato procured their dismissal, through fear, as Plutarch tells us,[2] lest their arts of disputation should corrupt the Roman youth. And when at length, by the authority of Scipio,[3] the literary treasures of Sylla, and the patronage of Lucullus, philosophical studies had gradually received the countenance of the higher classes of their countrymen, still, in consistency with the principle above laid down, we find them determined in their adoption of this or that system, not so much by the harmony of its parts, or by the plausibility of its reasonings, as by its suitableness to the particular profession and political station to which they severally belonged. Thus, because the Stoics were more minute than other sects in inculcating the moral and social duties, we find the Roman jurisconsults professing themselves followers of Zeno;[4] the orators, on the contrary, adopted the disputatious system of the later Academics;[5] while Epicurus was the master of the idle and the wealthy. Hence, too, they confined

[1] Lactantius, Inst. iii. 16.
[2] Plutarch, in Vitâ Caton. See also de Invent. i. 36.
[3] Paterculus, i. 12, etc. Plutarch, in Vitt. Lucull. et Syll.
[4] Gravin. Origin. Juris Civil. lib. i. c. 44.
[5] Quinct. xii. 2. Auct. Dialog. de Orator. 31.

the profession of philosophical science to Greek teachers; considering them the sole proprietors, as it were, of a foreign and expensive luxury, which the vanquished might suitably have the duty of furnishing, and which the conquerors could well afford to purchase.

Before the works of Cicero, no attempts worth considering had been made for using the Latin tongue in philosophical subjects. The natural stubbornness of the language conspired with Roman haughtiness to prevent this application.[1] The Epicureans, indeed, had made the experiment, but their writings were even affectedly harsh and slovenly,[2] and we find Cicero himself, in spite of his inexhaustible flow of rich and expressive diction, making continual apologies for his learned occupations, and extolling philosophy as the parent of everything great, virtuous, and amiable.[3]

Yet, with whatever discouragement his design was attended, he ultimately triumphed over the pride of an unlettered people, and the difficulties of a defective language. He was indeed possessed of that first requisite for eminence, an enthusiastic attachment to the studies he was recommending. But, occupied as he was with the duties of a statesman, mere love of literature would have availed little, if separated from that energy and breadth of intellect by which he was enabled to pursue a variety of objects at once, with equally perserving and indefatigable zeal. "He suffered no part of his leisure to be idle," says Middleton, "or the least interval of it to be lost; but what other people gave to the public shows, to

---

[1] De Nat. Deor. i. 4; de Off. i. 1; de Fin.; init. Acad. Quæst. init. etc.
[2] Tusc. Quæst. i. 3; ii. 3; Acad. Quæst. i. 2; de Nat. Deor. i. 21; de Fin. i. 3, etc.; de Clar. Orat. 35.
[3] Lucullus, 2; de Fin. i. 1—3; Tusc. Quæst. ii. 1, 2; iii. 2; v. 2; de Legg. i. 22—24; de Off. ii. 2; de Orat. 41, etc.

pleasures, to feasts, nay, even to sleep and the ordinary refreshments of nature, he generally gave to his books, and the enlargement of his knowledge. On days of business, when he had anything particular to compose, he had no other time for meditating but when he was taking a few turns in his walks, where he used to dictate his thoughts to his scribes who attended him. We find many of his letters dated before daylight, some from the senate, others from his meals, and the crowd of his morning levee."[1] Thus he found time, without apparent inconvenience, for the business of the State, for the turmoil of the courts, and for philosophical studies. During his Consulate he delivered twelve orations in the Senate, Rostrum, or Forum. His Treatises *de Oratore* and *de Republicâ*, the most finished perhaps of his compositions, were written at a time when, to use his own words, "not a day passed without his taking part in forensic disputes."[2] And in the last year of his life he composed at least eight of his philosophical works, besides the fourteen orations against Antony, which are known by the name of Philippics.

Being thus ardent in the cause of philosophy, he recommended it to the notice of his countrymen, not only for the honour which its introduction would reflect upon himself (which of course was a motive with him), but also with the fondness of one who esteemed it " the guide of life, the parent of virtue, the guardian in difficulty, and the tranquillizer in misfortune."[3] Nor were his mental endowments less adapted to the accomplishment of his object than the spirit with which he engaged in the work. Gifted with great versatility of talent, with acuteness, quickness of perception, skill in selection, art

[1] Middleton's Life, vol. ii. p. 254. [2] Ad Quinct. fratr. iii. 3.
[3] Tusc. Quæst. v. 2.

in arrangement, fertility of illustration, warmth of fancy, and extraordinary taste, he at once seizes upon the most effective parts of his subject, places them in the most striking point of view, and arrays them in the liveliest and most inviting colours. His writings have the singular felicity of combining brilliancy of execution with never-failing good sense. It must be allowed that he is deficient in depth; that he skims over rather than dives into the subjects of which he treats; that he had too great command of the plausible to be a patient investigator or a sound reasoner. Yet if he has less originality of thought than others, if he does not grapple with his subject, if he is unequal to a regular and lengthened disquisition, if he is frequently inconsistent in his opinions, we must remember that mere soundness of view, without talent for display, has few recommendations for those who have not yet imbibed a taste even for the outward form of knowledge,[1] that system nearly precludes freedom, and depth almost implies obscurity. It was this very absence of scientific exactness which constituted in Roman eyes a principal charm of Cicero's compositions.[2]

Nor must his profession as a pleader be forgotten in enumerating the circumstances which concurred to give his writings their peculiar character. For, however his design of interesting his countrymen in Greek literature, however too his particular line of talent, may have led him to explain rather than to invent; yet he expressly informs us it was principally with a view to his own improvement in Oratory that he devoted himself to

[1] De Off. i. 5. *init.*

[2] Johnson's observations on Addison's writings may be well applied to those of Cicero, who would have been eminently successful in short miscellaneous essays, like those of the Spectator, had the manners of the age allowed it.

philosophical studies.[1] This induced him to undertake successively the cause of the Stoic, the Epicurean, or the Platonist, as an exercise for his powers of argumentation; while the wavering and unsettled state of mind, occasioned by such habits of disputation, led him in his personal judgment to prefer the sceptical tenets of the New Academy.

6.

Here then, before enumerating Cicero's philosophical writings, an opportunity is presented to us of redeeming the pledge we have given elsewhere in our Encyclopædia,[2] to consider the system of doctrine which the reformers (as they thought themselves) of the Academic school introduced about 300 years before the Christian era.

We shall not trace here the history of the Old Academy, or speak of the innovations on the system of Plato, silently introduced by the austere Polemo. When Zeno, however, who was his pupil, advocated the same rigid tenets in a more open and dogmatic form,[3] the Academy at length took the alarm, and a reaction ensued. Arcesilas, who had succeeded Polemo and Crates, determined on reverting to the principles of the elder schools;[4] but mistaking the profession of ignorance, which Socrates had used against the Sophists on physical questions, for an actual scepticism on points connected with morals, he fell into the opposite extreme, and declared, first,

---

[1] Orat. iii. 4; Tusc. Quæst. ii. 3; de Off. i. 1. Paradox. *præfat.* Quinct. Instit. xii. 2.

[2] Article, Plato, in the Encyclopædia Metropolitana.

[3] Acad. Quæst. i. 10, etc.; Lucullus, 5; de Legg. i. 20; iii. 3, etc.

[4] Acad. Quæst. i. 4, 12, 13; Lucullus, 5 and 23; de Nat. Deor. i. 5; de Fin. ii. 1; de Orat. iii. 18. Augustin. contra Acad. ii. 6. Plutarch, in Colot. 26.

that nothing could be known, and therefore, secondly, nothing should be maintained.[1]

Whatever were his private sentiments (for some authors affirm his esoteric doctrines to have been dogmatic[2]), he brought forward these sceptical tenets in so unguarded a form, that it required all his argumentative powers, which were confessedly great, to maintain them against the obvious objections which were pressed upon him from all quarters. On his death, therefore, as might have been anticipated, his school was deserted for those of Zeno and Epicurus; and during the lives of Lacydes, Evander, and Hegesinus, who successively filled the Academic chair, being no longer recommended by the novelty of its doctrines,[3] or the talents of its masters, it became of little consideration amid the wranglings of more popular philosophies. Carneades,[4] therefore, who succeeded Hegesinus, found it necessary to use more cautious and guarded language; and, by explaining what was paradoxical, by reservations and exceptions, in short, by all the arts which an acute and active genius could suggest, he contrived to establish its authority, without departing, as far as we have the means of judging, from the principle of universal scepticism which Arcesilas had so pertinaciously advocated.[5]

[1] "Arcesilas negabat esse quidquam, quod sciri posset, ne illud quidem ipsum quod Socrates sibi reliquisset. Sic omnia latere censebat in occulto, neque esse quicquam quod cerni, quod intelligi, posset; quibus de causis nihil oportere neque profiteri neque affirmare quenquam, neque assentione approbare, etc."—*Acad. Quæst.* i. 12. See also Lucullus, 9 and 18. They were countenanced in these conclusions by Plato's doctrine of ideas.— *Lucullus*, 46.

[2] Sext. Empir. Pyrrh. Hypot. i. 33. Diogenes Laertius, lib. iv. in Arcesil. Vid. Lactant. Instit. iii. 6.

[3] Lucullus, 6.

[4] Augustin. contr. Acad. iii. 17.

[5] Lucullus, 18, 24. Augustin. contr. Acad. iii. 39.

The New Academy,[1] then, taught with Plato, that all things in their own nature were fixed and determinate ; but that, through the constitution of the human mind, it was impossible *for us* to see them in their simple and eternal forms, to separate appearance from reality, truth from falsehood.[2] For the conception we form of any object is altogether derived from and depends on the sensation, the impression, it produces on our own minds (πάθος ἐνεργείας, φαντασία). Reason does but deduce from premisses ultimately supplied by sensation. Our only communication, then, with actual existences being through the medium of our own impressions, we have no means of ascertaining the correspondence of the things themselves with the ideas we entertain of them; and therefore can in no case be certain of the truthfulness of our senses. Of their fallibility, however, we may easily assure ourselves ; for in cases in which they are detected contradicting each other, all cannot be correct reporters of the object with which they profess to acquaint us. Food, which is the same as far as *sight* and *touch* are concerned, *tastes* differently to different individuals; fire, which is the same to the *eye*, communicates a sensation of *pain* at one time, of *pleasure* at another ; the oar *appears* crooked in the water, while the *touch* assures us it is as straight as before it was immersed.[3] Again, in dreams, in intoxication, in madness, impressions are made upon the mind, vivid enough to incite to reflection and action, yet utterly at variance with those produced

---

[1] See Sext. Empir. adv. Log. i. 166., etc., p. 405.
[2] Acad. Quæst. i. 13; Lucullus, 23, 38; de Nat. Deor. i. 5; Orat. 71.
[3] " Tu autem te negas infracto remo neque columbæ collo commoveri. Primum cur ? nam et in remo sentio non esse id quod videatur, et in columbâ plures videri colores, nec esse plus uno, etc."—*Lucullus*, 25.

by the same objects when we are awake, or sober, or in possession of our reason.[1]

It appears, then, that we cannot prove that our senses are *ever* faithful to the things they profess to report about; but we do know they *often* produce erroneous impressions of them. Here then is room for endless doubt; for why may they not deceive us in cases in which we cannot detect the deception? It is certain they *often* act irregularly; is there any consistency *at all* in their operations, any law to which these varieties may be referred?

It is undeniable that an object often varies in the impression which it makes upon the mind, while, on the other hand, the same impression may arise from different objects. What limit is to be assigned to this disorder? is there any sensation strong enough to *assure* us of the presence of the object which it seems to intimate, any such as to preclude the possibility of deception? If, when we look into a mirror, our minds are impressed with the appearance of trees, fields, and houses, which are unreal, how can we ascertain beyond all doubt whether the scene we directly look upon has any more substantial existence than the former?[2]

From these reasonings the Academics taught that nothing was certain, nothing was to be known (καταληπτόν). For the Stoics themselves, their most determined opponents, defined the καταληπτικὴ φαντασία (the phantasy or impression which involved knowledge[3]) to be

[1] Lucullus, 16—18; 26—28.
[2] "Vehementer errare eos qui dicant ab Academiâ sensus eripi; à quibus nunquam dictum sit aut colorem aut saporem aut sonum nullum esse, [sed] illud sit disputatum, non inesse in his propriam, quæ nusquam alibi esset, veri et certi notam."—*Lucullus*, 32. See also 13, 24, 31; de Nat. Deor. i. 5.
[3] Οἱ γοῦν Στωϊκοὶ κατάληψιν εὐδὶ φασι καταληπτικῇ φαντασίᾳ συγκατάθεσιν. *Sext. Empir. Pyrrh. Hypot.* iii. 25. Vid. also Adv. Log. i. 152, p. 402.

one that was capable of being produced by no object except that to which it really belonged.[1]

Since then we cannot arrive at knowledge, we must suspend our decision, pronounce absolutely on nothing, nay, according to Arcesilas, never even form an opinion.[2] In the conduct of life, however, probability[3] must determine our choice of action; and this admits of different degrees. The lowest kind is that which suggests itself on the first view of the case (φαντασία πιθανή, or *persuasive phantasy*); but in all important matters we must correct the evidence of our senses by considerations derived from the nature of the medium, the distance of the object, the disposition of the organ, the time, the manner, and other attendant circumstances. When the impression has been thus minutely considered, the *phantasy* becomes περιωδευμένη, or *approved on circumspection;* and if during this examination no objection has arisen to weaken our belief, the highest degree of probability is attained, and the phantasy is pronounced *unembarrassed with doubt*, or ἀπερίσπαστος.[4]

Sextus Empiricus illustrates this as follows:[5] If on entering a dark room we discern a coiled rope, our first

[1] "Verum non posse comprehendi ex illâ Stoici Zenonis definitione arripuisse videbantur, qui ait id verum percipi posse, quod ita esset animo impressum ex eo unde esset, ut esse non posset ex eo unde non esset. Quod brevius planiusque sic dicitur, his signis verum posse comprehendi, quæ signa non potest habere quod falsum est."—*Augustin, contra Acad.* ii. 5. See also Sext. Empir. adv. Math. lib. vii. περὶ μεταβολῆς, and Cf. Lucullus, 6 with 13.

[2] Lucullus, 13, 21, 40.

[3] Τοῖς φαινομένοις οὖν προσέχοντες κατὰ τὴν βιωτικὴν τήρησιν ἀδοξάστως βιοῦμεν, ἐπεὶ μὴ δυνάμεθα ἀνενέργητοι παντάπασιν εἶναι.—*Sext. Empir. Pyrrh. Hypot.* I, 11.

[4] Cicero terms these three impressions, "visio probabilis; quæ ex circumspectione aliquâ et accuratâ consideratione fiat; quæ non impediatur." —*Lucullus*, 11.

[5] Pyrrh. Hypot. i. 33.

impression may be that it is a serpent—this is the *persuasive phantasy*. On a closer inspection, however, after *walking round it* (περιοδεύσαντες), or *on circumspection*, we observe it does not move, nor has it the proper colour, shape, or proportions; and now we conclude it is not a serpent; here we are determined in our belief by the περιωδευμένη φαντασία, and we assent to the *circumspective phantasy*. For an instance of the third and most accurate kind, viz., that with which no contrary impression interferes, we may refer to the conduct of Admetus on the return of Alcestis from the infernal regions. He believes he sees his wife; everything confirms it; but he cannot simply acquiesce in that opinion, because his mind is *embarrassed or distracted* (περισπᾶται) from the knowledge he has of her having died; he asks, "What! do I see my wife I just now buried?" (*Alc.* 1148.) Hercules resolves his difficulty, and his phantasy is in repose, or ἀπερίσπαστος.

The suspension then of assent (ἐποχή) which the Academics enjoined, was, at least from the time of Carneades,[1] almost a speculative doctrine;[2] and herein lay the chief difference between them and the Pyrrhonists; that the latter altogether denied the existence of the probable, while the former admitted there was sufficient to allow of action, provided we pronounced absolutely on nothing.

Little more can be said concerning the opinions of a sect whose fundamental maxim was that nothing could be known, and nothing should be taught. It lay midway between the other philosophies; and in the altercations of the various schools it was at once attacked by all,[3] yet appealed to by each of the contending parties, if

[1] Numen. apud Euseb. Præp. Evang. xiv. 7.
[2] Lucullus, 31, 34; de Off. ii. 2; de Fin. v. 26. Quinct. xii. 1.
[3] Lucullus, 22, et alibi; Tusc. Quæst. ii. 2.

not to countenance its own sentiments, at least to condemn those advocated by its opponents,[1] and thus to perform the office of an umpire.[2] From this necessity, then, of being prepared on all sides for attack,[3] it became as much a school of rhetoric as of philosophy,[4] and was celebrated among the ancients for the eloquence of its masters.[5] Hence also its reputation was continually varying: for, requiring the aid of great abilities to maintain its exalted and arduous post, it alternately rose and fell in estimation, according to the talents of the individual who happened to fill the chair.[6] And hence the frequent alterations which took place in its philosophical tenets; which, depending rather on the arbitrary determinations of its present head, than on the tradition of settled maxims, were accommodated to the views of each successive master, according as he hoped by sophistry or concession to overcome the repugnance which the mind ever will feel to the doctrines of universal scepticism.

And in these continual changes it is pleasing to observe that the interests of virtue and good order were

---

[1] See a striking passage from Cicero's Academics, preserved by Augustine, contra Acad. iii. 7, and Lucullus, 18.

[2] De Nat. Deor. passim; de Div. ii. 72. "Quorum controversiam solebat tanquam honorarius arbiter judicare Carneades."—*Tusc. Quæst.* v. 41.

[3] De Fin. ii. 1; de Orat. i. 18; Lucullus, 3; Tusc. Quæst. v. 11; Numen. apud Euseb. Præp. Evang. xiv. 6, etc. Lactantius, Inst. iii. 4.

[4] De Nat. Deor. i. 67; de Fat. 2; Dialog. de Orat. 31, 32.

[5] Lucullus, 6, 18; de Orat. ii. 38, iii. 18. Quint. Inst. xii. 2. Numen. apud Euseb. Præp. Evang. xiv. 6 and 8.

[6] "Hæc in philosophiâ ratio contra omnia disserendi nullamque rem apertè judicandi, profecta à Socrate, *repetita* ab Arcesilâ, *confirmata* à Carneade, usque ad nostram viguit ætatem; quam *nunc* propemodum *orbam* esse in ipsâ Græciâ intelligo. Quod non Academiæ vitio, sed *tarditate hominum* arbitror contigisse. Nam si singulas disciplinas percipere magnum est, quanto majus omnes? quod facere iis necesse est, quibus propositum est, veri reperiendi causâ, et contra omnes philosophos et pro omnibus dicere."—*De Nat. Deor.* i. 5.

uniformly promoted; interests to which the Academic doctrines were certainly hostile, if not necessarily fatal. Thus, although we find Carneades, in conformity to the plan adopted by Arcesilas,[1] opposing the *dogmatic* principles of the Stoics concerning moral duty,[2] and studiously concealing his private views even from his friends;[3] yet, by allowing that the suspense of judgment was not always a duty, that the wise man might sometimes *believe* though he could not *know*;[4] he in some measure restored the authority of those great instincts of our nature which his predecessor appears to have discarded. Clitomachus pursued his steps by innovations in the same direction;[5] Philo, who followed next, attempting to reconcile his tenets with those of the Platonic school,[6] has been accounted the founder of a fourth academy—while, to his successor Antiochus, who embraced the doctrines of the Porch,[7] and maintained the fidelity of the senses, it has been usual to assign the establishment of a fifth.

7.

We have already observed that Cicero in early life inclined to the doctrines of Plato and Antiochus, which, at the time he composed the bulk of his writings, he had abandoned for those of Carneades and Philo.[8] Yet he was never so entirely a disciple of the New Academy as

---

[1] De Nat. Deor. i. 25. Augustin. contra Acad. iii. 17. Numen. apud Euseb. Præp. Evang. xiv. 6.

[2] De Fin. ii. 13, v. 7; Lucullus, 42; Tusc. Quæst. v. 29.

[3] Lucullus, 45.

[4] Lucullus, 21. 24; for an elevated moral precept of his, see de Fin. ii. 18.

[5] Ἀνὴρ ἐν ταῖς τρισὶν αἱρέσεσι διατρίψας, ἔν τε τῇ Ἀκαδημαϊκῇ καὶ Περιπατητικῇ καὶ Στωϊκῇ.—*Diogenes Laertius*, lib. iv. sub fin.

[6] "Quanquam Philo, magnus vir, negaret in libris duas Academias esse; erroremque eorum qui ita putârunt coarguit."—*Acad. Quæst.* i. 4.

[7] De Fin. v. 5; Lucullus, 22, 43. Sext. Emp. Pyrrh. Hyp. i. 33.

[8] Acad. Quæst. i. 4; de Nat. Deor. i. 7.

to neglect the claims of morality and the laws. He is loud in his protestations that truth is the great object of his search : " For my own part, if I have applied myself especially to this philosophy, through any love of display or pleasure in disputation, I should condemn not only my folly, but my moral condition. And, therefore, unless it were absurd, in an argument like this, to do what is sometimes done in political discussions, I would swear by Jupiter and the divine Penates that I burn with a desire of discovering the truth, and really believe what I am saying."[1] And, however inappropriate this boast may appear, he at least pursues the useful and the magnificent in philosophy ; and uses his academic character as a pretext rather for a judicious selection from each system than for an indiscriminate rejection of all.[2] Thus, in the capacity of a statesman, he calls in the assistance of doctrines which, as an orator, he does not scruple to deride ; those of Zeno in particular, who maintained the truth of the popular theology, and the divine origin of augury, and (as we noticed above) was more explicit than the other masters in his views of social duty. This difference of sentiment between the magistrate and the pleader is strikingly illustrated in the opening of his treatise *de Legibus;* where, after deriving the principles of law from the nature of things, he is obliged to beg quarter of the Academics, whose reasonings he feels could at once destroy the foundation on which his argument rested. " My treatise throughout," he says, " aims at the strengthening of states and the welfare of peoples. I dread therefore to lay down any but well considered and carefully examined

---

[1] Lucullus, 20 ; see also de Nat. Deor. i. 7 ; de Fin. i. 5.

[2] "Nobis autem nostra Academia magnam licentiam dat, ut, quodcunque maximè probabile occurrat, id nostro jure liceat defendere."—*De Off.* iii. 4. See also Tusc. Quæst. iv. 4, v. 29 ; de Invent. ii. 3.

principles; I do not say principles which are universally received, for none are such, but principles received by those philosophers who consider virtue to be desirable for its own sake, and nothing whatever to be good, or at least a great good, which is not in its own nature praiseworthy." These philosophers are the Stoics; and then, apparently alluding to the arguments of Carneades against justice, which he had put into the mouth of Philus in the third book of his *de Republicâ*, he proceeds: "As to the Academy, which puts the whole subject into utter confusion, I mean the New Academy of Arcesilas and Carneades, let us persuade it to hold its peace. For, should it make an inroad upon the views which we consider we have so skilfully put into shape, it will make an extreme havoc of them. The Academy I cannot conciliate, and I dare not ignore."[1]

And as, in questions connected with the interests of society, he thus uniformly advocates the tenets of the Porch, so in discussions of a physical character we find him adopting the sublime and glowing sentiments of Pythagoras and Plato. Here, however, having no object of expediency in view to keep him within the bounds of consistency, he scruples not to introduce whatever is most beautiful in itself, or most adapted to his present purpose. At one time he describes the Deity as the all-pervading Soul of the world, the cause of life and motion;[2] at another He is the intelligent Preserver and Governor of every separate part.[3] At one time the soul of man is in its own nature necessarily eternal, without beginning or end of existence;[4] at another it is repre-

---

[1] De Legg. i. 13.
[2] Tusc. Quæst. i. 27; de Div. ii. 72; pro Milon. 31; de Legg. ii. 7.
[3] Fragm. de Rep. 3; Tusc. Quæst. i. 29.
[4] Tusc. Quæst. i. *passim;* de Senect. 21, 22; Somn. Scip. 8.

sented as a portion, or the haunt of the one infinite Spirit;[1] at another it is to enter the assembly of the Gods, or to be driven into darkness, according to its moral conduct in this life;[2] at another, it is only in its best and greatest specimens destined for immortality;[3] sometimes that immortality is described as attended with consciousness and the continuance of earthly friendships;[4] sometimes as but an immortality of name and glory;[5] more frequently however these separate notions are confused together in the same passage.

Though the works of Aristotle were not given to the world till Sylla's return from Greece, Cicero appears to have been a considerable proficient in his philosophy,[6] and he has not overlooked the important aid it affords in those departments of science which are alike removed from abstract reasoning and fanciful theorizing. To Aristotle he is indebted for most of the principles laid down in his rhetorical discussions,[7] while in his treatises on morals not a few of his remarks may be traced to the same acute philosopher.[8]

The doctrines of the Garden alone, though some of his most intimate friends were of the Epicurean school, he regarded with aversion and contempt; feeling no sort of interest in a system which cut at the very root of that activity of mind, industry, and patriotism, for which he

---

[1] De Div. i. 32, 49; Fragm. de Consolat.
[2] Tusc. Quæst. i. 30; Som. Scip. 9; de Legg. ii. 11.
[3] De Amic. 4; de Off. iii. 28; pro Cluent. 61; de Legg. ii. 17: Tusc. Quæst. i. 11; pro Sext. 21; de Nat. Deor. i. 17.
[4] De Senect. 23.
[5] Pro Arch. 11, 12; ad Fam. v. 21, vi. 21.
[6] He seems to have fallen into some misconceptions of Aristotle's meaning. De Invent. i. 35, 36, ii. 14; see Quinct. Inst. v. 14.
[7] De Invent. i. 7, ii. 51, *et passim*; ad. Fam. i. 9; de Orat. ii. 36.
[8] De Off. i. 1; de Fin. iv. 5.

himself both in public and private was so honourably distinguished.[1]

Such then was the New Academy, and such the variation of opinion which, in Cicero's judgment, was not inconsistent with the profession of an Academic. And, however his adoption of that philosophy may be in part referred to his oratorical habits, or his natural cast of mind, yet, considering the ambition which he felt to inspire his countrymen with a taste for literature and science,[2] we must conclude with Warburton[3] that, in acceding to the system of Philo, he was strongly influenced by the freedom of thought and reasoning which it allowed to his literary works, the liberty of illustrating the principles and doctrines, the strong and weak parts, of every Grecian school. Bearing then in mind his design of recommending the study of philosophy, it is interesting to observe the artifices of style and manner which, with this end, he adopted in his treatises; and though to enter minutely into this subject would be foreign to our present purpose, it may be allowed us to make some general remarks on the character of works so eminently successful in accomplishing the object for which they were undertaken.

8.

The obvious peculiarity of Cicero's philosophical discussions is the form of dialogue in which most of them are conveyed. Plato, indeed, and Xenophon, had, before his time, been even more strictly dramatic in their

---

[1] De Fin. ii. 21, iii. 1; de Legg. i. 13; de Orat. iii. 17; ad Fam. xiii. 1; pro Sext. 10.

[2] De Nat. Deor. i. 4; Tusc. Quæst. i. 1, v. 29; de Fin. i. 3, 4; de Off. i. 1; de Div. ii. 1, 2.

[3] Div. Leg. lib. iii. sec. 9.

compositions; but they professed to be recording the sentiments of an individual, and the Socratic mode of argument could hardly be displayed in any other shape. Of that interrogative and inductive conversation, however, Cicero affords but few specimens;[1] the nature of his dialogue being as different from that of the two Athenians as was his object in writing. His aim was to excite interest; and he availed himself of this mode of composition for the life and variety, the ease, perspicuity, and vigour which it gave to his discussions. His dialogue is of two kinds: according as the subject of it is beyond or under controversy, it assumes the shape of a continued treatise, or a free disputation; in the latter case imparting clearness to what is obscure, in the former relief to what is clear. Thus his practical and systematic treatises on rhetoric and moral duty, when not written in his own person, are merely divided between several speakers who are the mere organs of his own sentiments; while in questions of a more speculative cast, on the nature of the gods, on the human soul, on the greatest good, he uses his academic liberty, and brings forward the theories of contending schools under the character of their respective advocates. The advantages gained in both cases by the form of dialogue are evident. In controverted subjects he is not obliged to discover his own views, he can detail opposite arguments forcibly and luminously, and he is allowed the use of those oratorical powers in which, after all, his great strength lay. In those subjects, on the other hand, which are uninteresting because they are familiar, he may pause or digress before the mind is weary and the attention begins to flag; the reader is carried on by easy journeys and short stages, and novelty in the speaker supplies the want of novelty in the matter.

[1] See Tusc. Quæst. and de Republ.

Nor does Cicero discover less skill in the execution of these dialogues than address in their method. It were idle to enlarge upon the beauty, richness, and taste of compositions which have been the admiration of every age and country. In the dignity of his speakers, their high tone of mutual courtesy, the harmony of his groups, and the delicate relief of his contrasts, he is inimitable. The majesty and splendour of his introductions, which generally address themselves to the passions or the imagination, the eloquence with which both sides of a question are successively displayed, the clearness and terseness of his statements on abstract points, the grace of his illustrations, his exquisite allusions to the scene or time of the supposed conversation, his digressions in praise of philosophy or great men, his quotations from Grecian and Roman poetry; lastly, the melody and fulness of his style, unite to throw a charm round his writings peculiar to themselves. To the Roman reader they especially recommended themselves by their continual and most artful references to the heroes of the old republic, who now appeared but exemplars, and (as it were) patrons of that eternal philosophy, which he had before, perhaps, considered as the short-lived reveries of ingenious but inactive men. Nor is there any confusion, want of keeping, or appearance of effort in the introduction of the various beauties we have been enumerating, which are blended together with so much skill and propriety, that it is sometimes difficult to point out the particular sources of the admiration which they inspire.

9.

The series of his rhetorical works[1] has been preserved

[1] See Fabricius, Bibliothec. Latin.; Olivet. in Cic. opp. omn.; Middleton's Life.

nearly complete, and consists of the *De Inventione, De Oratore, Brutus sive de claris Oratoribus, Orator sive de optimo genere Dicendi, De partitione Oratoriâ, Topica,* and *de optimo genere Oratorum.* The last-mentioned, which is a fragment, is understood to have been the proem to his translation (now lost) of the speeches of Demosthenes and Æschines, *De Coronâ.* These he translated with the view of defending, by the example of the Greek orators, his own style of eloquence, which, as we shall afterwards find, the critics of the day censured as too Asiatic in its character; and hence the proem, which still survives, is on the subject of the Attic style of oratory. This composition and his abstracts of his own orations[1] are his only rhetorical works not extant, and probably our loss is not very great. The *Treatise on Rhetoric,* addressed to Herennius, though edited with his works, and ascribed to him by several of the ancients, is now generally attributed to Cornificius, or some other writer of the day.

The works, which we have enumerated, consider the art of rhetoric in different points of view, and thus receive from each other mutual support and illustration, while they prevent the tediousness which might else arise, if they were moulded into one systematic treatise on the general subject. Three are in the form of dialogue; the rest are written in his own person. In all, except perhaps the *Orator,* he professes to have availed himself of the principles of the Aristotelic and Isocratean schools, selecting what was best in each of them, and, as occasion might offer, adding remarks and precepts of his own.[2] The subject of Oratory is considered in three distinct lights;[3] with reference to the case, the speaker, and the speech. The

[1] Quinct. Inst. x. 7.   [2] De Invent. ii. 2 et 3; ad Fam. i. 9.
[3] Cf. de part. Orat. with de Invent.

case, as respects its nature, is definite or indefinite; with reference to the hearer, it is judicial, deliberative, or descriptive; as regards the opponent, the division is fourfold—according as the fact, its nature, its quality, or its propriety is called in question. The art of the speaker is directed to five points: the discovery of persuasives (whether ethical, pathetical, or argumentative), arrangement, diction, memory, delivery. And the speech itself consists of six parts: introduction, statement of the case, division of the subject, proof, refutation, and conclusion.

His treatises *De Inventione* and *Topica*, the first and nearly the last of his compositions, are both on the invention of arguments, which he regards, with Aristotle, as the very foundation of the art; though he elsewhere confines the term eloquence, according to its derivation, to denote excellence of diction and delivery, to the exclusion of argumentative skill.[1] The former of these works was written at the age of twenty, and seems originally to have consisted of four books, of which but two remain.[2] In the first of these he considers rhetorical invention generally, supplies commonplaces for the six parts of an oration promiscuously, and gives a full analysis of the two forms of argument, syllogism and induction. In the second book he applies these rules particularly to the three subject-matters of rhetoric, the deliberative, the judicial, and the descriptive, dwelling principally on the judicial, as affording the most ample field for discussion. This treatise seems for the most part compiled from the writings of Aristotle, Isocrates, and Hermagoras;[3] and as such he alludes to it in the opening of his *De Oratore* as deficient in the experience and judgment which

---

[1] Orat. 19.
[2] Vossius, de Nat. Rhet. c. xiii.; Fabricius, Bibliothec. Latin.
[3] De Invent. i. 5, 6; de clar. Orat. 76.

nothing but time and practice can impart. Still it is an entertaining, nay, useful work; remarkable, even among Cicero's writings, for its uniform good sense, and less familiar to the scholar only because the greater part has been superseded by the compositions of his riper years.

His *Topica*, or treatise on commonplaces, has less extent and variety of plan, being little else than a compendium of Aristotle's work on the same subject. It was, as he informs us in its proem, drawn up from memory on his voyage from Italy to Greece, soon after Cæsar's murder, and in compliance with the wishes of Trebatius, who had some time before urged him to undertake the translation.[1]

Cicero seems to have intended his *De Oratore*, *De claris Oratoribus*, and *Orator*, to form one complete system.[2] Of these three noble works the first lays down the principles and rules of the rhetorical art; the second exemplifies them in the most eminent speakers of Greece and Rome; and the third shadows out the features of that perfect orator, whose superhuman excellences should be the aim of our ambition. The *De Oratore* was written when the author was fifty-two, two years after his return from exile; and is a dialogue between some of the most illustrious Romans of the preceding age on the subject of oratory. The principal speakers are the orators Crassus and Antonius, who are represented unfolding the principles of their art to Sulpicius and Cotta, young men just rising in the legal profession. In the first book, the conversation turns on the subject-matter of rhetoric, and the qualifications requisite for the perfect orator. Here Crassus maintains the necessity of his being acquainted with the whole circle of the arts, while Antonius confines eloquence to the province of speaking well. The dispute

[1] Ad Fam. vii. 19.   [2] De Div. ii. 1.

for the most part seems verbal; for Cicero himself, though he here sides with Crassus, yet elsewhere, as we have above noticed, pronounces eloquence, strictly speaking, to consist in beauty of diction. Scævola, the celebrated lawyer, takes part in this preliminary discussion; but, in the ensuing meetings, makes way for Catulus and Cæsar, the subject leading to such technical disquisitions as were hardly suitable to the dignity of the aged Augur.[1] The next morning Antonius enters upon the subject of invention, which Cæsar completes by subjoining some remarks on the use of humour in oratory; and Antonius, relieving him, finishes the morning discussion with treating of arrangement and memory. In the afternoon the rules for propriety and elegance of diction are explained by Crassus, who was celebrated in this department of the art; and the work concludes with his handling the subject of delivery and action. Such is the plan of the *De Oratore*, the most finished perhaps of Cicero's compositions. An air of grandeur and magnificence reigns throughout. The characters of the aged senators are finely conceived, and the whole company is invested with an almost religious majesty, from the allusions interspersed to the melancholy destinies for which its members were reserved.

His treatise *De claris Oratoribus* was written after an interval of nine years, about the time of Cato's death, when he was sixty-one, and is thrown into the shape of a dialogue between Brutus, Atticus, and himself. He begins with Solon, and after briefly mentioning the orators of Greece, proceeds to those of his own country, so as to take in the whole period from the time of Junius Brutus down to himself. About the same time he wrote his *Orator;* in which he directs his attention principally to diction

[1] Ad Atticum, iv. 16.

and delivery, as in his *De Inventione* and *Topica* he considers the matter of an oration[1] This treatise is of a less practical nature than the rest.[2] It adopts the principles of Plato, and delineates the perfect orator according to the abstract conceptions of the intellect rather than the deductions of observation and experience. Hence he sets out with a definition of the perfectly eloquent man, whose characteristic it is to express himself with propriety on all subjects, whether humble, great, or of an intermediate character;[3] and here he has an opportunity of paying some indirect compliments to himself. With this work he was so well satisfied that he does not scruple to declare, in a letter to a friend, that he was ready to rest on its merits his reputation for judgment in Oratory.[4]

The treatise *De partitione Oratoriâ*, or on the three parts of rhetoric, is a kind of catechism between Cicero and his son, drawn up for the use of the latter at the same time with the two preceding. It is the most systematic and perspicuous of his rhetorical works, but seems to be but the rough draught of what he originally intended.[5]

10.

The connection which we have been able to preserve between the rhetorical writings of Cicero cannot be attained in his moral, political, and metaphysical treatises; partly from the extent of the subject, partly from the losses occasioned by time, partly from the inconsistency which we have warned the reader to expect in his sentiments. In our enumeration, therefore, we shall observe no other order than that which the date of their composition furnishes.

---

[1] Orat. 16. [2] Orat. 14, 31. [3] Orat. 21, 29.
[4] Ad Fam. vi. 18. [5] See Middleton, vol. ii. p. 147.

The earliest now extant is part of his treatise *De Legibus*, in three books; being a sequel to his work on Politics. Both were written in imitation of Plato's treatises on the same subjects.[1] The latter of these (*De Republicâ*) was composed a year after the *De Oratore*,[2] and seems to have vied with it in the majesty and interest of the dialogue. It consisted of a series of discussions in six books on the origin and principles of government, Scipio being the principal speaker, but Lælius, Philus, Manilius, and other personages of like gravity taking part in the conversation. Till lately, but a fragment of the fifth book was understood to be in existence, in which Scipio, under the fiction of a dream, inculcates the doctrine of the immortality of the soul. But in the year 1822, Monsignor Mai, librarian of the Vatican, published considerable portions of the first and second books, from a palimpsest manuscript of St. Austin's *Commentary on the Psalms*. In the part now recovered, Scipio discourses on the different kinds of constitutions and their respective advantages; with a particular reference to that of Rome. In the third book, the subject of justice was discussed by Lælius and Philus; in the fourth, Scipio treated of morals and education; while in the fifth and sixth, the duties of a magistrate were explained, and the best means of preventing changes and revolutions in the constitution itself. In the latter part of the treatise, allusion was made to the actual posture of affairs in Rome, when the conversation was supposed to have occurred, and the commotions excited by the Gracchi.

In his treatise *De Legibus*, which was written two years later than the *De Republicâ*, when he was fifty-five, and

---

[1] De Legg. i. 5.
[2] Ang. Mai. præf. in Remp. Middleton, vol. i. p. 486.

shortly after the murder of Clodius, he represents himself as explaining to his brother Quintus and Atticus, in their walks through the woods of Arpinum, the nature and origin of the laws and their actual state, both in other countries and in Rome. The first part only of the subject is contained in the books now extant; the introduction to which we have had occasion to notice, when speaking of his Stoical sentiments on questions connected with State policy. Law he pronounces to be the perfection of reason, the eternal mind, the divine energy, which, while it pervades and unites in one the whole universe, associates gods and men by the more intimate resemblance of reason and virtue, and still more closely men with men, by the participation of common faculties, affections, and situations. He then proves, at length, that justice is not merely created by civil institutions, from the power of conscience, the imperfections of human law, the moral sense, and the disinterestedness of virtue. He next proceeds to unfold the principles, first, of religious law, under the heads of divine worship; the observance of festivals and games; the office of priests, augurs, and heralds; the punishment of sacrilege and purjury; the consecration of land, and the rights of sepulchre; and, secondly, of civil law, which gives him an opportunity of noticing the respective duties of magistrates and citizens. In these discussions, though professedly speaking of the abstract question, he does not hesitate to anticipate the subject of the lost books, by frequent allusions to the history and customs of his own country. It must be added, that in no part of his writings do worse instances occur, than in this treatise, of that vanity which was notoriously his weakness, which are rendered doubly offensive by their being put into the mouth of his brother and Atticus.[1]

[1] Quinct. Inst. xi. 1.

Here a period of seven or eight years intervenes, during which he composed little of importance besides his Orations. He then published the *De claris Oratoribus* and *Orator;* and a year later, when he was sixty-three, his *Academicæ Quæstiones*, in the retirement from public business to which he was driven by the dictatorship of Cæsar. This work had originally consisted of two dialogues, which he entitled *Catulus* and *Lucullus*, from the names of the respective speakers in each. These he now remodelled and enlarged into four books, dedicating them to Varro, whom he introduced as advocating, in the presence of Atticus, the tenets of Antiochus, while he himself defended those of Philo. Of this most valuable composition, only the second book (*Lucullus*) of the first edition and part of the first book of the second are now extant. In the former of those two, Lucullus argues against, and Cicero for, the Academic sect, in the presence of Catulus and Hortensius; in the latter, Varro pursues the history of philosophy from Socrates to Arcesilas, and Cicero continues it down to the time of Carneades. In the second edition the style was corrected, the matter condensed, and the whole polished with extraordinary care and diligence.[1]

The same year he published his treatise *De Finibus*, or "On the chief good," in five books, in which are explained the sentiments of the Epicureans, Stoics, and Peripatetics on the subject. This is the earliest of his works in which the dialogue is of a disputatious character. It is opened with a defence of the Epicurean tenets, concerning pleasure, by Torquatus; to which Cicero replies at length. The scene then shifts from the Cuman villa to the library of young Lucullus (his father being dead), where the Stoic Cato expatiates on the sublimity of the system

[1] Ad Atticum, xiii. 13, 16, 19.

which maintains the existence of one only good, and is answered by Cicero in the character of a Peripatetic. Lastly, Piso, in a conversation held at Athens, enters into an explanation of the doctrine of Aristotle, that happiness is the greatest good. The general style of this treatise is elegant and perspicuous; and the last book in particular has great variety and splendour of diction.

It was about this time that Cicero was especially courted by the heads of the dictator's party, of whom Hirtius and Dolabella went so far as to declaim daily at his house for the benefit of his instructions.[1] A visit of this nature to the Tusculan villa, soon after the publication of the *De Finibus*, gave rise to his work entitled *Tusculanæ Quæstiones*, which professes to be the substance of five philosophical disputes between himself and friends, digested into as many books. He argues throughout after the manner of an Academic, even with an affectation of inconsistency; sometimes making use of the Socratic dialogue, sometimes launching out into the diffuse expositions which characterise his other treatises.[2] He first disputes against the fear of death; and in so doing he adopts the opinion of the Platonic school, as regards the nature of God and the soul. The succeeding discussions on enduring pain, on alleviating grief, on the other emotions of the mind, and on virtue, are conducted for the most part on Stoical principles.[3] This is a highly ornamental composition, and contains more quotations from the poets than any other of Cicero's treatises.

We have already had occasion to remark upon the singular activity of his mind, which becomes more and more conspicuous as we approach the period of his death. During the ensuing year, which is the last of his life, in

---

[1] Ad Fam. ix. 16, 18. [2] Tusc. Quæst. v. 4, 11.
[3] Ibid. iii. 10, v. 27.

the midst of the confusion and anxieties consequent on Cæsar's death, and the party warfare of his Philippics, he found time to write the *De Naturâ Deorum, De Divinatione, De Fato, De Senectute, De Amicitiâ, De Officiis,* and *Paradoxa*, besides the treatise on Rhetorical Common Places above mentioned.

Of these, the first three were intended as a full exposition of the conflicting opinions entertained on their respective subjects; the *De Fato*, however, was not finished according to this plan.¹ His treatise *De Naturâ Deorum*, in three books, may be reckoned the most splendid of all his works, and shows that neither age nor disappointment had done injury to the richness and vigour of his mind. In the first book, Velleius, the Epicurean, sets forth the physical tenets of his sect, and is answered by Cotta, who is of the Academic school. In the second, Balbus, the disciple of the Porch, gives an account of his own system, and is, in turn, refuted by Cotta in the third. The eloquent extravagance of the Epicurean, the solemn enthusiasm of the Stoic, and the brilliant raillery of the Academic, are contrasted with extreme vivacity and humour;—while the sublimity of the subject itself imparts to the whole composition a grander and more elevated character, and discovers in the author imaginative powers, which, celebrated as he justly is for playfulness of fancy, might yet appear more the talent of the poet than the orator.

His treatise *De Divinatione* is conveyed in a discussion between his brother Quintus and himself, in two books. In the former, Quintus, after dividing Divination into the heads of natural and artificial, argues with the Stoics for its sacred nature, from the evidence of facts, the agreement of all nations, and the existence of divine

---
¹De Nat. Deor. i. 6; de Div. i. 4; de Fat. 1.

intelligences. In the latter, Cicero questions its authority, with Carneades, from the uncertain nature of its rules, the absurdity and uselessness of the art, and the possibility of accounting from natural causes for the phenomena on which it was founded. This is a curious work, from the numerous cases adduced from the histories of Greece and Rome to illustrate the subject in dispute.

His treatise *De Fato* is quite a fragment; it purports to be the substance of a dissertation in which he explained to Hirtius (soon after Consul) the sentiments of Chrysippus, Diodorus, Epicurus, Carneades, and others, upon that abstruse subject. It is supposed to have consisted at least of two books, of which we have but the proem of the first, and a small portion of the second.

In his beautiful compositions, *De Senectute* and *De Amicitiâ*, Cato the censor and Lælius are respectively introduced, delivering their sentiments on those subjects. The conclusion of the former, in which Cato discourses on the immortality of the soul, has been always celebrated; and the opening of the latter, in which Fannius and Scævola come to console Lælius on the death of Scipio, is as exquisite an instance of delicacy and taste in composition as can be found in his works. In the latter he has borrowed largely from the eighth and ninth books of Aristotle's *Ethics*.

His treatise *De Officiis* was finished about the time he wrote his second Philippic, a circumstance which illustrates the great versatility of his mental powers. Of a work so extensively celebrated, it is enough to have mentioned the name. Here he lays aside the less authoritative form of dialogue, and, with the dignity of the Roman Consul, unfolds, in his own person, the principles of morals, according to the views of the older schools, particularly of the Stoics. It is written in three books, with great perspicuity and elegance of style; the first book treats of the *honestum*, or *virtue*, the second of the *utile*, or *expedience*, and the third adjusts the claims of the two, when they happen to interfere with each other.

His *Paradoxa Stoicorum* might have been more suitably, perhaps, included in his rhetorical works, being six short declamations in support of the positions of Zeno; in which that philosopher's subtleties are adapted to the comprehension of the vulgar, and the events of the times. The second, fourth, and sixth, are respectively directed against Antony, Clodius, and Crassus. They seem to have suffered from time.[1] The sixth is the most eloquent, but the argument of the third is strikingly maintained.

Besides the works now enumerated, we have a considerable fragment of his translation of Plato's *Timæus*, which he seems to have finished in his last year. His remaining philosophical works, viz.: the *Hortensius*, which was a defence of philosophy; *De Gloriâ; De Consolatione*, written upon Platonic principles on his daughter's death; *De Jure Civili, De Virtutibus, De Auguriis, Chorographia*, translations of Plato's *Protagoras*, and Xenophon's *Œconomics*, works on Natural History, Panegyric on Cato, and some miscellaneous writings, are, except a few fragments, entirely lost.

His Letters, about one thousand in all, are comprised in thirty-six books, sixteen of which are addressed to Atticus, three to his brother Quintus, one to Brutus, and sixteen to his different friends; and they form a history of his life from his fortieth year. Among those addressed to his friends, some occur from Brutus, Metellus, Plancius, Cælius, and others. For the preservation of

[1] Sciopp. in Olivet.

this most valuable department of Cicero's writings, we are indebted to Tyro, the author's freedman, though we possess, at the present day, but a part of those originally published. As his correspondence with his friends belongs to his character as a man and politician, rather than to his literary aspect, we have already noticed it in the first part of this memoir.

His Poetical and Historical works have suffered a heavier fate. The latter class, consisting of his commentary on his consulship and his history of his own times, is altogether lost. Of the former, which consisted of the heroic poems *Halcyone, Limon, Marius*, and his Consulate, the elegy of *Tamelastes*, translations of Homer and Aratus, epigrams, etc., nothing remains, except some fragments of the *Phænomena* and *Diosemeia* of Aratus. It may, however, be questioned whether literature has suffered much by these losses. We are far, indeed, from speaking contemptuously of the poetical talent of one who possessed so much fancy, so much taste, and so fine an ear.[1] But his poems were principally composed in his youth; and afterwards, when his powers were more mature, his occupations did not allow even to his active mind the time necessary for polishing a language still more rugged in metre than it was in prose. His contemporary history, on the other hand, can hardly have conveyed more explicit, and certainly would have contained less faithful, information than his private correspondence; while, with all the penetration he assuredly possessed, it may be doubted if his diffuse and graceful style was adapted for the deep and condensed thoughts and the grasp of facts and events which are the chief excellences of historical composition.

[1] See Plutarch, in Vitâ.

11.

The Orations which he is known to have composed amount in all to about eighty, of which fifty-nine, either entire or in part, are preserved. Of these some are deliberative, others judicial, others descriptive; some delivered from the rostrum, or in the senate; others in the forum, or before Cæsar; and, as might be anticipated from the character already given of his talents, he is much more successful in pleading or in panegyric than in debate or invective. In deliberative oratory, indeed, great part of the effect of the composition depends on its creating in the hearer a high opinion of the speaker; and, though Cicero takes considerable pains to interest the audience in his favour, yet his style is not simple and grave enough, he is too ingenious, too declamatory, discovers too much personal feeling, to elicit that confidence in him, without which argument has little influence. His invectives, again, however grand and imposing, yet, compared with his calmer and more familiar productions, have a forced and unnatural air. Splendid as is the eloquence of his Catilinarians and Philippics, it is often the language of abuse rather than of indignation; and even his attack on Piso, the most brilliant and imaginative of its kind, becomes wearisome from want of ease and relief. His laudatory orations, on the other hand, are among his happiest efforts. Nothing can exceed the taste and beauty of those for the Manilian law, for Marcellus, for Ligarius, for Archias, and the ninth Philippic, which is principally in praise of Servius Sulpicius. But it is in judicial eloquence, particularly on subjects of a lively cast, as in his speeches for Cælius and Muræna, and against Cæcilius, that his talents are displayed to the best advantage. In both these departments of oratory the grace and amiableness of his genius are manifested in their full lustre, though none of his orations are without tokens of those characteristic excellences. Historical allusions, philosophical sentiments, descriptions full of life and nature, and polite raillery, succeed each other in the most agreeable manner, without appearance of artifice or effort. Such are his pictures of the confusion of the Catilinarian conspirators on detection;[1] of the death of Metellus;[2] of Sulpicius undertaking the embassy to Antony;[3] the character he draws of Catiline;[4] and his fine sketch of old Appius, frowning on his degenerate descendant Clodia.[5]

These, however, are but incidental and occasional artifices to divert and refresh the mind, since his Orations are generally laid out according to the plan proposed in rhetorical works; the introduction, containing the ethical proof; the body of the speech, the argument, and the peroration addressing itself to the passions of the judges. In opening his case, he commonly makes a profession of timidity and diffidence, with a view to conciliate the favour of his audience; the eloquence, for instance, of Hortensius, is so powerful,[6] or so much prejudice has been excited against his client,[7] or it is his first appearance in the rostrum,[8] or he is unused to speak in an armed assembly,[9] or to plead in a private apartment.[10] He proceeds to entreat the patience of his judges; drops out some generous or popular sentiment, or contrives to excite prejudice against his opponent. He then states the circumstances of his case, and the intended plan of his oration; and here he is particularly clear. But it is

---

[1] In Catil. iii. 3-5.
[2] Pro Cæl. 24.
[3] Philipp. ix. 3.
[4] Pro Cæl. 6.
[5] Ibid. 14.
[6] Pro Quinct. 1, and In Verr. Act i. 13.
[7] Pro Cluent. 1.
[8] Pro Leg. Manil. 1.
[9] Pro Milon. 1.
[10] Pro Deiotar. 2.

when he comes actually to prove his point that his oratorical powers begin to have their full play. He accounts for everything so naturally, makes trivial circumstances tell so happily, so adroitly converts apparent objections into confirmations of his argument, connects independent facts with such ease and plausibility, that it becomes impossible to entertain a question on the truth of his statement. This is particularly observable in his defence of Cluentius, where prejudices, suspicions, and difficulties are encountered with the most triumphant ingenuity; in the antecedent probabilities of his *Pro Milone*;[1] in his apology for Muræna's public,[2] and Cælius's private life,[3] and his disparagement of Verres's military services in Sicily;[4] it is observable too in the address with which the Agrarian law of Rullus,[5] and the accusation of Rabirius,[6] both popular measures, are represented to be hostile to public liberty; with which Milo's impolitic unconcern is made a touching incident;[7] and Cato's attack upon the crowd of clients which accompanied the candidate for office, a tyrannical disregard for the feelings of the poor.[8] So great indeed is his talent, that he even hurts a good cause by an excess of plausibility.

But it is not enough to have barely proved his point; he proceeds, either immediately, or towards the conclusion of his speech, to heighten the effect by amplification.[9] Here he goes (as it were) round and round his object; surveys it in every light; examines it in all its parts; retires, and then advances; turns and re-turns it; compares and contrasts it; illustrates, confirms, enforces

---

[1] Pro Milon. 14, etc. [2] Pro Muræn. 9. [3] Pro Cæl. 7, etc.
[4] In Verr. vi. 2, etc. [5] Contra Rull. ii. 6, 7.
[6] Pro Rabir. 4. [7] Pro Milon. *init. et alibi.*
[8] Pro Muræn. 34. [9] De Orat. partit. 8, 16, 17.

his view of the question, till at last the hearer feels ashamed of doubting a position which seems built on a foundation so strictly argumentative. Of this nature is his justification of Rabirius in taking up arms against Saturninus;[1] his account of the imprisonment of the Roman citizens by Verres, and of the crucifixion of Gavius;[2] his comparison of Antony with Tarquin;[3] and the contrast he draws of Verres with Fabius, Scipio, and Marius.[4]

And now, having established his case, he opens upon his opponent a discharge of raillery, so delicate and good-natured, that it is impossible for the latter to maintain his ground against it. Or where the subject is too grave to admit this, he colours his exaggeration with all the bitterness of irony or vehemence of passion. Such are his frequent delineations of Gabinius, Piso, Clodius, and Antony;[5] particularly his vivid and almost humorous contrast of the two consuls, who sanctioned his banishment, in his oration for Sextius.[6] Such the celebrated account (already referred to) of the crucifixion of Gavius by Verres, which it is difficult to read, even at the present day, without having our feelings roused against the merciless Prætor. But the appeal to the gentler emotions of the soul is reserved (perhaps with somewhat of sameness) for the close of his oration; as in his defence of Cluentius, Muræna, Cælius, Milo, Sylla, Flaccus, and Rabirius Postumus; the most striking instances of which are the poetical burst of feeling with which he addresses his client Plancius,[7] and his picture of the desolate condition of

[1] Pro Rabir. 8.   [2] In Verr. v. 56, etc., and 64, etc.
[3] Philipp. iii. 4.   [4] In Verr. vi. 10.
[5] Post Redit. in Senat. i. 4—8; pro Dom. 9, 39, etc.; in Pis. 10, 11. Philipp. ii. 18, etc.
[6] Pro Sext. 8—10.   [7] Pro Planc. 41, 42

the Vestal Fonteia, should her brother be condemned.[1] At other times, his peroration contains more heroic and elevated sentiments; as in his invocation of the Alban groves and altars in the peroration of the *Pro Milone*, the panegyric on patriotism, and the love of glory in his defence of Sextius, and that on liberty at the close of the third and tenth Philippics.[2]

12.

But it is by the invention of a style, which adapts itself with singular felicity to every class of subjects, whether lofty or familiar, philosophical or forensic, that Cicero answers even more exactly to his own definition of a perfect orator[3] than by his plausibility, pathos, and brilliancy. It is not, however, here intended to enter upon the consideration of a subject so ample and so familiar to all scholars as Cicero's diction, much less to take an extended view of it through the range of his philosophical writings and familiar correspondence. Among many excellences, the greatest is its suitableness to the genius of the Latin language; though the diffuseness thence necessarily resulting has exposed it, both in his own days and since his time, to the criticisms of those who have affected to condemn its Asiatic character, in comparison with the simplicity of Attic writers, and the strength of Demosthenes.[4] Greek, however, is celebrated for its copiousness in vocabulary, for its perspicuity, and its reproductive power; and its consequent facility of expressing the most novel or abstruse ideas with precision and elegance. Hence the Attic style of

---

[1] Pro Fonteio, 17.

[2] Vid. his ideal description of an orator, in Orat. 40. Vid. also de clar. Orat. 93, his negative panegyric on his own oratorical attainments.

[3] Orat. 29.

[4] Tusc. Quæst. i. 1; de clar. Orat. 82, etc., de opt. gen. dicendi.

eloquence was plain and simple, because simplicity and plainness were not incompatible with clearness, energy, and harmony. But it was a singular want of judgment, an ignorance of the very principles of composition, which induced Brutus, Calvus, Sallust, and others to imitate this terse and severe beauty in their own defective language, and even to pronounce the opposite kind of diction deficient in taste and purity. In Greek, indeed, the words fall, as it were, naturally, into a distinct and harmonious order; and, from the exuberant richness of the materials, less is left to the ingenuity of the artist. But the Latin language is comparatively weak, scanty, and unmusical; and requires considerable skill and management to render it expressive and graceful. Simplicity in Latin is scarcely separable from baldness; and justly as Terence is celebrated for chaste and unadorned diction, yet, even he, compared with Attic writers, is flat and heavy.[1] Again, the perfection of strength is clearness united to brevity; but to this combination Latin is utterly unequal. From the vagueness and uncertainty of meaning which characterises its separate words, to be perspicuous it must be full. What Livy, and much more Tacitus, have gained in energy, they have lost in lucidity and elegance; the correspondence of Brutus with Cicero is forcible, indeed, but harsh and abrupt. Latin, in short, is not a philosophical language, not a language in which a deep thinker is likely to express himself with purity or neatness. Cicero found it barren and dissonant, and as such he had to deal with it. His good sense enabled him to perceive what could be done, and what it was in vain to attempt; and happily his talents answered precisely to the purpose required. He may be compared to a clever landscape-gardener, who gives

---

[1] Quinct. x. l.

depth and richness to narrow and confined premises by ingenuity and skill in the disposition of his trees and walks. Terence and Lucretius had cultivated simplicity; Cotta, Brutus, and Calvus had attempted strength; but Cicero rather made a language than a style; yet not so much by the invention as by the combination of words. Some terms, indeed, his philosophical subjects obliged him to coin;[1] but his great art lies in the application of existing materials, in converting the very disadvantages of the language into beauties,[2] in enriching it with circumlocutions and metaphors, in pruning it of harsh and uncouth expressions, in systematizing the structure of a sentence.[3] This is that *copia dicendi* which gained Cicero the high testimony of Cæsar to his inventive powers,[4] and which, we may add, constitutes him the greatest master of composition that the world has seen.

13.

Such, then, are the principal characteristics of Cicero's oratory; on a review of which we may, with some reason, conclude that Roman eloquence stands scarcely less indebted to his works than Roman philosophy. For, though in his *De claris Oratoribus* he begins his review from the age of Junius Brutus, yet, soberly speaking (and as he seems to allow in the opening of

---

[1] De Fin. iii. 1 and 4; Lucull. 6. Plutarch, in Vitâ.

[2] This, which is analogous to his address in pleading, is nowhere more observable than in his rendering the recurrence of the same word, to which he is forced by the barrenness or vagueness of the language, an elegance.

[3] It is remarkable that some authors attempted to account for the *invention* of the Asiatic style, on the same principle we have here adduced to account for Cicero's *adoption* of it in Latin; viz. that the Asiatics had a defective knowledge of Greek, and devised phrases, etc., to make up for the imperfection of their scanty vocubulary. See Quinct. xii. 10.

[4] De clar. Orat. 72.

the *De Oratore*), we cannot assign an earlier date to the rise of eloquence among his countrymen, than that of the same Athenian embassy which introduced the study of philosophy. To aim, indeed, at persuasion, by appeals to the reason or passions, is so natural, that no country, whether refined or barbarous, is without its orators. If, however, eloquence be the mere power of persuading, it is but a relative term, limited to time and place, connected with a particular audience, and leaving to posterity no test of its merits but the report of those whom it has been successful in influencing; but we are speaking of it as the subject-matter of an art.[1]

The eloquence of Carneades and his associates had made (to use a familiar term) a great sensation among the Roman orators, who soon split into two parties,—the one adhering to the rough unpolished manners of their forefathers, the other favouring the artificial graces which distinguished the Grecian rhetoricians. In the former class were Cato and Lælius,[2] both men of cultivated minds, particularly Cato, whose opposition to Greek literature was founded solely on political considerations. But, as might· have been expected, the Athenian cause had prevailed; and Carbo and the two Gracchi, who are the principal orators of the next generation, are praised as masters of an oratory learned, majestic, and harmonious in its character.[3] These were succeeded by Antonius, Crassus, Cotta, Sulpicius, and Hortensius; who, adopting greater liveliness and variety of manner, form a middle age in the history of Roman eloquence. But it was in

[1] "Vulgus interdum," says Cicero, "non probandum oratorem probat, sed probat sine comparatione, cùm à mediocri aut etiam à malo delectatur; eo est contentus: esse melius sentit: illud quod est, qualecunque est, probat."—De clar. Orat. 52.
[2] De clar. Orat. 72. Quinct. xii. 10.
[3] De clar. Orat. 25, 27; pro Harusp. resp. 19.

that which immediately followed that the art was adorned by an assemblage of orators, which even Greece will find it difficult to match. Of these Cæsar, Cicero, Curio, Brutus, Cælius, Calvus, and Callidius, are the most celebrated. The talents, indeed, of Cæsar were not more conspicuous in arms than in his style, which was noted for its force and purity.[1] Cælius, whom Cicero brought forward into public life, excelled in natural quickness, loftiness of sentiment, and politeness in attack;[2] Brutus in philosophical gravity, though he sometimes indulged himself in a warmer and bolder style.[3] Callidius was delicate and harmonious; Curio bold and flowing; Calvus, from studied opposition to Cicero's peculiarities, cold, cautious, and accurate.[4] Brutus and Calvus have been before noticed as the advocates of the dry sententious mode of speaking, which they dignified by the name of Attic; a kind of eloquence which seems to have been popular from the comparative facility with which it was attained.

In the Ciceronian age the general character of the oratory was dignified and graceful. The popular nature of the government gave opportunities for effective appeals to the passions; and, Greek literature being as yet a novelty, philosophical sentiments were introduced with corresponding success. The republican orators were long in their introductions, diffuse in their statements, ample in their divisions, frequent in their digressions, gradual and sedate in their perorations.[5] Under the Emperors, however, the people were less consulted in state affairs; and the judges, instead of possessing an

[1] Quinct. x. 1 and 2. De clar. Orat. 75.
[2] Ibid.
[3] Ibid. and ad Atticum, xiv. l.
[4] Ibid.
[5] Dialog. de Orat. 20 apud Tacit. and 22. Quinct. x. 2.

almost independent authority, being but delegates of the executive, from interested politicians became men of business; literature, too, was now familiar to all classes; and taste began sensibly to decline. The national appetite felt a craving for stronger and more stimulating compositions. Impatience was manifested at the tedious majesty and formal graces, the parade of arguments, grave sayings, and shreds of philosophy,[1] which characterized their fathers; and a smarter and more sparkling kind of oratory succeeded,[2] just as in our own country the minuet of the last century has been supplanted by the quadrille, and the stately movements of Giardini have given way to Rossini's brisker and more artificial melodies. Corvinus, even before the time of Augustus, had shown himself more elaborate and fastidious in his choice of expressions.[3] Cassius Severus, the first who openly deviated from the old style of oratory, introduced an acrimonious and virulent mode of pleading.[4] It now became the fashion to decry Cicero as inflated, languid, tame, and even deficient in ornament;[5] Mecænas and Gallio followed in the career of degeneracy; till flippancy of attack, prettiness of expression, and glitter of decoration prevailed over the bold and manly eloquence of free Rome.

[1] "It is not uncommon for those who have grown wise by the labour of others, to add a little of their own, and overlook their master."—*Johnson*. We have before compared Cicero to Addison as regards the purpose of sinpiring their respective countrymen with literary taste. They resembled each other in the return they experienced.
[2] Dialog. 18.   [3] Ibid.   [4] Dialog. 19.
[5] Dialog. 18 and 22. Quinct. xii. 10.

III.
APPOLLONIUS OF TYANA.
(From the ENCYCLOPÆDIA METROPOLITANA *of* 1824.)

APOLLONIUS OF TYANA.

                                                              PAGE

INTRODUCTION.—HIS LIFE WRITTEN BY PHILOSTRATUS, INDIRECTLY AGAINST CHRISTIANITY - - - - - - - - 305

1. HIS BIRTH, EDUCATION, PYTHAGOREAN TRAINING, AND TRAVELS 306

2. HIS POLITICAL ASPECT - - - - - - - - 309

3. HIS REPUTATION - - - - - - - - - 316

4. HIS PROFESSION OF MIRACLES - - - - - - - 319

5. NOT BORNE OUT BY THE INTERNAL CHARACTER OF THE ACTS THEMSELVES - - - - - - - - - 323

6. NOR BY THEIR DRIFT - - - - - - - - 326

7. BUT AN IMITATION OF SCRIPTURE MIRACLES - - - - 328

APOLLONIUS OF TYANA.

APOLLONIUS, the Pythagorean philosopher, was born at Tyana, in Cappadocia, in the year of Rome 750, four years before the common Christian era.[1] His reputation rests, not so much on his personal merits, as on the attempt made in the early ages of the Church, and since revived,[2] to bring him forward as a rival to the Divine Author of our Religion. A narrative of his life, which is still extant, was written with this object, about a century after his death (A.D. 217), by Philostratus of Lemnos, when Ammonius was systematizing the Eclectic tenets to meet the increasing influence and the spread of Christianity. Philostratus engaged in this work at the instance of his patroness Julia Domna, wife of the Emperor Severus, a princess celebrated for her zeal in the cause of Heathen Philosophy; who put into his hands a journal of the travels of Apollonius rudely written by one Damis, an Assyrian, his companion.[3] This manuscript, an account of his residence at Ægæ, prior to his acquaintance with Damis, by Maximus of that city, a collection of his letters, some private memoranda relative to his opinions and conduct, and lastly the public records of the cities he frequented, were the principal documents from which Philostratus compiled his elaborate narra-

---

[1] Olear. ad Philostr. i. 12.   [2] By Lord Herbert and Mr. Blount.   [3] Philostr. i. 3.

tive.[1] It is written with considerable elegance and command of Greek, but with more attention to ornament than is consistent with correct taste. Though it is not a professed imitation of the Gospels, it contains quite enough to show that it was written with a view of rivalling the sacred narrative; and accordingly, in the following age, it was made use of in a direct attack upon Christianity by Hierocles,[2] Prefect of Bithynia, a disciple of the Eclectic School, to whom a reply was made by Eusebius of Cæsarea. The selection of a Pythagorean Philosopher for the purpose of a comparison with our Lord was judicious. The attachment of the Pythagorean Sect to the discipline of the established religion, which most other philosophies neglected, its austerity, its pretended intercourse with heaven, its profession of extraordinary power over nature, and the authoritative tone of teaching which this profession countenanced,[3] were all in favour of the proposed object. But with the plans of the Eclectics in their attack upon Christianity we have no immediate concern.

I.

Philostratus begins his work with an account of the prodigies attending the philosopher's birth, which, with all circumstances of a like nature, we shall for the present pass over, intending to make some observations on them in the sequel. At the age of fourteen he was placed by his father under the care of Euthydemus, a distinguished rhetorician of Tarsus; but, being dis-

---

[1] Philostr. i. 2, 3.
[2] His work was called Λόγοι Φιλαλήθεις πρὸς Χριστιανούς· on this subject see Mosheim, *Dissertat. de turbatâ per recentiores Platonicos Ecclesiâ*, Sec. 25.
[3] Philostr. i. 17, vi. 11.

pleased with the dissipation of the place, he removed with his master to Ægæ, a neighbouring town, frequented as a retreat for students in philosophy.[1] Here he made himself master of the Platonic, Stoic, Epicurean, and Peripatetic systems; giving, however, an exclusive preference to the Pythagorean, which he studied with Euxenus of Heraclea, a man, however, whose life ill accorded with the ascetic principles of his Sect. At the early age of sixteen years, according to his biographer, he resolved on strictly conforming himself to the precepts of Pythagoras, and, if possible, rivalling the fame of his master. He renounced animal food and wine; restricted himself to the use of linen garments and sandals made of the bark of trees; suffered his hair to grow; and betook himself to the temple of Æsculapius, who is said to have regarded him with peculiar favour.[2]

On the news of his father's death, which took place not long afterwards, he left Ægæ for his native place, where he gave up half his inheritance to his elder brother, whom he is said to have reclaimed from a dissolute course of life, and the greater part of the remainder to his poorer relatives.[3]

Prior to composing any philosophical work, he thought it necessary to observe the silence of five years, which was the appointed initiation into the esoteric doctrines of his Sect. During this time he exercised his mind in storing up materials for future reflection. We are told that on several occasions he hindered insurrections in the cities in which he resided by the mute eloquence of his look and gestures;[4] but such an achievement is hardly consistent with the Pythagorean rule, which

[1] Philostr. i. 7.   [2] Ibid. i. 8.
[3] Ibid. i. 13.   [4] Ibid. i. 14, 15.

forbad its disciples during their silence the intercourse of mixed society.[1]

The period of silence being expired, Apollonius passed through the principal cities of Asia Minor, disputing in the temples in imitation of Pythagoras, unfolding the mysteries of his Sect to such as were observing their probationary silence, discoursing with the Greek Priests about divine rites, and reforming the worship of barbarian cities.[2] This must have been his employment for many years; the next incident in his life being his Eastern journey, which was not undertaken till he was between forty and fifty years of age.[3]

His object in this expedition was to consult the Magi and Brachmans on philosophical matters; still following the example of Pythagoras, who is said to have travelled as far as India with the same purpose. At Nineveh, where he arrived with two companions, he was joined by Damis, already mentioned as his journalist.[4] Proceeding thence to Babylon, he had some interviews with the Magi, who rather disappointed his expectations; and was well received by Bardanes the Parthian King, who, after detaining him at his Court for the greater part of two years, dismissed him with marks of peculiar

---

[1] Brucker, vol. ii. p. 104. [2] Philostr. i. 16.

[3] See Olear. *præfat. ad vitam*. As he died, U.C. 849, he is usually considered to have lived to a hundred. Since, however, here is an interval of almost twenty years in which nothing important happens, in a part also of his life unconnected with any public events to fix its chronology, it is highly probable that the date of his birth is put too early. Philostratus says that accounts varied, making him live eighty, ninety, or one hundred years; see viii. 29. See also ii. 12, where, by some inaccuracy, he makes him to have been in India twenty years *before* he was at Babylon.—Olear. *ad locum et præfat. ad vit.* The common date of his birth is fixed by his biographer's merely accidental mention of the revolt of Archelaus against the Romans, as taking place before Apollonius was twenty years old; see i. 12.

[4] Philostr. i. 19

honour.[1] From Babylon he proceeded, by way of the Caucasus and the Indus, to Taxila, the city of Phraotes, King of the Indians, who is represented as an adept in the Pythagorean Philosophy;[2] and passing on, at length accomplished the object of his expedition by visiting Iarchas, Chief of the Brachmans, from whom he is said to have learned many valuable theurgic secrets.[3]

On his return to Asia Minor, after an absence of about five years, he stationed himself for a time in Ionia; where the fame of his travels and his austere mode of life gained for him much attention to his philosophical harangues. The cities sent embassies to him, decreeing him public honours; while the oracles pronounced him more than mortal, and referred the sick to him for relief.[4]

From Ionia he passed over to Greece, and made his first tour through its principal cities;[5] visiting the temples and oracles, reforming the divine rites, and sometimes exercising his theurgic skill. Except at Sparta, however, he seems to have attracted little attention. At Eleusis his application for admittance to the Mysteries was unsuccessful; as was a similar attempt at the Cave of Trophonius at a later date.[6] In both places his reputation for magical powers was the cause of his exclusion.

2.

Hitherto our memoir has only set before us the life of

[1] Philostr. i. 27—41.
[2] Ibid. ii. 1—40. Brucker, vol. ii. p. 110.
[3] Ibid. iii. 51.
[4] Ibid. iv. 1. Acts xiii. 8; see also Acts viii. 9—11, and xix. 13—16.
[5] Ibid. iv. 11, *et seq*.
[6] When denied at the latter place he forced his way in.—Philostr. viii. 19.

an ordinary Pythagorean, which may be comprehended in three words, mysticism, travel, and disputation. From the date, however, of his journey to Rome, which succeeded his Grecian tour, it is in some degree connected with the history of the times; and, though for much of what is told us of him we have no better authority than the word of Philostratus himself, still there is neither reason nor necessity for supposing the narrative to be in substance untrue.

Nero had at this time prohibited the study of philosophy, alleging that it was made the pretence for magical practices;[1]—and the report of his tyrannical excesses so alarmed the followers of Apollonius as they approached Rome, that out of thirty-four who had accompanied him thus far, eight only could be prevailed on to proceed. On his arrival, his religious pretensions were the occasion of his being brought successively before the consul Telesinus and Tigellinus the Minister of Nero.[2] Both of them, however, dismissed him after an examination; the former from a secret leaning towards philosophy, the latter from fear (as we are told) of his extraordinary powers. He was in consequence allowed to go about at his pleasure from temple to temple, haranguing the people, and, as in Asia, prosecuting his reforms in the worship paid to the gods. This, however, can hardly have been the case, supposing the edict against philosophers was as severe as his biographer represents. In that case neither Apollonius, nor Demetrius the Cynic, who joined him after his arrival, would have been permitted to remain in Rome; certainly not Apollonius,

---

[1] Ibid. iv. 35. Brucker (vol. ii. p. 118) with reason thinks this prohibition extended only to the profession of magic.

[2] Ibid. iv. 40, etc.

after his acknowledgment of his own magical powers in the presence of Tigellinus.[1]

It is more probable he was sent out of the city; anyhow we soon find him in Spain, taking part in the conspiracy forming against Nero by Vindex and others.[2] The political partisans of that day seem to have made use of professed jugglers and magicians to gain over the body of the people to their interests. To this may be attributed Nero's banishing such men from Rome;[3] and Apollonius had probably been already serviceable in this way at the Capital, as he was now in Spain, and immediately after to Vespasian; and at a later period to Nerva.

His next expeditions were to Africa, to Sicily, and so to Greece,[4] but they do not supply anything of importance to the elucidation of his character. At Athens he obtained the initiation in the Mysteries, for which he had on his former visit unsuccessfully applied.

The following spring, the seventy-third of his life, according to the common calculation, he proceeded to Alexandria,[5] where he attracted the notice of Vespasian, who had just assumed the purple, and who seemed desirous of countenancing his proceedings by the sanction of religion. Apollonius might be recommended to him

---

[1] Brucker, vol. ii. p. 120.   [2] Philostr. v. 10.

[3] Astrologers were concerned in Libo's conspiracy against Tiberius, and punished. Vespasian, as we shall have occasion to notice presently, made use of them in furthering his political plans.—Tacit. Hist. ii. 78. We read of their predicting Nero's accession, the deaths of Vitellius and Domitian, etc. They were sent into banishment by Tiberius, Claudius, Vitellius, and Domitian. Philostratus describes Nero as issuing his edict *on leaving the Capital* for Greece, iv. 47. These circumstances seem to imply that astrology, magic, etc., were at that time of considerable service in political intrigues.

[4] Philostr. v. 11, etc.   [5] Ibid. v. 20, etc.

for this purpose by the fame of his travels, his reputation for theurgic knowledge, and his late acts in Spain against Nero. It is satisfactory to be able to detect an historical connexion between two personages, each of whom has in his turn been made to rival our Lord and His Apostles in pretensions to miraculous power. Thus, claims which appeared to be advanced on distinct grounds are found to proceed from one centre, and by their coalition to illustrate and expose one another. The celebrated cures by Vespasian are connected with the ordinary theurgy of the Pythagorean School; and Apollonius is found here, as in many other instances, to be the instrument of a political party.

His biographer's account of his first meeting with the Emperor, which is perhaps substantially correct, is amusing from the theatrical character with which it was invested.[1] The latter, on entering Alexandria, was met by the great body of the Magistrates, Prefects, and Philosophers of the city; but, not discovering Apollonius in the number, he hastily asked, "whether the Tyanean was in Alexandria," and when told he was philosophizing in the Serapeum, proceeding thither he suppliantly entreated him to make him Emperor; and, on the Philosopher's answering he had already done so in praying for a just and venerable Sovereign,[2] Vespasian avowed his determination of putting himself entirely into his hands, and of declining the supreme power, unless he could

[1] Philostr. v. 27.
[2] Tacitus relates, that when Vespasian was going to the *Serapeum, ut super rebus imperii consuleret*, Basilides, an Egyptian, who was at the time eighty miles distant, suddenly appeared to him; from his name the emperor drew an omen that the god sanctioned his assumption of the Imperial power.—Hist. iv. 82. This sufficiently agrees in substance with the narrative of Philostratus to give the latter some probability. It was on this occasion that the famous cures are said to have been wrought.

obtain his countenance in assuming it.¹ A formal consultation was in consequence held, at which, besides Apollonius, Dio and Euphrates, Stoics in the Emperor's train, were allowed to deliver their sentiments; when the latter philosopher entered an honest protest against the sanction which Apollonius was giving to the ambition of Vespasian, and advocated the restoration of the Roman State to its ancient republican form.² This difference of opinion laid the foundation of a lasting quarrel between the rival advisers, to which Philostratus makes frequent allusion in the course of his history. Euphrates is mentioned by the ancients in terms of high commendation; by Pliny especially, who knew him well.³ He seems to have seen through his opponent's religious pretences, as we gather even from Philostratus;⁴ and when so plain a reason exists for the dislike which Apollonius, in his Letters, and Philostratus, manifest towards him, their censure must not be allowed to weigh against the testimony, which unbiassed writers have delivered in his favour.

After parting from Vespasian, Apollonius undertook an expedition into Æthiopia, where he held discussions with the Gymnosophists, and visited the cataracts of the Nile.⁵ On his return he received the news of the

---

¹ As Egypt supplied Rome with corn, Vespasian by taking possession of that country almost secured to himself the Empire.—Tacit. Hist. ii. 82, iii. 8. Philostratus insinuates that he was already in possession of supreme power, and came to Egypt for the sanction of Apollonius. Τὴν μὲν αρχὴν κεκτημένος, διαλεξόμενος δὲ τῷ ανδρί. v. 27.

² Philostr. v. 31.

³ Brucker, vol. ii. p. 566, etc.

⁴ Philostr. v. 37, he makes Euphrates say to Vespasian, Φιλοσοφίαν, ὦ βασιλεῦ, τὴν μὲν κατὰ φύσιν ἐπαίνει καὶ ἀσπάζου· τὴν δὲ θεοκλυτεῖν φάσκουσαν παραιτοῦ· καταψευδόμενοι γὰρ τοῦ θείου πολλὰ καὶ ἀνόητα, ἡμᾶς ἐπαίρουσι. See Brucker; and Apollon. Epist. 8.

⁵ Ibid. vi. 1, etc.

destruction of Jerusalem; and being pleased with the modesty of the conqueror, wrote to him in commendation of it. Titus is said to have invited him to Argos in Cilicia, for the sake of his advice on various subjects, and obtained from him a promise that at some future time he would visit him at Rome.[1]

On the succession of Domitian, he became once more engaged in the political commotions of the day, exerting himself to excite the countries of Asia Minor against the Emperor.[2] These proceedings at length occasioned an order from the Government to bring him to Rome, which, however, according to his biographer's account, he anticipated by voluntarily surrendering himself, under the idea that by his prompt appearance he might remove the Emperor's jealousy, and save Nerva, and others whose political interests he had been promoting. On arriving at Rome he was brought before Domitian; and when, very inconsistently with his wish to shield his friends from suspicion, he launched out into praise of Nerva, he was forced away into prison to the company of the worst criminals, his hair and beard were cut short, and his limbs loaded with chains. After some days he was brought to trial; the charges against him being the singularity of his dress and appearance, his being called a god, his foretelling a pestilence at Ephesus, and his sacrificing a child with Nerva for the purpose of augury.[3] Philostratus supplies us with an ample defence, which, it seems, he was to have delivered,[4] had he not in the course of the proceedings suddenly vanished from the Court, and trans-

---

[1] Philostr. vi. 29, etc.
[2] Ibid. vii. 1, etc., see Brucker, vol. ii. p. 128.
[3] Ibid. viii. 5, 6, etc. On account of his foretelling the pestilence he was honoured as a god by the Ephesians, vii. 21. Hence this prediction appeared in the indictment.
[4] Euseb. in Hier. 41.

ported himself to Puteoli, whither he had before sent on Damis.

This is the only miraculous occurrence which forces itself into the history as a component part of the narrative; the rest being of easy omission without any detriment to its entireness.¹ And strictly speaking, even here, it is only his vanishing which is of a miraculous nature, and his vanishing is not really necessary for the continuity of events. His "liberation" and "transportation" are sufficient for that continuity; and to be set free from prison and sent out of Rome are occurrences which might happen without a divine interposition. And in fact they seem very clearly to have taken place in the regular course of business. Philostratus allows that just before the philosopher's pretended disappearance, Domitian had publicly acquitted him, and that after the miracle he proceeded to hear the cause next in order, as if nothing had happened;² and tells us, moreover, that Apollonius on his return to Greece gave out that he had pleaded his own cause and so escaped, no allusion being made to a miraculous preservation.³

After spending two years in the latter country in his usual philosophical disputations, he passed into Ionia. According to his biographer's chronology, he was now approaching the completion of his hundredth year. We may easily understand, therefore, that when invited to

---

¹ Perhaps his causing the writing of the indictment to vanish from the paper, when he was brought before Tigellinus, may be an exception, as being the alleged cause of his acquittal. In general, however, no consequence follows from his marvellous actions: *e. g.* when imprisoned by Domitian, in order to show Damis his power, he is described as drawing his leg out of the fetters, and then—as putting it back again, vii. 38. A great exertion of power with apparently a small object.

² Philostr. viii. 8, 9.   ³ Ibid. viii. 15.

Rome by Nerva, who had just succeeded to the Empire, he declined the proposed honour with an intimation that their meeting must be deferred to another state of being.[1] His death took place shortly after; and Ephesus, Rhodes, and Crete are variously mentioned as the spot at which it occurred.[2] A temple was dedicated to him at Tyana,[3] which was in consequence accounted one of the sacred cities, and permitted the privilege of electing its own Magistrates.[4]

He is said to have written[5] a treatise upon Judicial Astrology, a work on Sacrifices, another on Oracles, a Life of Pythagoras, and an account of the answers which he received from Trophonius, besides the memoranda noticed in the opening of our memoir. A collection of Letters ascribed to him is still extant.[6]

3.

It may be regretted that so elaborate a history, as that which we have abridged, should not contain more authentic and valuable matter. Both the secular transactions of the times and the history of Christianity might have been illustrated by the life of one, who, while he was an instrument of the partisans of Vindex, Vespasian, and Nerva, was a contemporary and in some respects a rival of the Apostles; and who, probably, was with St. Paul at Ephesus and Rome.[7] As

---

[1] Philostr. viii. 27.   [2] Ibid. viii. 30.   [3] Ibid. i. 5, viii. 29.

[4] A coin of Hadrian's reign is extant with the inscription, which seems to run Τύανα ἱερὰ, ἄσυλος, ἀυτόνομος. Olear. ad Philostr. viii. 31.

[5] See Bayle, Art. *Apollonius;* and Brucker.

[6] Bishop Lloyd considers them spurious, but Olearius and Brucker show that there is good reason from internal evidence to suppose them genuine. See Olear. Addend. ad præfat. Epistol.; and Brucker, vol. ii. p. 147.

[7] Apollonius continued at Ephesus, Smyrna, etc., from A.D. 50 to about 59, and was at Rome from A.D. 63 to 66. St. Paul passed through Ionia

far as his personal character is concerned, there is nothing to be lamented in these omissions. There is nothing very winning, or very commanding, either in his biographer's picture of him, or in his own letters. His virtues, as we have already seen, were temperance and a disregard of wealth; and that he really had these, and such as these, may be safely concluded from the fact of the popularity which he enjoyed. The great object of his ambition seems to have been to emulate the fame of his master; and his efforts had their reward in the general admiration he attracted, the honours paid him by the Oracles, and the attentions shown him by men in power.

We might have been inclined, indeed, to suspect that his reputation existed principally in his biographer's panegyric, were it not attested by other writers. The celebrity, which he has enjoyed since the writings of the Eclectics, by itself affords but a faint presumption of his notoriety before they appeared. Yet, after all allowances, there remains enough to show that, however fabulous the details of his history may be, there was something extraordinary in his life and character. Some foundation there must have been for statements which his eulogists were able to maintain in the face of those who would have spoken out had they been altogether novel. Pretensions never before advanced must have excited the surprise and contempt of the advocates of Christianity.[1] Yet Eusebius styles him a wise man, and seems to admit the correctness of Philostratus, except in the miraculous parts of the narrative.[2] Lac-

---

into Greece A.D. 53, and was at Ephesus A.D. 54, and again from A.D. 56 to 58; he was at Rome in A.D. 65 and 66, when he was martyred.

[1] Lucian and Apuleius speak of him as if his name were familiar to them. Olear. præf. ad Vit.   [2] In Hierocl. 5.

tantius does not deny that a statue was erected to him at Ephesus;[1] and Sidonius Apollinaris, who even wrote his life, speaks of him as the admiration of the countries he traversed, and the favourite of monarchs.[2] One of his works was deposited in the palace at Antium by the Emperor Hadrian, who also formed a collection of his letters;[3] statues were erected to him in the temples, divine honours paid him by Caracalla, Alexander Severus, and Aurelian, and magical virtue attributed to his name.[4]

It has in consequence been made a subject of dispute, how far his reputation was built upon that supposed claim to extraordinary power which, as was noticed in the opening of our memoir, has led to his comparison with Sacred Names. If it could be shown that he did advance such pretensions, and upon the strength of them was admitted as an object of divine honour, a case would be made out, not indeed so strong as that on which Christianity is founded, yet remarkable enough to demand our serious examination. Assuming, then, or overlooking this necessary condition, sceptical writers have been forward to urge the history and character of Apollonius as creating a difficulty in the argument for Christianity derived from miracles; while their opponents have sometimes attempted to account for a phenomenon of which they had not yet ascertained the existence, and have most gratuitously ascribed his supposed power to the influence of the Evil principle.[5]

---

[1] Inst. v. 3.
[2] See Bayle, Art. *Apollonius;* and Cudworth, Intell. Syst. iv. 14.
[3] Philostr. viii. 19, 20.
[4] See Eusebius, Vopiscus, Lampridius, etc., as quoted by Bayle.
[5] See Brucker on this point, vol. ii. p. 141, who refers to various authors. Eusebius takes a more sober view of the question, allowing the substance of the history, but disputing the extraordinary parts. See in Hierocl. 5 and 12.

On examination, we shall find not a shadow of a reason for supposing that Apollonius worked miracles in any proper sense of the word; or that he professed to work them; or that he rested his authority on extraordinary works of any kind; and it is strange indeed that Christians, with victory in their hands, should have so mismanaged their cause as to establish an objection where none existed, and in their haste to extricate themselves from an imaginary difficulty, to overturn one of the main arguments for Revealed Religion.

4

1. To state these pretended prodigies is in most cases a refutation of their claim upon our notice,[1] and even those which are not in themselves exceptionable become so from the circumstances or manner in which they took place. Apollonius is said to have been an incarnation of the God Proteus; his birth was announced by the falling of a thunderbolt and a chorus of swans; his death signalized by a wonderful voice calling him up to Heaven; and after death he appeared to a youth to convince him of the immortality of the soul.[2] He is reported to have known the language of birds; to have evoked the spirit of Achilles; to have dislodged a demon from a boy; to have detected an Empusa who was seducing a youth into marriage; when brought before Tigellinus, to have caused the writing of the indictment to vanish from the paper; when imprisoned by Domitian, to have miraculously released himself from his fetters; to have discovered the soul of Amasis in the body of a lion; to have cured a youth attacked

---

[1] Most of them are imitations of the miracles attributed to Pythagoras.

[2] See Philostr. i. 4, 5, viii. 30, 31. He insinuates (Cf. viii. 29 with 31), that Apollonius was taken up alive. See Euseb. 8.

by hydrophobia, whom he pronounced to be Telephus the Mysian.[1] In declaring men's thoughts and distant events, he indulged most liberally; adopting a brevity which seemed becoming the dignity of his character, while it secured his prediction from the possibility of an entire failure. For instance: he gave previous intimation of Nero's narrow escape from lightning; foretold the short reigns of his successors; informed Vespasian at Alexandria of the burning of the Capitol; predicted the violent death of Titus by a relative; discovered a knowledge of the private history of his Egyptian guide; foresaw the wreck of a ship he had embarked in, and the execution of a Cilician Proprætor.[2] His prediction of the Proprætor's ruin was conveyed in the words, "O that particular day!" that is, of execution; of the short reigns of the Emperors in his saying that many Thebans would succeed Nero. We must not omit his first predicting and then removing a pestilence at Ephesus, the best authenticated of his professed miracles, as being attested by the erecting of a statue to him in consequence. He is said to have put an end to the malady by commanding an aged man to be stoned, whom he pointed out as its author, and who when the stones were removed was found changed into the shape of a dog.[3]

That such marvellous occurrences are wanting either in the gravity, or in the conclusiveness, proper to true miracles, is very plain; moreover, that they gain no recommendation from the mode in which they are recorded will be evident, if we extract the accounts given us by Philostratus of those two which alone among Apollonius's acts,

[1] Philostr. iv. 3, 16, 20, 25, 44, v. 42, vi. 43, vii. 38.
[2] Ibid. i. 12, iv. 24, 43, 11—13, 18, 30, vi. 3, 32.
[3] Ibid. iv. 10.

from their internal character, demand our attention. These are the revival of a young maid at Rome, who was on her way to burial, and the announcement at Ephesus of Domitian's assassination at the very time of its occurrence.

As to the former of these, it will be seen to be an attempt, and an elaborate, pretentious attempt, to outdo certain narratives in the Gospels. It runs as follows :—

"A maiden of marriageable age seemed to have died, and the bridegroom was accompanying her bier, uttering wailing cries, as was natural on his marriage being thus cut short. And all Rome lamented with him, for the maiden belonged to a consular house. But Apollonius, coming upon this sad sight, said, 'Set down the bier, for I will stop your tears for her.' At the same time, he asked her name; and most of those present thought he was going to make a speech about her, after the manner of professed mourners. But he, doing nothing else than touching her, and saying over her some indistinct words, woke her from her seeming death. And the girl spoke, and returned to her father's house, as Alcestis, when restored to life by Hercules."[1]

As to his proclaiming at Ephesus the assassination of Domitian at the time of its occurrence, of course, if he was at a great distance from Rome and the synchronism of events could be proved, we should be bound to give it our serious consideration; but synchronisms are difficult to verify. Moreover, Apollonius is known to have taken part in the politics of the empire; and his words, if he used them, might be prompted by his knowledge, or by his furtherance, of some attempt upon Domitian's life. Apollonius was at this time busily engaged in promoting

[1] Vit. iv. 45; Cf. Mark v. 29, etc.; Luke vii. 16; also John xi. 41—43; Acts iii. 4—6. In the sequel, the parents offer him money, which he gives as a portion to the damsel. See 2 Kings v. 15, 16 [4 Kings], and other passages in Scripture.

Nerva's interests among the Ionians. Dion[1] tells us that his success was foretold by the astrologers, among whom Tzetzes reckons Apollonius; and he mentions a prediction of Domitian's death which had been put into circulation in Germany. It is true that Dion confirms Philostratus's statement so far as the prediction is concerned, expressing strongly his personal belief in it. "Apollonius," he says, "ascending upon a high stone at Ephesus or elsewhere, and calling together the people, cried out, 'Well done, Stephanus!'" He adds, "This really took place, though a man should ever so much disbelieve it."[2] But it must be recollected that Dion was writing his history when Philostratus wrote; and one of them may have taken the account from the other; moreover, he is well known to be of a credulous turn of mind, and far from averse from recording marvellous stories.

Let us now turn to the statement of Philostratus; it will be found to form as strong a contrast to the simplicity and dignity of the Gospel narratives, as the dabbling in politics, which is so marked a feature in Apollonius, differs from the conduct of Him who emphatically declared that His kingdom was not of this world.

"He was conversing," says Philostratus, "among the groves attached to the porticoes, about noon, that is, just at the time when the event was occurring in the imperial palace; and first he dropped his voice, as if in terror; then, with a faltering unusual to him, he described [an action], as if he beheld something external, as his words proceeded. Then he was silent, stopping abruptly; and looking with agitation on the ground, and advancing up three or four of the steps, 'Strike the tyrant, strike!' he cried out, not as drawing a mere image of the truth from some mirror, but as seeing the thing itself, and seeming to realize what was doing; and, to the consternation of all Ephesus, for it was thronging around while he

[1] Lib. 67. [2] Hist. 67.

was conversing, after an interval of suspense, such as happens when spectators are following some undecided action up to its issue, he said, 'Courage, my men, for the tyrant is slaughtered this day—nay, now, now.'"[1]

Only an eye-witness is warranted to write thus pictorially; Philostratus was born 86 years after Apollonius's death.

5.

2. But it is almost superfluous to speak either of the general character of his extraordinary acts, or of the tone and manner in which they are narrated, when, in truth, neither Apollonius nor his biographer had any notion or any intention of maintaining that, in our sense of the word "miracle," these acts were miracles at all, or were to be referred to the immediate agency of the Supreme Being. Apollonius neither claimed for himself, nor did Philostratus claim for him, any direct mission from on high; nor did he in consequence submit the exercise of his preternatural powers to such severe tests as may fairly be applied to the miracles of Christianity.

Of works, indeed, which are asserted to proceed from the Author of nature, sobriety, dignity, and conclusiveness may fairly be required; but when a man ascribes his extraordinary power to his knowledge of some merely human secret, impropriety does but evidence his own want of taste, and ambiguity his want of skill. We have no longer a right to expect a great end, worthy means, or a frugal and judicious application of the miraculous gift. Now, Apollonius claimed nothing beyond a fuller insight into nature than others had; a knowledge of the fated and immutable laws to which it is conformed, of

[1] Vit. viii. 26.

the hidden springs on which it moves.[1] He brought a secret from the East and used it; and though he professed to be favoured, and in a manner taught, by good spirits,[2] yet he certainly referred no part of his power to a Supreme Intelligence. Theurgic virtues, or those which consisted in communion with the Powers and Principles of nature, were high in the scale of Pythagorean excellence, and to them it was that he ascribed his extraordinary gift. By temperate living, it was said, the mind was endued with ampler and more exalted faculties than it otherwise possessed; partook more fully of the nature of the One Universal Soul, was gifted with prophetic inspiration, and a kind of intuitive perception of secret things.[3] This power, derived from the favour of the celestial deities, who were led to distinguish the virtuous and high-minded, was quite distinct from magic, an infamous, uncertain, and deceitful art, consisting in a compulsory power over infernal spirits, operating by means of Astrology, Auguries, and Sacrifices, and directed to the personal emolument of those who cultivated it.[4] To our present question, however, this dis-

[1] Philostr. v. 12; in i. 2, he associates Democritus, a natural philosopher, with Pythagoras and Empedocles. See viii. 7, § 8, and Brucker, vol. i. p. 1108, etc., and p. 1184.

[2] In his apology before Domitian, he expressly attributes his removal of the Ephesian pestilence to Hercules, and makes this ascription the test of a divine philosopher as distinguished from a magician, viii. 7, § 9, *ubi vid*. Olear.

[3] Vid. viii. 7, § 9. See also ii. 37, vi. 11, viii. 5.

[4] Philostr. i. 2, and Olear. *ad loc.* note 3, iv. 44, v. 12, vii. 39, viii. 7; Apollon. Epist. 8 and 52; Philostr. Prooem. vit. Sophist.; Euseb. in Hier. 2; Mosheim, de Simone Mago, Sec. 13. Yet it must be confessed that the views both of the Pythagoreans and Eclectics were very inconsistent on this subject. Eusebius notices several instances of γοητεία in Apollonius's miracles; in Hierocl. 10, 28, 29, and 31. See Brucker, vol. ii. p. 447. At Eleusis, and the Cave of Triphonius, Apollonius was, as we have seen, accounted a magician, and so also by Euphrates, Mœragenes, Apuleius, etc. See Olear. Præf. ad vit. p. 33; and Brucker, vol. ii. p. 136, note *k*.

tinction made by the genuine Pythagorean, is unimportant. To whichever principle the miracles of Apollonius be referred, theurgy or magic, in either case they are independent of the First Cause, and not granted with a view to the particular purpose to which they are to be applied.[1]

3. We have also incidentally shown that they did not profess to be miracles in the proper meaning of the word, that is, evident innovations on the laws of nature. At the utmost they do but exemplify the aphorism, "Knowledge is power."[2] Such as are within the range of human knowledge are no miracles. Those of them, on the contrary, which are beyond it, will be found on inspection to be unintelligible, and to convey no evidence. The prediction of an earthquake (for instance) is not necessarily superhuman. An interpretation of the discourse of birds can never be verified. In understanding languages, knowing future events, discovering the purposes of others, recognising human souls when enclosed in new bodies, Apollonius merely professes extreme penetration and extraordinary acquaintance with nature. The spell by which he evokes spirits and exorcises demons, implies the mere possession of a secret;[3] and so perfectly is his biographer aware of this, as almost to doubt the resuscitation of the Roman damsel, the only decisive miracle of them all, on the ground of its being supernatural, insinuating that perhaps she was dead only in appearance.[4] Accordingly, in

[1] See Mosheim, Dissertat. de turbatâ Ecclesiâ, etc., Sec. 27.
[2] See Quæst. ad Orthodox 24 as quoted by Olearius, in his Preface, p. 34.
[3] Eusebius calls it θειά τις καὶ ἀρρήτος σοφία in Hierocl. 2. In iii. 41, Philostratus speaks of the κλήσεις αἷς θεοὶ χαίρουσι, the *spells* for evoking them, which Apollonius brought from India; Cf. iv. 16, and in iv. 20 of the τεκμήριον used for casting out an Evil Spirit.
[4] Εἴ τε σπινθῆρα τῆς ψυχῆς εὗρεν ἐν αὐτῇ, etc.

the narrative which we have extracted above, he begins by saying that she "seemed to have died," or "was to all appearance dead;" and again at the end of it he speaks of her "seeming death." Hence, moreover, may be understood the meaning of the charge of magic, as brought against the early Christians by their heathen adversaries; the miracles of the Gospels being strictly interruptions of physical order, and incompatible with theurgic knowledge.[1]

When our Lord and His Apostles declare themselves to be sent from God, this claim to a divine mission illustrates and gives dignity to their profession of extraordinary power; whereas the divinity,[2] no less than the gift of miracles to which Apollonius laid claim, must be understood in its Pythagorean sense, as referring not to any intimate connection with a Supreme Agent, but to his partaking, through his theurgic skill, more largely than others in the perfections of the animating principle of nature.

6.

4. Yet, whatever is understood by his miraculous gift and his divine nature, certainly his works were not adduced as vouchers for his divinity, nor were they, in fact, the principal cause of his reputation. What we desiderate is a contemporary appeal to them, on the part of himself or his friends; as St. Paul speaks of his miracles to the Romans and Corinthians, even calling them in one place "the signs of an Apostle;" or as St. Luke, in the Acts of the Apostles, details the miracles of both St.

---

[1] Douglas (Criterion, p. 387, note), observes that some heretics affirmed that our Lord rose from the dead φαντασίωδως, only in appearance, *from an idea of the impossibility of a resurrection.*

[2] Apollon. Epist. 17.

Peter and St. Paul.[1] Far different is it with Apollonius: we meet with no claim to extraordinary power in his Letters; nor when returning thanks to a city for public honours bestowed on him, nor when complaining to his brother of the neglect of his townsmen, nor when writing to his opponent Euphrates.[2] To the Milesians, indeed, he speaks of earthquakes which he had predicted; but without appealing to the prediction in proof of his authority.[3] Since, then, he is so far from insisting on his pretended extraordinary powers, and himself connects the acquisition of them with his Eastern expedition,[4] we may conclude that credit for possessing magical secrets was a *part* of the reputation which that expedition conferred. A foreign appearance, singularity of manners, a life of travel, and pretences to superior knowledge, excite the imagination of beholders;[5] and, as in the case of a wandering people among ourselves, appear to invite the persons who are thus distinguished to fraudulent practices. Apollonius is represented as making converts as soon as seen.[6] It was not, then,

---

[1] Vid. Rom. xv. 69; 1 Cor. ii. 4; 2 Cor. xii. 2, and Acts *passim*.

[2] See Epist. 1, 2, etc., 11, 44; the last-mentioned addressed to his brother begins, "What wonder, that, while the rest of mankind think me godlike, and some even a god, my own country alone hitherto ignores me, for whose sake especially I wished to distinguish myself, when not even to you, my brother, as I perceive, has it become clear how much I excel this race of men in my *doctrine* and my *life?*"—Epist. ii. 44, vid. also i. 2. He does not say "in supernatural power." Cf. John xii. 37: "But though He had done so many *miracles* before them, yet they believed not in Him."

[3] Epist. 68. Claudius, in a message to the Tyanæans, Epist. 53, praises him merely as a benefactor to youth.

[4] Philostr. vi. 11. See Euseb. in Hierocl. 26, 27.

[5] Hence the first of the charges brought against him by Domitian was the strangeness of his dress.—Philostr. viii. 5. By way of contrast, Cf. 1 Cor. ii. 3, 4; 2 Cor. x. 10.

[6] Philostr. iv. 1. See also i. 19, 21, iv. 17, 20, 39, vii. 31, etc., and i. 10, 12, etc.

his display of marvels, but his Pythagorean dress and mysterious deportment, which arrested attention, and made him thought superior to other men, because he was different from them. Like Lucian's Alexander[1] (who was all but his disciple), he was skilled in medicine, professed to be favoured by Æsculapius, pretended to foreknowledge, was in collusion with the heathen priests, and was supported by the Oracles; and being more strict in conduct than the Paphlagonian,[2] he established a more lasting celebrity. His usefulness to political aspirants contributed to his success; perhaps also the real and contemporary miracles of the Christian teachers would dispose many minds easily to acquiesce in any claims of a similar character.

7.

5. In the foregoing remarks we have admitted the general fidelity of the history, because ancient authors allow it, and there was no necessity to dispute it. Tried however on his own merits, it is quite unworthy of serious attention. Not only in the miraculous accounts (as we have already seen), but in the relation of a multitude of ordinary facts, an effort to rival our Saviour's history is distinctly visible. The favour in which Apollonius from a child was held by gods and men; his conversations when a youth in the Temple of Æsculapius; his determination in spite of danger to go up to

---

[1] Brucker, vol. ii. p. 144.

[2] Brucker supposes that, as in the case of Alexander, gain was his object; but we seem to have no proof of this, nor is it necessary thus to account for his conduct. We discover, indeed, in his character, no marks of that high enthusiasm which would support him in his whimsical career without any definite worldly object; yet the veneration he inspired, and the notice taken of him by great men, might be quite a sufficient recompense to a conceited and narrow mind.

Rome;[1] the cowardice of his disciples in deserting him; the charge brought against him of disaffection to Cæsar; the Minister's acknowledging, on his private examination, that he was more than man; the ignominious treatment of him by Domitian on his second appearance at Rome; his imprisonment with criminals; his vanishing from Court and sudden reappearance to his mourning disciples at Puteoli;[2]—these, with other particulars of a similar cast, evidence a history modelled after the narrative of the Evangelists. Expressions, moreover, and descriptions occur, clearly imitated from the sacred volume. To this we must add[3] the rhetorical colouring of the whole composition, so contrary to the sobriety of truth;[4] the fabulous accounts of things and places

---

[1] Cf. also Acts xx. 22, 23; xxi. 4, 11—14.

[2] Philostr. i. 8, 11, iv. 36, 38, 44, vii. 34, viii. 5, 11.

[3] See the description of his raising the Roman maid as above given. Or take again the account of his appearance to Damis and Demetrius at Puteoli, after vanishing from Court, viii. 12; in which there is much incautious agreement with Luke xxiv. 14—17, 27, 29, 32, 36—40. Also more or less in the following: vii. 30, init. and 34, fin. with Luke xii. 11, 12; iii. 38, with Matt. xvii. 14, etc., where observe the contrast of the two narratives: viii. 30, fin. with Acts xii. 7—10: iv. 44, with John xviii. 33, etc.: vii. 34, init. with Mark xiv. 65: iv. 34, init. with Acts xvi. 8—10: i. 19, fin. with Mark vii. 27, 28. Brucker and Douglas notice the following in the detection of the Empusa: Δακρύοντι ἐῴκει τὸ φάσμα, καὶ ἐδεῖτο μὴ βασανίζειν αὐτό, μηδὲ ἀναγκάζειν ὁμολογεῖν ὅτι εἴη, iv. 25, Cf. Mark v. 7—9. Olearius compares an expression in vii. 30, with I Cor. ix. 9.

[4] E.G. his ambitious descriptions of countries, etc. In iv. 30, 32, v. 22, vi. 24, he ascribes to Apollonius regular Socratic disputations, and in vi. 11, a long and flowery speech in the presence of the Gymnosophists—modes of philosophical instruction totally at variance with the genius of the Pythagorean school, the Philosopher's Letters still extant, and the writer's own description of his manner of teaching, i. 17. Some of his exaggerations and mis-statements have been noticed in the course of the narrative. As a specimen of the rhetorical style in which the work is written, vid. his account of the restoration of the Roman damsel, Ὁ δὲ οὐδὲν ἀλλ' ἢ προσαψάμενος αὐτῆς ἀφύπνισε,—contrast this with the simplicity of the Scripture narrative. See also the last sentence of v. 17, and indeed *passim.*

interspersed through the history;[1] lastly, we must bear in mind the principle, recognised by the Pythagorean and Eclectic schools, of permitting exaggeration and deceit in the cause of philosophy.[2]

After all, it must be remembered, that were the pretended miracles as unexceptionable as we have shown them to be absurd and useless—were they plain interruptions of established laws—were they grave and dignified in their nature, and important in their object, and were there nothing to excite suspicion in the design, manner, or character of the narrator—still the testimony on which they rest is the bare word of an author writing one hundred years after the death of the person panegyrized, and far distant from the places in which most of the miracles were wrought, and who can give no better account of his information than that he gained it from an unpublished work,[3] professedly indeed composed by

---

[1] *E. G.* his accounts of Indian and Æthiopian monsters; of serpents whose eyes were jewels of magical virtue; of pygmies; of golden water; of the speaking tree; of a woman half white and half black, etc.; he incorporates in his narrative the fables of Ctesias, Agatharchidas, and other writers. His blunders in geography and natural philosophy may be added, as far as they arise from the desire of describing wonders, etc. See also his pompous description of the wonders of Babylon, which were not then in existence.—Prideaux, Connection, Part I. Book viii. For his inconsistencies, see Eusebius and Brucker. It must be remembered, that in the age of Philostratus the composition of romantic histories was in fashion.

[2] See Brucker, vol. i. p. 992, vol. ii. p. 378. Apollonius was only one out of several who were set up by the Eclectics as rivals to Christ. Brucker, vol. ii. p. 372. Mosheim, de turbatâ Ecclesiâ, etc. Secs. 25, 26.

[3] Philostr. i. 2, 3. He professes that his account contains much *news*. As to the sources, besides the journal of Damis, from which he pretends to derive his information, he neither tells us how he met with them, nor what they contained; nor does he refer to them in the course of his history. On the other hand (as we have above noticed), much of the detail of Apollonius's journey is derived from the writings of Ctesias, etc.

a witness of the extraordinary transactions, but passing into his hands through two intermediate possessors. These are circumstances which almost, without positive objections, are sufficient by their own negative force to justify a summary rejection of the whole account. Unless, indeed, the history had been perverted to a mischievous purpose, we should esteem it impertinent to direct argument against a mere romance, and to subject a work of imagination to a grave discussion.

IV.
PRIMITIVE CHRISTIANITY.
(*From the* BRITISH MAGAZINE, 1833—1836.)

PREFATORY NOTICE.

THE following Papers originally belonged to the "Church of the Fathers," as it appeared in the *British Magazine*, in the years 1833-1836, and as it was published afterwards in one volume, with additions and omissions, in 1840. They were removed from the subsequent Catholic editions, except the chapter on Apollinaris, as containing polemical matter, which had no interest for Catholic readers. Now they are republished under a separate title.

The date of their composition is a sufficient indication of the character of the theology which they contain. They are written under the assumption that the Anglican Church has a place, as such, in Catholic communion and Apostolic Christianity. This is a question of fact, which the Author would now of course answer in the negative, retaining still, and claiming as his own, the positive principles and doctrines which that fact is, in these Papers, taken to involve.

PRIMITIVE CHRISTIANITY.

CHAP.		PAGE
1. WHAT DOES ST. AMBROSE SAY ABOUT IT?		339
2. WHAT SAYS VINCENT OF LERINS?		375
3. WHAT SAYS THE HISTORY OF APOLLINARIS?		391
4. WHAT SAY JOVINIAN AND HIS COMPANIONS?		401
5. WHAT SAY THE APOSTOLICAL CANONS?		417

PRIMITIVE CHRISTIANITY.

CHAPTER I.

WHAT DOES ST. AMBROSE SAY ABOUT IT?

§ 1. *Ambrose and Justina.*

NO considerate person will deny that there is much in the spirit of the times, and in the actual changes which the British Constitution has lately undergone, which makes it probable, or not improbable, that a material alteration will soon take place in the relations of the Church towards the State, to which it has been hitherto united. I do not say that it is out of the question that things may return to their former quiet and pleasant course, as in the good old time of King George III.; but the very chance that they will not makes it a practical concern for every churchman to prepare himself for a change, and a practical question for the clergy, by what instruments the authority of Religion is to be supported, should the protection and patronage of the Government be withdrawn. Truth, indeed, will always support itself in the world by its native vigour; it will never die while heaven and earth last, but be handed down from saint to saint until the end of all things. But this was the case before our Lord came, and is still the case, as we may humbly trust, in heathen countries. My question concerns *the*

Church, that peculiar institution which Christ set up as a visible home and memorial of Truth; and which, as being in this world, must be manifested by means of this world. I know it is common to make light of this solicitude about the Church, under the notion that the Gospel may be propagated without it,—or that men are about the same under every Dispensation, their hearts being in fault, and not their circumstances,—or for other reasons, better or worse as it may be; to all which I am accustomed to answer (and I do not see how I can be in error), that, if Christ had not meant His Church to answer a purpose, He would not have set it up, and that our business is not to speculate about possible Dispensations of Religion, but to resign and devote ourselves to that in which we are actually placed.

Hitherto the English Church has depended on the State, *i. e.* on the ruling powers in the country—the king and the aristocracy; and this is so natural and religious a position of things when viewed in the abstract, and in its actual working has been productive of such excellent fruits in the Church, such quietness, such sobriety, such external propriety of conduct, and such freedom from doctrinal excesses, that we must ever look back upon the period of ecclesiastical history so characterized with affectionate thoughts; particularly on the reigns of our blessed martyr St. Charles, and King George the Good. But these recollections of the past must not engross our minds, or hinder us from looking at things as they are, and as they will be soon, and from inquiring what is intended by Providence to take the place of the time-honoured instrument, which He has broken (if it be yet broken), the regal and aristocratical power. I shall offend many men when I say, we must *look to the people;* but let them give me a hearing.

Well can I understand their feelings. Who at first sight does not dislike the thoughts of gentlemen and clergymen depending for their maintenance and their reputation on their flocks? of their strength, as a visible power, lying not in their birth, the patronage of the great, and the endowment of the Church (as hitherto), but in the homage of a multitude? I confess I have before now had a great repugnance to the notion myself; and if I have overcome it, and turned from the Government to the People, it has been simply because I was forced to do so. It is not we who desert the Government, but the Government that has left us; we are forced back upon those below us, because those above us will not honour us; there is no help for it, I say. But, in truth, the prospect is not so bad as it seems at first sight. The chief and obvious objection to the clergy being thrown on the People, lies in the probable lowering of Christian views, and the adulation of the vulgar, which would be its consequence; and the state of Dissenters is appealed to as an evidence of the danger. But let us recollect that we are an apostolical body; we were not made, nor can be unmade by our flocks; and if our influence is to depend on *them*, yet the Sacraments reside with *us*. We have that with us, which none but ourselves possess, the mantle of the Apostles; and this, properly understood and cherished, will ever keep us from being the creatures of a populace.

And what may become necessary in time to come, is a more religious state of things also. It will not be denied that, according to the Scripture view of the Church, though all are admitted into her pale, and the rich inclusively, yet, the poor are her members with a peculiar suitableness, and by a special right. Scripture is ever casting slurs upon wealth, and making much of poverty. "To the poor the Gospel is preached." "God hath chosen the poor of this world, rich in faith and heirs of the kingdom." "If thou wilt be perfect, sell all that thou hast, and give to the poor." To this must be added the undeniable fact that the Church, when purest and when most powerful, *has* depended for its influence on its consideration with the many. Becket's letters, lately published,[1] have struck me not a little; but of course I now refer, not to such dark ages as most Englishmen consider these, but to the primitive Church —the Church of St. Athanasius and St. Ambrose. With a view of showing the power of the Church at that time, and on what it was based, not (as Protestants imagine) on governments, or on human law, or on endowments, but on popular enthusiasm, on dogma, on hierarchical power, and on a supernatural Divine Presence, I will now give some account of certain ecclesiastical proceedings in the city of Milan in the years 385, 386,— Ambrose being bishop, and Justina and her son, the younger Valentinian, the reigning powers.

I.

Ambrose was eminently a popular bishop, as every one knows who has read ever so little of his history. His very promotion to the sacred office was owing to an unexpected movement of the populace. Auxentius, his Arian predecessor in the see of Milan, died, A. D. 374, upon which the bishops of the province wrote to the then Emperor, Valentinian the First, who was in Gaul, requesting him to name the person who was to succeed him. This was a prudent step on their part, Arianism having introduced such matter for discord and faction

---

[1] Vid. *British Magazine*, 1832, etc. And Froude's Remains, part II. vol. ii.

among the Milanese, that it was dangerous to submit the election to the people at large, though the majority of them were orthodox. Valentinian, however, declined to avail himself of the permission thus given him; the choice was thrown upon the voices of the people, and the cathedral, which was the place of assembling, was soon a scene of disgraceful uproar, as the bishops had anticipated. Ambrose was at that time civil governor of the province of which Milan was the capital: and, the tumult increasing, he was obliged to interfere in person, with a view of preventing its ending in open sedition. He was a man of grave character, and had been in youth brought up with a sister, who had devoted herself to the service of God in a single life; but as yet was only a catechumen, though he was half way between thirty and forty. Arrived at the scene of tumult, he addressed the assembled crowds, exhorting them to peace and order. While he was speaking, a child's voice, as is reported, was heard in the midst of the crowd to say, "Ambrose is bishop;" the populace took up the cry, and both parties in the Church, Catholic and Arian, whether influenced by a sudden enthusiasm, or willing to take a man who was unconnected with party, voted unanimously for the election of Ambrose.

It is not wonderful that the subject of this sudden decision should have been unwilling to quit his civil office for a station of such high responsibility; for many days he fought against the popular voice, and that by the most extravagant expedients. He absconded, and was not recovered till the Emperor, confirming the act of the people of Milan, published an edict against all who should conceal him. Under these strange circumstances, Ambrose was at length consecrated bishop. His ordination was canonical only on the supposition that it came under those rare exceptions, for which the rules of the Church allow, when they speak of election "by divine grace," by the immediate suggestion of God; and if ever a bishop's character and works might be appealed to as evidence of the divine purpose, surely Ambrose was the subject of that singular and extraordinary favour. From the time of his call he devoted his life and abilities to the service of Christ. He bestowed his personal property on the poor: his lands on the Church; making his sister tenant for life. Next he gave himself up to the peculiar studies necessary for the due execution of his high duties, till he gained that deep insight into Catholic truth, which is evidenced in his writings, and in no common measure in relation to Arianism, which had been the dominant creed in Milan for the twenty years preceding his elevation. Basil of Cæsarea, in Cappadocia, was at this time the main pillar of Catholic truth in the East, having succeeded Athanasius of Alexandria, who died about the time that both Basil and Ambrose were advanced to their respective sees. He, from his see in the far East, addresses the new bishop in these words in an extant Epistle:—

"Proceed in thy work, thou man of God; and since thou hast not received the Gospel of Christ of men, neither wast taught it, but the Lord himself translated thee from among the world's judges to the chair of the Apostles, fight the good fight, set right the infirmities of the people, wherever the Arian madness has affected them; renew the old foot-prints of the Fathers, and by frequent correspondence build up thy love towards us, of which thou hast already laid the foundation."—*Ep.* 197.

I just now mentioned St. Thomas Becket. There is at once a similarity and a contrast between his history and that of Ambrose. Each of the two was by education and society what would now be called a gentleman.

Each was in high civil station when he was raised to a great ecclesiastical position; each was in middle age. Each had led an upright, virtuous life before his elevation; and each, on being elevated, changed it for a life of extraordinary penance and saintly devotion. Each was promoted to his high place by the act, direct or concurrent, of his sovereign; and each showed to that sovereign in the most emphatic way that a bishop was the servant, not of man, but of the Lord of heaven and earth. Each boldly confronted his sovereign in a great religious quarrel, and staked his life on its issue;—but then comes the contrast, for Becket's earthly master was as resolute in his opposition to the Church as Becket was in its behalf, and made him a martyr; whereas the Imperial Power of Rome quailed and gave way before the dauntless bearing and the grave and gracious presence of the great prelate of Milan. Indeed, the whole Pontificate of Ambrose is a history of successive victories of the Church over the State; but I shall limit myself to a bare outline of one of them.

2.

Ambrose had presided in his see about eleven years at the time when the events took place which are here to be related. Valentinian was dead, as well as his eldest son Gratian. His second son, who bore his own name, was Emperor of the West, under the tutelage of Justina, his second wife.

Justina was an Arian, and brought up her son in her own heretical views. This was about the time when the heresy was finally subdued in the Eastern Churches; the Ecumenical Council of Constantinople had lately been held, many Arian bishops had conformed, and laws had been passed by Theodosius against those who held out. It was natural under such circumstances that a number of the latter should flock to the court of Milan for protection and patronage. The Gothic officers of the palace were Arians also, as might be supposed, after the creed of their nation. At length they obtained a bishop of their persuasion from the East; and having now the form of an ecclesiastical body, they used the influence of Valentinian, or rather of his mother, to extort from Ambrose one of the churches of Milan for their worship.

The bishop was summoned to the palace before the assembled Court, and was formally asked to relinquish St. Victor's Church, then called the Portian Basilica, which was without the walls, for the Arian worship. His duty was plain; the churches were the property of Christ; he was the representative of Christ, and was therefore bound not to cede what was committed to him in trust. This is the account of the matter given by himself in the course of the dispute :—

"Do not," he says, "O Emperor, embarrass yourself with the thought that you have an Emperor's right over sacred things. Exalt not yourself, but, as you would enjoy a continuance of power, be God's subject. It is written, God's to God, and Cæsar's to Cæsar. The palace is the Emperor's, the churches are the bishop's."—*Ep*. 20.

This argument, which is true at all times, was much more convincing in an age like the primitive, before men had begun to deny that Christ had left a visible representative of Himself in His Church. If there was a body to whom the concerns of religion were intrusted, there could be no doubt it was that over which Ambrose presided. It had been there planted ever since Milan became Christian, its ministers were descended from the Apostles, and it was the legitimate trustee of the sacred property. But in our day men have been taught to doubt whether there *is* one Apostolic Church, though it is mentioned in the Creed: nay, it is grievous to say, clergymen have sometimes forgotten, sometimes made light of their own privileges. Accordingly, when a question arises now about the spoliation of the Church, we are obliged to betake ourselves to the rules of *national* law; we appeal to precedents, or we urge the civil consequences of the measure, or we use other arguments, which, good as they may be, are too refined to be very popular. Ambrose rested his resistance on grounds which the people understood at once, and recognized as irrefragable. They felt that he was only refusing to surrender a trust. They rose in a body, and thronged the palace gates. A company of soldiers was sent to disperse them; and a riot was on the point of ensuing, when the ministers of the Court became alarmed, and despatched Ambrose to appease the tumult, with the pledge that no further attempt should be made on the possessions of the Church.

Now some reader will here interrupt the narrative, perhaps, with something of an indignant burst about connecting the cause of religion with mobs and outbreaks To whom I would reply, that the multitude of men is always rude and intemperate, and needs restraint, —religion does not make them so. But being so, it is better they should be zealous about religion, and repressed by religion, as in this case, than flow and ebb again under the irrational influences of this world. A mob, indeed, is always wayward and faithless; but it is a good sign when it is susceptible of the hopes and fears of the world to come. Is it not probable that, when religion is thus a popular subject, it may penetrate, soften, or stimulate hearts which otherwise would know nothing of its power? However, this is not, properly speaking, my present point, which is to show how a Church may be in "favour with all the people" without any subserviency to them. To return to our history.

3.

Justina, failing to intimidate, made various underhand attempts to remove the champion of orthodoxy. She endeavoured to raise the people against him. Failing in this object, next, by scattering promises of place and promotion, she set on foot various projects to seize him in church, and carry him off into banishment. One man went so far as to take lodgings near the church, and had a carriage in readiness, in order to avail himself of any opportunity which offered to convey him away. But none of these attempts succeeded.

This was in the month of March; as Easter drew on, more vigorous steps were taken by the Court. On April 4th, the Friday before Palm Sunday, the demand of a church for the Arians was renewed; the pledges which the government had given, that no further steps should be taken in the matter, being perhaps evaded by changing the church which was demanded. Ambrose was now asked for the New or Roman Basilica, which was within the walls, and larger than the Portian. It was dedicated to the Apostles, and (I may add, for the sake of the antiquarian,) was built in the form of a cross. When the bishop refused in the same language as before, the imperial minister returned to the demand of the Portian Church; but the people interfering, and being clamorous against the proposal, he was obliged to retire to the palace to report how matters stood.

On Palm Sunday, after the lessons and sermon were over in the Basilica, in which he officiated, Ambrose was engaged in teaching the creed to the candidates for baptism, who, as was customary, had been catechized during Lent, and were to be admitted into the Church on the night before Easter-day. News was brought him that the officers of the Court had taken possession of the Portian Church, and were arranging the imperial hangings in token of its being confiscated to the Emperor; on the other hand, that the people were flocking thither. Ambrose continued the service of the day; but, when he was in the midst of the celebration of the Eucharistical rite, a second message came that one of the Arian priests was in the hands of the populace.

"On this news (he says, writing to his sister,) I could not keep from shedding many bitter tears, and, while I made oblation, I prayed God's protection that no blood might be shed in the Church's quarrel: or if so, that it might be mine, and that not for my people only, but for those heretics."—*Ep.* 20.

At the same time he despatched some of his clergy to the spot, who had influence enough to rescue the unfortunate man from the mob.

Though Ambrose so far seems to have been supported only by a popular movement, yet the proceedings of the following week showed that he had also the great mass of respectable citizens on his side. The imprudent measures of the Court, in punishing those whom it considered its enemies, disclosed to the world their number and importance. The tradesmen of the city were fined two hundred pounds of gold, and many were thrown into prison. All the officers, moreover, and place-men of the courts of justice, were ordered to keep in-doors during the continuance of the disorders; and men of higher rank were menaced with severe consequences, unless the Basilica were surrendered.

Such were the acts by which the Imperial Court solemnized Passion week. At length a fresh interview was sought with Ambrose, which shall be described in his own words :—

"I had a meeting with the counts and tribunes, who urged me to give up the Basilica without delay, on the ground that the Emperor was but acting on his undoubted rights, as possessing sovereign power over all things. I made answer, that if he asked me for what was my own—for instance, my estate, my money, or the like—I would make no opposition: though, to tell the truth, all that was mine was the property of the poor; but that he had no sovereignty over things sacred. If my patrimony is demanded, seize upon it; my person, here I am. Would you take to prison or to death? I go with pleasure. Far be it from me to entrench myself within the circle of a multitude, or to clasp the altar in supplication for my life; rather I will be a sacrifice for the altar's sake.

"In good truth, when I heard that soldiers were sent to take possession of the Basilica, I was horrified at the prospect of bloodshed, which might issue in ruin to the whole city. I prayed God that I might not survive the destruction, which might ensue, of such a place, nay, of Italy itself. I shrank from the odium of having occasioned slaughter, and would sooner have given my own throat to the knife. ... I was ordered to calm the people. I replied, that all I could do was not to inflame them; but God alone could appease them. For myself, if I appeared to have instigated them, it was the duty of the government to proceed against me, or to banish me. Upon this they left me."

Ambrose spent the rest of Palm Sunday in the same Basilica in which he had been officiating in the morning: at night he went to his own house, that the civil power might have the opportunity of arresting him, if it was thought advisable.

4

The attempt to gain the Portian seems now to have been dropped; but on the Wednesday troops were marched before day-break to take possession of the New Church, which was within the walls. Ambrose, upon the news of this fresh movement, used the weapons of an apostle. He did not seek to disturb them in their possession; but, attending service at his own church, he was content with threatening the soldiers with a sentence of excommunication. Meanwhile the New Church, where the soldiers were posted, began to fill with a larger congregation than it ever contained before the persecution. Ambrose was requested to go thither, but, desirous of drawing the people away from the scene of imperial tyranny, lest a riot should ensue, he remained where he was, and began a comment on the lesson of the day, which was from the book of Job. First, he commended them for the Christian patience and resignation with which they had hitherto borne their trial, which indeed was, on the whole, surprising, if we consider the inflammable nature of a multitude. "We petition your Majesty," they said to the Emperor; "we use no force, we feel no fear, but we petition." It is common in the leader of a multitude to profess peaceableness, but very unusual for the multitude itself to persevere in doing so. Ambrose went on to observe, that both they and he had in their way been tempted, as Job was, by the powers of evil. For himself, his peculiar trial had lain in the reflection that the extraordinary measures of the government, the movements of the Gothic guards, the fines of the tradesmen, the various sufferings of the faithful, all arose from, as it might be called, his obstinacy in not yielding to what seemed an overwhelming necessity, and giving the Basilica to the Arians. Yet he felt that to do so would be to peril his soul; so that the request was but the voice of the tempter, as he spoke in Job's wife, to make him "say a word against God, and die," to betray his trust, and incur the sentence of spiritual death.

Before this time the soldiers who had been sent to the New Church, from dread of the threat of excommunication, had declared against the sacrilege, and joined his own congregation; and now the news came that the royal hangings had been taken down. Soon after, as he was continuing his address to the people, a fresh message came to him from the Court to ask him whether he had an intention of domineering over his sovereign? Ambrose, in answer, showed the pains he had taken to be obedient to the Emperor's will, and to hinder disturbance: then he added:—

"Priests have by old right bestowed sovereignty, never assumed it; and it is a common saying, that sovereigns have coveted the priesthood more than priests the sovereignty. Christ hid Himself, lest He should be made a king. Yes! we have a dominion of our own. The dominion of the priest lies in his helplessness, as it is said, 'When I am weak, then am I strong.'"

And so ended the dispute for a time. On Good Friday the Court gave way; the guards were ordered from the Basilica, and the fines were remitted. I end for the present with the view which Ambrose took of the prospect before him :—

"Thus the matter rests; I wish I could say, has ended : but the Emperor's words are of that angry sort which shows that a more severe contest is in store. He says I domineer, or worse than domineer. He implied this when his ministers were entreating him, on the petition of the soldiers, to attend church. 'Should Ambrose bid you,' he made answer, 'doubtless you would give me to him in chains.' I leave you to judge what these words promise. Persons present were all shocked at hearing them; but there are parties who exasperate him."

§ 2. *Ambrose and Valentinian.*

I.

IN the opposition which Ambrose made to the Arians, as already related, there is no appearance of his appealing to any law of the Empire in justification of his refusal to surrender the Basilica to them. He rested it upon the simple basis of the Divine Law, a common-sense argument which there was no evading. "The Basilica has been made over to Christ; the Church is His trustee; I am its ruler. I dare not alienate the Lord's property. He who does so, does it at his peril." Indeed, he elsewhere expressly repudiates the principle of dependence in this matter on human law. "Law," he says, "has not brought the Church together, but the faith of Christ." However, Justina determined to have human law on her side. She persuaded her son to make it a capital offence in any one, either publicly or privately, even by petition, to interfere with the assemblies of the Arians; a provision which admitted a fair, and might also bear, and did in fact receive, a most tyrannical interpretation. Benevolus, the Secretary of State, from whose office the edict was to proceed, refused to draw it up, and resigned his place; but of course others less scrupulous were easily found to succeed him. At length it was promulgated on the 21st of January of the next year, A.D. 386, and a fresh attempt soon followed on the part of the Court to get possession of the Portian Basilica, which was without the walls.

The line of conduct which Ambrose had adopted

remained equally clear and straight, whether before or after the promulgation of this edict. It was his duty to use all the means which Christ has given the Church to prevent the profanation of the Basilica. But soon a new question arose for his determination. An imperial message was brought to him to retire from the city at once, with any friends who chose to attend him. It is not certain whether this was intended as an absolute command, or (as his words rather imply) a recommendation on the part of government to save themselves the odium, and him the suffering, of public and more severe proceedings. Even if it were the former, it does not appear that a Christian bishop, so circumstanced, need obey it; for what was it but in other words to say, "Depart from the Basilica, and leave it to us?"—the very order which he had already withstood. The words of Scripture, which bid Christians, if persecuted in one city, flee to another, are evidently, from the form of them, a discretionary rule, grounded on the expediency of each occasion, as it arises. A mere threat is not a persecution, nor is a command; and though we are bound to obey our civil rulers, the welfare of the Church has a prior claim upon our obedience. Other bishops took the same view of the case with Ambrose; and, accordingly, he determined to stay in Milan till removed by main force, or cut off by violence.

2.

The reader shall hear his own words in a sermon which he delivered upon the occasion:—

"I see that you are under a sudden and unusual excitement," he said, "and are turning your eyes on me. What can be the reason of this? Is it that you saw or heard that an imperial message had been brought to me by the tribunes desiring me to depart hence whither I would, and to take with me all who would follow me?

What! did you fear that I would desert the Church, and, for fear of my life, abandon you? Yet you might have attended to my answer. I said that I could not, for an instant, entertain the thought of deserting the Church, in that I feared the Lord of all more than the Emperor of the day: in truth that, should force hurry me off, it would be my body, not my mind, that was got rid of; that, should he act in the way of kingly power, I was prepared to suffer after the manner of a priest.

"Why, then, are you thus disturbed? I will never leave you of my own will; but if compelled, I may not resist. I shall still have the power of sorrowing, of weeping, of uttering laments: when weapons, soldiers, Goths, too, assail me, tears are my weapons, for such are the defences of a priest. In any other way I neither ought to resist, nor can; but as to retiring and deserting the Church, this is not like me; and for this reason, lest I seem to do so from dread of some heavier punishment. Ye yourselves know that it is my wont to submit to our rulers, but not to make concessions to them; to present myself readily to legal punishment, and not to fear what is in preparation.

"A proposal was made to me to deliver up at once the Church plate. I made answer, that I was ready to give anything that was my own, farm or house, gold or silver; but that I could withdraw no property from God's temple, nor surrender what was put into my hands, not to surrender, but to keep safely. Besides, that I had a care for the Emperor's well-being; since it was as little safe for him to receive as for me to surrender: let him bear with the words of a free-spoken priest, for his own good, and shrink from doing wrong to his Lord.

"You recollect to-day's lesson about holy Naboth and his vineyard. The king asked him to make it over to him, as a ground, not for vines, but for common pot-herbs. What was his answer? 'God forbid I should give to thee the inheritance of my fathers!' The king was saddened when another's property was justly denied him; but he was beguiled by a woman's counsel. Naboth shed his blood rather than give up his vines. Shall he refuse his own vineyard, and we surrender the Church of Christ?

"What contumacy, then, was there in my answer? I did but say at the interview, 'God forbid I should surrender Christ's heritage!' I added, 'the heritage of our fathers;' yes, of our Dionysius, who died in exile for the faith's sake, of Eustorgius the Confessor, of Myrocles, and of all the other faithful bishops back. I answered as a priest: let the Emperor act as an Emperor; he shall rob me of my life sooner than of my fidelity.

"In what respect was my answer other than respectful? Does the Emperor wish to tax us? I make no opposition. The Church lands pay taxes. Does he require our lands? He has power to claim them; we will not prevent him. The contributions of the people will suffice for the poor. Let not our enemies take offence at our lands; they may away with them, if it please the Emperor; not that I give them, but I make no opposition. Do they seek my gold? I can truly say, silver and gold I seek not. But they take offence at my raising contributions. Nor have I any great fear of the charge. I confess I have stipendiaries; they are the poor of Christ's flock; a treasure which I am well used in amassing. May this at all times be my offence, to exact contributions for the poor. And if they accuse me of defending myself by means of them, I am far from denying, I court the charge. The poor *are* my defenders, but it is by their prayers. Blind though they be, lame, feeble, and aged, yet they have a strength greater than that of the stoutest warriors. In a word, gifts made to them are a claim upon the Lord; as it is written, 'He who giveth to the poor, lendeth to God;' but a military guard oftentimes has no title to divine grace.

"They say, too, that the people are misled by the verses of my hymns. I frankly confess this also. Truly those hymns have in them a high strain above all other influence. For can any strain have more of influence than the confession of the Holy Trinity, which is proclaimed day by day by the voice of the whole people? Each is eager to rival his fellows in confessing, as he well knows how, in sacred verses, his faith in Father, Son, and Holy Spirit. Thus all are made teachers, who else were scarce equal to being scholars.

"No one can deny that in what we say we pay to our sovereign due honour. What indeed can do him higher honour than to style him a son of the Church? In saying this, we are loyal to him without sinning against God. For the Emperor is within the Church, but not over the Church; and a religious sovereign seeks, not rejects, the Church's aid. This is our doctrine, modestly avowed, but insisted on without wavering. Though they threaten fire, or the sword, or transportation, we, Christ's poor servants, have learned not to fear. And to the fearless nothing is frightful; as Scripture says, 'Their blows are like the arrows of a child.'"—*Serm. contr. Auxent.*

3.

Mention is made in this extract of the Psalmody which Ambrose adopted about this time. The history of its introduction is curiously connected with the subject before us, and interesting, inasmuch as this was the beginning of a change in the style of Church music, which spread over the West, and continues even among ourselves to this day; it is as follows :—

Soldiers had been sent, as in the former year, to surround his church, in order to prevent the Catholic service there; but being themselves Christians, and afraid of excommunication, they went so far as to allow the people to enter, but would not let them leave the building. This was not so great an inconvenience to them as might appear at first sight: for the early Basilicas were not unlike the heathen temples, or our own collegiate chapels, that is, part of a range of buildings, which contained the lodgings of the ecclesiastics, and formed a fortress in themselves, which could easily be fortified from within or blockaded from without. Accordingly, the people remained shut up within the sacred precincts for some days, and the bishop with them. There seems to have been a notion, too, that he was to be seized for exile, or put to death; and they naturally kept about him to "see the end," to suffer with him or for him, according as their tempers and principles led them. Some went so far as to barricade the doors of the Basilica;[1] nor could Ambrose prevent this proceeding, unnecessary as it was, because of the good feelings of the soldiery towards them, and indeed impracticable in such completeness as might be sufficient for security.

Some persons may think that Ambrose ought to

[1] Vid. 2 [4] Kings vi. 32.

have used his utmost influence against it, whereas in his sermon to the people he merely insists on its uselessness, and urges the propriety of looking simply to God, and not at all to such expedients, for deliverance. It must be recollected, however, that he and his people in no sense drew the sword from its sheath; he confined himself to passive resistance. He had violated no law; the Church's property was sought by a tyrant: without using any violence, he took possession of that which he was bound to defend with his life. He placed himself upon the sacred territory, and bade them take it and him together, after St. Laurence's pattern, who submitted to be burned rather than deliver up the goods with which he had been intrusted for the sake of the poor. However, it was evidently a very uncomfortable state of things for a Christian bishop, who might seem to be responsible for all the consequences, yet was without control over them. A riot might commence any moment, which it would not be in his power to arrest. Under these circumstances, with admirable presence of mind, he contrived to keep the people quiet, and to direct their minds to higher objects than those around them, by Psalmody. Sacred chanting had been one especial way in which the Catholics of Antioch had kept alive, in Arian times, the spirit of orthodoxy. And from the first a peculiar kind of singing—the antiphonal or responsorial, answering to our cathedral chanting—had been used in honour of the sacred doctrine which heresy assailed. Ignatius, the disciple of St. Peter, was reported to have introduced the practice into the Church of Antioch, in the doxology to the Trinity. Flavian, afterwards bishop of that see, revived it during the Arian usurpation, to the great edification and encouragement of the oppressed Catholics. Chrysostom used it in the vigils at Constantinople, in opposition to the same heretical party; and similar vigils had been established by Basil in the monasteries of Cappadocia. The assembled multitude, confined day and night within the gates of the Basilica, were in the situation of a monastic body without its discipline, and Ambrose rightly considered that the novelty and solemnity of the oriental chants, in praise of the Blessed Trinity, would both interest and sober them during the dangerous temptation to which they were now exposed. The expedient had even more successful results than the bishop anticipated; the soldiers were affected by the music, and took part in it; and, as we hear nothing more of the blockade, we must suppose that it thus ended, the government being obliged to overlook what it could not prevent.

It may be interesting to the reader to see Augustine's notice of this occurrence, and the effect of the Psalmody upon himself, at the time of his baptism.

"The pious populace (he says in his Confessions) was keeping vigils in the church prepared to die, O Lord, with their bishop, Thy servant. There was my mother, Thy handmaid, surpassing others in anxiety and watching, and making prayers her life.

"I, uninfluenced as yet by the fire of Thy Spirit, was roused however by the terror and agitation of the city. Then it was that hymns and psalms, after the oriental rite, were introduced, lest the spirits of the flock should fail under the wearisome delay."—*Confess.* ix. 15.

In the same passage, speaking of his baptism, he says:—

"How many tears I shed during the performance of Thy hymns and chants, keenly affected by the notes of Thy melodious Church! My ears drank up those sounds, and they distilled into my heart as sacred truths, and overflowed thence again in pious emotion, and gushed forth into tears, and I was happy in them."—*Ibid.* 14.

Elsewhere he says :—

> "Sometimes, from over-jealousy, I would entirely put from me and from the Church the melodies of the sweet chants which we use in the Psalter, lest our ears seduce us; and the way of Athanasius, Bishop of Alexandria, seems the safer, who, as I have often heard, made the reader chant with so slight a change of note, that it was more like speaking than singing. And yet when I call to mind the tears I shed when I heard the chants of Thy Church in the infancy of my recovered faith, and reflect that at this time I am affected, not by the mere music, but by the subject, brought out, as it is, by clear voices and appropriate tune, then, in turn, I confess how useful is the practice."—*Confess.* x. 50.

Such was the influence of the Ambrosian chants when first introduced at Milan by the great bishop whose name they bear; there they are in use still, in all the majestic austerity which gave them their original power, and a great part of the Western Church uses that modification of them which Pope Gregory introduced at Rome in the beginning of the seventh century.

4.

Ambrose implies, in the sermon from which extracts were given above, that a persecution, reaching even to the infliction of bodily sufferings, was at this time exercised upon the bishops of the Exarchate. Certainly he himself was all along in imminent peril of his life, or of sudden removal from Milan. However, he made it a point to frequent the public places and religious meetings as usual; and indeed it appears that he was as safe there as at home, for he narrowly escaped assassination from a hired ruffian of the Empress's, who made his way to his bed-chamber for the purpose. Magical arts were also practised against him, as a more secret and certain method of ensuring his destruction.

I ought to have mentioned, before this, the challenge sent to him by the Arian bishop to dispute publicly with him on the sacred doctrine in controversy; but was unwilling to interrupt the narrative of the contest about the Basilica. I will here translate portions of a letter sent by him, on the occasion, to the Emperor.

"To the most gracious Emperor and most happy Augustus
"Valentinian, Ambrosius Bishop,—

"Dalmatius, tribune and notary, has come to me, at your Majesty's desire, as he assures me, to require me to choose umpires, as Auxentius[1] has done on his part. Not that he informed me who they were that had already been named; but merely said that the dispute was to take place in the consistory, in your Majesty's presence, as final arbitrator of it.

"I trust my answer will prove sufficient. No one should call me contumacious, if I insist on what your father, of blessed memory, not only sanctioned by word of mouth, but even by a law: —That in cases of faith, or of ecclesiastics, the judges should be neither inferior in function nor separate in jurisdiction—thus the rescript runs; in other words, he would have priests decide about priests. And this extended even to the case of allegations of wrong conduct.

"When was it you ever heard, most gracious Emperor, that in a question of faith laymen should be judges of a bishop? What! have courtly manners so bent our backs, that we have forgotten the rights of the priesthood, that I should of myself put into another's hands what God has bestowed upon me? Once grant that a layman may set a bishop right, and see what will follow. The layman in consequence discusses, while the bishop listens; and the bishop is the pupil of the layman. Yet, whether we turn to Scripture or to history, who will venture to deny that in a question of faith, in a question, I say, of faith, it has ever been the bishop's business to judge the Christian Emperor, not the Emperor's to judge the bishop?

"When, through God's blessing, you live to be old, then you will

---

[1] The Arian bishop, who had lately come from the East to Milan, had taken the name of Auxentius, the heretical predecessor of Ambrose.

know what to think of the fidelity of that bishop who places the rights of the priesthood at the mercy of laymen. Your father, who arrived, through God's blessing, at maturer years, was in the habit of saying, 'I have no right to judge between bishops;' but now your Majesty says, 'I ought to judge.' He, even though baptized into Christ's body, thought himself unequal to the burden of such a judgment; your Majesty, who still have to earn a title to the sacrament, claims to judge in a matter of faith, though you are a stranger to the sacrament to which that faith belongs.

"But Ambrose is not of such value, that he must degrade the priesthood for his own well-being. One man's life is not so precious as the dignity of all those bishops who have advised me thus to write; and who suggested that Auxentius might be choosing some heathen perhaps or Jew, whose permission to decide about Christ would be a permission to triumph over Him. What would pleasure them but blasphemies against Him? What would satisfy them but the impious denial of His divinity—agreeing, as they do, full well with the Arian, who pronounces Christ to be a creature with the ready concurrence of Jews and heathens?

"I would have come to your Majesty's Court, to offer these remarks in your presence; but neither my bishops nor my people would let me; for they said that, when matters of faith were discussed in the Church, this should be in the presence of the people.

"I could have wished your Majesty had not told me to betake myself to exile somewhere. I was abroad every day; no one guarded me. I was at the mercy of all the world; you should have secured my departure to a place of your own choosing. Now the priests say to me, 'There is little difference between voluntarily leaving and betraying the altar of Christ; for when you leave, you betray it.'

"May it please your Majesty graciously to accept this my declining to appear in the Imperial Court. I am not practised in attending it, except in your behalf; nor have I the skill to strive for victory within the palace, as neither knowing, nor caring to know, its secrets."—*Ep.* 21.

The reader will observe an allusion in the last sentence of this defence to a service Ambrose had rendered the Emperor and his mother, upon the murder of Gratian; when, at the request of Justina, he undertook the difficult embassy to the usurper Maximus, and was the means of preserving the peace of Italy. This Maximus now interfered to defend him against the parties whom he had on a former occasion defended against Maximus; but other and more remarkable occurrences interposed in his behalf, which shall be mentioned in the next section.

§ 3. *Ambrose and the Martyrs.*

I.

A TERMINATION was at length put to the persecution of the Church of Milan by an occurrence of a very different nature from any which take place in these days. And since such events as I am to mention do not occur now, we are apt to argue, not very logically, that they did not occur then. I conceive this to be the main objection which will be felt against the following narrative. Miracles never took place then, because we do not see reason to believe that they take place now. But it should be recollected, that if there are no miracles at present, neither are there at present any martyrs. Might we not as cogently argue that no martyrdoms took place then, because no martyrdoms take place now? And might not St. Ambrose and his brethren have as reasonably disbelieved the possible existence of parsonages and pony carriages in the nineteenth century, as we the existence of martyrs and miracles in the primitive age? Perhaps miracles and martyrs go together. Now the account which is to follow does indeed relate to miracles, but then it relates to martyrs also.

Another objection which may be more reasonably urged against the narrative is this: that in the fourth century there were many miraculous tales which even Fathers of the Church believed, but which no one of any way of thinking believes now. It will be argued, that because some miracles are alleged which did not really take place, that therefore none which are alleged took place either. But I am disposed to reason just the contrary way. Pretences to revelation make it probable that there is a true Revelation; pretences to miracles make it probable that there are real ones; falsehood is the mockery of truth; false Christs argue a true Christ; a shadow implies a substance. If it be replied that the Scripture miracles are these true miracles, and that it is they, and none other but they, none after them, which suggested the counterfeit; I ask in turn, if so, what becomes of the original objection, that *no* miracles are true, because some are false? If this be so, the Scripture miracles are to be believed as little as those after them; and this is the very plea which infidels have urged. No; it is not reasonable to limit the scope of an argument according to the exigency of our particular conclusions; we have no leave to apply the argument *for* miracles only to the first century, and that *against* miracles only to the fourth. If forgery in some miracles proves forgery in all, this tells against the first as well as against the fourth century; if forgery in some argues truth in others, this avails for the fourth as well as for the first.

And I will add, that even credulousness on other occasions does not necessarily disqualify a person's evidence for a particular alleged miracle; for the sight of one true miracle could not but dispose a man to believe others readily, nay, too readily, that is, would make him what is called credulous.

Now let these remarks be kept in mind while I go on to describe the alleged occurrence which has led to them. I know of no direct objection to it in particular, viewed in itself; the main objections are such antecedent considerations as I have been noticing. But if Elisha's bones restored a dead man to life, I know of no antecedent reason why the relics of Gervasius and Protasius should not, as in the instance to be considered, have given sight to the blind.

2.

The circumstances were these:—St. Ambrose, at the juncture of affairs which I have described in the foregoing pages, was proceeding to the dedication of a certain church at Milan, which remains there to this day, with the name of "St. Ambrose the Greater;" and was urged by the people to bury relics of martyrs under the altar, as he had lately done in the case of the Basilica of the Apostles. This was according to the usage of those times, desirous thereby both of honouring those who had braved death for Christ's sake, and of hallowing religious places with the mortal instruments of their triumph. Ambrose in consequence gave orders to open the ground in the church of St. Nabor, as a spot likely to have been the burying-place of martyrs during the heathen persecutions.

Augustine, who was in Milan at the time, alleges that Ambrose was directed in his search by a dream. Ambrose himself is evidently reserved on the subject in his letter to his sister, though he was accustomed to make her his confidant in his ecclesiastical proceedings; he only speaks of his heart having burnt within him in presage of what was to happen. The digging commenced, and in due time two skeletons were discovered, of great size, perfect, and disposed in an orderly way; the head of each, however, separated from the body, and a quantity of blood about. That they were the remains of martyrs, none could reasonably doubt; and their names were ascertained to be Gervasius and Protasius; how, it does not appear, but certainly it was not so alleged on any traditionary information or for any popular object, since they proved to be quite new names to the Church of the day, though some elderly men at length recollected hearing them in former years. Nor is it wonderful that these saints should have been forgotten, considering the number of the Apostolic martyrs, among whom Gervasius and Protasius appear to have a place.

It seems to have been usual in that day to verify the genuineness of relics by bringing some of the *energumeni*, or possessed with devils, to them. Such afflicted persons were present with St. Ambrose during the search; and, before the service for exorcism commenced, one of them gave the well-known signs of horror and distress which were customarily excited by the presence of what had been the tabernacle of divine grace.

The skeletons were raised and transported to the neighbouring church of St. Fausta. The next day, June 18th, on which they were to be conveyed to their destination, a vast concourse of people attended the procession. This was the moment chosen by Divine Providence to give, as it were, signal to His Church, that, though years passed on, He was still what He had been from the beginning, a living and a faithful God, wonder-working as in the lifetime of the Apostles, and true to His word as spoken by His prophets unto a thousand generations. There was in Milan a man of middle age, well known in the place, by name Severus, who, having become blind, had given up his trade, and was now supported by charitable persons. Being told the cause of the shoutings in the streets, he persuaded his guide to lead him to the sacred relics. He came near; he touched the cloth which covered them; and he regained his sight immediately.

This relation deserves our special notice from its distinct miraculousness and its circumstantial character; but numerous other miracles are stated to have followed. Various diseases were cured and demoniacs dispossessed by the touch of the holy bodies or their envelopments.

3.

Now for the evidence on which the whole matter rests. Our witnesses are three: St. Augustine, St. Ambrose, and Paulinus, the secretary of the latter, who after his death addressed a short memoir of his life to the former.

1. St. Augustine, in three separate passages in his works, two of which shall here be quoted, gives his testimony. First, in his City of God, in an enumeration of miracles which had taken place since the Apostles' time. He begins with that which he himself had witnessed in the city of St. Ambrose:—

"The miracle," he says, "which occurred at Milan, while I was there, when a blind man gained sight, was of a kind to come to the knowledge of many, because the city is large, and the Emperor was there at the time, and it was wrought with the witness of a vast multitude, who had come together to the bodies of the martyrs Protasius and Gervasius; which, being at the time concealed and altogether unknown, were discovered on the revelation of a dream to Ambrose the bishop; upon which that blind man was released from his former darkness, and saw the day."—xxii. 8.

And next in his sermon upon the feast-day of the two martyrs:—

"We are celebrating, my brethren, the day on which, by Ambrose the bishop, that man of God, there was discovered, precious in the sight of the Lord, the death of His Saints; of which so great glory of the martyrs, then accruing, even I was a witness. I was there, I was at Milan, I know the miracles which were done, God attesting to the precious death of His Saints; that by those miracles henceforth, not in the Lord's sight only, but in the sight of men also, that death might be precious. A blind man, perfectly well known to the whole city, was restored to sight; he ran, he caused himself to be brought near, he returned without a guide. We have not yet heard of his death; perhaps he is still alive. In the very church where their bodies are, he has vowed his whole life to religious service. We rejoiced in his restoration, we left him in service."—*Serm.* 286. *vid.* also 318.

The third passage will be found in the ninth book of St. Augustine's Confessions, and adds to the foregoing extracts the important fact that the miracle was the cause of Justina's relinquishing her persecution of the Catholics.

2. Now let us proceed to the evidence of St. Ambrose, as contained in the sermons which he preached upon the occasion. In the former of the two he speaks as follows of the miracles wrought by the relics:—

"Ye know, nay, ye have yourselves seen, many cleansed from evil spirits, and numbers loosed from their infirmities, on laying their hands on the garment of the saints. Ye see renewed the miracles of the old time, when, through the advent of the Lord Jesus, a fuller grace poured itself upon the earth; ye see most men healed by the very shadow of the sacred bodies. How many are the napkins which pass to and fro! what anxiety for garments which are laid upon the most holy relics, and made salutary by their very touch! It is an object with all to reach even to the extreme border, and he who reaches it will be made whole. Thanks be to Thee, Lord Jesus, for awakening for us at this time the spirits of the holy martyrs, when Thy Church needs greater guardianship. Let all understand the sort of champions I ask for—those who may act as champions, not as assailants. And such have I gained for you, my religious people, such as benefit all, and harm none. Such defenders I solicit, such soldiers I possess, not the world's soldiers, but soldiers of Christ. I fear not that such will give offence; because the higher is their guardianship, the less exceptionable is it also. Nay, for them even who grudge me the martyrs, do I desire the martyrs' protection. So let them come and see my body-guard; I own I have such arms about me. 'These put their trust in chariots and these in horses; but we will glory in the name of the Lord our God.'

"Elisæus, as the course of Holy Scripture tells us, when hemmed in by the Syrian army, said to his frightened servant, by way of calming him, 'There are more that are for us than are against us.' And to prove this, he begged that Gehazi's eyes might be opened; upon which the latter saw innumerable hosts of Angels present to the prophet. We, though we cannot see them, yet are sensible of them. Our eyes were held as long as the bodies of the saints lay hid in their graves. The Lord has opened our eyes: we have seen those aids by which we have often been defended. We had not the sight of these, yet we had the possession. And so, as though the Lord said to us in our alarm, 'Behold what martyrs I have given you!' in like manner our eyes are unclosed, and we see the glory of the Lord, manifested, as once in their passion, so now in their power. We have got clear, my brethren, of no slight disgrace; we had patrons, yet we knew it not. We have found this one thing, in which we have the advantage of our forefathers—they lost the knowledge of these holy martyrs, and we have obtained it.

"Bring the victorious victims to the spot where is Christ the sacrifice. But He upon the altar, who suffered for all; they under it, who were redeemed by His passion. I had intended this spot for myself, for it is fitting that where the priest had been used to offer, there he should repose; but I yield the right side to the sacred victims; that spot was due to the martyrs. Therefore let us bury the hallowed relics, and introduce them into a fitting home; and celebrate the whole day with sincere devotion."—*Ep.* 22.

In his latter sermon, preached the following day, he pursues the subject:—

"This your celebration they are jealous of, who are wont to be; and, being jealous of it, they hate the cause of it, and are extravagant enough to deny the merits of those martyrs, whose works the very devils confess. Nor is it wonderful; it commonly happens that unbelievers who deny are less bearable than the devil who confesses. For the devil said, 'Jesus, Son of the living Son, why hast Thou come to torment us before the time?' And, whereas the Jews heard this, yet they were the very men to deny the Son of God. And now ye have heard the evil spirits crying out, and confessing to the martyrs, that they cannot bear their pains, and saying, 'Why are ye come to torment us so heavily?' And the Arians say, 'They are not martyrs, nor can they torment the devil, nor dispossess any one;' while the torments of the evil spirits are evidenced by their own voice, and the benefits of the martyrs by the recovery of the healed, and the tokens of the dispossessed.

"The Arians say, 'These are not real torments of evil spirits, but they are pretended and counterfeit.' I have heard of many things pretended, but no one ever could succeed in feigning himself a devil. How is it we see them in such distress when the hand is laid on them? What room is here for fraud? what suspicion of imposture?

"They deny that the blind received sight; but he does not deny that he was cured. He says, 'I see, who afore saw not.' He says, 'I ceased to be blind,' and he evidences it by the fact. They deny the benefit, who cannot deny the fact. The man is well known; employed as he was, before his affliction, in a public trade, Severus his name, a butcher his business: he had given it up when this misfortune befell him. He refers to the testimony of men whose charities were supporting him; he summons them as evidence of his present visitation, who were witnesses and judges of his blindness. He cries out that, on his touching the hem of the martyrs' garment, which covered the relics, his sight was restored to him. We read in the Gospel, that when the Jews saw the cure of the blind man, they sought the testimony of the parents. Ask others, if you distrust me; ask persons unconnected with him, if you think that his parents would take a side. The obstinacy of these Arians is more hateful than that of the Jews. When the latter doubted, at least they inquired of the parents; these inquire secretly, deny openly, as giving credit to the fact, but denying the author."—*Ibid.*

3. We may corroborate the evidence of those two Fathers with that of Paulinus, who was secretary to St. Ambrose, and wrote his life, about A.D. 411.

"About the same time," he says, "the holy martyrs Protasius and Gervasius revealed themselves to God's priest. They lay in the Basilica, where, at present, are the bodies of the martyrs Nabor and Felix; while, however, the holy martyrs Nabor and Felix had crowds to visit them, as well the names as the graves of the martyrs

Protasius and Gervasius were unknown; so that all who wished to come to the rails which protected the graves of the martyrs Nabor and Felix, were used to walk on the graves of the others. But when the bodies of the holy martyrs were raised and placed on litters, thereupon many possessions of the devil were detected. Moreover, a blind man, by name Severus, who up to this day performs religious service in the Basilica called Ambrosian, into which the bodies of the martyrs have been translated, when he had touched the garment of the martyrs, forthwith received sight. Moreover, bodies possessed by unclean spirits were restored, and with all blessedness returned home. And by means of these benefits of the martyrs, while the faith of the Catholic Church made increase, by so much did Arian misbelief decline."—§ 14.

4.

Now I want to know what reason is there for stumbling at the above narrative, which will not throw uncertainty upon the very fact that there was such a Bishop as Ambrose, or such an Empress as Justina, or such a heresy as the Arian, or any Church at all in Milan. Let us consider some of the circumstances under which it comes to us.

1. We have the concordant evidence of three distinct witnesses, of whom at least two were on the spot when the alleged miracles were wrought, one writing at the time, another some years afterwards in a distant country. And the third, writing after an interval of twenty-six years, agrees minutely with the evidence of the two former, not adding to the miraculous narrative, as is the manner of those who lose their delicate care for exactness in their admiration of the things and persons of whom they speak.

2. The miracle was wrought in public, on a person well known, on one who continued to live in the place where it was professedly wrought, and who, by devoting himself to the service of the martyrs who were the instru-

ments of his cure, was a continual memorial of the mercy which he professed to have received, and challenged inquiry into it, and refutation if that were possible.

3. Ambrose, one of our informants, publicly appealed, at the time when the occurrence took place, to the general belief, claimed it for the miracle, and that in a sermon which is still extant.

4. He made his statement in the presence of bitter and most powerful enemies, who were much concerned, and very able to expose the fraud, if there was one; who did, as might be expected, deny the hand of God in the matter; but who, for all that appears, did nothing but deny what they could not consistently confess, without ceasing to be what they were.

5. A great and practical impression was made upon the popular mind in consequence of the alleged miracles: or, in the words of an historian, whose very vocation it is to disbelieve them, "Their effect on the minds of the people was rapid and irresistible; and the feeble sovereign of Italy found himself unable to contend with the favourite of heaven."[1]

6. And so powerfully did all this press upon the Court, that, as the last words of this extract intimate, the persecution was given up, and the Catholics left in quiet possession of the churches.

On the whole, then, are we not in the following dilemma? If the miracle did not take place, then St. Ambrose and St. Augustine, men of name, said they had ascertained a fact which they did not ascertain, and said it in the face of enemies, with an appeal to a whole city, and that continued during a quarter of a century. What instrument of refutation shall we devise against a case like this, neither so violently *à priori* as to supersede the testimony

---

[1] Gibbon, Hist. ch. 27.

of Evangelists, nor so fastidious of evidence as to imperil Tacitus or Cæsar? On the other hand, if the miracle did take place, a certain measure of authority, more or less, surely must thereby attach to St. Ambrose—to his doctrine and his life, to his ecclesiastical principles and proceedings, to the Church itself of the fourth century, of which he is one main pillar. The miracle gives a certain sanction to three things at once, to the Catholic doctrine of the Trinity, to the Church's resistance of the civil power, and to the commemoration of saints and martyrs.

Does it give any sanction to Protestantism and its adherents? shall we accept it or not? shall we retreat, or shall we advance? shall we relapse into scepticism upon all subjects, or sacrifice our deep-rooted prejudices? shall we give up our knowledge of times past altogether, or endure to gain a knowledge which we think we have already—the knowledge of divine truth?

CHAPTER II.

WHAT SAYS VINCENT OF LERINS?

I.

IT is pretty clear that most persons of this day will be disposed to wonder at the earnestness shown by the early bishops of the Church in their defence of the Catholic faith. Athanasius, Hilary, Basil, Gregory, and Ambrose resisted the spread of Arianism at the risk of their lives. Yet their repeated protests and efforts were all about what? The man of the world will answer, "strifes of words, perverse disputings, curious questions, which do not tend to advance what ought to be the one end of all religion, peace and love. This is what comes of insisting on orthodoxy; putting the whole world into a fever!" *Tantum religio potuit*, etc., as the Epicurean poet says.

Such certainly is the phenomenon which we have to contemplate: theirs was a state of mind seldom experienced, and little understood, in this day; however, for that reason, it is at least interesting to the antiquarian, even were it not a sound and Christian state also. The highest end of Church union, to which the mass of educated men now look, is quiet and unanimity; as if the Church were not built upon faith, and truth really the first object of the Christian's efforts, peace but the second. The one idea which statesmen, and lawyers, and journalists, and men of letters have of a clergyman is, that he is by profession " a man of peace : " and if he has occasion to denounce, or to resist, or to protest, a cry is raised, " O how disgraceful in a minister of peace ! " The Church is thought invaluable as a promoter of good order and sobriety; but is regarded as nothing more. Far be it from me to seem to disparage what is really one of her high functions; but still a part of her duty will never be tantamount to the whole of it. At present the *beau idéal* of a clergyman in the eyes of many is a " reverend gentleman," who has a large family, and " administers spiritual consolation." Now I make bold to say, that confessorship for the Catholic faith is one part of the duty of Christian ministers, nay, and Christian laymen too. Yet, in this day, if at any time there is any difference in matters of doctrine between Christians, the first and last wish—the one sovereign object—of so-called judicious men, is to hush it up. No matter what the difference is about; *that* is thought so little to the purpose, that your well-judging men will not even take the trouble to inquire what it is. It may be, for what they know, a question of theism or atheism ; but they will not admit, whatever it is, that it can be more than secondary to the preservation of a good understanding between Christians. They think, whatever it is, it may safely be postponed for future consideration—that things will right themselves—the one pressing object being to present a bold and extended front to our external enemies, to prevent the outward fabric of the Church from being weakened by dissensions, and insulted by those who witness them. Surely the Church exists, in an especial way, for the sake of the faith committed to her keeping. But our practical men forget there may be remedies worse than the disease ; that latent heresy may be worse than a contest of "party;" and, in their treatment of the Church, they fulfil the satirist's well-known line:—

"Propter vitam vivendi perdere causas."

No wonder they do so, when they have been so long accustomed to merge the Church in the nation, and to talk of "Protestantism" in the abstract as synonymous with true religion; to consider that the characteristic merit of our Church is its "tolerance," as they call it, and that its greatest misfortune is the exposure to the world of those antagonistic principles and views which are really at work within it. But talking of exposure, what a scandal it was in St. Peter to exert his apostolical powers on Ananias; and in St. John, to threaten Diotrephes! What an exposure in St. Paul to tell the Corinthians he had "a rod" for them, were they disobedient! One should have thought, indeed, that weapons were committed to the Church for use as well as for show; but the present age apparently holds otherwise, considering that the Church is then most primitive, when it neither cares for the faith itself, nor uses the divinely ordained means by which it is to be guarded. Now, to people who acquiesce in this view, I know well that Ambrose or Augustine has not more of authority than an English non-juror; still, to those who do not acquiesce in it, it may be some little comfort, some encouragement, some satisfaction, to see that they themselves are not the first persons in the world who have felt and judged of religion in that particular way which is now in disrepute.

2.

However, some persons will allow, perhaps, that doctrinal truth ought to be maintained, and that the clergy ought to maintain it; but then they will urge that we should not make the path of truth too narrow; that it is a royal and a broad highway by which we travel heavenward, whereas it has been the one object of theologians, in every age, to encroach upon it, till at length it has become scarcely broad enough for two to walk abreast in. And moreover, it will be objected, that over-exactness was the very fault of the fourth and fifth centuries in particular, which refined upon the doctrines of the Holy Trinity and our Lord's Incarnation, till the way of life became like that razor's edge, which is said in the Koran to be drawn high over the place of punishment, and must be traversed by every one at the end of the world.

Now I cannot possibly deny, however disadvantageous it may be to their reputation, that the Fathers do represent the way of faith as narrow, nay, even as being the more excellent and the more royal for that very narrowness. Such is orthodoxy certainly; but here it is obvious to ask whether this very characteristic of it may not possibly be rather an argument for, than against, its divine origin. Certain it is, that such nicety, as it is called, is not unknown to other religious dispensations, creeds, and covenants, besides that which the primitive Church identified with Christianity. Nor is it a paradox to maintain that the whole system of religion, natural as well as revealed, is full of similar appointments. As to the subject of ethics, even a heathen philosopher tells us, that virtue consists in a mean—that is, in a point between indefinitely-extending extremes; "men being in one way good, and many ways bad." The same principle, again, is seen in the revealed system of spiritual communications; the grant of grace and privilege depending on positive ordinances, simple and definite—on the use of a little water, the utterance of a few words, the imposition of hands, and the like; which, it will perhaps be granted, are really essential to the conveyance of spiritual blessings, yet are confessedly as formal and technical as any creed can be represented to be. In a word, such technicality is involved in the very idea of a *means*, which may even be defined to be a something appointed, at God's inscrutable pleasure, as the necessary condition of something else; and the simple question before us is, merely the *matter of fact*, viz., whether any doctrine *is* set forth by Revelation as necessary to be believed *in order* to salvation? Antecedent difficulty in the question there is none; or rather, the probability is in favour of there being some necessary doctrine, from the analogy of the other parts of religion. The question is simply about the matter of fact.

This analogy is perspicuously expressed in one of the sermons of St. Leo :—" Not only," he says, "in the exercise of virtue and the observance of the commandments, but also in the path of faith, strait and difficult is the way which leads to life; and it requires great pains, and involves great risks, to walk without stumbling along the one footway of sound doctrine, amid the uncertain opinions and the plausible untruths of the unskilful, and to escape all peril of mistake when the toils of error are on every side."—*Serm.* 25.

St. Gregory Nazianzen says the same thing :—"We have bid farewell to contentious deviations of doctrine, and compensations on either side, neither Sabellianizing nor Arianizing. These are the sports of the evil one, who is a bad arbiter of our matters. But we, pacing along the middle and royal way, *in which also the essence of the virtues lies*, in the judgment of the learned, believe in Father, Son, and Holy Ghost."—*Orat.* 32.

On the whole, then, I see nothing very strange either in

orthodoxy lying in what at first sight appears like subtle and minute exactness of doctrine, or in its being our duty to contend even to confessorship for such exactness. Whether it be thus exact, and whether the exactness of Ambrose, Leo, or Gregory be the true and revealed exactness, is quite another question: all I say is, that it is no great difficulty to believe that it may be what they say it is, both as to its truth and as to its importance.

3.

But now supposing the question is asked, are Ambrose, Leo, and Gregory right? and is our Church right in maintaining with them the Athanasian doctrine on those sacred points to which it relates, and condemning those who hold otherwise? what answer is to be given? I answer by asking in turn, supposing any one inquired how we know that Ambrose, Leo, or Gregory was right, and our Church right, in receiving St. Paul's Epistles, what answer we should make? The answer would be, that it is a matter of history that the Apostle wrote those letters which are ascribed to him. And what is meant by its being a matter of history? why, that it has ever been so believed, so declared, so recorded, so acted on, from the first down to this day; that there is no assignable point of time when it was not believed, no assignable point at which the belief was introduced; that the records of past ages fade away and vanish *in* the belief; that in proportion as past ages speak at all, they speak in one way, and only fail to bear a witness, when they fail to have a voice. What stronger testimony can we have of a past fact?

Now evidence such as this have we for the Catholic doctrines which Ambrose, Leo, or Gregory maintained; they have never and nowhere *not* been maintained; or in other words, wherever we know anything positive of ancient times and places, there we are told of these doctrines also. As far as the records of history extend, they include these doctrines. as avowed always, everywhere, and by all. This is the great canon of the *Quod semper, quod ubique, quod ab omnibus,* which saves us from the misery of having to find out the truth for ourselves from Scripture on our independent and private judgment. He who gave Scripture, also gave us the interpretation of Scripture; and He gave the one and the other gift in the same way, by the testimony of past ages, as matter of historical knowledge, or as it is sometimes called, by Tradition. We receive the Catholic doctrines as we receive the canon of Scripture, because, as our Article expresses it, "*of their authority*" there "*was never any doubt in the Church.*"

We receive them on Catholic Tradition, and therefore they are called Catholic doctrines. And that they are Catholic, is a proof that they are Apostolic; they never could have been universally received in the Church, unless they had had their origin in the origin of the Church, unless they had been made the foundation of the Church by its founders. As the separate successions of bishops in various countries have but one common origin, the Apostles, so what has been handed down through these separate successions comes from that one origin. The Apostolic College is the only point in which all the lines converge, and from which they spring. Private traditions, wandering unconnected traditions, are of no authority, but permanent, recognised, public, definite, intelligible, multiplied, concordant testimonies to one and the same doctrine, bring with them an overwhelming evidence of apostolical origin. We ground the claims of orthodoxy on no powers of reasoning, however great, on the credit of no names, however imposing, but on an external fact, on an argument the same as that by which we prove the genuineness and authority of the four gospels. The unanimous tradition of all the churches to certain articles of faith is surely an irresistible evidence, more trustworthy far than that of witnesses to certain facts in a court of law, by how much the testimony of a number is more cogent than the testimony of two or three. That this really is the ground on which the narrow line of orthodoxy was maintained in ancient times, is plain from an inspection of the writings of the very men who maintained it, Ambrose, Leo, and Gregory, or Athanasius and Hilary, and the rest, who set forth its Catholic character in more ways than it is possible here to instance or even explain.

4

However, in order to give the general reader some idea of the state of the case, I will make some copious extracts from the famous tract of Vincent of Lerins on Heresy, written in A.D. 434, immediately after the third Ecumenical Council, held against Nestorius. The author was originally a layman, and by profession a soldier. In after life he became a monk and took orders. Lerins, the site of his monastery, is one of the small islands off the south coast of France. He first states what the principle is he would maintain, and the circumstances under which he maintains it ; and if his principle is reasonable and valuable in itself, so does it come to us with great weight under the circumstances which he tells us led him to his exposition of it:[1]

"Inquiring often," he says, "with great desire and attention, of very many excellent, holy, and learned men, how and by what means I might assuredly, and as it were by some general and ordi-

[1] The Oxford translation of 1837 is used in the following extracts.

nary way, discern the true Catholic faith from false and wicked heresy; to this question I had usually this answer from them all, that whether I or any other desired to find out the fraud of heretics, daily springing up, and to escape their snares, and to continue in a sound faith himself safe and sound, that he ought, by two ways, by God's assistance, to defend and preserve his faith; that is, first, by the authority of the law of God; secondly, by the tradition of the Catholic Church."—*Ch.* 2.

It will be observed he is speaking of the *mode* in which an *individual* is to seek and attain the truth; and it will be observed also, as the revered Bishop Jebb has pointed out, that he is allowing[1] and sanctioning the use of personal inquiry. He proceeds:—

"Here some man, perhaps, may ask, seeing the canon of the Scripture is perfect, and most abundantly of itself sufficient for all things, what need we join unto it the authority of the Church's understanding and interpretation? The reason is this, because the Scripture being of itself so deep and profound, all men do not understand it in one and the same sense, but divers men diversely, this man and that man, this way and that way, expound and interpret the sayings thereof, so that to one's thinking, 'so many men, so many opinions' almost may be gathered out of them : for Novatian expoundeth it one way, Photinus another; Sabellius after this sort, Donatus after that; Arius, Eunomius, Macedonius will have this exposition, Apollinaris and Priscilian will have that; Jovinian, Pelagius, Celestius, gather this sense, and, to conclude, Nestorius findeth out that; and therefore very necessary it is for the avoiding of so great windings and turnings, of errors so various, that the line of expounding the Prophets and Apostles be directed and drawn, according to the rule of the Ecclesiastical and Catholic sense.

"Again, within the Catholic Church itself we are greatly to consider that we hold that which hath been believed *everywhere*,

---

[1] [He allows of it in the *absence* at the time of the Church's authoritative declaration concerning the particular question in debate. He would say, "There was no need of any Ecumenical Council to condemn Nestorius; he was condemned by Scripture and tradition already."—1872.]

always, and *of all men :* for that is truly and properly *Catholic* (as the very force and nature of the word doth declare) which comprehendeth all things in general after an universal manner, and that shall we do if we follow *universality, antiquity, consent.* Universality shall we follow thus, if we profess that one faith to be true which the whole Church throughout the world acknowledgeth and confesseth. Antiquity shall we follow, if we depart not any whit from those senses which it is plain that our holy elders and fathers generally held. Consent shall we likewise follow, if in this very Antiquity itself we hold the definitions and opinions of all, or at any rate almost all, the priests and doctors together."—*Ch.* 2, 3.

It is sometimes said, that what is called orthodoxy or Catholicism is only the opinion of one or two Fathers—fallible men, however able they might be, or persuasive—who created a theology, and imposed it on their generation, and thereby superseded Scriptural truth and the real gospel. Let us see how Vincent treats such individual teachers, however highly gifted. He is speaking in the opening sentence of the Judaizers of the time of St. Paul :—

"When, therefore, such kind of men, wandering up and down through provinces and cities to set their errors to sale, came also unto the Galatians, and these, after they had heard them, were delighted with the filthy drugs of heretical novelty, loathing the truth, and casting up again the heavenly manna of the Apostolic and Catholic doctrine : the authority of his Apostolic office so puts itself forth as to decree very severely in this sort. 'But although (quoth he) we or an Angel from heaven evangelize unto you beside that which we have evangelized, be he Anathema.'[1] What meaneth this that he saith, 'But although we?' why did he not rather say, 'But although I?' that is to say, Although Peter, although Andrew, although John, yea, finally, although the whole company of the Apostles, evangelize unto you otherwise than we have evangelized, be he accursed. A terrible censure, in that for maintaining the possession of the first faith, he spared not himself, nor any other of the Apostles ! But this is a small matter : 'Although an Angel from

[1] Gal. i. 8.

heaven (quoth he) evangelize unto you, beside that which I have evangelized, be he Anathema,' he was not contented for keeping the faith once delivered to make mention of man's weak nature, unless also he included those excellent creatures the Angels... But peradventure he uttered those words slightly, and cast them forth rather of human affection than decreed them by divine direction. God forbid : for it followeth, and that urged with great earnestness of repeated inculcation, 'As I have foretold you (quoth he), and now again I tell you, If anybody evangelize unto you beside that which you have received, be he Anathema.' He said not, If any man preach unto you beside that which you have received, let him be blessed, let him be commended, let him be received, but let him be *Anathema*, that is, separated, thrust out, excluded, lest the cruel infection of one sheep with his poisoned company corrupt the sound flock of Christ."—*Ch.* 12 and 13.

5.

Here, then, is a point of doctrine which must be carefully insisted on. The Fathers are primarily to be considered as *witnesses*, not as *authorities*. They are witnesses of an existing state of things, and their treatises are, as it were, *histories*,—teaching us, in the first instance, matters of fact, not of opinion. Whatever they themselves might be, whether deeply or poorly taught in Christian faith and love, they speak, not their own thoughts, but the received views of their respective ages. The especial value of their works lies in their opening upon us a state of the Church which else we should have no notion of. We read in their writings a great number of high and glorious principles and acts ; and our first thought thereupon is, "All this must have had an existence somewhere or other in those times. These very men, indeed, may be merely speaking by rote, and not understand what they say ; but it matters not to the profit of their writings what they were themselves." It matters not to the profit of their writings, nor again to the authority resulting from them; for the *times* in which they wrote of course *are* of authority, though the Fathers themselves may have none. Tertullian or Eusebius may be nothing more than bare witnesses; yet so much as this they have a claim to be considered.

This is even the strict Protestant view. We are not obliged to take the Fathers as *authorities*, only as *witnesses*. Charity, I suppose, and piety will prompt the Christian student to go further, and to believe that men who laboured so unremittingly, and suffered so severely in the cause of the Gospel, really did possess some little portion of that earnest love of the truth which they professed, and were enlightened by that influence for which they prayed; but I am stating the strict Protestant doctrine, the great polemical principle ever to be borne in mind, that the Fathers are to be adduced in controversy merely as testimonies to an existing state of things, not as authorities. At the same time, no candid Protestant will be loth to admit, that the state of things to which they bear witness, *is*, as I have already said, a most grave and conclusive authority in guiding us in those particulars of our duty about which Scripture is silent; succeeding, as it does, so very close upon the age of the Apostles.

Thus much I claim of consistent Protestants, and thus much I grant to them. Gregory and the rest may have been but nominal Christians. Athanasius himself may have been very dark in all points of doctrine, in spite of his twenty years' exile and his innumerable perils by sea and land; the noble Ambrose, a high and dry churchman; and Basil, a mere monk. I do not dispute these points; though I claim "the right of private judgment," so far as to have my own very definite opinion in the matter, which I keep to myself.

6.

Such being the plain teaching of the Fathers, and such the duty of following it, Vincentius proceeds to speak of the misery of doubting and change:—

"Which being so, he is a true and genuine Catholic that loveth the truth of God, the Church, the body of Christ; that preferreth nothing before the religion of God; nothing before the Catholic faith; not any man's authority, not love, not wit, not eloquence, not philosophy; but contemning all these things, and in faith abiding fixed and stable, whatsoever he knoweth the Catholic Church universally in old times to have holden, that only he purposeth with himself to hold and believe; but whatsoever doctrine, new and not before heard of, such an one shall perceive to be afterwards brought in of some one man, beside all or contrary to all the saints, let him know that doctrine doth not pertain to religion, but rather to temptation, especially being instructed with the sayings of the blessed Apostle St. Paul. For this is that which he writeth in his first Epistle to the Corinthians: 'There must (quoth he) be heresies also, that they which are approved may be made manifest among you.' . . .

"O the miserable state of [waverers]! with what seas of cares, with what storms, are they tossed! for now at one time, as the wind driveth them, they are carried away headlong in error; at another time, coming again to themselves, they are beaten back like contrary waves; sometime with rash presumption they allow such things as seem uncertain, at another time of pusillanimity they are in fear even about those things which are certain; doubtful which way to take, which way to return, what to desire, what to avoid, what to hold, what to let go; which misery and affliction of a wavering and unsettled heart, were they wise, is as a medicine of God's mercy towards them.

"Which being so, oftentimes calling to mind and remembering the selfsame thing, I cannot sufficiently marvel at the great madness of some men, at so great impiety of their blinded hearts, lastly, at so great a licentious desire of error, that they be not content with the rule of faith once delivered us, and received from our ancestors, but do every day search and seek for new doctrine, ever desirous to add to, to change, and to take away something from religion; as though that were not the doctrine of God, which it is enough to have once revealed, but rather man's institution, which cannot but by continual amendment (or rather correction) be perfected."—*Ch.* 25, 26.

7.

Then he takes a text, and handles it as a modern preacher might do. His text is this :—

"O Timothy, keep the *depositum*, avoiding the profane novelties of words, and oppositions of falsely-called knowledge, which certain professing have erred about the faith."

He dwells successively upon *Timothy*, on the *deposit*, on *avoiding*, on *profane*, and on *novelties*.

First, *Timothy* and the "*deposit:*"—

"Who at this day is Timothy, but either generally the whole Church, or especially the whole body of prelates, who ought either themselves to have a sound knowledge of divine religion, or who ought to infuse it into others? What is meant by *keep the deposit?* Keep it (quoth he) for fear of thieves, for danger of enemies, lest when men be asleep, they oversow cockle among that good seed of wheat, which the Son of man hath sowed in His field. 'Keep (quoth he) the deposit.' What is meant by this deposit? that is, that which is committed to thee, not that which is invented of thee; that which thou hast received, not that which thou hast devised; a thing not of wit, but of learning; not of private assumption, but of public tradition; a thing brought to thee, not brought forth of thee; wherein thou must not be an author, but a keeper; not a beginner, but a follower; not a leader, but an observer. Keep the deposit. Preserve the talent of the Catholic faith safe and undiminished; that which is committed to thee, let that remain with thee, and that deliver. Thou hast received gold, render then gold; I will not have one thing for another; do not for gold render either impudently lead, or craftily brass; I will, not the show, but the very nature of gold itself. O Timothy, O priest, O teacher, O doctor, if God's gift hath made thee meet and sufficient by thy wit, exercise, and learning, be the Beseleel of the spiritual tabernacle, engrave the precious stones of God's doctrine, faithfully set them, wisely adorn them, give them brightness, give them grace, give them beauty. That which men before believed obscurely, let them by thy exposition understand more clearly. Let posterity rejoice for coming to the understanding of that by thy means, which antiquity without that understanding had in veneration. Yet for all this, in such sort deliver the same things which thou hast learned, that albeit thou teachest after a new manner yet thou never teach new things."

Next, "*avoiding:*"—

"'O Timothy (quoth he), keep the deposit, avoid profane novelties of words.' Avoid (quoth he) as a viper, as a scorpion, as a basilisk, lest they infect thee not only by touching, but also with their very eyes and breath. What is meant by *avoid?*[1] that is, not so much as to eat with any such. What importeth this *avoid?* 'If any man (quoth he) come unto you, and bring not this doctrine,'[2] what doctrine but the Catholic and universal, and that which, with incorrupt tradition of the truth, hath continued one and the selfsame, through all successions of times, and that which shall continue for ever and ever? What then? 'Receive him not (quoth he) into the house, nor say God speed; for he that saith unto him God speed, communicateth with his wicked works.'"

Then, "*profane:*"—

"'Profane novelties of words' (quoth he); what is *profane?* Those which have no holiness in them, nought of religion, wholly external to the sanctuary of the Church, which is the temple of God. 'Profane novelties of words (quoth he), of words, that is, novelties of doctrines, novelties of things, novelties of opinions, contrary to old usage, contrary to antiquity, which if we receive, of necessity the faith of our blessed ancestors, either all, or a great part of it, must be overthrown; the faithful people of all ages and times, all holy saints, all the chaste, all the continent, all the virgins, all the clergy, the deacons, the priests, so many thousands of confessors, so great armies of martyrs, so many famous and populous cities and commonwealths, so many islands, provinces, kings, tribes, kingdoms, nations; to conclude, almost now the whole world, incorporated by the Catholic faith to Christ their Head, must needs

---

[1] 1 Cor. v. 11. [2] 2 John 10, 11.

be said, so many hundreds of years, to have been ignorant, to have erred, to have blasphemed, to have believed they knew not what."

Lastly, "*novelties:*"—

"'Avoid (quoth he) profane *novelties* of words,' to receive and follow which was never the custom of Catholics, but always of heretics. And, to say truth, what heresy hath ever burst forth, but under the name of some certain man, in some certain place, and at some certain time? Who ever set up any heresy, but first divided himself from the consent of the universality and antiquity of the Catholic Church? Which to be true, examples do plainly prove. For who ever before that profane Pelagius presumed so much of man's free will, that he thought not the grace of God necessary to aid it in every particular good act? Who ever before his monstrous disciple Celestius denied all mankind to be bound with the guilt of Adam's transgression? Who ever before sacrilegious Arius durst rend in pieces the Unity of Trinity? Who ever before wicked Sabellius durst confound the Trinity of Unity? Who ever before cruel Novatian affirmed God to be merciless, in that He had rather the death of a sinner than that he should return and live? Who ever before Simon Magus, durst affirm that God our Creator was the Author of evil, that is, of our wickedness, impieties, and crimes; because God (as he said) so with His own hands made man's very nature, that by a certain proper motion and impulse of an enforced will, it can do nothing else, desire nothing else, but to sin. Such examples are infinite, which for brevity-sake I omit, by all which, notwithstanding, it appeareth plainly and clearly enough, that it is, as it were, a custom and law in all heresies, ever to take great pleasure in profane novelties, to loath the decrees of our forefathers, and to make shipwreck of faith, by oppositions of falsely-called knowledge; contrariwise that this is usually proper to all Catholics, to keep those things which the holy Fathers have left, and committed to their charge, to condemn profane novelties, and, as the Apostle hath said, and again forewarned, 'if any man shall preach otherwise than that which is received,' to anathematize him."—*Ch.* 27—34.

From these extracts, which are but specimens of the whole Tract, I come to the conclusion that Vincent was a very sorry Protestant.

CHAPTER III.

WHAT SAYS THE HISTORY OF APOLLINARIS?

IN the judgment of the early Church, the path of doctrinal truth is narrow; but, in the judgment of the world in all ages, it is so broad as to be no path at all. This I have said above; also, that the maintenance of the faith is considered by the world to be a strife of words, perverse disputings, curious questionings, and unprofitable technicality, though by the Fathers it is considered necessary to salvation. What they call heresy, the man of the world thinks just as true as what they call orthodoxy, and only then wrong when pertinaciously insisted on by its advocates, as the early Fathers insisted on orthodoxy. Now do, or do not, Protestants here take part with the world in disliking, in abjuring doctrinal propositions and articles, such as the early Church fought for? Certainly they do. Well, then, if they thus differ from the Church of the Fathers, how can they fancy that the early Church was Protestant?

In the Treatise I have been quoting, Vincent gives us various instances of heresiarchs, and tells us what he thinks about them. Among others, he speaks of Apollinaris and his fall; nor can we have a better instance than that of Apollinaris of the grave distress and deep commiseration with which the early Fathers regarded those whom the present Protestant world thinks very good kind of men, only fanciful and speculative, with some twist or hobby of their own. Apollinaris, better than any one else, will make us understand what was thought of the guilt of heresy in times which came next to the Apostolic, because the man was so great, and his characteristic heresy was so small. The charges against Origen have a manifest breadth and width to support them; Nestorius, on the other hand, had no high personal merits to speak for him; but Apollinaris, after a life of laborious service in the cause of religion, did but suffer himself to teach that the Divine Intelligence in our Lord superseded the necessity of His having any other, any human intellect; and for this apparently small error, he was condemned. Of course it was not small really; for one error leads to another, and did eventually in his case; but to all appearance it was small, yet it was promptly and sternly denounced and branded by East and West; would it be so ruthlessly smitten by Protestants now?

A brief sketch of his history, and of the conduct of the Church towards him, may not be out of place in the experiments I am making with a view of determining the relation in which modern Protestantism stands towards primitive Christianity.

I.

His father, who bore the same name, was a native of Alexandria, by profession a grammarian or schoolmaster; who, passing from Berytus to the Syrian Laodicea, married and settled there, and eventually rose to the presbyterate in the Church of that city. Apollinaris, the son, had been born there in the early part of the fourth century, and was educated for the profession of rhetoric. After a season of suspense, as to the ultimate destination of his talents, he resolved on dedicating them to the service of the Church; and, after being admitted into reader's orders, he began to distinguish himself by his opposition to philosophical infidelity. His work against Porphyry, the most valuable and elaborate of his writings, was extended to as many as thirty books. During the reign of Julian, when the Christian schools were shut up, and the Christian youth were debarred from the use of the classics, the two Apollinares, father and son, exerted themselves to supply the inconvenience thence resulting from their own resources. They wrote heroical pieces, odes, tragedies, and dialogues, after the style of Homer and Plato, and other standard authors, upon Christian subjects; and the younger, who is the subject of this Chapter, wrote and dedicated to Julian a refutation of Paganism, on grounds of reason.

Nor did he confine himself to the mere external defence of the Gospel, or the preparatory training of its disciples. His expositions on Scripture were the most numerous of his works; he especially excelled in eliciting and illustrating its sacred meaning, and he had sufficient acquaintance with the Hebrew to enable him to translate or comment on the original text. There was scarcely a controversy of the age, prolific as it was in heresies, into which he did not enter. He wrote against the Arians, Eunomians, Macedonians, and Manichees; against Origen and Marcellus; and in defence of the Millenarians. Portions of these doctrinal writings are still extant, and display a vigour and elegance of style not inferior to any writer of his day.

Such a man seemed to be raised up providentially for the Church's defence in an evil day; and for awhile he might be said resolutely and nobly to fulfil his divinely appointed destiny. The Church of Laodicea, with the other cities of Syria, was at the time in Arian possession; when the great Athanasius passed through on his return to Egypt, after his second exile (A.D. 348), Apollinaris communicated with him, and was in consequence put out of the Church by the bishop in possession. On the death of Constantius (A.D. 361), the Catholic cause prevailed; and Apollinaris was consecrated to that see, or to that in Asia Minor which bears the same name.

2.

Such was the station, such the reputation of Apollinaris, at the date of the Council thereupon held at Alexandria, A.D. 362, for settling the disorders of the Church; and yet, in the proceedings of this celebrated assembly, the first intimation occurs of the existence of that doctrinal error by which he has been since known in history, though it is not there connected with his name. The troubles under Julian succeeded, and diverted the minds of all parties to other objects. The infant heresy slept till about the year 369; when it gives us evidence of its existence in the appearance of a number of persons, scattered about Syria and Greece, who professed it in one form or other, and by the solemn meeting of a Council in the former country, in which its distinctive tenets were condemned. We find that even at this date it had run into those logical consequences which make even a little error a great one; still the name of Apollinaris is not connected with them.

The Council, as I have said, was held in Syria, but the heresy which occasioned it had already, it seems, extended into Greece; for a communication, which the there assembled bishops addressed to Athanasius on the subject, elicited from him a letter, still extant, addressed to Epictetus, bishop of Corinth, who had also written to him upon it. This letter, whether from tenderness to Apollinaris, or from difficulty in bringing the heresy home to him, still does not mention his name. Another work written by Athanasius against the heresy, at the very end of his life, with the keenness and richness of thought which distinguish his writings generally, is equally silent; as are two letters to friends about the same date, which touch more or less on the theological points in question. All these treatises seem to be forced from the writer, and are characterized by considerable energy of expression: as if the Catholics addressed were really perplexed with the novel statements of doctrine, and doubtful how Athanasius would meet them, or at least required his authority before pronouncing upon them; and, on the other hand, as if Athanasius himself were fearful of conniving at them, whatever private reasons he might have for wishing to pass them over. Yet there is nothing in the history or documents of the times to lead one to suppose that more than a general suspicion attached to Apollinaris; and, if we may believe his own statement, Athanasius died in persuasion of his orthodoxy. A letter is extant, written by Apollinaris on this subject, in which he speaks of the kind intercourse he had with the Patriarch of Alexandria, and of their agreement in faith, as acknowledged by Athanasius himself. He claims him as his master, and at the same time slightly hints that there had been points to settle between them, in which he himself had given way. In another, written to an Egyptian bishop, he seems to refer to the very epistle to Epictetus noticed above, expressing his approbation of it. It is known, moreover, that Athanasius gave the usual letters of introduction to Timotheus, Apollinaris's intimate friend, and afterwards the most extravagant teacher of his sect, on his going to the Western Bishops, and that, on the ground of his controversial talents against the Arians.

Athanasius died in A.D. 371 or 373; and that bereavement of the Church was followed, among its calamities, by the open avowal of heresy on the part of Apollinaris. In a letter already referred to, he claims Athanasius as agreeing with him, and then proceeds to profess one of the very tenets against which Athanasius had written. In saying this, I have no intention of accusing so considerable a man of that disingenuousness which is almost the characteristic mark of heresy. It was natural that Athanasius should have exercised an influence over his mind; and it was as natural that, when his fellow-champion was taken to his rest, he should have found himself able to breathe more freely, yet have been unwilling to own it. While indulging in the speculations of a private judgment, he might still endeavour to persuade himself that he was not outstepping the teaching of the Catholic Church. On the other hand, it appears that the ecclesiastical authorities of the day, even when he professed his heresy, were for awhile incredulous about the fact, from their recollection of his former services and his tried orthodoxy, and from the hope that he was but carried on into verbal extravagances by his opposition to Arianism. Thus they were as unwilling to impute to him heresy, as he to confess it. Nay, even when he had lost shame, attacked the Catholics with violence, and formed his disciples into a sect, not even then was he himself publicly animadverted on, though his creed was anathematized. His first condemnation was at Rome, several years after Athanasius's death, in company with Timotheus, his disciple. In the records of the General Council of Constantinople, several years later, his sect is mentioned as existing, with directions how to receive back into the Church those who applied for reconciliation. He outlived this Council about ten years; his sect lasted only twenty years beyond him; but in that short time it had split into three distinct denominations, of various degrees of heterodoxy, and is said to have fallen more or less into the errors of Judaism.

3.

If this is a faithful account of the conduct of the Church towards Apollinaris, no one can accuse its rulers of treating him with haste or harshness; still they accompanied their tenderness towards him personally with a conscientious observance of their duties to the Catholic Faith, to which our Protestants are simply dead. Who now in England, except very high churchmen, would dream of putting a man out of the Church for what would be called a mere speculative or metaphysical opinion? Why could not Apollinaris be a "spiritual man," have "a justifying faith," "apprehend" our Lord's merits, have "a personal interest in redemption," be in possession of "experimental religion," and be able to recount his "experiences," though he had some vagaries of his own about the nature of our Lord's soul? But such ideas did not approve themselves to Christians of the fourth century, who followed up the anathemas of Holy Church with their own hearty adhesion to them. Epiphanius speaks thus mournfully:—

"That aged and venerable man, who was ever so singularly dear to us, and to the holy Father, Athanasius, of blessed memory, and to all orthodox men, Apollinaris, of Laodicea, he it was who originated and propagated this doctrine. And at first, when we were assured of it by some of his disciples, we disbelieved that such a man could admit such an error into his path, and patiently waited in hope, till we might ascertain the state of the case. For we argued that his youths, who came to us, not entering into the profound views of so learned and clear-minded a master, had invented these statements of themselves, not gained them from him. For there were many points in which those who came to us were at variance with each other: some of them ventured to say that Christ had brought down His body from above (and this strange theory, admitted into the mind, developed itself into worse notions); others of them denied that Christ had taken a soul; and some ventured to say that Christ's body was consubstantial with the Godhead, and thereby caused great confusion in the East."—*Hær.* lxxvii. 2.

He proceeds afterwards:—

"Full of distress became our life at that time, that between brethren so exemplary as the forementioned, a quarrel should at all have arisen, that the enemy of man might work divisions among us. And great, my brethren, is the mischief done to the mind from such a cause. For were no question ever raised on the subject, the matter would be most simple (for what gain has accrued to the world from such novel doctrine, or what benefit to the Church? rather has it not been an injury, as causing hatred and dissension?): but when the question was raised, it became formidable; it did not tend to good; for whether a man disallows this particular point, or even the slightest, still it is a denial. For we must not, even in a trivial matter, turn aside from the path of truth. No one of the ancients ever maintained it—prophet, or apostle, or evangelist, or commentator—down to these our times, when this so perplexing doctrine proceeded from that most learned man aforesaid. His was a mind of no common cultivation; first in the preliminaries of literature in Greek education, then as a master of dialectics and argumentation. Moreover, he was most grave in his whole life, and reckoned among the very first of those who ever deserved the love of the orthodox, and so continued till his maintenance of this doctrine. Nay, he had undergone banishment for not submitting to the Arians;—but why enlarge on it? It afflicted us much, and gave us a sorrowful time, as is the wont of our enemy."—*Ibid.* 24.

St. Basil once got into trouble from a supposed intimacy with Apollinaris. He had written one letter to him on an indifferent matter, in 356, when he himself was as yet a layman, and Apollinaris orthodox and scarcely in orders. This was magnified by his opponent Eustathius into a correspondence and intercommunion between the archbishop and heresiarch. As in reality Basil knew very little even of his works, the description which the following passages give is valuable, as being, in fact, a sort of popular opinion about Apollinaris, more than an individual judgment. Basil wrote the former of the two in defence of himself; in the latter, other errors of Apollinaris are mentioned, besides those to which I have had occasion to allude, for, as I have said, errors seldom are found single.

"For myself," says Basil, "I never indeed considered Apollinaris as an enemy; nay, there are respects in which I reverence him; however, I did not so connect myself with him as to make myself answerable for his alleged faults, considering, too, that I have a complaint of my own against him, on reading some of his compositions. I hear, indeed, that he is become the most copious of all writers; yet I have fallen in with but few of his works, for I have not leisure to search into such, and besides, I do not easily form the acquaintance of recent writers, being hindered by bodily health from continuing even the study of inspired Scripture laboriously, and as is fitting."—*Ep.* 244, § 3.

The other passage runs thus :—

"After Eustathius comes Apollinaris; he, too, no slight disturber of the Church; for, having a facility in writing and a tongue which served him on every subject, he has filled the world with his compositions, despising the warning, 'Beware of making many books,' because in the many are many faults. For how is it possible, in much speaking, to escape sin?"—*Ep.* 263, § 4.

And then he goes on to mention some of the various gross errors, to which by that time he seemed to be committed.

Lastly, let us hear Vincent of Lerins about him :—

"Great was the heat and great the perplexity which Apollinaris created in the minds of his auditory, when the authority of the Church drew them one way, and the influence of their teacher drew them the other, so that, wavering and hesitating between the two, they could not decide which was to be chosen. You will say, he ought at once to have been put aside; yes, but he was so great a man, that his word carried with it an extraordinary credence. Who indeed was his superior in acumen, in long practice, in view of doctrine? As to the number of his volumes against heresies, I will but mention as a specimen of them that great and noble work of his against Porphyry, in not less than thirty books, with its vast collection of arguments. He would have been among the master-builders of the Church, had not the profane lust of heretical curiosity incited him to strike out something new, to pollute withal his labours throughout with the taint of leprosy, so that his teaching was rather a temptation to the Church than an edification."—*Ch.* 16.

It is a solemn and pregnant fact, that two of the most zealous and forward of Athanasius's companions in the good fight against Arianism, Marcellus and Apollinaris, fell away into heresies of their own; nor did the Church spare them, for all their past services. "Let him that thinketh he standeth, take heed lest he fall."

> " Alas, my brother! round thy tomb,
>   In sorrow kneeling, and in fear,
> We read the pastor's doom,
>   Who speaks and will not hear.
>
> "The gray-haired saint may fail at last,
>   The surest guide a wanderer prove;
> Death only binds us fast
>   To the bright shore of love."

CHAPTER IV.

AND WHAT SAY JOVINIAN AND HIS COMPANIONS?

I.

VINCENTIUS wrote in the early part of the fifth century, that is, three good centuries and more after the death of St. John; accordingly, we sometimes hear it said that, true though it be, that the Catholic system, as we Anglicans maintain it, existed at that time, nevertheless it was a system quite foreign to the pure Gospel, though introduced at a very early age; a system of Pagan or Jewish origin, which crept in unawares, and was established on the ruins of the Apostolic faith by the episcopal confederation, which mainly depended on it for its own maintenance. In other words, it is considered by some persons to be a system of priestcraft, destructive of Christian liberty.

Now, it is no paradox to say that *this* would be a sufficient answer to such a speculation, were there no other, viz., that no answer *can* be made to it. I say, supposing it could not be answered at all, that fact would be a fair answer. All discussion must have data to go upon; without data, neither one party can dispute nor the other. If I maintained there were negroes in the moon, I should like to know how these same philosophers would answer me. Of course they would not attempt it: they would confess they had no grounds for denying it, only they would add, that I had no grounds for asserting it. They would not prove that I was wrong, but call upon me to prove that I was right. They would consider such a mode of talking idle and childish, and unworthy the consideration of a serious man; else, there would be no end of speculation, no hope of certainty and unanimity in anything. Is a man to be allowed to say what he will, and bring no reasons for it? Even if his hypothesis fitted into the facts of the case, still it would be but an hypothesis, and might be met, perhaps, in the course of time, by another hypothesis, presenting as satisfactory a solution of them. But if it would not be necessarily true, though it were adequate, much less is it entitled to consideration before it is proved to be adequate—before it is actually reconciled with the facts of the case ; and when another hypothesis has, from the beginning, been in the possession of the field. From the first it has been believed that the Catholic system is Apostolic; convincing reasons must be brought against this belief, and in favour of another, before that other is to be preferred to it.

Now the new and gratuitous hypothesis in question does not appear, when examined, even to harmonize with the facts of the case. One mode of dealing with it is this:—Take a large view of the faith of Christians during the centuries before Constantine established their religion. Is there any family likeness in it to Protestantism? Look at it, as existing during that period in different countries, and is it not one and the same, and a reiteration of itself, as well as singularly unlike Reformed Christianity? Hermas with his visions, Ignatius with his dogmatism, Irenæus with his praise of tradition and of the Roman See, Clement with his allegory and mysticism, Cyprian with his " Out of the Church is no salvation," and Methodius with his praise of Virginity, all of them writers between the first and fourth centuries, and witnesses of the faith of Rome, Africa, Gaul, Asia Minor, Syria, and Egypt, certainly do not represent the opinions of Luther and Calvin. They stretch over the whole of Christendom; they are consistent with each other; they coalesce into one religion; but it is not the religion of the Reformation. When we ask, "Where was your Church before Luther?" Protestants answer, "Where were you this morning before you washed your face?" But, if Protestants can clean themselves into the likeness of Cyprian or Irenæus, they must scrub very hard, and have well-nigh learned the art of washing the blackamoor white.

2

If the Church system be not Apostolic, it must, some time or other, have been introduced, and then comes the question, when? We maintain that the known circumstances of the previous history are such as to preclude the possibility of any time being assigned, ever so close upon the Apostles, at which the Church system did not exist. Not only cannot a time be shown when the free-and-easy system now in fashion did generally exist, but no time can be shown in which it can be colourably maintained that the Church system was brought in. It will be said, of course, that the Church system was gradually introduced. I do not say there have never been introductions of any kind; but let us see what they amount to here. Select for yourself your doctrine, or your ordinance, which you say was introduced, and try to give the history of its introduction. Hypothetical that history will be, of course; but we will not scruple at that;—we will only ask one thing, that it should cut clean between the real facts of the case, though it bring none in its favour; but it will not be able to do even this. The rise of the doctrine of the Holy Trinity, of the usage of baptizing infants, of the eucharistic offering, of the episcopal prerogatives, do what one will, can hardly be made short of Apostolical times. This is not the place to prove all this; but so fully is it felt to be so, by those who are determined not to admit these portions of Catholicism, that in their despair of drawing the line between the first and following centuries, they make up their minds to intrude into the first, and boldly pursue their supposed error into the very presence of some Apostle or Evangelist. Thus St. John is sometimes made the voluntary or involuntary originator of some portions of our creed. Dr. Priestley, I believe, conjectures that his amanuensis played him false, as regards his teaching upon the sacred doctrine which that philosopher opposed. Others take exceptions to St. Luke, because he tells us of the "handkerchiefs, or aprons," which "were brought from St. Paul's body" for the cure of diseases. Others have gone a step further, and have said, "Not Paul, but Jesus." Infidel, Socinian, and Protestant, agree in assailing the Apostles, rather than submitting to the Church.

3.

Let our Protestant friends go to what quarter of Christendom they will, let them hunt among heretics or schismatics, into Gnosticism outside the Church, or Arianism within it, still they will find no hint or vestige anywhere of that system which they are now pleased to call Scriptural. Granting that Catholicism be a corruption, is it possible that it should be a corruption springing up everywhere at once? Is it conceivable that at least no opponent should have retained any remnant of the system it supplanted?—that no tradition of primitive purity should remain in any part of Christendom?—that no protest, or controversy, should have been raised, as a monument against the victorious error? This argument, conclusive against modern Socinianism, is still more cogent and striking when directed against Puritanism. At least, there *were* divines in those early days who denied the sacred doctrine which Socinianism also disowns, though commonly they did not profess to do so on authority of tradition; but who ever heard of Erastians, Supralapsarians, Independents, Sacramentarians, and the like, before the sixteenth and seventeenth centuries? It would be too bold to go to prove a negative: I can only say that I do not know in what quarter to search for the representatives, in the early Church, of that "Bible religion," as it is called, which is now so much in favour. At first sight, one is tempted to say that all errors come over and over again; that this and that notion now in vogue has been refuted in times past. This is indeed a general truth—nay, for what I know, these same bold speculatists will bring it even as an argument for their not being in error, that Antiquity says nothing at all, good or bad, about their opinions. I cannot answer for the extent to which they will throw the *onus probandi* on us; but I protest—be it for us, or be it against us—I cannot find this very religion of theirs in ancient times, whether in friend or foe, Jew or Pagan, Montanist or Novatian; though I find surely enough, and in plenty, the general characteristics, which are conspicuous in their philosophy, of self-will, eccentricity, and love of paradox.

So far from it, that if we wish to find the rudiments of the Catholic system clearly laid down in writing, those who are accounted least orthodox will prove as liberal in their information about it as the strictest Churchman.

We can endure even the heretics better than our opponents can endure the Apostles. Tertullian, though a Montanist, gives no sort of encouragement to the so-called Bible Christians of this day; rather he would be the object of their decided abhorrence and disgust. Origen is not a whit more of a Protestant, though he, if any, ought, from the circumstances of his history, to be a witness against us. It is averred that the alleged revolution of doctrine and ritual was introduced by the influence of the episcopal system; well, here is a victim of episcopacy, brought forward by our opponents as such. Here is a man who was persecuted by his bishop, and driven out of his country; and whose name after his death has been dishonourably mentioned, both by Councils and Fathers. He surely was not in the episcopal conspiracy, at least; and perchance may give the latitudinarian, the anabaptist, the Erastian, and the utilitarian, some countenance. Far from it; he is as high and as keen, as removed from softness and mawkishness, as ascetic and as reverential, as any bishop among them. He is as superstitious (as men now talk), as fanatical, as formal, as Athanasius or Augustine. Certainly, there seems something providential in the place which Origen holds in the early Church, considering the direction which theories about it are now taking; and much might be said on that subject.

Take another instance:—There was, in the fourth century, a party of divines who were ecclesiastically opposed to the line of theologians, whose principles had been, and were afterwards, dominant in the Church, such as Athanasius, Jerome, and Epiphanius; I mean, for instance, Eusebius, Cyril of Jerusalem, and others who were more or less connected with the Semi-Arians. If, then, we see that in all points, as regards the sacraments and sacramentals, the Church and its ministers, the form of worship, and other religious duties of Christians, Eusebius and Cyril agree entirely with the most orthodox of their contemporaries, with those by party and country most separated from them, we have a proof that that system, whatever it turns out to be, was received before their time—*i.e.* before the establishment of Christianity under Constantine; in other words, that we must look for the gradual corruption of the Church, if it is to be found, not when wealth pampered it, and power and peace brought its distant portions together, but while it was yet poor, humble, and persecuted, in those times which are commonly considered pure and primitive. Again, the genius of Arianism, as a party and a doctrine, was to discard antiquity and mystery; that is, to resist and expose what is commonly called priestcraft. In proportion, then, as Cyril and Eusebius partook of that spirit, so far would they be in their own cast of mind indisposed to the Catholic system, both considered in itself and as being imposed on them.

Now, have the writers in question any leaning or tenderness for the theology of Luther and Calvin? rather they are as unconscious of its existence as of modern chemistry or astronomy. That faith is a closing with divine mercy, not a submission to a divine announcement, that justification and sanctification are distinct, that good works do not benefit the Christian, that the Church is not Christ's ordinance and instrument, and that heresy and dissent are not necessarily and intrinsically evil: notions such as these they do not oppose, simply because to all appearance they never heard of them. To take a single passage, which first occurs, in which Eusebius, one of the theologians in question, gives us his notion of the Catholic Church:—

"These attempts," he says, speaking of the arts of the enemy, "did not long avail him, Truth ever consolidating itself, and, as time went on, shining into broader day. For while the devices of adversaries were extinguished at once, confuted by their very activity,—one heresy after another presenting its own novelty, the former specimens ever dissolving and wasting variously in manifold and multiform shapes,—the brightness of the Catholic and only true Church went forward increasing and enlarging, yet ever in the same things and in the same way, beaming on the whole race of Greeks and barbarians with the awfulness, and simplicity, and nobleness, and sobriety, and purity of its divine polity and philosophy. Thus the calumny against our whole creed died with its day, and there continued alone our discipline, sovereign among all, and acknowledged to be pre-eminent in awfulness and sobriety, in its divine and philosophical doctrines; so that no one of this day dares to cast any base reproach upon our faith, nor any such calumny such as it was once customary for our enemies to use."—*Hist.* iv. 7.

Or to take a passage on a different subject, which almost comes first to hand, from St. Cyril, another of this school of divines:—

"Only be of good cheer, only work, only strive cheerfully; for nothing is lost. Every prayer of thine, every psalm thou singest is recorded; every alms-deed, every fast is recorded; every marriage duly observed is recorded; continence kept for God's sake is recorded; but the first crowns in record are those of virginity and purity; and thou shalt shine as an Angel. But as thou hast gladly listened to the good things, listen without shrinking to the contrary. Every covetous deed of thine is recorded; every fleshly deed, every perjury, every blasphemy, every sorcery, every theft, every murder. All these things are henceforth recorded, if thou do these after baptism; for thy former deeds are blotted out."—*Cat.* xv. 23.

Cyril and Eusebius, I conceive, do not serve at all better than Origen to show that faith is a feeling, that it makes a man independent of the Church, and is efficacious apart from baptism or works. I do not know any ancient divines of whom more can be made.

4.

Where, then, is primitive Protestantism to be found? There is one chance for it, not in the second and third centuries, but in the fourth; I mean in the history of Aerius, Jovinian, and Vigilantius,—men who may be called, by some sort of analogy, the Luther, Calvin, and Zwingle, of the fourth century. And they have been so considered both by Protestants and by their opponents; so covetous, after all, of precedent are innovators, so prepared are Catholics to believe that there is nothing new under the sun. Let me, then, briefly state the history and tenets of these three religionists.

1. Aerius was an intimate friend of Eustathius, bishop of Sebaste, in Armenia, whose name has already occurred above. Both had embraced a monastic life; and both were Arians in creed. Eustathius, being raised to the episcopate, ordained his friend presbyter, and set him over the almshouse or hospital of the see. A quarrel followed, from whatever cause; Aerius left his post, and accused Eustathius of covetousness, as it would appear, unjustly. Next he collected a large number of persons of both sexes in the open country, where they braved the severe weather of that climate. A congregation implies a creed, and Aerius founded or formed his own on the following points: 1. That there was no difference between bishop and presbyter. 2. That it was judaical to observe Easter, because Christ is our Passover. 3. That it was useless, or rather mischievous, to name the dead in prayer, or to give alms for them. 4. That fasting was judaical, and a yoke of bondage. If it be right to fast, he added, each should choose his own day; for instance, Sunday rather than Wednesday and Friday: while Passion Week he spent in feasting and merriment,

And this is pretty nearly all we know of Aerius, who flourished between A.D. 360 and 370.

2. Jovinian was a Roman monk, and was condemned, first by Siricius at Rome, then by St. Ambrose and other bishops at Milan, about A.D. 390. He taught, 1. That eating with thanksgiving was just as good as fasting. 2. That, *cæteris paribus*, celibacy, widowhood, and marriage, were on a level in the baptized. 3. That there was no difference of rewards hereafter for those who had preserved their baptism; and, 4. That those who had been baptized with full faith could not fall; if they did, they had been baptized, like Simon Magus, only with water. He persuaded persons of both sexes at Rome, who had for years led a single life, to desert it. The Emperor Honorius had him transported to an island on the coast of Dalmatia; he died in the beginning of the fifth century.

3. Vigilantius was a priest of Gaul or Spain, and flourished just at the time Jovinian died: he taught, 1. That those who reverenced relics were idolaters; 2. That continence and celibacy were wrong, as leading to the worst scandals; 3. That lighting candles in churches during the day, in honour of the martyrs, was wrong, as being a heathen rite; 4. That Apostles and Martyrs had no presence at their tombs; 5. That it was useless to pray for the dead; 6. That it was better to keep wealth and practice habitual charity, than to strip one's-self of one's property once for all; and 7. That it was wrong to retire into the desert. This is what we learn of these three (so-called) reformers, from the writings of Epiphanius and Jerome.

Now you may say, "What can we require more than this? Here we have, at the time of a great catastrophe, Scriptural truth come down to us in the burning matter which melted and preserved it, in the persecuting language of Epiphanius and Jerome. When corruptions began to press themselves on the notice of Christians, here you find three witnesses raising their distinct and solemn protest in different parts of the Church, independently of each other, in Gaul, in Italy, and in Asia Minor, against prayers for the dead, veneration of relics, candles in the day-time, the merit of celibacy, the need of fasting, the observance of days, difference in future rewards, the defectibility of the regenerate, and the divine origin of episcopacy. Here is pure and scriptural Protestantism." Such is the phenomenon on which a few remarks are now to be offered.

5.

1. I observe then, first, that this case so presented to us, does not answer the purpose required. The doctrine of these three Protestants, if I am to be forced into calling them so, is, after all, but negative. We know what they protested *against*, not what they protested *for*. We do not know what the system of doctrine and ritual was which they substituted for the Catholic, or whether they had any such. Though they differed from the ancients, there is no proof that they agreed with the moderns. Parties which differ from a common third, do not necessarily agree with each other; from two negative propositions nothing is inferred. For instance, the moral temper and doctrinal character of the sixteenth century is best symbolized by its views about faith and justification, to which I have already referred, and upon the duty of each individual man drawing his own creed from the Scriptures. This is its positive shape, as far as it may be considered positive at all. Now does any one mean to maintain that Aerius, Jovinian, or Vigilantius, held justification by faith only in the sense of John Wesley, or of John

Newton? Did they consider that baptism was a thing of nought; that faith did everything; that faith was trust, and the perfection of faith assurance; that it consisted in believing that "I am pardoned;" and that works might be left to themselves, to come as they might, as being *necessary* fruits of faith, without our trouble? Did they know anything of the "apprehensive" power of faith, or of man's proneness to consider his imperfect services, done in and by grace, as adequate to purchase eternal life? There is no proof they did. Let then these three protesters be ever so cogent an argument against the Catholic creed, this does not bring them a whit nearer to the Protestant; though in fact there is nothing to show that their protest was founded on historical grounds, or on any argument deeper than such existing instances of superstition and scandal in detail as are sure to accumulate round revelation.

Further, even if a modern wished, he would not be able to put up with even the negative creed of these primitive protesters, whatever his particular persuasion might be. Their protest suits no sect whatever of this day. It is either too narrow or too liberal. The Episcopalian, as he is styled, will not go along with Aerius's notions about bishops; nor will the Lutheran subscribe to the final perseverance of the saints; nor will the strict Calvinist allow that all fasting is judaical; nor will the Baptist admit the efficacy of baptism: one man will wonder why none of the three protested against the existence of the Church itself; another that none of them denied the received doctrine of penance; a third that all three let pass the received doctrine of the Eucharist. Their protestations are either too much or too little for any one of their present admirers. There is no one of any of the denominations of this day but will think them wrong in some points or other; that is all we know about them; but if we all think them wrong on some points, is that a good reason why we should take them as an authority on others?

Or, again, do we wish to fix upon what *can* be detected in their creed of a positive character, and distinct from their protests? We happen to be told what it was in the case of one of them. Aerius was an Arian; does this mend matters? Is there any agreement at all between him and Luther here? If Aerius is an authority against bishops, or against set fasts, why is he not an authority against the Creed of St. Athanasius?

2. What has been last said leads to a further remark. I observe, then, that if two or three men in the fourth century are sufficient, against the general voice of the Church, to disprove one doctrine, then still more are two or three of an earlier century able to disprove another. Why should protesters in century four be more entitled to a hearing than protesters in century three? Now it so happens, that as Aerius, Jovinian, and Vigilantius in the fourth protested against austerities, so did Praxeas, Noetus, and Sabellius in the third protest against the Catholic or Athanasian doctrine of the Holy Trinity. A much stronger case surely could be made out in favour of the latter protest than of the former. Noetus was of Asia Minor, Praxeas taught in Rome, Sabellius in Africa. Nay, we read that in the latter country their doctrine prevailed among the common people, then and at an earlier date, to a very great extent, and that the true faith was hardly preached in the churches.

3. Again, the only value of the protest of these three men would be, of course, that they *represented* others; that they were exponents of a state of opinion which

prevailed either in their day or before them, and which was in the way to be overpowered by the popular corruptions. What are Aerius and Jovinian to me as individuals? They are worth nothing, unless they can be considered as organs and witnesses of an expiring cause. Now, it does not appear that they themselves had any notion that they were speaking in behalf of any one, living or dead, besides themselves. They argued against prayers for the departed from reason, and against celibacy, hopeless as the case might seem, from Scripture. They ridiculed one usage, and showed the ill consequence of another. All this might be very cogent in itself, but it was the conduct of men who stood by themselves and were conscious of it. If Jovinian had known of writers of the second and third centuries holding the same views, Jovinian would have been as prompt to quote them as Lutherans are to quote Jovinian. The protest of these men shows that certain usages undeniably existed in the fourth century; it does not prove that they did not exist also in the first, second, and third. And how does the fact of their living in the fourth century prove there were Protestants in the first? What we are looking for is a Church of primitive heretics, of baptists and independents of the Apostolic age, and we must not be put off with the dark and fallible protests of the Nicene era.

Far different is the tone of Epiphanius in his answer to Aerius:—

"If one need refer," he says, speaking of fasting, "to the constitution of the Apostles, why did they there determine the fourth and sixth day to be ever a fast, except Pentecost? and concerning the six days of the Pascha, why do they order us to take nothing at all but bread, salt, and water? . . Which of these parties is the rather correct? this deceived man, who is now among us, and is still alive, or they who were witnesses before us, possessing before our time the tradition in the Church, and they having received it from their fathers, and those very fathers again having learned it from those who lived before them? . . The Church has received it, and it is unanimously confessed in the whole world, before Aerius and Aerians were born."—*Hær.* 75, § 6.

4. Once more, there is this very observable fact in the case of each of the three, that their respective protests seem to have arisen from some personal motive. Certainly what happens to a man's self often brings a thing home to his mind more forcibly, makes him contemplate it steadily, and leads to a successful investigation into its merits. Yet still, where we know personal feelings to exist in the maintenance of any doctrine, we look more narrowly at the proof for ourselves; thinking it not impossible that the parties may have made up their minds on grounds short of reason. It is natural to feel distrust of controversialists, who, to all appearance, would not have been earnest against a doctrine or practice, except that it galled themselves. Now it so happens that each of these three Reformers lies open to this imputation. Aerius is expressly declared by Epiphanius to have been Eustathius's competitor for the see of Sebaste, and to have been disgusted at failing. *He* is the preacher against bishops. Jovinian was bound by a monastic vow, and *he* protests against fasting and coarse raiment. Vigilantius was a priest; and, therefore, *he* disapproves the celibacy of the clergy. No opinion at all is here ventured in favour of clerical celibacy; still it is remarkable that in the latter, as in the two former cases, private feeling and public protest should have gone together.

6.

These distinct considerations are surely quite sufficient to take away our interest in these three Reformers.

These men are not an historical clue to a lost primitive creed, more than Origen or Tertullian; and much less do they afford any support to the creed of those moderns who would fain shelter themselves behind them. That there were abuses in the Church then, as at all times, no one, I suppose, will deny. There may have been extreme opinions and extreme acts, pride and pomp in certain bishops, over-honour paid to saints, fraud in the production of relics, extravagance in praising celibacy, formality in fasting; and such errors would justify a protest, which the Catholic Fathers themselves are not slow to make; but they would not justify that utter reprobation of relics, of celibacy, and of fasting, of episcopacy, of prayers for the dead, and of the doctrine of defectibility, which these men avowed—avowed without the warrant of the first ages—on grounds of private reason, under the influence of personal feeling, and with the accompaniment of but a suspicious orthodoxy. It does certainly look as if our search after Protestantism in Antiquity would turn out a simple failure;—whatever Primitive Christianity was or was not, it was not the religion of Luther. I shall think so, until I find Ignatius and Aerius, in spite of their differences about bishops, agreeing in his doctrine of justification; until Irenæus and Jovinian, though at daggers drawn about baptism, shall yet declare Scripture to be the sole rule of faith; until Cyprian and Vigilantius, however at variance about the merit of virginity, uphold in common the sacred right and duty of private judgment.

CHAPTER V.

AND WHAT DO THE APOSTOLICAL CANONS SAY?

1.

SUCH, then, is the testimony borne in various ways by Origen, Eusebius, and Cyril, by Aerius, Jovinian, and Vigilantius, to the immemorial reception among Christians of those doctrines and practices which the private judgment of this age considers to be unscriptural. I have been going about from one page to another of the records of those early times, prying and extravagating beyond the beaten paths of orthodoxy, for the chance of detecting some sort of testimony in favour of our opponents. With this object I have fallen upon the writers aforesaid; and, since they have been more or less accused of heterodoxy, I thought there was at least a chance of their subserving the cause of Protestantism, which the Catholic Fathers certainly do not subserve; but they, though differing from each other most materially, and some of them differing from the Church, do not any one of them approximate to the tone or language of the movement of 1517. Every additional instance of this kind does but go indirectly to corroborate the testimony of the Catholic Church.

It is natural and becoming in all of us to make a brave struggle for life; but I do not think it will avail the Protestant who attempts it in the medium of ecclesiastical history. He will find himself in an element in which he cannot breathe. The problem before him is to draw a line between the periods of purity and alleged corruption, such, as to have all the Apostles on one side, and all the Fathers on the other; which may insinuate and meander through the dove-tailings and inosculations of historical facts, and cut clean between St. John and St. Ignatius, St. Paul and St. Clement; to take up a position within the shelter of the book of Acts, yet safe from the range of all other extant documents besides. And at any rate, whether he succeeds or not, so much he must grant, that if such a system of doctrine as he would now introduce ever existed in early times, it has been clean swept away as if by a deluge, suddenly, silently, and without memorial; by a deluge coming in a night, and utterly soaking, rotting, heaving up, and hurrying off every vestige of what it found in the Church, before cock-crowing; so that "when they rose in the morning" her true seed "were all dead corpses"—nay, dead and buried—and without grave-stone. "The waters went over them; there was not one of them left; they sunk like lead in the mighty waters." Strange antitype, indeed, to the early fortunes of Israel!—then the enemy was drowned, and "Israel saw them dead upon the sea-shore." But now, it would seem, water proceeded as a flood "out of the serpent's mouth," and covered all the witnesses, so that not even their dead bodies "lay in the streets of the great city." Let him take which of his doctrines he will,—his peculiar view of self-righteousness, of formality, of superstition; his notion of faith, or of spirituality in religious worship; his denial of the virtue of the sacraments, or of the ministerial commission, or of the visible Church; or his doctrine of the divine efficacy of the Scriptures as the one appointed instrument of religious teaching; and let him consider how far

Antiquity, as it has come down to us, will countenance him in it. No; he must allow that the alleged deluge has done its work; yes, and has in turn disappeared itself; it has been swallowed up in the earth, mercilessly as itself was merciless.

2.

Representations such as these have been met by saying that the extant records of Primitive Christianity are scanty, and that, *for what we know*, what is not extant, had it survived, would have told a different tale. But the hypothesis that history *might* contain facts which it does *not* contain, is no positive evidence for the truth of those facts; and this is the present question, what is the *positive* evidence that the Church ever believed or taught a Gospel substantially different from that which her extant documents contain? All the evidence that is extant, be it much or be it little, is on our side: Protestants have none. Is none better than some? Scarcity of records—granting for argument's sake there is scarcity—may be taken to account for Protestants having no evidence; it will not account for our having some, for our having all that is to be had; it cannot become a positive evidence in their behalf. That records are few, does not show that they are of none account.

Accordingly, Protestants had better let alone facts; they are wisest when they maintain that the Apostolic system of the Church was certainly lost;—lost, when they know not, how they know not, without assignable instruments, but by a great revolution lost—of *that* there can be no doubt; and then challenge us to prove it was not so. "Prove," they seem to say, "if you can, that the real and very truth is not so entirely hid in primitive history as to leave not a particle of evidence betraying it. This is the very thing which misleads you, that all the arguments are in your favour. Is it not possible that an error has got the place of the truth, and has destroyed all the evidence but what witnesses on its side? Is it not possible that all the Churches should everywhere have given up and stifled the scheme of doctrine they received from the Apostles, and have substituted another for it? Of course it is; it is plain to common sense it may be so. Well, we say, what *may be, is;* this is our great principle: we say that the Apostles considered episcopacy an indifferent matter, though Ignatius says it is essential. We say that the table is not an altar, though Ignatius says it is. We say there is no priest's office under the Gospel, though Clement affirms it. We say that baptism is not an enlightening, though Justin takes it for granted. We say that heresy is scarcely a misfortune, though Ignatius accounts it a deadly sin; and all this, because it is our right, and our duty, to interpret Scripture in our own way. We uphold the pure unmutilated Scripture; the Bible, and the Bible only, is the religion of Protestants; the Bible and our own sense of the Bible. We claim a sort of parliamentary privilege to interpret laws in our own way, and not to suffer an appeal to any court beyond ourselves. We know, and we view it with consternation, that all Antiquity runs counter to our interpretation; and therefore, alas, the Church was corrupt from *very* early times indeed. But mind, we hold all this in a truly Catholic spirit, not in bigotry. We allow in others the right of private judgment, and confess that we, as others, are fallible men. We confess facts are against us; we do but claim the liberty of theorizing in spite of them. Far be it from us to say that we are certainly right; we only say that the whole early Church was certainly wrong. We do not impose our belief on any one; we only say that those who take the contrary side are Papists, firebrands, persecutors, madmen, zealots, bigots, and an insult to the nineteenth century."

To such an argument, I am aware, it avails little to oppose historical evidence, of whatever kind. It sets out by protesting against all evidence, however early and consistent, as the testimony of fallible men; yet at least, the imagination is affected by an array of facts; and I am not unwilling to appeal to the imagination of those who refuse to let me address their reason. With this view I have been inquiring into certain early works, which, or the authors of which, were held in suspicion, or even condemned by the ruling authorities of the day, to see if any vestige of an hypothetical Protestantism could be discovered in them; and, since they make no sign, I will now interrogate a very different class of witnesses. The consent of Fathers is one kind of testimony to Apostolical Truth; the protest of heretics is another; now I will come, thirdly, to received usage. To give an instance of the last mentioned argument, I shall appeal to the Apostolical Canons, though a reference to them will involve me in an inquiry, interesting indeed to the student, but somewhat dry to the general reader.

3.

These Canons, well known to Antiquity, were at one time supposed to be, strictly speaking, Apostolical, and published before A.D. 50. On the other hand, it has been contended that they are later than A.D. 450, and the work of some heretics. Our own divines take a middle course, considering them as published before A.D. 325, having been digested by Catholic authorities in the course of the two preceding centuries, or at the end of the second, and received and used in most parts of Christendom. This judgment has since been acquiesced in by the theological world, so far as this—to suppose the matter and the enactments of the Canons to be of the highest antiquity, even though the edition which we possess was not published so early as Bishop Beveridge, for instance, supposes. At the same time it is acknowledged by all parties, that they, as well as some other early documents, have suffered from interpolation, and perhaps by an heretical hand.

They are in number eighty-five,[1] of which the first fifty are considered of superior authority to the remaining thirty-five. What has been conjectured to be thei origin will explain the distinction. It was the custom of the early Church, as is well known, to settle in Council such points in her discipline, ordinances, and worship, as the Apostles had not prescribed in Scripture, as the occasion arose, after the pattern of their own proceedings in the fifteenth chapter of the Acts; and this, as far as might be, after their unwritten directions, or after their practice, or at least, after their mind, or as it is called in Scripture, their "minding" or "spirit." Thus she decided upon the question of Easter, upon that of heretical baptism, and the like. And, after that same precedent in the Acts, she recorded her decisions in formal decrees, and " delivered them for to keep" through the cities in which her members were found. The Canons in question are supposed to be some of these decrees, of which, first and nearest to the Apostles' times, or in the time of their immediate successors, were published fifty; and in the following age, thirty-five more, which had been enacted in the interval. They claim, then, to be, first,

---

[1] This account is for the most part taken from Bishops Beveridge and Pearson.

the recorded judgment of great portions of the Ante-Nicene Church, chiefly in the eastern provinces, upon certain matters in dispute, and to be of authority so far as that Church may be considered a representative of the mind of the Apostles; next, they profess to embody in themselves positive decisions and injunctions of the Apostles, though without clearly discriminating how much is thus directly Apostolical, and how much not. I will here attempt to state some of the considerations which show both their antiquity and their authority, and will afterwards use them for the purpose which has led me to mention them.

4.

1. In the first place, it would seem quite certain that, as, on the one hand, Councils were held in the primitive Church, so, on the other, those Councils enacted certain Canons. When, then, a Collection presents itself professing to consist of the Ante-Nicene Canons, there is nothing at all to startle us; it only professes to set before us that which we know anyhow must have existed. We may conjecture, if we please, that the fact that there were Canons may have suggested and encouraged a counterfeit. Certainly; but though the fact that there were Canons will account for a counterfeit, it will not account for those original Canons being lost; on the contrary, what is known to have once existed as a rule of conduct, is likely to continue in existence, except under particular circumstances. Which of the two this existing Collection is, the genuine or the counterfeit, must depend on other considerations; but if these considerations be in favour of its genuineness, then this antecedent probability will be an important confirmation.

Canons, I say, must have existed, whether these be

the real ones or no; and the circumstance that there were real ones existing must have tended to make it difficult to substitute others. It would be no easy thing in our own Church to pass off another set of Articles for the Thirty-nine, and to obliterate the genuine. Canons are public property, and have to be acted upon by large bodies. Accordingly, as might be expected, the Nicene Council, when enacting Canons of its own, refers to certain Canons as already existing, and speaks of them in that familiar and indirect way which would be natural under the circumstances, just as we speak of our Rubrics or Articles. The Fathers of that Council mention certain descriptions of persons whom "*the Canon* admits into holy orders;" they determine that a certain rule shall be in force, "according to the Canon which says so and so;" they speak of a transgression of the Canon, and proceed to explain and enforce it. Nor is the Nicene the only Council which recognizes the existence of certain Canons, or rules, by which the Church was at that time bound. The Councils of Antioch, Gangra, Constantinople, and Carthage, in the same century, do so likewise; so do individual Fathers, Alexander, Athanasius, Basil, Julius, and others.

Now here we have lighted upon an important circumstance, whatever becomes of the particular Collection of Canons before us. It seems that at the Nicene Council, only two centuries and a quarter after St. John's death, about the distance of time at which we live from the Hampton Court Conference, all Christendom confessed that from time immemorial it had been guided by certain ecclesiastical rules, which it considered of authority, which it did not ascribe to any particular persons or synods (a sign of great antiquity), and which writers of the day assigned to the Apostles. I suppose we know pretty well, at this day, what the customs of our Church have been since James the First's time, or since the Reformation; and if respectable writers at present were to state some of them,—for instance, that it is and has been the rule of our Church that the king should name the bishops, that Convocation should not sit without his leave, or that Easter should be kept according to the Roman rule,—we should think foreigners very unreasonable who doubted their word. Now, in the case before us, we find the Church Catholic, the first time it had ever met together since the Apostles' days, speaking as a matter of course of the rules to which it had ever been accustomed to defer.

If we knew no more than this, and did not know what the rules were; or if, knowing what they were, we yet decided, as we well might, that the particular rules are not of continual obligation; still, the very circumstance that there *were* rules from time immemorial would be a great fact in the history of Christianity. But we do know, from the works of the Fathers, the *subjects* of these Canons, and that to the number of thirty or forty of them; so that we might form a code, as far as it goes, of primitive discipline, quite independent of the particular Collection which is under discussion. However, it is remarkable that all of these thirty or forty are found in this Collection, being altogether nearly half the whole number, so that the only question is, whether the rest are of that value which we know belongs to a great proportion of them. It is worth noticing, that *no* Ecclesiastical Canon is mentioned in the historical documents of the primitive era which is not found in this Collection, for it shows that, whoever compiled it, the work was done with considerable care. The opponents to its genuineness bring, indeed, several exceptions, as they wish to consider them; but these admit of so satisfactory an explanation as to illustrate the proverb, that *exceptio probat regulam.*

Before going on to consider the whole Collection, let us see in what terms the ancient writers speak of those particular Canons to which they actually refer.

(1.) Athanasius speaks as follows:—" Canons and forms," he says, when describing the extraordinary violences of the Arians, " were not given to the Churches in this day, but were *handed down* from our fathers well and securely. Nor, again, has the faith had its beginning in this day, but has passed on even to us from the Lord through His disciples. Rouse yourselves, then, my brethren, to prevent that from perishing unawares in the present day *which has been observed in the Churches from ancient times down to us*, and ourselves from incurring a responsibility in what has been intrusted to us."—*Ep. Encycl.* 1. It is remarkable, in this extract, that St. Athanasius accurately distinguishes between the Faith which came from Christ, and the Canons received from the Fathers of old time: which is just the distinction which our divines are accustomed to make.

(2) Again: the Arians, by simoniacal dealings with the civil power, had placed Gregory in the see of Alexandria. Athanasius observes upon this:—"Such conduct is both *a violation of the Ecclesiastical Canons*, and forces the heathen to blaspheme, as if appointments were made, not by Divine ordinance, but by merchandise and secular influence."—*Ibid.* 2.

(3) Arsenius, bishop of Hypsela, who had been involved in the Meletian[1] schism, and had acted in a hostile way towards Athanasius, at length reconciled himself to the Church. In his letter to Athanasius he promises " to be

---

[1] The Egyptian Meletius, from which this schism has its name, must not be confounded with Meletius of Antioch.

obedient to *the Ecclesiastical Canon*, according to ancient usage, and never to put forth any regulation, whether about bishops or any other public ecclesiastical matter, without the sanction of his metropolitan, but to *submit to all the established Canons."—Apol. contr. Arian.* 69.

(4) In like manner, St. Basil, after speaking of certain crimes for which a deacon should be reduced to lay communion, proceeds, "for *it is an ancient Canon*, that they who lose their degree should be subjected to this kind of punishment only."—*Ep.* 188. Again: "*The Canon* altogether excludes from the ministry those who have been twice married."

(5) When Arius and his abettors were excommunicated by Alexander of Alexandria, they betook themselves to Palestine, and were re-admitted into the Church by the bishops of that country. On this, Alexander observes as follows :—" A very heavy imputation, doubtless, lies upon such of my brethren as have ventured on this act, in that it is *a violation of the Apostolical Canon.*" —*Theod. Hist.* i. 4.

(6) When Eusebius declined being translated from the see of Cæsarea to Antioch, Constantine complimented him on his "observance of the commandments of God, *the Apostolical Canon*, and the rule of the Church,"—*Vit. Constant.* iii. 61,—which last seems to mean the regulation passed at Nicæa.

(7) In like manner, Julius, bishop of Rome, speaks of a violation of "*the Apostles' Canons ;*" and a Council held at Constantinople, A.D. 394, which was attended by Gregory Nyssen, Amphilochius, and Flavian, of a determination of "*the Apostolical Canons.*"

It will be observed that in some of these instances the Canons are spoken of in the plural, when the particular infraction which occasions their mention relates only to one of them. This shows they were collected into a code, if, indeed, that need be proved; for, in truth, that various Canons should exist, and be in force, and yet not be put together, is just as unlikely as that no collection should be made of the statutes passed in a session of Parliament.

With this historical information about the existence, authority, and subject-matter of certain Canons in the Church from time immemorial, we should come to many anti-Protestant conclusions, even if the particular code we possess turned out to have no intrinsic authority. And now let us see how the matter stands on this point as regards this code of eighty-five Canons.

5.

2. If this Collection existed *as* a Collection in the time of the above writers and Councils, then, considering they allude to nearly half its Canons, and that no Canons are anywhere producible which are not in it, and that they do seem to allude to a Collection, and that no other Collection is producible, we certainly could not avoid the conclusion that they referred to *it*, and that, therefore, in quoting parts of it they sanction the whole. If no book is to be accounted genuine except such parts of it as happen to be expressly cited by other writers,—if it may not be regarded as a whole, and what is actually cited made to bear up and carry with it what is not cited,— no ancient book extant can be proved to be genuine. We believe Virgil's Æneid to be Virgil's, because we know he wrote an Æneid, and because particular passages which we find in it, and in no other book, are contained, under the name of Virgil, in subsequent writers or in criticisms, or in accounts of it. We do not divide it into rhapsodies, *because* it only exists in fragments in the testimony of later literature. For the same

reason, if the Canons before us can be shown to have existed as one book in Athanasius's time, it is natural to conceive that they are the very book to which he and others refer. All depends on this. If the Collection was made after his time, of course he referred to some other; but if it existed in his time, it is more natural to suppose that there was one Collection than two distinct ones, so similar, especially since history is silent about there being two.

However, I conceive it is not worth while to insist upon so early a formation of the existing Collection. Whether it existed in Athanasius's time, or was formed afterwards, and formed by friend or foe, heretic or Catholic, seems to me immaterial, as I shall by-and-by show. First, however, I will state, as candidly as I can, the arguments for and against its antiquity *as* a Collection.

Now there can be no doubt that the early Canons were formed into one body; moreover, certain early writers speak of them under the name of "the Apostles'. Canons," and "Apostolical Canons." So far I have already said. Now, certain collectors of Canons, of A.D. (more or less) 550, and they no common authorities, also speak of "the Apostolical Canons," and incorporate them into their own larger collections; and these which they speak of are the very body of Canons which we now possess under the name. We know it, for the digest of these collectors is preserved. No reason can be assigned why they should not be speaking of the *same* Collection which Gregory Nyssen and Amphilochius speak of, who lived a century and a half before them; no reason, again, why Nyssen and Amphilochius should not mean the same as Athanasius and Julius, who lived fifty to seventy years earlier than themselves. The writers of A.D. 550 might be just as certain that they and St. Athanasius quoted the same work, as we, at this day, that our copy of it is the same as Beveridge's, Pearson's, or Ussher's.

The authorities at the specified date (A.D. 550) are three—Dionysius Exiguus, John of Antioch, patriarch of Constantinople, and the Emperor Justinian. The learning of Justinian is well known, not to mention that he speaks the opinion of the ecclesiastical lawyers of his age. As to John of Antioch and Dionysius, since their names are not so familiar to most of us, it may be advisable to say thus much—that John had been a lawyer, and was well versed both in civil and ecclesiastical matters,—hence he has the title of Scholasticus; while Dionysius is the framer of the Christian era, as we still reckon it. They both made Collections of the Canons of the Church, the latter in Latin, and they both include the Apostolical Canons, as we have them, in their editions; with this difference, however (which does not at present concern us), that Dionysius published but the first fifty, while John of Antioch enumerates the whole eighty-five.

Such is the main argument for the existence of our Collection at the end of the third century; viz., that, whereas *a* Collection of Apostolic Canons is acknowledged at that date, *this* Collection is acknowledged by competent authorities to be that Apostolic record at the end of the fifth. However, when we inspect the language which Dionysius uses concerning them, in his prefatory epistle, we shall find something which requires explanation. His words are these, addressed to Stephen, bishop of Salona:—"We have, in the first place, translated from the Greek what are called the Canons of the Apostles; *which, as we wish to apprise your holiness, have not gained an easy credit from very many persons.* At the same time, some of the decrees of the [Roman] pontiffs, at a later date, seem to be taken from these very Canons." Here Dionysius must only mean, that they were not received *as* Apostolic; for that they were received, or at least nearly half of them, is, as I have said, an historical fact, whatever becomes of the Collection as a Collection. He must mean that a claim had been advanced that they were to be received as part of the apostolic *depositum;* and he must be denying that they had more than *ecclesiastical* authority. The distinction between divine and ecclesiastical injunctions requires little explanation: the latter are imposed by the Church for the sake of decency and order, as a matter of expedience, safety, propriety, or piety. Such is the rule among ourselves, that dissenting teachers conforming must remain silent three years before they can be ordained; or that a certain form of prayer should be prescribed for universal use in public service. On the other hand, the appointment of the Sacraments is apostolic and divine. So, again, that no one can be a bishop unless consecrated by a bishop, is apostolic; that three bishops are necessary in consecration, is ecclesiastical; and, though ordinarily an imperative rule, yet, under circumstances, admits of dispensation. Or again, it has, for instance, in this day been debated whether the sanctification of the Lord's-day is a divine or an ecclesiastical appointment. Dionysius, then, in the above extract, means nothing more than to deny that the Apostles enacted these Canons; or, again, that they enacted them *as* Apostles; and he goes on to say that the Popes had acknowledged the *ecclesiastical* authority of some of them by embodying them in their decrees. At the same time, his language certainly seems to show as much as this, and it is confirmed by that of other writers, that the Latin Church, though using them separately as authority, did not receive them as a Collection with the implicit deference which they met with in the East; indeed, the last thirty-five, though two of them were cited at Niçæa, and one at Constantinople, A.D. 394, seem to have been in inferior account. The Canons of the General Councils took their place, and the Decrees of the Popes.

6.

This, then, seems to be the state of the case as regards the Collection or Edition of Canons, whether fifty or eighty-five, which is under consideration. Speaking, not of the Canons themselves, but of this particular edition of them, I thus conclude about it—that, whether it was made at the end of the third century, or later, there is no sufficient proof that it was strictly of authority; but that it is not very material that it should be proved to be of authority, nay, or even to have been made in early times. Give us the Canons themselves, and we shall be able to prove the point for which I am adducing them, even though they were not at first formed into a collection. They are, one by one, witnesses to us of a state of things.

Indeed, it must be confessed, that probability is against this Collection having ever been regarded as an authority by the ancient Church. It was an *anonymous* Collection; and, as being anonymous, seemed to have no claim upon Christians. They would consider that a collection or body of Canons could only be imposed by a *Council;* and since the Council could not be produced which imposed this in particular, they had no reason to admit it. They might have been in the practice of acting upon this Canon, and that, and the third, and so on to the eighty-fifth, from time immemorial, and that as Canons, not as mere customs, and might confess the obligation of each: and yet might say, "We never looked upon them as a *code*," which should be something complete and limited to itself. The true sanction of each was the immemorial observance of each, not its place in the Collection, which implied a competent framer. Moreover, in proportion as General Councils were held, and enacted Canons, so did the vague title of mere usage, without definite sanction, become less influential, and the ancient Canons fell into disregard. And what made this still more natural was the circumstance that the Nicene Council did re-enact a considerable number of those which it found existing. It substituted then a definite authority, which, in after ages, would be much more intelligible than what would have by that time become a mere matter of obscure antiquity. Nor did it tend to restore their authority, when their advocates, feeling the difficulty of their case, referred the Collection to the Apostles themselves: first, because this assertion could not be maintained; next, because, if it could, it would have seemingly deprived the Church of the privilege of making Canons. It would have made those usages divine which had ever been accounted only ecclesiastical. It would have raised the question whether, under such circumstances, the Church had more right to add to the code of really Apostolic Canons than to Scripture; discipline, as well as doctrine, would have been given by direct revelation, and have been included in the fundamentals of religion.

If, however, all this be so, it follows that we are not at liberty to argue, from one part of this Collection having been received, that therefore every other was also; as if it were one authoritative work. No number of individual Canons being proved to be of the first age will tend to prove that the remainder are of the same. It is true;

and I do not think it worth while to contest the point. For argument-sake I will grant that the bond, which ties them into one, is not of the most trustworthy and authoritative description, and will proceed to show that even those Canons which are not formally quoted by early writers ought to be received as the rules of the Ante-Nicene Church, independently of their being found in one compilation.

· 7·

3. I have already said that nearly half of the Canons, as they stand in the Collection, are quoted as Canons by early writers, and thus placed beyond all question, as remains of the Ante-Nicene period: the following arguments may be offered in behalf of the rest :—

(1) They are otherwise known to express *usages* or *opinions* of the Ante-Nicene centuries. The simple question is, whether they had been reflected on, recognized, converted into principles, enacted, obeyed; whether they were the unconscious and unanimous result of the one Christian spirit[1] in every place, or were formal determinations from authority claiming obedience. This being the case, there is very little worth disputing about; for (whether we regard them as being religious practices or as religious antiquities) if uniform custom was in favour of them, it does not matter whether they were enacted or not. If they were not, their universal observance is a still greater evidence of their extreme antiquity, which, in that case, can be hardly short of the Apostolic age; and we shall refer to them in the existing Collection, merely for the sake of convenience, as being brought together in a short compass.

Nay, a still more serious conclusion will follow, from

---

[1] The ἐκκλησιαστικὸν φρόνημα.

supposing them not to be enactments—much more serious than any I am disposed to draw. If it be maintained that these observances, though such, did not arise from injunctions on the part of the Church, then, it might be argued, the Church has no power over them. As not having imposed, she cannot abrogate, suspend, or modify them. They must be referred to a higher source, even to the inspired Apostles; and their authority is not ecclesiastical, but divine. We are almost forced, then, to consider them as enactments, even when they are not recognized by ancient writers as such, lest we should increase the authority of some of them more than seems consistent with their subject-matter.

Again, if such Canons as are not appealed to by ancient writers are nevertheless allowed to have been really enacted, on the ground of our finding historically that usage corresponds to them; it may so be that others, about which the usage is not so clearly known, are real Canons also. There is a *chance* of their being genuine; for why, in drawing the line, should we decide by the mere accident of the usage admitting or not admitting of clear historical proof?

(2) Again, all these Canons, or at least the first fifty, are composed in uniform style; there is no reason, as far as the internal evidence goes, why one should be more primitive than another, and many, we know, were certainly in force as Canons from the earliest times.

(3) This argument becomes much more cogent when we consider *what* that style is. It carries with it evident marks of primitive simplicity, some of which I shall instance. The first remark which would be made on reading them relates to their brevity, the breadth of the rules which they lay down, and their plain and unartificial mode of stating them. An instance of this, among

others which might be taken, is supplied by a comparison of the 7th of them with one of a number of Canons passed at Antioch by a Council held A. D. 341, and apparently using the Apostolical Canons as a basis for its own. The following, read with the words in brackets, agrees, with but slight exceptions, with the Antiochene Canon, and, without them, with the Apostolical:—

"All who come [to church] and hear the [holy] Scriptures read, but do not remain to prayer [with the people,] and [refuse] the holy communion [of the Eucharist, these] must be put out of the Church, as disorderly, [until, by confession, and by showing fruits of penitence, and by entreaty, they are able to gain forgiveness."]

(4) Now this contrast, if pursued, will serve to illustrate the antiquity of the Apostolical Canons in several ways, besides the evidence deducible from the simplicity of their structure. Thus the word "metropolitan" is introduced into the thirty-fifth Canon of Antioch; no such word occurs in the Apostolical Canon from which it is apparently formed. There it is simply said, "the principal bishop;" or, literally, the primus. This accords with the historical fact, that the word metropolitan was not introduced till the fourth century. The same remark might be made on the word "province," which occurs in the Canon of Antioch, not in the other. This contrast is strikingly brought out in two other Canons, which correspond in the two Collections. Both treat of the possessions of the Church; but the Apostolical Canon says simply, "the interests of the Church," "the goods of the Church;" but the Antiochene, composed after Christianity had been acknowledged by the civil power, speaks of "the revenue of the Church," and "the produce of the land."

Again, when attempts have been made to show that certain words are contained in the Canons before us which were not in use in the Ante-Nicene times, they have in every case failed in the result, which surely may be considered as a positive evidence in favour of their genuineness. For instance, the word "clergy," for the ministerial body, which is found in the Apostolical Canons, is also used by Origen, Tertullian, and Cyprian. The word "reader," for an inferior order in the clergy, is used by Cornelius, bishop of Rome; nay, by Justin Martyr. "Altar," which is used in the Canons, is the only word used for the Lord's table by St. Cyprian, and, before him, by Tertullian and Ignatius. "Sacrifice" and "oblation," for the consecrated elements, found in the Canons, are also found in Clement of Rome, Justin Irenæus, and Tertullian.

This negative evidence of genuineness extends to other points, and surely is of no inconsiderable weight. We know how difficult it is so to word a forgery as to avoid all detection from incongruities of time, place, and the like. A forgery, indeed, it is hardly possible to suppose this Collection to be, both because great part of it is known to be genuine, and because no assignable object would be answered by it; but let us imagine the compiler hastily took up with erroneous traditions, or recent enactments, and joined them to the rest. Is it possible to conceive, under such circumstances, that there would be no anachronisms or other means of detection? And if there are none such, and much more if the compiler, who lived perhaps as early as the fourth century, found none such (supposing we may assume him willing and qualified to judge of them), nay, if Dionysius Exiguus found none such, what reasons have we for denying that they are the produce of those early times to which they claim to belong? Yet so it is; neither rite, nor heresy, nor observance, nor phrase, is found in them which is foreign to the Ante-Nicene period. Indeed, the only reason one or two persons have thrown suspicion on them has been an unwillingness on their part to admit episcopacy, which the Canons assert; a necessity which led the same parties to deny the genuineness of St. Ignatius' epistles.[1]

(5) I will make one more remark:—First, these Canons come to us, not from Rome, but from the East, and were in a great measure neglected, or at least superseded in the Church, after Constantine's day, especially in the West, where Rome had sway; these do not embody what are called "Romish corruptions." Next, there is ground for suspecting that the Collection or Edition which we have was made by heretics, probably Arians, though they have not meddled with the main contents of them. Thus, while the neglect of them in later times separates them from Romanism, the assent of the Arians is a second witness, in addition to their recognition by the first centuries, in evidence of their Apostolical origin. Those first centuries observe them; contemporary heretics respect them; only later and corrupt times pass them by. May they not be taken as a fair portrait, as far as they go, of the doctrines and customs of Primitive Christianity?

8.

I do wish out-and-out Protestants would seriously lay to heart where they stand when they would write a history of Christianity. Are there any traces of Luther before Luther? Is there anything to show that what they call the religion of the Bible was ever professed by any persons, Christians, Jews, or heathen? Again, are there any traces

---

[1] Vid. the parallel case of the Ignatian Epistles in the Author's Essays, vol. i., p. 266.

in history of a process of change in Christian belief and practice, so serious, or so violent, as to answer to the notion of a great corruption or perversion of the Primitive Religion? Was there ever a time, what was the time, when Christianity was not that which Protestants protest against, as if formal, unspiritual, self-righteous, superstitious, and unevangelic? If that time cannot be pointed out, is not "the Religion of Protestants" a matter, not of past historical fact, but of modern private judgment? Have they anything to say in defence of their idea of the Christianity of the first centuries, except that that view of it is necessary to their being Protestants. "Christians," they seem to say, "*must* have been in those early times different from what the record of those times shows them to have been, and they must, as time went on, have fallen from that faith and that worship which they had at first, though history is quite silent on the subject, *or else* Protestantism, which is the apple of our eye, is not true. We are driven to hypothetical facts, or else we cannot reconcile with each other phenomena so discordant as those which are presented by ancient times and our own. We claim to substitute *à priori* reasoning for historical investigation, by the right of self-defence and the duty of self-preservation."

I have urged this point in various ways, and now I am showing the light which the Canons of the Apostles throw upon it. There is no reasonable doubt that they represent to us, on the whole, and as far as they go, the outward face of Christianity in the first centuries;—now will the Protestant venture to say that he recognizes in it any likeness of his own Religion? First, let him consider what is conveyed in the very idea of Ecclesiastical Canons? This: that Christians could not worship according to their fancy, but must think and pray by rule, by a set of rules issuing from a body of men, the Bishops, over whom the laity had no power whatever. If any men at any time have been priest-ridden, such was the condition of those early Christians. And then again, what becomes of the Protestant's watchword, "the Bible, the whole Bible, and nothing but the Bible," if a set of Canons might lawfully be placed upon their shoulders, as if a second rule of faith, to the utter exclusion of all free-and-easy religion? and what room was there for private judgment, if they had to obey the bidding of certain fallible men? and what is to be done with the great principle, "Unity, not Uniformity," if Canons are to be recognized, which command uniformity as well as unity?

So much at first sight; but when we go on to examine what these Canons actually contain, their incompatibility with the fundamental principles of Protestantism becomes still more patent. I will set down some instances in proof of this. Thus, we gather from the Canons the following facts about Primitive Christianity :—viz., that,

1. There was a hierarchy of ordained ministers, consisting of the three orders of Bishops, Priests, and Deacons.

2. Their names were entered on a formal roll or catalogue.

3. There were inferior orders, such as readers and chanters.

4. Those who had entered into the sacred orders might not afterwards marry.

5. There were local dioceses, each ruled by a Bishop.

6. To him and him only was committed the care of souls in his diocese.

7. Each Bishop confined himself to his own diocese.

8. No secular influence was allowed to interfere with the appointment of Bishops.

9. The Bishops formed one legislative body, and met in Council twice a year, for the consideration of dogmatic questions and points in controversy.

10. One of them had the precedence over the rest, and took the lead; and, as the priests and people in each diocese obeyed their Bishop, so in more general matters the Bishops deferred to their Primus.

11. Easter and Pentecost were great feasts, and certain other days feasts also. There was a Lent Fast; also a Fast on Easter Eve; and on Wednesdays and Fridays.

12. The state of celibacy was recognized

13. Places of worship were holy.

14. There was in their churches an altar, and an altar service.

15. There was a sacrifice in their worship, of which the materials were bread and wine.

16. There were oblations also of fruits of the earth, in connection with the sacrifice.

17. There were gold and silver vessels in the rite, and these were consecrated.

18. There were sacred làmps, fed with olive oil, and incense during the holy rite.

19. Baptism was administered in the name of Father, Son, and Holy Ghost.

20. Excommunication was inflicted on Christians who disgraced their profession.

21. No one might pray, even in private, with excommunicated persons, except at the cost of being excommunicated himself.

22. No one might pray with heretics, or enter their churches, or acknowledge their baptism, or priesthood.

These rules furnish us with large portions, and the

more important, of the outline of the religion of their times; and are not only definitive in themselves, but give us the means of completing those parts of it which are not found in them. Considered, then, as a living body, the primitive Christian community was distinguished by its high sacerdotal, ceremonial, mystical character. Which among modern religious bodies was it like? Was it like the Wesleyans? was it like the Society of Friends? was it like the Scotch Kirk? was it like any Protestant denomination at all? Fancy any model Protestant of this day in a state of things so different from his own! With his religious societies for the Church, with his committees, boards, and platforms instead of Bishops, his *Record* and *Patriot* newspapers instead of Councils, his concerts for prayer instead of anathemas on heresy and schism, his spoutings at public meetings for exorcisms, his fourths of October for festivals of the Martyrs, his glorious memories for commemorations of the dead, his niggard vestry allowances for gold and silver vessels, his gas and stoves for wax and oil, his denunciations of self-righteousness for fasting and celibacy, and his exercise of private judgment for submission to authority—would he have a chance of finding himself at home in a Christianity such as this? is it his own Christianity?

I end, then, as I began:—If Protestantism is another name for Christianity, then the Martyrs and Bishops of the early Church, the men who taught the nations, the men who converted the Roman Empire, had themselves to be taught, themselves to be converted. Shall we side with the first age of Christianity, or with the last?

NOTE ON P. 366.

Lately the relics of St. Ambrose have been discovered in his Church at Milan, as were the relics of St. Gervasius and St. Protasius several years since. On this subject I received a month since a letter from a friend, who passed through Milan, and saw the sacred remains. I will quote a portion of his letter to me:—

"*Sept.* 17, 1872.

"I am amazed at the favour which was shown me yesterday at the Church of St. Ambrogio. I was accidentally allowed to be present at a private exposition of the relics of St. Ambrose and the Saints Gervasius and Protasius. I have seen complete every bone in St. Ambrose's body. There were present a great many of the clergy, three *medici*, and Father Secchi, who was there on account of his great knowledge of the Catacombs, to testify to the age, etc., of the remains. It was not quite in chance, for I wanted to go to Milan, solely to venerate St. Ambrose once more, and to thank him for all the blessings I have had as a Catholic and a Priest, since the day that I said Mass over his body. The churches were shut when I arrived; so I got up early next morning and went off to the Ambrosian. I knelt down before the high altar, and thought of all that had happened since you and I were there, twenty-six years ago. As I was kneeling, a cleric came out; so I asked him to let me into the *scurolo*, which was boarded up all round for repairs. He took me there, but he said:. 'St. Ambrose is not here; he is above; do you wish to see him?' He took me round through the corretti into a large room, where, on a large table, surrounded by ecclesiastics and medical men, were three skeletons. The two were of immense size, and very much alike, and bore the marks of a violent death; their age was determined to be about twenty-six years. When I entered the room, Father Secchi was examining the marks of martyrdom on them. Their throats had been cut with great violence, and the neck vertebræ were injured on the inside. The *pomum Adami* had been broken, or was not there; I forget which. This bone was quite perfect in St. Ambrose; his body was wholly uninjured; the lower jaw (which was broken in one of the two martyrs) was wholly uninjured in him, beautifully formed, and every tooth, but one molar in the lower jaw, quite perfect and white and regular. His face had been long, thin, and oval, with a high arched forehead. His bones were nearly white; those of the other two were very dark. His fingers long and very delicate; his bones were a marked contrast to those of the two martyrs.

"The finding, I was told, was thus :—In the ninth century the Bishop of Milan translated the relics of St. Ambrose, which till then had laid side by side with the martyrs in one great stone coffin of two compartments, St. Gervase being, according to the account, nearest to St. Ambrose. He removed St. Ambrose from this coffin into the great porphyry urn which we both saw in the *scurolo;* leaving the martyrs where they were. In 1864 the martyrs' coffin was opened, and one compartment was found empty, except a single bone, the right-ankle bone, which lay by itself in that empty compartment. This was sent to the Pope as all that remained of St. Ambrose; in the other compartment were the two skeletons complete. St. Ambrose's urn was not opened till the other day, when it was removed from its place for the alterations. The bones were found perfect all but the ankle bone. They then sent for it to Rome, and the President of the Seminary showed me how it fitted exactly in its place, having been separated from it for nine centuries.

"The Government seems very desirous to make a handsome restoration of the whole chapel, and the new shrine will be completed by May next."

Thus far my friend's letter.

I have not been able in such historical works as are at my command to find notice of Archbishop Angelbert's transferring St. Ambrose's body from the large coffin of the martyrs to the porphyry urn which has been traditionally pointed out as the receptacle of the Saint, and in which he was recently found. That the body, however, recently disinterred actually was once in the coffin of the martyrs is evidenced by its right-ankle bone being found there. Another curious confirmation arises from my friend's remark about the missing tooth, when compared with the following passage from Ughelli, Ital. Sacr. t. iv. col. 82 :—

"Archbishop Angelbert was most devout to the Church of St. Ambrose, and erected a golden altar in it, at the cost of 30,000 gold' pieces. The occasion of this gift is told us by Galvaneus, among others, in his Catalogue, when he is speaking of Angelbert. His words are these:— 'Angelbert was Archbishop for thirty-five years, from A.D. 826, and out of devotion he extracted a tooth from the mouth of St. Ambrose, and placed it in his [episcopal] ring. One day the tooth fell out from the ring; and, on the Archbishop causing a thorough search to be made for it, an old woman appeared to him, saying, "You will find the tooth in the place from which you took it." On hearing this, the Archbishop betook himself to the body of St. Ambrose, and found it in the mouth of the blessed Ambrose. Then, to make it impossible for anything in future [or anything else, de cætero] to be taken from his body, he hid it under ground, and caused to be made the golden altar of St. Ambrose, etc.

Castellionæus in his Antiquities of Milan (apud Burman. Antiqu. Ital. t. 3, part I. col. 487) tells us that the Archbishop lost his relic "as he was going in his pontifical vestments to the Church of St. Lawrence on Palm Sunday. He found he had lost it in the way thither, for, on taking off his gloves, he saw it was gone

It would seem from my friend's letter that either the Archbishop took away the tooth a second time, or the miracle of its restoration did not take place.

It should be added that the place in which Angelbert hid the sacred relics was so well known, that in the twelfth century Cardinal Bernard, Bishop of Parma, was allowed to see and venerate them,—Vid. Puricelli's Ambros. Basil. Descriptio. c. 58 and c. 352, ap. Burman. Thesaur. Antiqu. Ital. t. 4, part 1.

That St. Ambrose was buried in his own church, called even from the time of his death the "Ambrosian," and the church where he had placed the bones of the two martyrs, Gervasius and Protasius, by the side of whom he proposed to have his own body placed, is plain from his own words and those of Paulinus his Secretary.

For the controversy on the subject vid. Castellion. *ubi supra.*

THE END.

PUBLICATIONS OF JOHN HENRY NEWMAN, D.D.

1—8. PAROCHIAL AND PLAIN SERMONS. (*Rivingtons.*)

9. SERMONS ON SUBJECTS OF THE DAY. (*Rivingtons.*)

10. UNIVERSITY SERMONS. (*Rivingtons.*)

11. DOCTRINE OF JUSTIFICATION. (*Rivingtons.*)

12. DISCUSSIONS AND ARGUMENTS. 1. How to accomplish it. 2. The Antichrist of the Fathers. 3. Scripture and the Creed. 4. Tamworth Reading-Room. 5. Who's to blame? 6. An Argument for Christianity. (*Pickering.*)

13. TWO ESSAYS ON MIRACLES. 1. Of Scripture. 2. Of Ecclesiastical History. (*Pickering.*)

14, 15. ESSAYS CRITICAL AND HISTORICAL, TWO VOLUMES WITH NOTES. 1. Poetry. 2. Rationalism. 3. De la Mennais. 4. Palmer on Faith and Unity. 5. St. Ignatius. 6. Prospects of the Anglican Church. 7. The Anglo-American Church. 8. Countess of Huntingdon. 9. Catholicity of the Anglican Church. 10. The Antichrist of Protestants. 11. Milman's Christianity. 12. Reformation of the Eleventh Century. 13. Private Judgment. 14. Davison. 15. Keble. (*Pickering.*)

16, 17. VIA MEDIA, TWO VOLUMES WITH NOTES. 1. Vol. Prophetical Office of the Church. 2. Vol. Occasional Letters and Tracts. (*Pickering.*)

18. ESSAY ON THE DEVELOPMENT OF CHRISTIAN DOCTRINE. (*Pickering.*)

19, 20. DIFFICULTIES OF ANGLICANS, TWO VOLUMES. 1. Vol. Twelve Lectures. 2. Vol. Letters to Dr. Pusey, and to the Duke of Norfolk. (*Burns and Oates, and Pickering.*)

PUBLICATIONS *(continued).*

21. PRESENT POSITION OF CATHOLICS IN ENGLAND. (*Burns and Oates.*)
22. SERMONS TO MIXED CONGREGATIONS. (*Burns and Oates.*)
23. OCCASIONAL SERMONS. (*Burns and Oates.*)
24. IDEA OF A UNIVERSITY. 1. Nine Discourses. 2. Occasional Lectures and Essays. (*Pickering.*)
25. ESSAY ON ASSENT. (*Burns and Oates.*)

26. ANNOTATED TRANSLATION OF ATHANASIUS. (*Parker.*)
27. THEOLOGICAL TRACTS. 1. Dissertatiunculæ. 2. Doctrinal Causes of Arianism. 3. Apollinarianism. 4. St. Cyril's Formula. 5. Ordo de Tempore. 6. Douay Version of Scripture. (*Pickering.*)
28. THE ARIANS OF THE FOURTH CENTURY. (*Pickering.*)
29—31. HISTORICAL SKETCHES. THREE VOLUMES. 1. The Turks. 2. Cicero. 3. Apollonius. 4. Primitive Christianity. 5. Church of the Fathers. 6. St. Chrysostom. 7. Theodoret. 8. St. Benedict. 9. Benedictine Schools. 10. Universities. 11. Northmen and Normans. 12. Medieval Oxford. 13. Convocation of Canterbury. (*Pickering.*)

32. LOSS AND GAIN. (*Burns and Oates, and Pickering.*)
33. CALLISTA. (*Burns and Oates, and Pickering.*)
34. VERSES ON VARIOUS OCCASIONS. (*Burns and Oates.*)
35. APOLOGIA PRO VITÂ SUÂ. (*Longman.*)

Important Works

PUBLISHED BY

PICKERING & Co.,

196, Piccadilly, London, W.

ACROSTICS, a Hundred new, on Old Subjects, written by Two Poor Women, with a Preface by Mrs. GREVILLE. 12mo, 2s 6d

ACROSTICS.—Corn and Chaff, or Double Acrostics. Square 12mo, *frontispiece, cloth, gilt leaves*, 3s 6d

ALTAR SERVICE.—The Second Year of the Reign of King Edward VI.; the Altar Service of the Church of England for that Year, with that of the Third Year, 1549. Edited by W. J. BLEW. 16mo, 1s 6d

BALL (F. J.) S. Augustine upon Fasting Communion. 8vo, 6d.

——— Our Fears and our Confidence, a Sermon at S. Lawrence's, Reading, June 26th, 1877. 8vo, *sewed*, 6d

BAYNE (EMILY) Sighs of Hope. (Verse.) 12mo, 3s

BELANEY (R.) Mr. Gladstone Himself Reviewed and Analysed. Crown 8vo, *sewed*, 2s

BISHOPS.—Are the Bishops Mad? a Letter to the Rt. Hon. J. Bright, by a CLERGYMAN. 8vo, 1s

BLEW (W.) Privy Council Infallibility; the Mere Mistake in the Knightsbridge Judgment, excused by Mr. Fremantle, explained by Dr. Cardwell, exposed by WM. BLEW. 8vo, *sewed*, 1s

BONN RE-UNION.—Report of the Proceedings of the Re-Union Conference held at Bonn (1875), translated from German, with a Preface by CANON LIDDON, edited by M. MACCOLL. Crown 8vo, 3s 6d

BLAKE (WILLIAM) Poems: comprising Songs of Innocence and of Experience, together with Poetical Sketches and some Copyright Poems not in any other Edition. 12mo, 2s 6d

"The songs only require to be known to be loved with a tenderness and enthusiasm which it is not given to many poets to arouse."—*The Saturday Review.*

"The admirers of W. Blake as a poet—and they are rapidly increasing in number—owe much to Mr. Pickering for this reprint."—*Notes and Queries.*

—— Songs of Innocence and Experience, new edition, printed from the text of the Original Volumes published in 1789 and 1794, with Miscellaneous Poems, now first printed from the Author's MSS. 12mo, 4s

—— Poetical Sketches. Now first reprinted from the Original Edition of 1783, with a short Critical Preface. 12mo, 3s 6d

"A charming reprint of a most musical and dainty little book of songs. Turn where we will, throughout its hundred pages, we are sure to light on something that sparkles up into the light, as the sound of rippling water, the songs of birds, amid the breath of spring."—*The Standard.*

BOOKER (E.) Parthenia, a Drama. 12mo, 3s

BOURNE (V.) Poems, Latin and English, with Memoir and Notes by the Rev. J. MITFORD. 12mo, *printed with ornamental head and tail pieces, cloth,* 5s

Kept in various styles of binding.

"I love the memory of Vinny Bourne; I think him a better Latin poet than Tibullus, Propertius, Ausonius, or any of the writers in his way, except Ovid, and not at all inferior to him."—COWPER.

"Vincent Bourne's Latin translations in sweetness of numbers and elegant expression are at least equal to the originals, and scarce inferior to anything in Ovid or Tibullus."—DR. BEATTIE.

BRITTLEBANK (W.) Persia during the Famine of 1872, a Personal Narrative of Travel in the East. Crown 8vo, *frontispiece*, 7s 6d

"It is long since we have read a book of travel with so much satisfaction as that of Mr. Brittlebank's short narrative affords."—*The Examiner.*

"These pages evince the adventurous spirit of a true traveller."—*The Athenæum.*

BURIAL SERVICE.—The Order for the Burial of the Dead. 16mo, *printed in red and black from the sealed Copy of the Book of Common Prayer. In limp cloth, for the use of "Mourners,"* £2 10s *per hundred.*

This little book can be made to answer the purpose of a memorial card by having the name of the departed person printed on the back of the title.

BURKE (U. R.) Spanish Salt: a Collection of all the Proverbs which are to be found in Don Quixote, with a literal English Translation, Notes and Introduction, by ULICK RALPH BURKE. 12mo, *cloth*, 3s 6d
"We cordially recommend this little daintily-printed volume to those who care to con in a concentrated form those wise saws which, in connection with Squire Sancho, the shield-bearer of the immortal Don, have made him and his master immortal. The translations are adequate and satisfactory, the work has evidently been a labour of love," &c., &c.—*The Athenæum.*

CALCOEN (CALICUT) Facsimile of a Dutch Narrative of the Second Voyage of Vasco da Gama to Calicut. Printed at Antwerp, *circa* 1504, with Introduction and Translation, by J. PH. BERJEAU. Small 4to, 5s
This book, unnoticed by both biographers and bibliographers, is in the British Museum. Although the name of the great navigator to India is not mentioned in it, the dates, events, and places recorded perfectly agree with the second voyage of Vasco de Gama round the Cape of Good Hope. This valuable narrative supplies a number of interesting details of the voyage which will be looked for in vain in Galvao, Ramusio, Castanheda, Faria, Barros, &c.

CAPEL (MONSIGNORE) and the Ritualists, a Review of a Recent Controversy, by a ENGLISH CATHOLIC. 8vo, *sewed*, 1s

CASWALL (E., *of the Oratory, Birmingham*) Poems and Hymns, original and translated, comprising Hymns for the Week, the Christian Seasons, and Saints' Days, translated from the Breviary, the Missal, and other sources: Original Meditative Pieces and Hymns: also upwards of Seventy Poems and Odes. 12mo, 5s.
From the above Poems and Hymns, originally published under the titles, Lyra Catholica, Masque of Angels, and in other works, now for the first time collected in one volume, it is not too much to say that the compilers of all the best known Hymn books during the last twenty years have borrowed, and in some cases very largely.

—— Tale of Tintern; a May Pageant. Second Edition, square 16mo, 2s

CASWALL (M. E.) Old Man's Review of his Past Life (a Fragment). Crown 8vo, *sewed*, 6d

CATECHISM, THE CHURCH, from the Book of Common Prayer; with Pictures and Explanations. Second Edition, 16mo, *with* 42 *cuts*, single copies, 1s 3d each; for distribution, 11s 6d per dozen
The above-named Manual has been read and approved by the Venerable Archdeacon Denison and other eminent clergy of the Church.

CEREMONIAL for Servers at Choral and Plain Celebrations of the Holy Eucharist. 18mo, 1s

—— Notes on Ceremonial, Sarum Use. 12mo, *cuts*, 4s 6d

"A very useful manual."—*The Church Times.*
Containing directions for the Celebrant and Ministers of the Altar and the Communion Service, with the Secreta translated from the Sarum Missal.

CERVANTES.—Sancho Panza's Proverbs, with others which occur in Don Quixote; with literal translation, Notes, and Introduction, by ULICK RALPH BURKE. 12mo, 3s; LARGE PAPER, crown 8vo, 8s 6d

CHAMBERS (J. D.) The Principles of Divine Worship, the Book of Common Prayer, Illustrated by references to the Sarum Rites and Ceremonies. *With numerous Illustratious, new edition, revised, with additions*, 4to, £1 1s

CHATELAIN (Chevalier de) L'Hostellerie des Sept Péchés Capitaux. Crown 8vo, *sewed*, 1s

—— (Le Chevalier de) Les Noces de la Lune. Crown 8vo, *sewed*, 1s

—— (Clara de) Photographs of Familiar Faces, edited by the CHEVALIER DE CHATELAIN. Crown 8vo, 5s

CHAUCER (G.) La Fleur et la Feuille; poëme avec le Texte Anglais en Regard, traduit en vers Français par le CHEVALIER DE CHATELAIN. 12mo, *cloth, gilt leaves*, 2s

"A very clever translation of Chaucer's 'Floure and the Leafe.'"—*English Journal of Education.*

—— Contes de Cantorbéry traduits en vers Français, par le CHEVALIER DE CHATLAIN. 3 vols, 12mo, *printed in the old style, portrait and cuts*, £1 5s

"There are evidences of great industry in it, and still more of sound judgment and good taste."—*Athenæum.*

CHRISTMAS CHIMES and New Year Rhymes, Serious and Comic, with a gallery of not-ables drawn and quartered in various verse, sense, and non-sense. Square 8vo, 3s

"There is badinage, sarcasm brilliant and telling, and wit at once scholarly, tender, but biting, on almost each page, such as will delight everybody who owns the power to appreciate the clever satire of an unusually original and pointed writer."—*Morning Post.*

CHURTON (E.) The Early English Church. New edition, 12mo, *maps and woodcuts*, 4s

CHURCH SERVICE, THE ADULT'S; being the Liturgy according to the use of the Church of England, for use in Church; with Homely Explanations, Forms of Self-Examination and Confession, &c., &c. Fourth Thousand, 16mo, *with 22 cuts*, 1s 3d each, 11s 6d per dozen.

"Our readers will be good enough to consider all that we have said of the first issue (the Child's Church Service) said also of this. We trust and believe that it will be very widely circulated."—*The Church Times.*

CHURCH SERVICE, THE CHILD'S; being the Liturgy according to the use of the Church of England, for use in Church, with Homely Explanations to be read at Home or at School. Third edition (6th thousand) 18mo, *with 22 cuts, in cloth*, 1s 3d each, 11s 6d per dozen nett.

"That admirable little manual."—*The Church Times.*
"This is really a miracle of beauty and cheapness! It is only 1s. 3d., and each of the twenty-two woodcuts would be cheap at the money!"—*The Illustrated Review.*

CLAUDET (A., *F.R.S.*) A Memoir reprinted from "The Scientific Review." 8vo, *sewed*, 2s

COLERIDGE (S. T.) The Poetical and Dramatic Works of Samuel Taylor Coleridge. An entirely new edition, revised and enlarged, founded on that published in three volumes by the late WILLIAM PICKERING in 1834. 4 vols, fcap. 8vo, 30s

Large Paper Copies (only 100 *printed)* £2 12s 6d.

While containing everything which appeared in the earlier Edition, the present Re-issue includes a number of pieces of considerable value and interest, now for the first time collected.

CONSTABLE (HENRY) Diana, Spiritual Sonnets, and other Poems, now first collected, with some Account of the Author, by W. C. HAZLITT, and Notes by THOMAS PARK. 1859, crown 8vo, *only* 230 *copies printed*, 6s

—— Ditto, LARGE PAPER, *only* 20 *copies printed, uncut*, 15s

COX (F. E.) Hymns from the German, the Originals and Translations side by side, translated and edited by F. E. COX. Second edition, revised and enlarged 12mo, 5s

Hymns in the original German, accompanied with English verse translation, selected from Gerhard, Angelus, and several hundred different collections, most of the Hymns were pointed out as "National Treasures" by the learned and famous collector of German Hymns, Baron Bunsen, on whose authority the names and dates of the authors are given.

COPINGER (W. A.) A Testimony of Antiquity, showing the Ancient Faith in the Church of England touching the Sacrament of the Body and Blood of Christ. 18mo, 1s

DANIEL (GEORGE) Love's Last Labour Not Lost. 12mo, pp. 300, *cloth*, 7s 6d
  Contents :—Recollections of Charles Lamb ; Samuel Johnson ; Father Christmas ; The Loving Cup and Horace Walpole ; New Year's Eve ; The Presumed Disinterment of Milton ; Moorfields in the Olden Time ; Dreams ; Recollections of Siddons and John Kemble ; Tom Durfey ; Old Ballads ; Robert Cruikshauk ; A Book of Fools, etc., etc.

DAWSON (A.) Theory of Gravity, and of the Solar Process. 8vo, *sewed*, 6d

—— English Landscape Art in the year 1877. Crown 8vo, 1s

DE VERE (SIR AUBREY) Julian the Apostate, the Duke of Mercia ; two Dramas. 1 vol, 12mo, 8s 6d

—— Irish Odes and other Poems. Crown 8vo, 6s

—— Sonnets. New edition, 12mo, 3s 6d

DORE (J. R.) Old Bibles ; or an Account of the various Versions of the English Bible. Crown 8vo, 2s 6d
  " Mr. Dore in the volume before us has endeavoured to give a plain, unvarnished account of the English Bible. In the account of Tyndale's work Mr. Dore is careful and succinct. . . . It is beautifully printed."
  —*Saturday Review.*

DUNN (REV. JAMES) The Honesty of our Position, a Paper read before the Clifton Branch of the E. C. U. 8vo, *sewed*, 6d

EDEN (ROBERT) Some Thoughts on the Inspiration of the Holy Scriptures. 12mo, pp. 294, *handsomely printed in the old style*, 5s

ELLIS (EDWARD) The Two Ysondes and other Verses. Crown 8vo, 2s 6d

EWALD (ALEX. CHAS.) The Public Records, a Brief Handbook to the National Archives, by ALEX. CHAS. EWALD, one of the Senior Clerks of Her Majesty's Public Records. 8vo, 9s
  This book is an Alphabetical Index of the Principal Matters contained in the Public Records, with a reference directing the student of history under what heading they may be found, and a Glossary of Words to be found in the Public Records, with a Prefatory Essay on the most remarkable of these Records.
  " For the students of the Public Records and the National Archives Mr. Ewald's New Hand-Book will be found extremely useful. . . . "—*Westminste Review.*

ELLIS (JOSEPH) Meletæ: Poems by Joseph Ellis. Cr. 8vo, 6s

——— Cæsar in Egypt, Costanza, and other Poems. Cr 8vo, 9s

"Cæsar in Egypt" comprises the history of the Alexandrine War, also the Journey of Caius Julius Cæsar with Queen Cleopatra up the Nile.

FANSHAWE (C. M.) The Literary Remains of Catherine Maria Fanshawe, with Notes, by the late Rev. WM. HARNESS. Fcap. 8vo, *only 250 printed*, 3s

FISHER (RICHARD TROTT) Lays of Ancient Babyland, to which are added divers small Histories not known to the Ancients. Square 12mo, *printed in the old style, with head and grotesque tail pieces, cloth, gilt leaves*, 4s 6d

Suitable for a Christmas present to a child, containing many of the old popular stories versified, with the addition of several tales.

——— The Travellers, an Argument in three parts— 1. The Night Watch; 2. The Day Watch; 3. The Repose. Crown 8vo, 5s

——— The Minster, with some common Flowers picked in the Close. 12mo, 4s 6d

"Contains many good verses carefully written."—*Athenæum*.

——— Rakings over Many Seasons. Crown 8vo, *cloth*, 8s 6d

FONBLANQUE (E. BARRINGTON) Cluck Cluck; a Fairy Tale, *with* 11 *illustrations by T. W. Y.* Sq. 8vo, 3s 6d

——— Account of a New System of Elementary Teaching. 8vo, 1s

FRANKUM (R.) The Bee and the Wasp, a Fable in Verse. Square 12mo, *with etchings by George Cruikshank, executed in early life and in his best manner*, 5s

——— The Same. Square 12mo, with the plates on INDIA PAPER, *only fifty copies so printed*, 7s 6d

FRERE (J. H.) The Works in Prose and Verse of the Right Honourable John Hookham Frere. Now first collected with a Memoir by W. E. and Sir BARTLE FRERE. Second edition, 3 vols, crown 8vo, *with two portraits engraved by C. H. Jeens*, 24s

——— LARGE PAPER, 3 vols, 8vo, £2 2s

FULLER (MORRIS, *M.A.*) A Voice in the Wilderness, being Sermons preached at Dartmoor. Crown 8vo, 7s 6d

—— Our Established Church, its History, Philosophy, Advantages, and Claims. Crown 8vo,

FULLER (T.) David's Hainous Sinne, Heartie Repentance, Heavie Punishment. Crown 8vo, 7s 6d

—— Life, with Notices of his Books, his Kinsmen, and his Friends, by J. EGLINGTON BAILEY. Thick 8vo, pp. 826, *numerous illustrations*, £1 5s

"If ever there was an amusing writer in this world, the facetious Thomas Fuller was one. There was in him a combination of those qualities which minister to our entertainment, such as few have possessed in an equal degree."—*Retrospective Review*.

GUILEVILLE (GUILLAUME DE) The Ancient Poem entitled "Le Pèlerinage de l'Homme," by GUILLAUME DE GUILEVILLE (1330), compared with "The Pilgrim's Progress" of JOHN BUNYAN, with Illustrations, and an Appendix containing the English Version, by JOHN LYDGATE. Crown 4to, *with numerous illustrations*, 15s

"A volume full of deep interest to the admirers of John Bunyan, and of no small value in illustrating the history of religious allegories."—*Notes and Queries*.

—— A Modern Prose Translation of the Ancient Poem of G. de Guileville, entitled the Pylgrymage of Man, with Appendix. Crown 4to, *twenty-six illustrations*, 5s

—— The Booke of the Pylgrymage of the Sowle, translated from the French, printed by Caxton, 1483, *with illustrations taken from a MS. copy in the British Museum*, edited by K. I. CUST. Crown 4to, *coloured plates*, 15s

HOBSON (W. F.) Church Innovations, an Examination and Plea for Tolerance. 8vo, 1s

—— Letter to the Right Hon. Montague Bernard. 12mo, 4d

—— The Ridsdale Judgement on Vestments. 12mo, 6d.

HOME (F. WYVILLE) Songs of a Wayfarer. Extra fcap, 7s 6d

HORE (P. H.) Explanation of Ancient Terms and Measures of Land, with some Account of Old Tenures. 8vo, 4s

HUGO (T.) Prayers before and after a Chapter of Order of S. John of Jerusalem in England. Crown 8vo, 2s 6d

——— LARGE PAPER, 4to, *only 12 so printed*, 10s 6d

HURCOMB (F. B.) Sermons with Memoir by F. ARNOLD. 8vo, 10s 6d

HYETT (W. H.) Flowers of the South from the Hortus Siccus of an old Collector. 4to, 12s

JESSE (GEORGE R., *Author of "Researches into the History of the British Dog," &c.*) Unabridged Evidence given before the Royal Commission on Vivisection, on the 1st and 6th November, and 20th December, 1875. Crown 8vo, 2s 6d

N.B.—The Blue Book Report, issued by the Royal Commission, presents the above evidence in a mutilated condition only.

KARSLAKE (W. H., *Preacher at Lincoln's Inn, Vicar of Westcott, late Fellow and Tutor of Merton College, Oxford*) The Litany of the English Church considered in its History, its Plan, and the Manner in which it is intended to be used. 8vo, 8s 6d

KEBLE (J.) The Christian Year; Thoughts in Verse for the Sundays and Holy Days throughout the Year. 8vo, *beautifully printed*, 9s

KEN (BISHOP) Christian Year; or Hymns and Poems for the Holy Days and Festivals of the Church. 8vo, *pp. 478, every page surrounded by an elaborate woodcut border in the style of Geoffrey Tory.* £1 1s

These borders are entirely new, never having been used in any other work. They are larger and more elaborate than those used in the "Elizabeth Prayer," or the other bordered Prayer Book.

Bishop Ken was the author of "Awake my soul and with the Sun!" and of "Glory to Thee, my God, this night."

"Bishop Ken's 'Christian Year,' published by Mr. Pickering, is an exquisite edition of a book which would have been welcome in any shape."—*Times*.

——— Christian Year; Hymns and Poems for the Festivals and Holidays of the Church. Third edition, fcap. 8vo, 6s, *and may be had in various bindings*

KERSHAW (S. W., *Librarian of Lambeth Library*) The Art Treasures of Lambeth Library : a Description of the Illuminated MSS. and Illustrated Books, with Outline Illustrations from the most remarkable MSS. 8vo, *uniform with Maitland's Catalogues of the Early Printed Books, only 225 copies printed*, 14s

—— 4to size, *on hand-made paper, plates on India paper, half Roxburghe morocco, only 25 copies printed*, £2 12s 6d

LAMB (CHARLES AND MARY) Poetry for Children, Edited and Prefaced by R. H. SHEPHERD. 12mo, 106 *pp. with woodcut initials, head, and tail-pieces, a pretty volume*, 3s 6d

"These delightful poems for children, in spite of their extraordinary merit, and marked superiority to other productions of a similar class, seem altogether to have escaped the notices of modern readers, and even of those lovers of Lamb's genius who have during late years rescued from oblivion all the waifs and strays of which the authorship is traceable to him."

LENDRUM (REV. ALEXANDER) The Reformation and Deformation, their Principles and Results as Affecting Doctrine, Worship, and Discipline, a Letter to the Archbishop of Canterbury. Thick 8vo, 15s

LONGFELLOW (HENRY WADSWORTH) Early Poems now first collected and edited by R. H. SHEPHERD. 12mo, 3s

"Seldom, if ever, have verses fuller of rich promise or of actual fulfilment been composed by a boy of seventeen."—*Examiner*.

LOVE'S TRIUMPH : a Play. 12mo, 3s 6d

"A light dramatic five-act play, cast rather in the style of thought and expression which belong to the age succeeding that of Shakespeare. The author is evidently a man of poetic taste, as well as a great admirer of those golden days and golden writers, and tells his light and pleasant ove-story in a quiet and simple fashion."—*The Morning Herald*.

LYRICS OF LIGHT AND LIFE.—Original Poems, by Dr. John Henry Newman, Alexander Lord Bishop of Derry, Miss Christiana G. Rossetti, Rev. Gerard Moultrie, Rev. J. S. B. Monsell, Rev. W. J. Blew, Aubrey de Vere, Rev. H. N. Oxenham, Rev. Ed. Caswall, &c., &c., edited by Dr. F. G. Lee. Second edition, revised and enlarged, *handsomely printed with head and tail-pieces*, fcap. 8vo, 6s

—— LARGE PAPER. Crown 8vo, *printed on hand-made paper, only 24 so printed*, £1 1s

MACGILL (HAMILTON M., *D.D.*) Songs of the Christian Creed and Life, selected from Eighteen Centuries. Crown 8vo, 7s

> The representative hymns included in this volume range from the Second Century to the Nineteenth. In each case the original and a translation are given, and where the hymn was originally in English, a Latin rendering is given. A few are Greek and English; all the others have the Latin and English side by side. Among the authors may be enumerated Clement of Alexandria, Hilary, Ambrose, Augustine, Gregory of Nazianzus, Anselm, Thomas A. Kempis, Xavier, Watts. Toplady, Cowper, Heber, Keble, Newman, Bonar, and many others.

MACKENZIE (J.) An Appeal for a New Nation. 8vo, 3d

———— Mainoc Evline, and other Poems. 12mo, 5s

MANNING (CARDINAL) and History: An Answer to the Cardinal's Appeal to the History of the Venerable Bede, by TWO PRIESTS. Sewed, 1s 6d

MANUEL (PRINCE DON JUAN, *the Spanish Boccaccio*) Count Lucanor, or the Fifty Pleasant Stories of Patronio, written by the Prince Don Juan Manuel, A.D. 1335—1347, and now first translated from the Spanish into English, by James York, M.D. 12mo (*pp.* xvi. 246), 6s

> "This curious collection of 'Pleasant Stories,' composed a century before the invention of printing, has already been translated into French and German, and was well worth putting into an English dress. . . . In his brief account of Don Juan Manuel, Dr. James York has told the readers of 'Fifty Pleasant Stories' as much, perhaps, as they will require to know of them. . . . The notes explanatory or illustrative of the stories are, as notes should be, brief, instructive, and to the point."—*The Saturday Review.*

MARTYN (REV. THOMAS, M.A.) Greek Testament Studies; or, a Revision of the Translation for Private Use. 8vo, 2s 6d

MARY (QUEEN) Two Plays by Dekker, Webster, and by Thos. Heywood, newly edited, with Essay on the Relation of the Old and Modern Dramas in this Chapter of History, by W. J. BLEW. 12mo, 4s 6d

MILTON'S PARADISE LOST, in Ten Books, the text exactly reproduced from the First Edition of 1667, with Appendix, containing the additions made i'n later Issues, and a Monograph on the original publication of the Poem. Crown 4to, 18s

———— LARGE PAPER, £1 4s

> The reproduction of Milton's "Paradise Lost" has an interest superior to that of most reprints, as no edition subsequent to the first has preserved the system of emphasis adopted by Milton.

NEWMAN (DR. JOHN HENRY) The Arians of the Fourth Century, third edition. Crown 8vo, 6s

——— Callista ; a Sketch of the Third Century. Crown 8vo, 5s 6d

——— Certain Difficulties felt by Anglicans in Catholic Teaching Considered, in a Letter addressed to the Rev. E. B. Pusey, D.D., on occasion of his Eirenicon of 1864 ; and in a Letter addressed to the Duke of Norfolk on occasion of Mr. Gladstone's Expostulation of 1874. Crown 8vo, 5s 6d

——— Discussions, 6s

Containing : I.—The celebrated "Letters of Catholicus" on Education (The Tamworth Reading Room). II.—An Internal Argument for Christianity. III.—On English Jealousy of "The Army" and "The Church." IV.—On the Relation between Scripture and the Catholic Creed, &c.

——— The Miscellaneous and Critical Essays of John Henry Newman (formerly Fellow of Oriel College, Oxford, now D.D., and of the Oratory, Birmingham), now first collected ; comprising Articles on Poetical, Historical, and Biographical subjects, written 1829—71. 2 vols, crown 8vo, 12s

I.—The Nature of Poetry. II.—Rationalism. III.—Fall of De la Mennais. IV.—Palmer's View of the Church. V.—Epistles of Saint Ignatius. VI.—Anglican Prospects. VII.—The Anglo-American Church. VIII.—The Countess of Huntingdon. IX.—Catholicity of Anglican Church. X.—Antichrist. XI.—Milman's View of Christianity. XII.—The Reformation of the Eleventh Century. XIII.—Private Judgment. XIV.—John Davison. XV.—John Keble.

——— Historical Sketches. Vol. I., 6s

Containing : I.—The History of the Turks in their relation to Europe. II.—Life of Apollonius of Tyana. III.—The Personal and Literary Character of Cicero. IV.—Of Primitive Christianity.

——— Historical Sketches. Vol. II., 6s

Containing: I.—A Sketch of the Life of Theodoret (*now first printed*). II.—A Sketch of the Life of St. Chrysostom. III.—Of the Mission of St. Benedict. IV.—Of the Benedictine Schools. V.—The Church of the Fathers, containing Sketches of St. Basil, St. Gregory, St. Anthony, St. Augustine, Demetrius, and St. Martin.

——— Historical Sketches. Vol. III., 6s

Containing : I.—A Sketch of the Rise and Progress of Universities. II.—An Essay on the Northmen and Normans in England and Ireland. III.—A Review of Mediæval Oxford. IV.—An Historical Sketch of the Convocation of Canterbury.

NEWMAN (DR. JOHN HENRY) An Essay on the Development of Christian Doctrine, new edition, revised by the author. Crown 8vo, 6s

—— Loss and Gain; the Story of a Convert, sixth edition, with a New Advertisement. Crown 8vo, *pp.* 442, 5s 6d

—— On Miracles.—Two Essays on Scripture Miracles, and on Ecclesiastical. Crown 8vo, *pp.* 406, 6s

—— Tracts, Theological and Ecclesiastical, Crown 8vo, 8s
Containing: I.—Dissertatlunculæ. II.—The Doctrinal Causes of Arianism. III.—Apollonarianism. IV.—St. Cyril's Formula. V.—Ordo de Tempore. VI.—On the various revisions of the Douay Versions of Scripture.
Several of the above have NEVER BEEN PREVIOUSLY PRINTED, others are from periodicals now inaccessible.

—— The Via Media of the Anglican Church. Vol. I. containing the whole of the "Lectures on the Prophetical Office of the Church Viewed Relatively to Romanism and Popular Protestantism," as published in 1837; with New Preface and Notes [1877]. Vol. II., containing Occasional Letters and Tracts written between 1830 and 1841. 2 vols, crown 8vo, 6s each

—— Idea of a University, Considered in Nine Discourses, Occasional Lectures, and Essays. Crown 8vo, *uniform in cloth (double volume)*, 7s

NOWELL (T. W.) Sacrifice or no Sacrifice? John Wesley an Unconscious Romanist: Notes on a Suggested Alteration in the English Communion Office. 8vo, sewed, 2s

PANIZZI (ANTONIO) Chi Era Francesco da Bologna? Seconda edizione con nuova appendice. 12mo, *only 265 copies printed, with five facsimiles of the types used by Francesco da Bologna*, 2s 6d

—— LARGE HAND-MADE PAPER, *only 12 printed*, 10s 6d
This essay is written to establish the identity of Francesco da Bologna, who designed and cut the Aldine cursive type, with the celebrated sculptor and artist Francesco Raibolini, usually called Il Francia, the contemporary of Leonardo da Vinci, Rafaelle, and Michael Angelo.

PAYNE (JOHN) The Masque of Shadows, and other Poems. Fcap. 8vo, *cloth*, 7s

—— Intaglios, Sonnets. 12mo, *finely printed with head and tail-pieces, ornamented with initial letters*, 3s 6d

"Excellent scholar's work in poetry. The spirit of his work is much akin to the earlier writings of Mr. Rossetti and Mr. Morris."—*The Academy.*

—— Lautrec, a Poem. 12mo

PEARCE (M.) Philip of Konigsmarkt, and Poems. 12mo, 8s 6d

POCOCK (N.) The Principles of the Reformation shown to be in Contradiction to the Book of Common Prayer. 8vo, 1s

—— Recovery from the Principles of the Reformation. 8vo, 1s

POETS.—Birthdays with the Poets, a birthday book of quotations from the poets. Square 16mo, *ornamented cloth, gilt leaves*, 3s

PRAYER, A Service of, A Litany and an Office of the Holy Communion. 16mo, 1s

PUNCHARD (E. G.) King Saul and other Poems. 12mo, 2s 6d

—— Seven Times a Day: a Manual of the Hours of Prayer, with Notes thereon. 18mo, 1s

RALEIGH (SIR WALTER) Poems, edited by J. Hannah. 12mo, *handsomely printed, with ornamental head and tail-pieces*, 5s

SANDYS (R. H.) In the Beginning, Remarks on Certain Modern Views of the Creation. 8vo. Part I. 1s; Part II. 1s 6d; Part III. 1s 6d; Part IV. 1s 6d

SCOTT (PATRICK) Christianity and a Personal Devil. Second Edition, revised and re-arranged. 12mo, 5s

"We think every impartial inquirer will agree with Mr. Scott."—*Pall Mall Gazette.*

SHIPLEY (OBBY) Ought we to obey the New Court created by the Public Worship Regulation Act? Second Edition. 8vo, 6d

SHIRLEY (E. P.) A History of the County of Monaghan. Part I. Folio, *with numerous Illustrations, Antiquarian and Heraldic, only* 250 *copies printed*, 12s

—— Part II. 16s

—— Part III. 12s

—— Part IV. *In the Press.*

SINGLETON (LUCY) Some Statistics to Show the Necessity for more Bishops and Clergy. Royal 8vo, *sewed*, 1s

SKETCHES OF NONCONFORMITY chiefly taken from the Old Testament. 8vo, *sewed*, 6d

TENNYSONIANA.—Notes Critical and Bibliographical on the Works of Alfred Tennyson, D.C.L., Poet Laureate, Second Edition, revised and enlarged. 12mo

TONES, Sad, for Sick Times, by the Author of "Hints of Horace." Crown 8vo, 3s

TONDINI (C.) Anglicanism, Old Catholicism, and the Union of the Christian Episcopal Churches. 8vo, *sewed*, 1s 6d

—— The Future of the Russian Church. 8vo, *sewed*, 1s

TOWNSEND.—Sunday Utterances of Prayer and Praise. Square 18mo, *sewed*, 1s

TRACTS.—Privy Council. 4s 6d

No. 1—Dr. Stephens on the Ornaments Rubric, Dedicated to His Grace the ARCHBISHOP OF YORK, 1s

No. 2—The Case of "The Seven Bishops"—The Case of "The 4,700," dedicated to the LORD BISHOP OF LONDON, 1s

No. 3—A Handy Book of Privy Council Law.—I. Ecclesiastical Cases.—II. Patent Cases.—Dedicated to the Right Honourable BARON HATHERLEY, royal 8vo, *pp.* 75, 1s 6d

"This is No. III. of a series of which the first two are already well known, and duly appreciated wherever they are known."—*The Church Review.*

TRELAWNY (E. J.) Records of Shelley, Byron, and the Author, New edition, greatly enlarged. 2 vols, crown 8vo, *with portraits and plates*, 12s

WACE (H.) Christianity and Morality: being the Boyle Lectures for 1874-5, by Henry Wace, M.A., Chaplain of Lincoln's Inn, Professor of Ecclesiastical History, King's College, London, Bampton Lecturer for 1879 in the Univ. of Oxford, &c. Fourth Edition. Crown 8vo, 6s

WALKER (C.) An Order for Matins and Evensong, and the Celebration of the Holy Communion, commonly called the Mass, chiefly after the First Prayer Book of Edward VI. 16mo, 2s

WALTON (IZAAK) Reliquiæ Waltonianæ: Inedited Remains of Izaak Walton, Author of "The Complete Angler," edited by R. H. Shepherd. 12mo, 6s

WARBURTON (R. E. EGERTON) Poems and Epigrams. Crown 8vo, *only 250 printed*, 7s 6d

—— Hunting Songs, Sixth Edition. 12mo, *with vignette title, uncut*, 5s

"We have to thank Mr. Egerton Warburton, a sportsman of the best stamp, for the agreeable collection of hunting songs before us. They are fresh, lively, not deficient in point, and frequently characterized by a healthy and genial humour."—*Vide review of two columns in the "Saturday Review" of Jan.* 24, 1874.

WILBERFORCE (R. T.) The Five Empires; an Outline of Ancient History, Fifteenth Edition. 12mo, *maps and plates*, 3s 6d

WINSCOM (CAVE) Tsoé, and other Poems. 12mo, 3s 6d

—— Waves and Caves, and other Poems 12mo, 3s 6d

—— Camden, and other Poems. 12mo, 3s 6d

PICKERING & CO.,,

196, PICCADILLY, LONDON, W

www.ingramcontent.com/pod-product-compliance
Lightning Source LLC
Chambersburg PA
CBHW051853300426
44117CB00006B/376